Praise for

The Good Society

"*The Good Society* is not only thought-provoking but also deeply moving....This book should be widely read, discussed, and argued about in public. It is the beginning of a conversation that must continue and expand."
—*Utne Reader*

"Vital truth."
—*L.A. Times*

"[*The Good Society*] is more direct, more cogently argued, more readable, and ultimately may prove to be more important than *Habits of the Heart*."
—*St. Petersburg Times*

"Instructive...a revelation, one can imagine it being used quite effectively, for instance, as a discussion text."
—*Kansas City Star*

"*The Good Society* has the ambition and the sweep of *Habits of the Heart*."
—*Entertainment Weekly*

"Likely to generate...quite a stir in sociological circles."
—*Dallas Morning News*

Also by the authors of *The Good Society*

HABITS OF THE HEART

ABOUT THE AUTHORS

Robert N. Bellah and Ann Swidler teach at the
University of California, Berkeley; Richard Madsen
at the University of California, San Diego; William
M. Sullivan at LaSalle University; and Steven M.
Tipton at Emory University.

The Good Society

THE GOOD SOCIETY

Robert N. Bellah

Richard Madsen

William M. Sullivan

Ann Swidler

Steven M. Tipton

Vintage Books

A Division of Random House, Inc.

New York

First Vintage Books Edition, September 1992

Copyright © 1991 by Robert N. Bellah, Richard Madsen,
William M. Sullivan, Ann Swidler, and Steven M. Tipton

Library of Congress Cataloging-in-Publication Data
The Good Society / Robert Bellah...[et al.].
—1st Vintage Books ed.
p.   cm.
Originally published: New York: Knopf, 1991.
ISBN 0-679-73359-0
1. United States—Civilization—1970–   2. United States—
Economic conditions—1981–   3. United States—Social
conditions—1980–
I. Bellah, Robert Neelly, 1927–
[E169.12.G645   1992]
973.92—dc20   92-50103
CIP

Author photograph by Jean Margolis

Manufactured in the United States of America
10 9 8 7 6 5 4 3

Contents

Acknowledgments

We have asked scholars from various fields, as well as civic leaders, clergy, and students, to respond critically to early drafts of *The Good Society*—even more than we did in composing *Habits of the Heart*. Since well over a hundred people read parts of the manuscript and discussed it with us, it is impossible to mention all their names, but we are most grateful for their assistance and their thoughtful criticism. We also learned a great deal, as we did with *Habits*, from those we interviewed during our research for the book. We take responsibility for what we have written; but whatever there is of value in it comes out of and contributes to a continuation of an ongoing conversation among fellow citizens.

John Chan gave us valuable research assistance. Harlan Stelmach beautifully organized for us a series of consultations held at the Graduate Theological Union in Berkeley. Eli Sagan and Melanie Bellah were kind enough to give us their comments on the complete manuscript. Our editor, Elisabeth Sifton, helped us greatly to improve the clarity of what we wanted to say.

The research for and writing of this book were made possible by generous funding from the National Endowment for the Humanities, which supports work in the humanistic social sciences as well as the traditional humanities. The NEH grant was administered by the Department of Sociology of the University of California at Berkeley. The later stages of our work were supported by a grant from the Religion and the Third Sector Program of the Lilly Endowment administered by the Center for Ethics and Social Policy of the Graduate Theological Union at Berkeley. We are grateful for the moral as well as material support from both endowments and the administering institutions. Richard Madsen's research was supported in part by a grant from the Social Science Research Council's Foreign Policy Studies Program, funded by the Ford Foundation.

The final draft of this book was finished in the early summer of 1990 and reflects to some extent the atmosphere created by the "velvet revolutions" in Eastern Europe and the destruction of the Berlin Wall. We anticipated that the struggle to build genuine democracy in the Soviet Union and Eastern Europe would be a difficult one, and indeed pointed out that creating the trust essential to democratic institutions is a long slow process, subject to many reversals, and by no means inevitable. We did not anticipate Saddam Hussein's invasion of Kuwait in August 1990, or the war in the Persian Gulf in January and February of 1991. But the Gulf War dramatizes many of our main themes—especially the dangers and opportunities inherent in the interdependence that so preeminently characterizes the modern world. The war makes us aware of how fragile are the international institutions nurturing that interdependence, and also how important it is to strengthen them. As this century draws to a close there remain, we believe, vital opportunities—as well as the urgent necessity—for transforming our national and international institutions so as to bring about a new, more democratic, more peaceful world order under the leadership of the United Nations. Without excessive optimism, we continue to be hopeful about our capacity to pay attention to and take responsibility for realizing those possibilities.

The Good Society

Introduction

We Live Through Institutions

In the last few years, the world democratic revolution that began in the seventeenth and eighteenth centuries in Europe and America, having suffered severe setbacks earlier in the twentieth century, entered a new stage of intensity in many parts of the world: in Eastern Europe, the Soviet Union, South Africa, and elsewhere. This new stage of political development will have significant repercussions in the United States, even though Americans' initial reaction was more or less to stay home and watch what was happening on television. In ways we could not have imagined when we began work on this book, it has turned out to be concerned with the shape of a new democratic transformation in the United States as part of the world democratic revolution. But if such a transformation is to be successful here, we must understand the peculiar obstacles we face—apparently less daunting than the obstacles faced, for example, in the Soviet Union, yet in their own way quite daunting enough.

Democracy requires a degree of trust that we often take for granted. In a democratic society citizens must be able to trust that if they are defeated by opponents in a political struggle, for example, they will not be killed, and that if they win an election, their opponents will let them take power peacefully.[1] Building that kind of trust in the nations of Central and Eastern Europe will not be easy: it is much harder to build trust than to lose it. But that is our problem in the United States: we have begun to lose trust in our institutions—not yet, fortunately, in the electoral transfer of political power, though cynicism about elections is growing. The heritage of trust that has been the basis of our stable democracy is eroding.[2] This trust is not a nonrenewable resource, but it is much easier to destroy than to renew. That is why our problems are ominous in their implications for our future.

I. INSTITUTIONS AS PATTERNED WAYS OF LIVING TOGETHER

Walking in any American city today, one participates in a ritual that perfectly expresses the difficulty of being a good person in the absence of a good society. In the midst of affluence, perhaps with a guilty sense of the absurd wastefulness of the expensive meal, new blouse, or electronic gadget that has brought us to town, we pass homeless men or, often, women with children asking money for food and shelter. Whether we give or withhold our spare change, we know that neither personal choice is the right one. We may experience the difficulty of helping the plight of homeless people as a painful individual moral dilemma, but the difficulty actually comes from failures of the larger institutions on which our common life depends.

The problem of homelessness, like many of our problems, was created by social choices. The market-driven conversion of single-room-occupancy hotels into upscale tourist accommodations, government urban-renewal projects that revitalized downtowns while driving up rents and reducing housing for the poor, economic changes that eliminated unskilled jobs paying enough to support a family, the states' "deinstitutionalization" of the mentally ill and reduced funding of local community health programs, have together created the crisis of homelessness. But with this issue, as with many others, we tend to feel helpless to shape the institutional order that made these choices meaningful—or meaningless.[3]

In *Habits of the Heart* we asked, "How ought we to live? How do we think about how to live?" and we focused on cultural and personal resources for thinking about our common life.[4] In *The Good Society* we are concerned with the same questions, but we are now focusing on the patterned ways Americans have developed for living together, what sociologists call institutions.[5] In a world undergoing enormous technological, economic, and political change, many of the established ways we have of living together are not working well. Some of them are not working as they were intended to. Others are having alarming and unintended consequences that affect not only people but the natural environment.

It is hardly surprising that institutions established at different times and under different conditions might need to be reformed from time to time. Some of our institutions date from the eighteenth century, when the United States was a small country with a largely agricultural economy, far from, and well insulated against, the major centers of world power. Other American institutions date from the postwar years when the United States was embarking on a gigantic militant effort to save the "free world" from Communist oppression—and indeed some of the institutions established then are serving us less well than some of those that date from the eighteenth century.

It is tempting to think that the problems that we face today, from the homeless in our streets and poverty in the Third World to ozone depletion and the greenhouse effect, can be solved by technology or technical expertise alone. But even to begin to solve these daunting problems, let alone problems of emptiness and meaninglessness in our personal lives, requires that we greatly improve our capacity to think about our institutions. We need to understand how much of our lives is lived in and through institutions, and how better institutions are essential if we are to lead better lives. In surveying our present institutions we need to discern what is healthy in them and what needs to be altered, particularly where we have begun to destroy the nonrenewable natural and nearly nonrenewable human resources upon which all our institutions depend.

Our present situation requires an unprecedented increase in the ability to attend to new possibilities, moral as well as technical, and to put the new technical possibilities in a moral context. The challenges often seem overwhelming, but there are possibilities for an immense enhancement of our lives, individual and collective, an enhancement based on a significant moral advance. One of the greatest challenges, especially for individualistic Americans, is to understand what institutions are—how we form them and how they in turn form us—and to imagine that we can actually alter them for the better.

Habits of the Heart offered a portrait of middle-class Americans and of the cultural resources they have for making sense of their society and their lives. We described a language of individualistic achievement and self-fulfillment that often seems to make it difficult for people to sustain their commitments to others, either in intimate relationships or in the public sphere. We held up older traditions, biblical and civic republican, that had a better grasp on the truth that the individual is realized only in and through community; but we showed that contemporary Americans have difficulty understanding those traditions today or seeing how they apply to their lives. We called for a deeper understanding of the moral ecology that sustains the lives of all of us, even when we think we are making it on our own. "Moral ecology" is only another way of speaking of healthy institutions, yet the culture of individualism makes the very idea of institutions inaccessible to many of us. We Americans tend to think that all we need are energetic individuals and a few impersonal rules to guarantee fairness; anything more is not only superfluous but dangerous—corrupt, oppressive, or both. As we showed in *Habits of the Heart*, Americans often think of individuals pitted against institutions.[6] It is hard for us to think of institutions as affording the necessary context within which we become individuals; of institutions as not just restraining but enabling us; of institutions not as an arena of hostility within which our character is tested but an indispensable source from which character is formed. This is in part because some of our institutions have indeed grown out of control and beyond our comprehension. But the answer is to change them, for it is illusory to imagine that we can escape them.

The problems with which *Habits of the Heart* and *The Good Society* are concerned are rooted in changes that began a long while ago. These changes have been preoccupying not only social theorists but religious and political leaders for several centuries, ever since the emergence of modern science and the modern economy made it clear that a radically new and rapidly changing kind of society was coming into existence. Recently one way of posing the argument about how to deal with the problems emerging in this new form of society has been to pit philosophical liberals against communitarians; *Habits of the Heart* was often termed communitarian.[7]

If philosophical liberals are those who believe that all our problems can be solved by autonomous individuals, a market economy, and a procedural state, whereas communitarians believe that more substantive ethical identities and a more active participation in a democratic polity are necessary for the functioning of any decent society, then we are indeed communitarians. But we feel that the word "communitarian" runs the risk of being misunderstood if one imagines that only face-to-face groups—families, congregations, neighborhoods— are communities and that communitarians are opposed to the state, the economy, and all the larger structures that so largely dominate our life today. Indeed, it is our sense that only greater citizen participation in the large structures of the economy and the state will enable us to surmount the deepening problems of contemporary social life.[8] In order not to be misunderstood, we are reaching back into the earlier twentieth century for terminology that will put the issues in terms that are helpful.

II. IS THE GREAT SOCIETY A GOOD SOCIETY?

In 1915 Graham Wallas published a book entitled *The Great Society*[9] which had an enormous influence, notably on two major American public philosophers, John Dewey and Walter Lippmann. By "the Great Society" Wallas meant the "invisible environment" of communication and commerce that was linking the whole modern world in ever more coercive ways but was almost beyond human capacity to understand, much less to manage. For Wallas the great society was a neutral, indeed rather frightening, term for modernity. In 1927 John Dewey, in *The Public and Its Problems*, posed the central problem of modernity as he saw it as follows: "Our concern at this time is to state how it is that the machine age in developing the Great Society has invaded and partially disintegrated the small communities of former times without generating a Great Community."[10] Dewey had no nostalgia for the old small communities, too enthralled by custom as they were to release the energies of individual and social growth. "The Great Community," a term Dewey probably derived from Josiah Royce, who published a book by that title in 1916,[11] was not to be a mere revival of the old small communities, what the Germans call *Gemeinschaft*, but something new that would infuse public spirit and public consciousness into those now largely invisible structures characterized by the Great Society. For Dewey, hope lay in the enlargement and enhancement of democracy throughout our institutional life.

It was that great twentieth-century advocate of political realism Walter Lippmann who used another contrast term to "the Great Society," namely "the Good Society," which was the title of a book he published in 1937.[12] Because "community" can be misunderstood if interpreted too narrowly, we have adopted Lippmann's term and his title for this book. Lippmann kept reminding Americans of his day that they were living through a vast period of global transformation, the greatest since the coming of settled agriculture. For several centuries now the great society, particularly in the form of the division of labor and the exchange economy, but even, ironically, through the increased level of international violence, has been pushing more and more of human society toward an interconnected planetary whole. The process has been anything but smooth, causing repeated crises of moral meaning and solidarity, as well as breakdowns into extraordinary violence and anger, as the units and conditions of life develop unevenly.

The same process has given rise to possibilities unique to human history thus far. As Lippmann put it in *The Good Society*: "Until the division of labor had begun to make men dependent upon the free collaboration of other men, the worldly policy was to be predatory. The claims of the spirit were other-worldly." The news, according to Lippmann, is that with the coming of interdependence and technological abundance "the vista was opened at the end of which men could see the possibility of the Good Society on this earth. At long last," he continued, "the ancient schism between the world and the spirit, between self-interest and disinterestedness, was potentially closed, and a wholly new orientation of the human race became theoretically conceivable and, in fact, necessary."[13]

The necessity of the new orientation became clearest, Lippmann thought, in modern wars. These are more and more not battles between aliens but "internecine" struggles "within one closely related, intricately interdependent community." According to Lippmann, "Modern war tears apart huge populations which have become dependent upon one another for the maintenance of their standard of life—in some degree for the maintenance of life itself."[14] Certainly the development of nuclear weaponry has only strengthened Lippmann's argument.

Lippmann proposed that the reason war-mongering now elicits such strong moral sanction is that war makes less and less rational, practical sense as an instrument of long-term national self-interest. The great moral aspiration toward a global order of security based on equity increasingly seemed to him, a strategic realist, to be demanded by any sober calculation of interests. The good society emerges not only as an idealistic project but as the long-term practical necessity of the new era.

We shall draw from a number of observers and analysts of the modern world besides John Dewey and Walter Lippmann, but it is their spirit that we wish to emulate. Both were critical of much they saw around them. Neither was nostalgic for a vanished past. Both were moderately hopeful that Americans could meet the enormous challenges facing them, the challenge of transforming the great society into the good society. But as we look at the reality of our society today we can see that though we can learn from their suggestions about reforming our institutions, they provide only the beginnings for the constructive task that lies ahead. We shall build on the work of these and other predecessors, but we shall inevitably push beyond them into areas that they did not explore.

At this point, the reader may wish to know exactly what we mean by "the good society," how we would define it, how we would recognize it if we saw it. Some readers may also well ask, "A good society for whom?" or "A good society in whose opinion?" Even though throughout the book we shall try to sketch out some of its features, our ultimate answer is that there is no pattern of a good society that we or anyone else can simply discern and then expect people to conform to. It is central to our very notion of a good society that it is an open quest, actively involving all its members. As Dennis McCann has put it, the common good is the pursuit of the good in common.[15]

As we understand it, pluralism does not contradict the idea of a good society, for the latter would be one that would allow a wide scope for diversity and would draw on resources from its pluralistic communities in discerning those things that are necessarily matters of the good of all. Some of the ideas we have just found in Dewey and Lippmann are part of our definition: a widening of democratic participation and the accountability of institutions; an interdependent prosperity that counteracts predatory relations among individuals and groups and enables everyone to participate in the goods of society; a peaceful world, without which the search for a good society is surely illusory.

Freedom, for most Americans, is an essential ingredient in a definition of a good society, and one we affirm. But, as with all the great moral terms, we need to probe more deeply to find out what "freedom" really means. For many of us, "freedom" still has the old meaning of the right to be left alone. In an older America, where one could spend most of one's life on one's own homestead, that kind of notion had a certain plausibility. But in the great society of today, freedom cannot mean simply getting away from other people. Freedom must exist within and be guaranteed by institutions, and must include the right to participate in the economic and political decisions that affect our lives. Indeed, the great classic criteria of a good society—peace, prosperity, freedom, justice—all depend today on a new experiment in democracy, a newly extended and enhanced set of democratic institutions, within which we citizens can better discern what we really want and what we ought to want to sustain a good life on this planet for ourselves and the generations to come.

III. WHY AMERICANS HAVE TROUBLE
UNDERSTANDING INSTITUTIONS

We need to understand why the very idea of institutions is so intim-
idating to Americans and why it is so important to overcome this
anxiety and think creatively about institutions. In its formal sociological definition, an institution is a pattern of expected action of individuals or groups enforced by social sanctions, both positive and
negative. For example, institutions may be such simple customs as
the confirming handshake in a social situation,[16] where the refusal to
respond to an outstretched hand might cause embarrassment and some
need for an explanation; or they may be highly formal institutions
such as taxation upon which social services depend, where refusal to
pay may be punished by fines and imprisonment. Institutions always
have a moral element. A handshake is a sign of social solidarity, at
least a minimal recognition of the personhood of the other. Taxation,
especially in a democracy, is for the purpose of attaining agreed-upon
common aims and is supposed to be fair in its assessment.

Individualistic Americans fear that institutions impinge on their
freedom. In the case of the handshake this impingement may give rise
only to a very occasional qualm. More powerful institutions seem
more directly to threaten our freedom. For just this reason, the classical liberal view held that institutions ought to be as far as possible
neutral mechanisms for individuals to use to attain their separate
ends—a view so persuasive that most Americans take it for granted,
sharing with liberalism the fear that institutions that are not properly
limited and neutral may be oppressive. This belief leads us to think
of institutions as efficient or inefficient mechanisms, like the Department of Motor Vehicles, that we learn to use for our own purposes,
or as malevolent "bureaucracies" that may crush us under their impersonal wheels. It is not that either of these beliefs is wholly mistaken.
In modern society we do indeed need to learn how to manipulate
institutions. And all of us, particularly but not only the poor and the
powerless, find ourselves at the mercy of institutions that control our
lives in ways we often do not fully understand. Yet if this is our only
conception of institutions we have a very impoverished idea of our
common life, an idea that cannot effectively help us deal with our
problems but only worsens them.

There is an ambiguity about the idea of institutions that it is hard
to avoid but that we will try to be clear about. Institutions are nor-

mative patterns embedded in and enforced by laws and mores (informal customs and practices). In common usage the term is also used to apply to concrete organizations. Organizations certainly loom large in our lives, but if we think only of organizations and not of institutions we may greatly oversimplify our problems. The corporation is a central institution in American life about which we will have much to say in this book. As an institution it is a particular historical pattern of rights and duties, of powers and responsibilities, that make it a major force in our lives. Individual corporations are organizations that operate within the legal and other patterns that define what a corporation is. If we do not distinguish between institution and organization, we may think that our only problem with corporations is to make them more efficient or more responsible. But there are problems with how corporations are institutionalized in American society, with the underlying pattern of power and responsibility, and we cannot solve the problems of corporate life simply by improving individual organizations: we have to reform the institution itself. If we confuse organizations and institutions, then when we believe we are being treated unfairly we may retreat into private life or flee from one organization to another—a different company or a new marriage—hoping that the next one will treat us better. But changes in how organizations are conceived, changes in the norms by which they operate—institutional changes—are the only way to get at the source of our difficulties.

The same logic applies throughout our social life. There are certainly better families and worse, happier and more caring families and ones that are less so. But the very way Americans institutionalize family life, the very pressures and temptations that American society presents to all families, are themselves the source of serious problems, so just asking individual families to behave better, important though that is, will not get to the root of the difficulties. Indeed, there is a kind of reductionism in our traditional way of thinking about society. We think in the first place that the problem is probably with the individual; if not, then with the organization. This pattern of thinking hides from us the power of institutions and their great possibilities for good and for evil.

What is missing in this American view of society? Just the idea that in our life with other people we are engaged continuously, through words and actions, in creating and re-creating the institutions that make that life possible. This process is never neutral but is always ethical and political, since institutions (even such an intimate institution as the family) live or die by ideas of right and wrong and conceptions of the good. Conversely, while we in concert with others create institutions, they also create us: they educate us and form us—especially through the socially enacted metaphors they give us, metaphors that provide normative interpretations of situations and actions. The metaphors may be appropriate or inappropriate, but they are inescapable. A local congregation may think of itself as a "family." A corporate CEO may speak of management and workers all being "team players." Democracy itself is not so much a specific institution as a metaphoric way of thinking about an aspect of many institutions.

In short, we are not self-created atoms manipulating or being manipulated by objective institutions. We form institutions and they form us every time we engage in a conversation that matters, and certainly every time we act as parent or child, student or teacher, citizen or official, in each case calling on models and metaphors for the rightness and wrongness of action. Institutions are not only constraining but also enabling. They are the substantial forms through which we understand our own identity and the identity of others as we seek cooperatively to achieve a decent society.

The idea that institutions are objective mechanisms that are essentially separate from the lives of the individuals who inhabit them is an ideology that exacts a high moral and political price. The classical liberal view has elevated one virtue, autonomy, as almost the only good, but has failed to recognize that even autonomy depends on a particular kind of institutional structure and is not an escape from institutions altogether. By imagining a world in which individuals can be autonomous not only from institutions but from each other, it has forgotten that autonomy, valuable as it is in itself, is only one virtue among others and that without such virtues as responsibility and care, which can be exercised only through institutions, autonomy itself becomes, as we argued in *Habits of the Heart*, an empty form without substance.

IV. INSTITUTIONAL RESPONSIBILITY IN PRACTICE

The policy analyst David Kirp, in his book *Learning by Heart*,[17] gives moving examples of a richer conception of institutions. He and his associates studied a number of public school systems faced with the challenge of admitting children with AIDS. In a situation of extraordinary anxiety superintendents, principals, teachers, and parents were called upon to decide what kind of school and what kind of community they wanted to have. The speech and behavior of institutional authorities took on enormous importance, as did the capacity of parents to respond. Doctors could explain that the risks were exceedingly small, but school administrators and parents had to decide whether any risk at all should be taken to extend the moral community to include a child in great need. Finding the right metaphor—seeing the child primarily as a human being in need of special compassion or primarily as a source of dangerous contamination—was critical to the outcome.

An example like this illustrates the truth that the anthropologist Mary Douglas expressed in these words: "The most profound decisions about justice are not made by individuals as such, but by individuals thinking within and on behalf of institutions."[18] We can extend her insight by saying that responsibility is something we exercise as individuals but within and on behalf of institutions. The character of certain individuals, particularly superintendents and principals, significantly influenced the outcome in school districts confronting AIDS panic. But that very character in part reflected the history and moral resources of the community as a whole. Administrators and parents changed the institutional definition of their schools and communities by how they responded to this major challenge. Those for whom the virtues of responsibility and care were determinative (and it is important that those virtues were located not only in them as individuals but in their sense of themselves as institutional representatives) thought not only that they had done the right thing but that they had taught their children a lesson more valuable than most of what they learn in the classroom. Those who, desiring to protect what was theirs, opted to reject the stigmatized child, remained closed, bitter, and defensive long after the event. Their children too had learned a lesson. The process was one of institutional learning for everyone. It was not just that some school systems acted better than others. It was that some learned to understand what a good school system would really be like, and then tried to make theirs embody this more deeply understood institutional ideal.

But many of the institutions that are most important in our lives are, on the face of it, less accessible to understanding and participation than the patterns of decision-making in local school districts. We know that we are affected by changes in the national and international economies, by the policies of the federal government and its relations with other nations, by industrial and agricultural developments that threaten the global environment, and by the mass media; but we feel overwhelmed by the problem of understanding these complex aspects of the great society and helpless to do much about changing them.

The current burst of environmental awareness might seem to be an exception to this aversion to complexity. The first Earth Day, in 1970, took place in the United States. Since that time the environmental concerns expressed in Green politics have become a powerful world-wide current. Laws have been enacted in many nations and even transnationally, as in the Law of the Sea, to protect natural resources, regions, and species. Citizens in the tens of millions have begun to modify their styles of consumption and activity to accord with what they judge to be the requirements of planetary health, even survival. Most remarkably, the groundswell of ecological sentiment seems to fly in the face of conventional beliefs about what modern populations respect and value.

A rare species of squirrel examining an acorn on the intended site of a power plant, as shown in a television sequence, can remind millions that wonder is a gift not monopolized by humans. In such public reactions we see the capacity to identify our destiny with fellow creatures in the great web of nature. The particular concerns of "Green consciousness," whether they are the local ecosystem, trees, whales, or wilderness in a distant part of the planet, serve to focus attention on this larger context, which we are able to shape, but cannot dominate unilaterally. The term used for ecological end-in-view is "sustain-ability." It indicates recognition that the "carrying capacity" of any ecosystem is limited and must be respected. This attitude requires at the least a long-term view of utility, but many environmentalists go even further in their vision of global nurturance. Ecological awareness, then, is one area where people do see what is at stake and believe their actions can make a difference.

It is equally remarkable that this strong new awareness of the non-utilitarian context of life mostly operates at two quite disconnected levels. There is very local, even personal "Green behavior"—such as recycling trash, using only certain products, and driving less. And then there is a second, planetary level of concern, as in campaigns to protect endangered species, the tropical rain forests, or the ozone layer. The mediating relationships that link the individual household with the planetary ecosystem are left out—the bonds of human in-stitutions and culture. There is a void in awareness, a gap in our thinking at the crucial point, the middle range between the local and the global level. Planetary environmental degradation is rarely under-stood as connected with human poverty and hunger. Why is it that it is easier to think about the whole planetary ecosphere than to un-derstand the social effects of our everyday relationships within household, economy, and polity? Environmentalists sometimes forget that human culture is itself, as Cicero put it, a "second nature," whose true aim is not to exploit the rest of nature but to cultivate it, raising the potentials emergent in humanity toward harmonious completion.

Our growing sensitivity to the natural ecological context, rightly understood, should inspire a new focus on our social institutions; natural and social ecology are, profoundly, mutually implicated. Most of the threats to the planetary ecosystem are the results of habitual human ways of relating to the physical world, ways dictated by institutional arrangements. Inversely, our relations with nature—the way we have used land, materials, and other species—both reveal and shape the institutions through which we deal with each other. But we still have a long way to go in finding a realistic institutional approach to environmental problems.

We shall argue in this book that, in spite of the complexities and the difficulties, large-scale institutions can and indeed must be better understood, and they are amenable to citizen action and the influence of global public opinion. To imagine them as autonomous systems operating according to their own mysterious internal logic, to be fine-tuned only by experts, is to opt for some kind of modern gnosticism that sees the world as controlled by the powers of darkness and encourages us to look only to our private survival. We believe that the modern ideal of a democracy governed by intelligent public opinion and participation not only is worth redeeming in our own society but requires, as far as possible, extension to the human community as a whole. In making this argument we shall attempt to renew earlier efforts to create an American public philosophy less trapped in the clichés of rugged individualism and more open to an invigorating, fulfilling sense of social responsibility. But responsible social participation, with an enlightened citizenry that can deal with moral and intellectual complexity, does not come about just from exhortation. It is certainly not enough simply to implore our fellow citizens to "get involved." We must create the institutions that will enable such participation to occur, encourage it, and make it fulfilling as well as demanding.

Institutions are very much dependent on language: what we cannot imagine and express in language has little chance of becoming a sociological reality. In this book, as in *Habits of the Heart*, we hearken to the insights that our religious as well as our political traditions may have for us and the language they teach us for thinking about the renewal of our common concern. These traditions can help us think and talk about the new level of self-discipline that an interdependent world requires, and the renewed celebration of our common life on this planet in the light of transcendent reality.

V. OUR INSTITUTIONAL PROBLEMS TODAY

In Chapter 1, "Making Sense of It," we consider some of the problems Americans are facing today, why institutional dilemmas are also moral dilemmas, and why our cultural resources for dealing with them are impoverished. Chapter 2, "The Rise and Fall of the American Century," describes the immediate postwar American society that many Americans still think of as "normal" and against which they measure subsequent developments, and then considers the historical forces that gave rise to that society. Chapter 3, "The Political Economy: Market and Work," deals with the economy not simply as an objective mechanism but as a set of institutional arrangements, created by human beings, and profoundly influencing the kind of people we become. Chapter 4 considers government, law, and politics. Most of the founders of the United States imagined a nation with a modest central administration and a great deal of local control. The growth of a massive centralized state and an ever more pervasive legal system must be understood as human responses to human needs, but also as responses that have sometimes shaped us in ways we neither expected nor desired. Chapter 5 considers educational institutions—schools and colleges—that have become so central to so many of us, though it is one of the arguments of our book that all institutions are educative. Since schools take children from the family and neighborhood and give them skills to operate in the large-scale structures of economy and state, they are institutions crucial to the functioning of society and also to the formation of our character. The school, particularly the university, is the "church" of our secular society, and we shall consider how well it fulfills that function. In particular we ask if our schools and universities can become democratic learning communities, whether they can help us deal with the moral as well as the technical problems of a complex society.

Chapter 6 considers how religious institutions relate to American society, how they do or do not remain faithful to their defining messages, and how they shape or fail to shape our capacity as individuals and as a society to meet our current challenges, and particularly to provide the meaning that seems to be slipping from the lives of so many of us. Religious traditions, interpreted in a way respectful of the views of others (including those who are entirely secular), have much to contribute to the democratic debate about a good form of life for our society and our world, if only we know how to draw on them. Chapter 7, "America and the World," describes the impact on our lives of the changing place of the United States in the world system of powers. It describes the traditional ways we have thought about and acted in the world, how global pressures affect the kind of people we are, and the growing necessity to increase our democratic learning capacity. The Conclusion returns to the issue of creativity and vitality in American institutional life, the importance of individual and social responsibility within and for institutions, and suggests some of the ways we might indeed transform the great society into the good society. In an appendix we defend, philosophically and sociologically, the conception of institutions that is central to this book, and we consider in somewhat greater depth the resources in American public philosophy that might help us today.

The Good Society, like *Habits of the Heart*, is very much a group effort. Every chapter has gone through multiple revisions on the basis of intensive group discussion, with Bellah being responsible for the final revision. Although all the authors contributed to the framing chapters, Bellah had primary responsibility for them, and Sullivan made especially extensive contributions to them. With respect to the substantive chapters, the division of labor among us has been according to institutional spheres, roughly correlating with specific chapters. Each of us has carried out research and in several cases field studies and interviews in the areas allotted to us, as we did for *Habits of the Heart*. Sullivan was responsible for political history and political economy, Swidler for the regulatory state and the legal system, Bellah for education, Tipton for religion, and Madsen for America's place in the world. Our interviews were fewer and more selective than they were in the case of *Habits*, for we were not trying to get a sense of the cultural predicaments of ordinary people so much as to discern how managers, government experts, church functionaries, and foreign-policy advisors think.

Some readers of early drafts of this book have worried about who might be the "we" whom we so frequently mention and the complementary "you" to whom the book is addressed. In *The Good Society* "we" has a number of references that must be discerned in context. Sometimes "we" means the five authors. Sometimes "we" means Americans. Sometimes "we" means all the inhabitants of the earth. As in *Habits of the Heart*, we the authors do not intend to put ourselves above our readers or those we describe. Our "we" is meant not as coercion but as invitation. We invite "you" to join "us" in the effort to discern what our common problems are and how we might better meet them. Joining our "we" does not mean that you accept our solutions, however tentative, or even our descriptions, but only that you join the conversation itself. We do not agree with those who imagine that the United States (or the world) is divided into closed "communities" that differ radically on all significant moral and political issues. It is our sense that the many communities that make up the world overlap greatly in their basic concerns. Without underestimating the difficulty of intercultural translation, we are nonetheless optimistic about the capacity to converse even across forbidding boundaries. Of course, those who think we have nothing to say and so do not wish to join the conversation are free to ignore or dismiss us. We claim no "authorial authority" over them. We do not apologize for having views, sometimes strong views, and we expect many of our readers to have equally strong views in return. Only through argument can the discussion continue.

I

Making Sense of It

In America, finding ourselves, learning how to live our lives, and with whom, are exacting tasks. It is not surprising that our personal lives are so challenging and complex that they take just about all our energy. The individualistic assumptions of our culture lead us to believe that we can live as we choose, using the big institutions—the agencies of the state, the companies or organizations we work for, the schools we attend—for our own ends, without being fundamentally influenced by them. This attitude is the current expression of our long-standing frontier mentality: when you can see the smoke from your neighbor's chimney, it's time to move west. But today there is no West we can go to (if there ever was) that will not involve us with other people in ever more complex interrelations. Most of us really know that, so just behind the bravado of the assertion that our lives are completely in our own hands is a fear that our future will be determined by forces beyond our control. Focusing on what is close at hand, then, may be as much an expression of fatalism as of self-confidence.

Whether we like it or not, we are formed by the opportunities and barriers, the temptations and threats that the larger world, what in this book we are calling the great society, presents to us. If we would be the kind of people we most want to be, we cannot ignore that larger world. For individual Americans to allow the operations of government and the economy to go on "over our heads," as though we had nothing to do with them, is to abandon just the democratic impulse that much of the rest of the world has admired in the United States. Our problem is how to educate ourselves as citizens so that we really can "make a difference" in the institutions that have such an impact on our lives.

Complexity is real enough, but it should not be a cover beneath which undemocratic managers and experts can hide. Our culture or our institutions may lead us to believe that the big issues are beyond us; but then we need to change those assumptions, and a social science that takes its public responsibility seriously can help us do so. The modern world is complex, but in its very complexity there are rich possibilities for us as individuals and in our relations with others. There is no reason a modern citizenry cannot participate in this larger world much more knowledgeably and actively than is presently the case. Active and informed participation can enhance our lives and counter the anxiety we experience when we focus too exclusively on the quest for purely private satisfactions. Indeed, finding the institutional forms to make this participation possible is a necessary condition for solving the economic and political problems that beset us.

As we Americans watched on television the candlelight vigils in Leipzig, the celebrations as the Berlin Wall fell, or the gathering of thousands of people in Wenceslas Square in Prague, in the last weeks of 1989, we rejoiced in what we saw, but it did not occur to most of us that American problems demanded that sort of action. We know that the success of democracy in Czechoslovakia or the Soviet Union or South Africa will depend on a long process of institutionalizing democratic participation. Democracy is an ongoing moral quest, not an end state, and we in America need to continue that long process in our society as well.

In this chapter we will meet a number of Americans who have had to try to make sense of how the country's large institutions affect their lives and the lives of those around them. From their difficulties we hope to learn more about what the barriers are to thinking effectively about institutions and acting responsibly within them. To face the modern world with confidence, those barriers must be overcome.

I. A SUDDEN VULNERABILITY

"I had been recognized and promoted, and then—*bang*—it was all over!" Marian Metzger was describing the climax and sudden termination of her career in business, a career that had been, on the whole, very successful. In her mid-forties, she was the only woman to have risen to important management status in her company, a midwestern paint manufacturer. The firm, which we shall call Persis Paints, was prospering, having weathered the recession of the early 1980s and the departure of many of its old industrial customers. Marian was proud of the successful new marketing strategy she devised that had won her promotion: customized attention to individual customer needs. This strategy had enabled Persis to expand sales in a difficult time—and, ironically, helped make Persis a good target for corporate takeover.

In the late 1980s, it came without warning. Persis was suddenly bought out by a much larger paint producer, whose management decided to merge the Persis operation into its own. This made the Persis plant in Indiana superfluous, and as part of the reorganization Metzger's position, like that of most of Persis's employees, was terminated. Marian's last assignment had a touch of irony: she was to coordinate the transfer of Persis Paints' central office from the Indiana plant to the new headquarters in New Jersey and see to its smooth merger into the enlarged operation.

"The whole thing—the takeover, the sudden change of management, all that—made my work seem basically futile," she said when she reflected on her experience. "I mean, I'd done a lot, without much initial support from my boss, to get the marketing operations going successfully in a new direction." Despite her sense of futility, she proceeded energetically with her final management task. "I've always taken pride," she explained, "in doing the job well, whatever it is. I'm not going to stop now. It's a personal thing for me."

One reason that Marian Metzger could finish out her tenure at Persis with relatively little bitterness was that the new company was providing displaced management personnel like herself with generous severance terms, and she would also receive her pension earnings. When asked what she planned to do next, Marian responded enthusiastically: "Actually, I have an interesting prospect. I'm planning to do something I've always wanted to do—I'm going to open an antique store with my father-in-law. He's a retired school administrator, and we've both had this interest in antiques for a long time." Marian's husband was a college professor, and their two children were well along toward financial independence.

Thanks to good severance terms, pension earnings, and a sound educational background, Marian could look forward securely to expanding her horizons into another career. At the same time she was quite aware that many of Persis Paints' employees, especially the shop workers, faced more difficult times, and she felt "very sad" for many of these workers and their families. These considerations roused her to some anger at the top managements of both the new company and Persis. "In the end," she declared, "they care only about profit. Unless they've been personally affected by this thing, they're not really very bothered." The Persis top brass had liked her work in marketing after it began to pay off, but not for the same reasons she had. Marian had loved her work because her innovations created more team spirit and cooperation both within the firm and between Persis and its customers. "They were suspicious of all that," she noted. And now, "with new owners and all, they're quite willing to destroy all the good morale" that had been built up.

Finally, what was her judgment about the whole process? Personal considerations apart, was the acquisition on balance a good or a bad thing? Was this the way to run businesses? Here Marian Metzger hesitated: "I'm not really sure." On the one hand, the combined operation would represent a more efficient economic unit, a more efficient use of investors' resources; and particularly in the face of "overseas competition," she thought the larger company "probably will benefit the economy as a whole." On the other hand, "it sure isn't a benefit to northwest Indiana, where I live, and it's not a plus for all the people who lost their jobs. The sad part is that after the former people are gone, if the firm survives, they'll declare the whole thing a success and forget the people and their pain."

Marian Metzger's situation, like her perception of it, is far from unique. During the past two decades more and more Americans discovered that their economy had become highly porous. Long accustomed to a fairly stable but dynamic economic environment, they first were made aware of their new dependence on a less predictable world market by the oil shortages of the early 1970s. Soon the United States was dependent on the world market for half the oil it needed. By the end of the 1980s it was feeling the effects of stiff foreign competition both within its own markets and overseas.

Americans have always believed that a dynamic market system will produce progress; in this respect Marian Metzger is typical. We have also known the painful swings of the business cycle and the pitiless forces of "creative destruction" that market growth unleashes. But what we have often forgotten is that though economic markets operate in some ways through an autonomous logic of their own, they can exist only because of certain institutional arrangements that brought them into being, most notably the law of contract and the law of corporations as they have developed over the past two or three centuries, and also the less formal maxims and understandings that frame business life and give it its shape.

Marian Metzger considers herself to be a responsible person—responsible in her personal life, responsible to the company she worked for, and responsible for improving the way she related to others, customers and suppliers. In all these senses she is indeed an admirable person, the kind of person upon whom the strength and integrity of American society depend. But when faced with the merger that brought one phase of her professional life to a close, she also came up against the limits of her capacity for responsible action. With bemusement and regret, she was torn between accepting the dictates of the market as somehow rational and rejecting the callousness of people who claimed to be working on the market's behalf. What she lacked was a way to think responsibly about the institutional forms that had brought about her quandary. In some states, such as Connecticut, there are state agencies with funding and expert advice that can help the workers in a plant like Persis Paints to buy out the company and run it themselves. Some of our major economic competitor nations put stringent limitations on the kind of buyouts and takeovers that we have allowed to occur in the United States. At the moment of decision in her company, Marian Metzger had little time to think about such alternatives; but it is also true that her sense of responsible citizenship stopped short, on the whole, of seeing herself in a responsible relation to the institutions, economic and otherwise, that influenced her life. Those institutions she took for granted, imagining that, like the weather, there was very little she could do about them. In this respect she is like most of us. Yet clearly she has the capacity for that larger sense of citizenship that includes critical reflection on the nature of those institutions. In that respect too she is like the rest of us.

Increasingly in the twentieth century, when faced with market outcomes that seem repugnant to their moral sense or personal welfare, Americans have turned to the government for immediate relief—a reflex that makes Marian Metzger and many other Americans uneasy. We tend to believe that we should handle most of our problems ourselves, relying on the support of voluntary associations when necessary, and that government intervention beyond a very narrow sphere is preferably a matter of last resort. Yet, as a result of continual pressures from diverse constituencies, government has become intensely involved in all sectors of the private economy, albeit in an ad hoc way. There has been little general discussion about the public purposes and responsibilities of our economic institutions, and we thus have also failed to clarify government's legitimate function in this realm.

II. SEEKING COMMON GROUND

In July 1988 millions of television viewers witnessed a historically remarkable event. A black American, a minister born and reared in the South during the years of legal segregation, addressed a major political party and the nation as a candidate for the party's presidential nomination. Perhaps equally remarkable was the introduction Jesse Jackson received from his five children: delegates and millions of viewers heard a series of articulate testimonies delivered with aplomb by his well-turned-out sons and daughters. In a statement more powerful than "The Cosby Show," the Jacksons manifestly staked the claim of the black family upon the mainstream of American life.

In the speech,[1] Jesse Jackson referred to the civil rights movement of barely a quarter-century before and to its martyred leader, the Reverend Martin Luther King, Jr. "We sit here together," said Jackson, "the sons and daughters of slavemasters and the sons and daughters of slaves sitting together around a common table, to decide the direction of our party and our country." Martin Luther King's heart, declared Jackson, who had been an associate of King's in the 1960s, "would be full tonight." Jackson stressed the need to find what he called "common ground." The choice was between "a false sense of independence" rooted in "our capacity to survive and endure," and "interdependency . . . our capacity to act, to unite for the greater good." Later, in a departure from his prepared text, he exhorted—and thereby brought for a moment into public view—"the poor and the vulnerable and the many in the world" not to lose hope and dignity.

Jackson's children belong to the successor generation to those like their father who waged the battle for civil rights, and they as well as he embody the struggle's great achievements. The "underclass" for whom Jackson claimed to speak is the shocking reminder of that movement's incomplete results.

The civil rights movement, like World War II, profoundly reshaped American national consciousness and changed the country's moral order. Racial equality became an uncontested central belief and a basic legal commitment. But, unlike the victory in World War II, victory for this cause has been elusive. The valid but limited victory that the civil rights legislation of the mid-1960s represents produced unexpected consequences.

The great burst of freedom made possible by open housing and antidiscrimination laws found black Americans by the millions wanting to leave overcrowded, decaying urban ghettoes and poorly rewarded occupations. As the fortunate and determined entered middle-class neighborhoods and middle-class occupations, they left behind people unable to get a toehold in the labor market, for at the same time industrial jobs were drying up in inner cities. The isolation and demoralization of an "underclass" had begun.

School integration and affirmative action to help blacks—well-intended national efforts to make restitution for the old evils of racism—produced their own conundrums. They made possible educational and economic gains for many black Americans, but they also pitted the "rights" of one group against the "rights" of others. The resulting distrust and anguish have made it seem that the gains of the civil rights era are slipping away under our feet. Only now, unlike in the triumphant days of "the Movement," it is often unclear to persons of good will what the government can or should do.

Jesse Jackson stressed the importance of government, and in one sense he was surely right to do so. Not only in efforts to gain racial justice but in many other ways Americans today are deeply dependent upon the national government. In the economic realm, many of the great recent bursts of entrepreneurial energy we pride ourselves on, even the electronics boom of Silicon Valley, rest on technology that was developed and paid for by federal defense spending. Americans today refuse to accept the continued poisoning of the air and water; they do not see the risk of being maimed or killed as a normal part of holding a job, just as they less and less see cancer, emphysema, or AIDS as an inevitable part of the human condition. And they expect government to protect them from preventable risk, injury, or death caused by workplaces, food, or the toys they buy for their children. Increasingly, we recognize that what we formerly saw as private difficulties and sufferings are matters of public responsibility, just as much as national security or relief from natural disasters.

At the same time, Americans' traditional suspicion of governmental power has not died out. In the past Americans tried to achieve the positive effects of government while avoiding its tyrannical potentials by using it only to control abuses in the private economy; rarely was the government given clear public mandates and purposes. However, such a "regulatory state" produces its own difficulties. For example, consider health care. The expansion of publicly financed health insurance for the elderly that occurred as part of Lyndon Johnson's War on Poverty has been a godsend for millions; yet as a result of efforts to reduce the abuse of the system, the federal government reshaped the priorities of the medical establishment by favoring shorter hospital stays and less rather than more expensive treatment; the government now has data on the quality of health care in each hospital; and it soon will be able to provide such data for individual physicians. So as the federal government pays for or underwrites health care, it also begins to regulate how that health care is provided. And soon its policy planners begin to ask questions such as, for example, whether it is reasonable to fund expensive new medical technologies of primary benefit to the elderly in preference to prenatal care for indigent mothers. Further questions concern the potential trade-offs between health care and other public goods.

But the very language of "trade-offs" is inadequate, for it suggests that the problems are merely technical, when we need a richer moral discourse with which to conduct public discussion about these problems.

This is not to say that we would be healthier or better off without such government interventions. We clearly would not be; our overall provision of health care still lags behind that of Western Europe. But increasing government interventions represent a centralization of authority as well as responsibility. It is troubling that we lack a common moral grounding for these new decisions our government is making, and that the decisions have been made without any broad public discussion of the ends our health-care system should seek, who should pay for it, and who should control its several parts. We have more government, but less political and moral capacity to make it accountable.

If Marian Metzger was listening to Jesse Jackson that July evening of his convention address, she might well have posed a question that concerned both his themes and her own experience. She might have asked, "How can we use government to enhance everyone's freedom, and benefit those at the margins of the market, without simultaneously creating excessive and rigid governmental controls?" Government intervention, as we have seen in the case of health care, can include not just the "red tape" of bureaucratic regulation but the intrusiveness of data collection and its use as a tool for control. For a considerable time, one favored answer was that expert management would handle this conundrum. American business has long depended upon professional experts as part of the practice of "scientific management." And expert management seemed a way to address problems and design solutions in the public realm that was both socially efficient and "above politics." Today, however, this apparently tried-and-true approach is confronting baffling dilemmas of its own. And if the rule of experts is not the solution but part of the problem, where are we to turn for answers?

As in the case of the economy, it is important to realize that government operates only within the context of institutions. We are now torn between our long-standing commitment to "limited government" and the realization that many of our problems require urgent government response; rather than veering from too much government regulation and intervention to too much *de*regulation and then back again, we would do better to rethink the entire institutional context of government in a modern society. The question is not just what should government do but how it can do it in a way that strengthens the initiative and participation of citizens, both as individuals and within their communities and associations, rather than reducing them to the status of clients.

To answer that question effectively is to challenge powerful groups with vested interests in present arrangements, but it is the only direction to go if we believe that democracy is more than an ideological facade for what is fast becoming an administered society. In short, government as such is not the answer to our problems. The question is, what kind of government? Jesse Jackson and other liberal leaders have not ignored that question, but neither have they proposed ways to think about the public participation and accountability that alone will keep administrative structures from being despotic. Politicians focus on the ends that government is supposed to achieve more than on means, the texture of relationships, and the institutional forms that will ensure that the ends enhance rather than diminish our possibilities for responsible citizenship.

III. WHAT IS THE VALUE OF A LIFE?

Though he would probably wince at the term, Bud Chapin is a government expert. As a senior regulatory analyst at the Occupational Safety and Health Administration (OSHA), he is charged with determining standards of acceptable job-related risk and safety for industries like Marian Metzger's Persis Paints. Bud Chapin expresses considerable discomfort with the standard economic techniques his agency uses to determine acceptable trade-offs between the often high costs of safe technology and risks to human life. The use of what is known as "cost-benefit" analysis, standard at OSHA, is, to Bud

Chapin, when applied to areas of health, "mind-boggling. It's nuts. It's wrong, totally wrong.

"Can lives be valued? I guess I'm saying, 'With very great difficulty; and I don't know what that value is.' " This was Chapin's response to a direct question about the basis of what his agency was charged to do. Like the Environmental Protection Agency (EPA), OSHA was established after the upsurge in national awareness of new social problems in the aftermath of the 1960s. And like the EPA, OSHA is charged with regulating what economists call "externalities," which involves an effort to measure and make sense of the increasing degree to which our activities impinge on one another—the overloaded sewer systems, the crowded highways, the waste dumps, the use of dangerous materials in manufacturing. The problem has been how to set standards to regulate these once unforeseen impingements. The technique of cost-benefit analysis leads to the construction of a market, with incentives and costs, where none naturally exists, as in the case of the disposal of toxic waste. To create such a fictive market requires one to set a price on everything, from human lives to scenic vistas, so that trade-offs among these goods can be calculated as costs and benefits. Analysts like Bud Chapin are charged with devising regulations that in effect create economic incentives for firms to take problems of safety and risk seriously as intrinsic costs of doing business.

How, then, does Chapin proceed? By means of what he calls "a simplistic approach at this point—what will do the most good for the most number for the least price." This is the classic formula of welfare economics, as it is of philosophical utilitarianism, the intellectual parent of economics.

As Chapin sees it, university-trained economists like himself think about trade-offs. They try to work out reasonable answers to the question of whether money spent to clean up a toxic dump, saving one life over fifty years, might not be better spent on regulating toxic substances in the factory or on providing health care to poor mothers, which would save more lives for less cost. "But," continues Chapin, "I stop short, if I can, of putting dollars on the injury and on the people." Asked why, he replies: "The kinds of machinations and formulae and techniques and designs that we can put into the things that we do to make sense of supply-and-demand intersections—these are apart from, and don't relate to, anything other than market considerations." These techniques can tell us that "if you spend a million dollars today in this industry, here's what you will be getting in terms of benefits today and tomorrow and into the future in real people terms. If you wait, here's what you get . . . and here are the streams of benefits in terms of illnesses and injuries avoided."

Dissident experts such as Chapin acknowledge the limitations. According to him, "there is something missing" in cost-benefit and similar techniques that propose to calculate "objectively" how to take account of the growing interconnectedness of American society. But even for Chapin cost-benefit reasoning is powerful, despite his fundamental disagreement with it, and he has difficulty imagining a real alternative. He finally recommends using it with reservations and moderation.

Where might we look for intellectual resources more adequate to the challenges of the new era? The major blind spot in the economic theory that Bud Chapin has to rely on is that it sees only disaggregated individuals, not the institutions that give them meaning and a place in the world. In the theoretical perspective he works from, there are only the goods or interests of individuals, assumed to be fixed preferences which can only be aggregated but not discussed. This typically economistic way of thinking blocks out the truth that such goods and interests are culturally constituted and historically variable, and any notion of a common good embodied in the institutional life of society is ruled out in advance as illusory. Thus what experts like Chapin overlook is the value of public discussion that could clarify popular preferences and very possibly alter them in the light of a deeper moral consensus. Nor do they see that the legislative mandates under which they must work are too fragile, too much the result of momentary compromise and too little the result of sustained public discussion, to justify the moral logic they use.

Jesse Jackson was affirming an old American tradition as well as his own biography when he used religious language to conjure a vision of an expanded and inclusive society in which the search for a common good would be central. Can our religious institutions still provide such resources? Can they, as in the days of abolition, the Social Gospel, or civil rights, provide the needed inspiration?

IV. THE LEAST OF THESE

The gleaming towers of commerce rising from the Piedmont mark Atlanta, capital of the New South. A short walk from the ultramodern hall in which Jesse Jackson gave his address on seeking common ground runs the aging urban corridor of Ponce de Leon Avenue. A wave of recent redevelopment has begun to dot its two-mile length with new supermarkets, shopping centers, small office blocks, and refurbished apartment buildings. But the markets employ round-the-clock guards, the apartments feature ironclad security systems, and clerks in the liquor stores keep baseball bats at hand under the checkout counter; for the avenue is also lined with rundown welfare and transient hotels, single-room apartments, and trash-strewn vacant lots that provide a kind of base for Atlanta's homeless, jobless poor. For them, Ponce de Leon contains no beckoning fountain of youth. They wander the avenue's broad sidewalks, cluster in front of its neon-lit diners and bars, and panhandle their better-off neighbors in its parking lots.

Almost ten years ago two Presbyterian ministers and a lay couple moved into a rambling old Ponce de Leon building, once the Women's Union Mission, and began the Open Door Community. Described as "a Presbyterian Catholic Worker House," it provides the homeless with a place to live, the hungry with a soup kitchen, the unwashed with public showers, and the uprooted with a group of resident "partners" and "volunteers" who share household tasks, communal care, and prayer with their "house guests" from the streets.

One of the Open Door's founders is Ed Loring. He first came to the neighborhood in the mid-1970s as pastor of a small, aging Presbyterian congregation. Then approaching forty, he planned on staying just a few years while he and his wife, Murphy Davis, finished their doctoral studies at a nearby university, and then moving on to teach at a church college. Things did not work out that way. From a small Bible-study group on Sunday evenings whose members asked how to live out the Gospel's message, Loring and Davis gradually developed a new sense of mission. "We recognized that the call to serve God is the call to serve the poor," relates Davis, citing the "Great Judgment" passage in Matthew 25, where Jesus says, "Truly, I say to you, as you did it to one of the least of these my brethren, you did it to me." It is in the suffering of the poor, she says, that "we come to understand the suffering of Christ."

Loring and Davis inaugurated a night shelter for Atlanta's homeless in the sanctuary of their church with the help of another young couple, Rob and Carolyn Johnson. The example of Dorothy Day's Catholic Worker Houses gave some guidance. As Murphy Davis recalls, "Ed just drove around in this old blue van we had, stopping and asking people if they wanted to come and spend the night in our church. You can imagine that most people thought we were crazy, but after that, word got around." So effectively did the word get around that the number of homeless soon filled the church. "We take seriously the word 'hospitality,' and we are attempting to offer hospitality and not just shelter," Loring explained. "Hospitality, theologically, means trying to offer space where the people are not only sheltered and fed but also given friendship. And the basis for that is God's friendship with us."

At that point problems arose. Some members of the congregation refused to join in the night-shelter work and resisted its expanding presence. Others worried that it would threaten the church's own fellowship and distract Ed from his work as their pastor. Meanwhile, Loring, Davis, and the Johnsons felt pulled between their full-time jobs and their growing responsibility for the shelter. Both couples recall wondering if they could truly follow Christ and feed the hungry without living together with them.

Finally, in 1981, the Open Door moved into its own home, financed in part by the sale of Loring and Davis's house and help from the Atlanta Presbytery. "We felt a new vocation emerging from our experience of serving God in the midst of the poor," said Loring. "We wanted to form an alternative style of Christian community—a residential community."

The Open Door has sustained a pattern of community life, service to the homeless, and public advocacy on their behalf. But it has been a struggle. The Open Door contrasts its biblical ideal of hospitality given freely to strangers as fellow creatures and neighbors with the professional services that state and public agencies give to their clients. Unwilling to do "intake evaluations" of "neediness" to determine their "clients' " eligibility for help, or to keep the precise records required by the United States Department of Agriculture to receive surplus food, the Open Door has given up getting government aid, but it sorely misses this help.

Two of the community's four original partners, the Johnsons, are now gone. Continually seeking to help those who have not always helped themselves, and who may be drunk, abusive, and violent as well as needy, is a heavy burden. Some of the people who came through the Open Door "were carrying a lot of things they had done wrong," says a partner who left. Some of them had put themselves in that situation. "I struggled with the theology of Jesus Christ coming through the door for soup. I had a difficult time saying they are still Jesus Christ."

Meanwhile, some of the (mostly black, mostly less well educated) house guests protested against the authority reserved by the Open Door's partners. "I don't know how you can have a real community," challenges one, "when half the people here have no decision-making position." Ed Loring responds, "The purpose of the church, the purpose of Pentecost, is to undo the damage of the tower of Babel so we can live in a new unity as in Ephesians 2 ["So then you are no more strangers and sojourners, but you are fellow citizens with the saints"]. What is painful, and what I have not found a way to address, is how we open that reality to class and race distinctions. . . . But I'm not now thinking, as I was five, six, or seven years ago, that we're going to pull off a kind of equality and mutuality inside this house that we can't do outside this house. The world is too much here. We're not doing much, but it's something. We're here, living with the diversity, together."

Even in its most idealistic and exemplary form as a community of moral witness, then, the church cannot escape or ignore the larger society. Nor, as Loring sees, can it heal every wound. Selfless service as a way of life, which a few Americans choose, and the more measured charity of many others are important but, as Murphy Davis concludes, "our little crumbs are not enough. What the poor and the downtrodden need is not our piecemeal charity but justice. Wholeness. Enough for all God's children."

Sometimes members of the overcrowded and underfunded Open Door Community question the effect of their message for the church and for society as a whole. "Perhaps," Davis reflects, "one reason that God calls us to love the poor is because the reality of the poor mocks our assumptions about progress and success." This somber insight is related to the Open Door's impulse to stand apart from a society it perceives as at odds with its ideals of social justice, voluntary poverty, and solidarity with the poor. At the same time, it engages in vigorous public education, advocacy, and discussion in the hope that society can come to feed the hungry, shelter the homeless, and enable the poor, too, to work for the common good. This complicated stance expresses the tension between any religious vision and an imperfect world, but it also suggests the great problem that dogs any efforts at spontaneous religious service: the problem of embodying ethical ideals in the individual actions of people working with others when one cannot alter the larger institutional context that produces the suffering one is trying to alleviate.

Radical Christians like Murphy Davis are rarely accustomed to imagine themselves in situations like that of Bud Chapin. Yet in one important way their aims and even their views are not so far apart. Both are dismayed at what they perceive as the coldness of a society so heavily focused on competitive market calculation. Davis writes: "How difficult to hear that the Gospel calls us to be failures. . . . It is hard to learn that salvation comes not because our work builds steady progress toward the coming of God's kingdom, but because God is full of love and grace for us and the whole of creation." Davis and Chapin concur in wanting somehow to redeem the narrowness of self-interested calculation by invoking reasons of the heart. Both see head and heart sundered in contemporary society and wish actively to reunite them.

Murphy Davis and Ed Loring are proceeding from a richer understanding of this problem than Bud Chapin is. Chapin lacks a community and a tradition capable of providing a concrete alternative meaning to his qualms about "valuing" lives. By contrast, Davis and Loring have opted to free themselves from dealing with the larger economic and governmental institutions as much as possible; having avoided the responsibilities Chapin took on, they are not involved in the unsatisfying compromises he must make. However, as we have seen, they pay a significant price for this purity and freedom. In spite of their commitment, their community cannot cope with the depth and complexity of the problems facing those people unlucky enough to fall into the perhaps permanent underclass. What solutions can they offer to the problems of education and participation in an economy driven by rapidly changing and ever more complex technology? Their witness is a profound and moving gesture of hope; but it remains a gesture, a sign but not a pattern for transforming the whole of society. What Davis and Loring have come to know very painfully is that converting individuals, however important, does not take the place of converting institutions. Yet that does not detract from their vision of what a better society would be: one more deeply inclusive, one oriented to human wholeness rather than private acquisition—a vision that our current institutions badly need to embody. They know the church does not have a blueprint for that institutional conversion, but they also know it belongs in the conversation of those seeking the right answers.[2]

V. REALISTS AND IDEALISTS

By no means all religious believers, certainly not all Christians, believe that concern for the poor and the problems of injustice require disengagement from the systems of worldly power. The Protestant theologian Reinhold Niebuhr, for one, argued with great public effect that because of the tragic limitations of human nature, human beings could not help doing some evil in the course of doing good; yet, he continued, God commanded sinful men and women to bring justice

to bear on human efforts, despite the ironic consequences that often
meet such attempts.[3] During the key years of American dominance
in world affairs that followed World War II, Niebuhr's views established a powerful rationale for a stance known as "realist." Today, as
then, many Americans of good will worry that the receptive charity
of the Open Door Community is not a reasonable or proper metaphor
for the way America should act in the international world.

Richard Nixon was for long a prominent spokesman for his own
kind of "realism." "Americans prefer to conduct their peacetime con-
tests in the international arena by Marquess of Queensbury rules,"
he wrote in his 1980 book *The Real War*. "For the Soviet leaders,
however, the same rules apply in peace as in war, and those are the
rules of the street-fighter: anything goes. To meet their challenge, the
American President must use all the power at his command in an
effective and responsible way. . . . This means that he think realistically, not naïvely . . . and finally that he accept the reality that moral
perfection in the conduct of nations cannot be expected and should
not be demanded."[4]

Published during the beleaguered last year of Jimmy Carter's administration, Nixon's *cri de coeur* was a harsh criticism of the ideals that
Jimmy Carter had voiced during his presidential campaign. Carter,
who acknowledged Reinhold Niebuhr as a spiritual mentor, had vig-
orously criticized the Nixon-Kissinger approach to foreign policy and
had promised an alternative to it. "The question, I think," Carter said
in one of his campaign statements, "is whether in recent years our
highest officials have not been too pragmatic, even cynical, and as a
consequence have ignored those moral values that had often distinguished our country." He warned that "military strength alone is not
enough," that the country's real strength lay in the values embodied
in its founding documents. "These principles have made us great,"
he stated, "and unless our foreign policy reflects them, we make a
mockery of all those values." In his inaugural address he quoted Micah
6:8: "What doth the Lord require of thee, but to do justly, and to
love mercy, and to walk humbly with thy God?"[5]

After the 1980 election, a photo in *Time* magazine showed Ronald
Reagan sitting at a clean desk topped by a copy of Nixon's *The Real
War*. To many it must have seemed that the debate had come full
circle.[6] Actually, the argument between Nixon and Carter and Reagan
was part of a long public debate between "realists" and "idealists" in
foreign affairs, a debate as old as the republic. "No nation," observed
George Washington, "is to be trusted farther than it is bound by its
interest." Yet from the beginning, Americans saw themselves as an

exemplary people, a vision called up by both Presidents Carter and Reagan, albeit with different emphases.

Harriet Beecher Stowe wrote in the nineteenth century of Americans as a people "commissioned to bear the light of liberty and religion through all the earth and to bring in the great millennial day, when wars should cease and the whole world, released from the thralldom of evil, should rejoice in the light of the Lord."[7] This messianic conception of the United States in the world was especially easy to proclaim during the nineteenth century, when the country was able to stand aloof and secure on what its citizens saw as their own continent. Woodrow Wilson brought this American millennialism into the world of twentieth-century power politics when he announced of American entry into World War I: "We have come to redeem the world by giving it liberty and justice."[8] However, all idealists have not been hopeless dreamers, nor all realists disillusioned cynics. Public figures like the diplomat George Kennan and the historian Arthur Schlesinger, Jr., tried to enact Niebuhr's "moral realism" as a responsible moral practice of power politics in a complicated, ambiguous, tragically immoral world. Theirs was an example of the subtlety, and difficulty, of public moral understanding that could be achieved through a serious debate between realism and idealism.

During the past two decades, however, as American preeminence in the world has receded and new forces have grown, idealism and realism have become strangely detached from the actual practice of foreign relations. The contrast between the aura of Wilsonian idealism in Carter's rhetoric and the acrid sensation of hard-edged realism in Nixon's or the forceful millennialism of Reagan's did not correspond to fundamental differences in their actual conduct of foreign affairs. Neither does it explain their successes and failures in this realm.

By the end of his term in office, Carter was popularly regarded as a failure in foreign affairs. The public's idea was that although—or perhaps because—Carter was good and decent, his administration was weak and incompetent, as could be seen in setbacks like the Soviet invasion of Afghanistan and especially the Iranian hostage seizure. One might argue to the contrary that it was the implementation of Carter's idealistic aspirations that led to his greatest triumph, his brokering of the Camp David accords between Israel and Egypt. Further, Carter's policies were by no means softly idealistic. Under the tutelage of National Security Adviser Zbigniew Brzezinski, Carter's administration adopted a geopolitical strategy that, like Nixon's, aimed soberly and systematically to maximize America's advantage in the international balance of power.[9]

The problem with Carter's foreign policy was not that it was weakened by softhearted idealism or inconsistency, as critics charged, but that the international political economy was becoming too complicated to permit effective use of the standard instruments of the geopolitical strategies beloved by the realists. "A flaw in our strategy," admits a former member of Carter's National Security Council staff, "was in not having full ideas about what were the appropriate instruments of power. There was a recognition that military response was inadequate for many of the problems we faced. In matters of East-West policy, you can use military power. But [for many of our basic problems] military power is not of much use. You have to rely on the power of ideas and the power of economics."

For more than a decade it has been clear that the United States government, like the governments of all other nation states, is no longer able to control the international flow of information and the dynamics of the global economy. So when the Carter administration tried to punish the Soviet Union for its invasion of Afghanistan by means of a grain embargo, the result was that other grain-exporting nations promptly filled the gap left by the American withdrawal from Soviet trade. When revolutionary Iranians seized fifty-two American hostages in Teheran, international media coverage turned the event into a huge psychodrama that intensified the pain, frustration, and humiliation caused by the event in the United States.

The Reagan administration tried to avoid the kinds of foreign-policy defeats suffered by Carter, and to a degree it succeeded. Certain demonstrations of American power, such as the invasion of Grenada, were militarily successful and boosted morale. Many others, such as the stationing of Marines in Lebanon, the mining of harbors in Nicaragua, or the dispatching of the Navy to the Persian Gulf, were not. The Reagan White House greatly expanded the military budget, already increased under Carter, and sought to achieve unquestioned military superiority over the Soviet Union, reestablishing American world hegemony. But ultimately how successful was this strategy? The great breakthrough in controlling strategic arms, for which Reagan will be remembered most, came as a dramatic reversal rather than a steady continuation of his earlier policy. The effort to bankrupt the USSR through the arms race may have succeeded, though with a nearly similar result at home, measured by an indebtedness that threatens to debilitate our entire international strategic position by making the country increasingly dependent upon the goodwill of other nations. What appeared to Ronald Reagan and his advisers at the beginning of his administration as tough-minded realism now appears as a kind of quixotic idealism. The reasons do not lie in the traditional realist-idealist debate; the change stems rather from seismic global shifts.

The dynamics of the international economy led to increasing competition with the European Economic Community, Japan, and the newly industrializing countries of East Asia. Our military might was useless to prevent this. The same dynamic, with some inadvertent help from U.S. economic policies, produced increasing poverty in Latin America and Africa. Again, all our military power was irrelevant to these problems, producing instead a policy of proxy warfare in Central America and elsewhere. The new complexities of international interdependence rendered obsolete our commonly accepted categories for understanding foreign-policy challenges.[10]

The terms of the current foreign policy debates concern a world that no longer exists. The realist says that the United States should do whatever it takes to protect its national self-interest. However, we are entering an era when, as Daniel Bell put it recently, "the nation-state is becoming too small for the big problems of life, and too big for the small problems of life."[11] Our economic life is dominated by the dynamics of a vast world market that cannot be controlled by the action of any single nation-state. Problems of environmental pollution transcend national boundaries. The proliferation of nuclear weapons threatens the security of all. Vast disparities in global wealth and power lead to festering conflicts that endanger economic health and political security around the world.

Under these circumstances, the self-interest of our nation, which the realists stress, cannot always be clearly distinguished from the self-interest of other societies, let alone be conceived in opposition to it. The idealistic approach, for its part, assumes that the United States has ideals that are uniquely its own and that we have it in our power to spread them around the world. If that is still true, and in some ways it surely is, we do not understand very well what it is that others seek to learn from us or how to provide them an example that will neither stifle nor oppress them. It would appear, then, that both our ideals and our interests require reformulation from a new, more global perspective. And it is also clear that that global perspective is an institutional perspective.

The realistic perspective was based on the notion that nation-states were in a "state of nature" and had to act as though they were perpetually in an actual or potential "war of all against all." The idealistic perspective also imagined nations to be isolated "individuals" among which the United States stands out as an uplifting example for others.

But we are finally realizing a truth that has long been clear to perceptive observers: that nation-states are enmeshed in a global great society which puts severe constraints on the power of even the strongest of them. International institutions—treaties, agreements, covenants—have grown immensely since the end of World War II, and an international public opinion has developed that no nation can easily ignore. In view of the military, economic, and ecological threats that endanger every human being, the challenge today is to strengthen and expand the international institutions essential to the common good of our planet as a whole.

VI. INSTITUTIONAL DILEMMAS AS MORAL DILEMMAS

Up to this point we have been examining instances of serious individuals having difficulty making sense of and knowing how to act in the complex economic, political, and international institutions that go to make up the great society. If well-educated managers, experts, political leaders, and elected officials seem to lack an adequate public philosophy to help them assess facts and determine goals, it is hardly surprising that ordinary citizens are often baffled by what they see.

When faced with issues we do not understand, we grasp for contexts that are more immediately intelligible. Familiar institutions, such as the family, function as metaphors by means of which we extend meaning to unfamiliar situations and events, so Americans can extend sympathy and concern to the lives of people in other cities or other countries by seeing their lives as like those experienced in families and kin networks at home. When we see a picture of an injured child being carried from the rubble of an earthquake-devastated building in Mexico or Armenia, we immediately understand the needs of those people far away. Another familiar institution that we use in this metaphorical way is sports. The triumphs and failures of business organizations, for example, make sense when described—and lived—as the life of a "team." But much of the information coming to us in newspapers or on the television news remains incomprehensible because we lack a sense of institutional context that would make it seem human.

As we have said, the very idea of institutions is often repugnant to Americans. But whatever their conscious attitude, Americans are deeply fascinated by the moral drama of institutions, at least when they understand them, or think they do, as in the case of sports.

Consider baseball, the national pastime. Tens of millions of fans depend for the excitement of a season not only upon the practice of the sport but on the institution of the leagues, with their complex athletic, economic, and legal rules. The drama of the annual pennant races is what it is only because the skills of players and teams are supported and guided by the less visible structure of coaches, umpires, accountants, and contracts. Equally crucial is the moral infrastructure of collective honor, loyalty, and devotion to the sport. For many fans the drama of baseball is heightened at those moments when the larger institutional patterns come into view—especially in moments of crisis, as when a team is separated from a city long identified with it, or when scandal shocks the public's sense of the honor and propriety that ought to govern the sport.

It is expected that star players are extraordinarily well paid; but when they allow their own image or their own self-indulgence to become more important than their contribution to the team, the enjoyment of the game changes to moral outrage, as it does when owners appear to be acting for private gain at the expense of the honest life of the sport. Why this indignation? At such moments the public acknowledges that moral norms are woven throughout baseball; shared indignation expresses the fans' tremendous moral identification with the sport as an institution. Clearly baseball in such moments is not being understood as a neutral device for individual satisfaction—if it were, who would care about scandals? Rather, baseball, with its purposes, codes, and standards, is a collective moral enterprise, an institution in the full sense, and many Americans care deeply about it. As an institution, baseball is more than the actual players and organizations who play the game during any given season. That is why we can see the sport as sometimes succeeding, sometimes failing, in becoming what baseball really ought to be. This understanding of things was beautifully expressed by the late Baseball Commissioner A. Bartlett Giamatti in his statement of August 10, 1989, concerning his decision to banish from the game for life the former star player and then-manager of the Cincinnati Reds, Pete Rose, as a result of Mr. Rose's gambling activities:

> I believe baseball is a beautiful and exciting game, loved by millions—I among them—and I believe that baseball is an important, enduring American institution. It must assert and aspire to the highest of principles—of integrity, of professionalism of performance, of fair play within its rules. It will come as no surprise that like any institution

composed of human beings, this institution will not always fulfill its highest aspirations. I know of no earthly institution that does. But this one, because it is so much a part of our history as a people and because it has such a purchase on our national soul, has an obligation to the people for whom it is played—to its fans and its well-wishers—to strive for excellence in all things and to promote the highest ideals.

I will be told that I am an idealist. I hope so. I will continue to locate ideals I hold for myself and for my country in the national game as well as in other of our national institutions. And there will be debate and dissent about this or that or another occurrence on or off the field, and while the game's nobler parts will always be enmeshed in the human frailties of those who, whatever their role, have stewardship of this game, let there be no doubt or dissent about the goal of baseball or our dedication to it. Nor about our vigilance and vigor—and patience—in protecting the game from blemish or stain or disgrace.[12]

Sports fans intuitively understand things important for all Americans to know. Their enthusiasm for institutionalized sports enables them to recognize that individual excellence depends on collectively maintained codes of honor and discipline. As generations of coaches have claimed and athletes have affirmed, sports teach and form character. But so do all institutions: in this they are not so much unique as exemplary.

Institutions are patterns of social activity that give shape to collective and individual experience. An institution is a complex whole that guides and sustains individual identity, as a family gives sense and purpose to the lives of its members, enabling them to realize themselves as spouses, parents, and children. Institutions form individuals by making possible or impossible certain ways of behaving and relating to others. They shape character by assigning responsibility, demanding accountability, and providing the standards in terms of which each person recognizes the excellence of his or her achievements. Each individual's possibilities depend on the opportunities opened up within the institutional contexts to which that person has access. Without the collective effort represented by the teams on the field, there could be no grand slams.

Institutions, then, are essential bearers of ideals and meanings; yet in the real world the embodiment is imperfect. The achievement of individual ends, like the carrying out of patterned social activity on which it always depends, requires material resources. It also involves the use of power. For this reason all institutions—armies, teams, and even families—are necessarily involved to some degree with both wealth and power. These means all too easily become ends in themselves. Institutions become corrupt, some more so than others. The enormous amount of money at stake in professional sports has introduced an element of corruption so profound that many fans are deeply cynical about the sport that at the same time they also deeply love. Indeed, it is just at the point where the relative clarity of the game is clouded over by purely business considerations and power conflicts that disillusionment sets in. Suddenly an institution we thought we understood well begins to look like the institutions we don't understand at all. What seemed morally clear is now morally ambiguous. It is no wonder that Americans have an often-noted allergy to large institutions—though, as in the case of sports, even in our cynicism we continue to depend on them.

But corruption can be recognized and criticized. If the ideals embodied in an institution are not totally dead, they stand as a judgment against the corruption of their embodiment. This is something we often overlook. The heroic individual who cleans up the corrupt institution is a staple figure of our lore in movies and television. It is easy not to notice that the honest cop and the crusading reporter, in the very act of resisting corruption, are drawing upon and enacting norms and ideals at the core of the institutions with which they struggle. When heroism has a lasting effect, it is because it has worked catalytically to reignite the dedication of others to the highest codes of the police or of journalism. That is, it must find expression in reformed institutions.

But that we all too easily think of economic or political programs as "game plans" and of our leaders as "quarterbacks" should give us pause. Sports institutions give us intelligible metaphors in situations we do not understand very well, and a careful consideration of that fact can be instructive; but there are features of sports that make them limited and finally misleading as a way of thinking about the central institutions of today's great society. The formal properties of the game of baseball, for example, give it an objectivity that appears to be timeless. One can tinker with the rules, to be sure, but the basic pattern of the game is untouchable; to change it drastically would be to invent another game (something that has certainly happened historically, but that we do not usually contemplate when thinking about sports). Yet to think that our economic and political institutions are given, timeless, "natural," is fundamentally the wrong way to think about them in a rapidly changing world.

Sports help us to see that at the core of any viable institution there is a moral code which must be periodically reinvigorated so that the institution may survive and flourish. Sports do not help us to see when our institutions are in such serious difficulty that drastic institutional innovations are required. Family and sports often serve us well as institutional metaphors to help us make sense of our world. But the problems our society faces today require that we expand our repertory far beyond these familiar examples, that we think hard and critically about what has too long been taken for granted.

The unprecedented problems now challenging most of our country's major institutions, our established ways of doing things, are so new that their precise nature and significance are still being debated. One thing is clear, however: between now and the turn of the new millennium we as a people will have to respond to profound challenges to our beliefs, habits, and ways of life. The decisions that are made about our economy, our schools, our government, or our national position in the world cannot be separated from the way we live in practical terms, the moral life we lead as a people.

The decisions we are making and will make about the future of our institutions will reshape us as moral beings. And as we respond to challenge and change, our economic and governmental institutions, like our families, schools, universities, churches, and synagogues, will be crucially important—as the bearers of our collective memories and our cultural traditions, as the expression of important, but often barely conscious, patterns of meaning and self-definition.

Perhaps no maxim can better provide guidance than the Socratic admonition to "know thyself." To reflect on our institutions will serve as a primary means toward growing self-knowledge.

VII. MAKING SENSE OF OUR LIVES

We began this chapter by arguing that it is easier to understand what we know at first hand than it is to understand the institutions and structures of the great society. Yet we are all aware of those situations, frequent enough in our own lives and the lives of those closest to us, when things don't make sense. Our dilemmas seem related to our freedom. In societies where there are well-established expectations, life may be difficult, but it is not confusing.

It is not that we have no rules. In a sense the rules are clearer than ever. A successful life in American society depends on the ability to negotiate competently a series of requirements, primarily to show technical competence and secondarily to demonstrate the ability to deal effectively with other people. The educational system dovetails with the occupational system in maintaining these emphases. Socialization in the middle-class family reinforces this pattern through its emphasis on doing well in school, being competitive (in sports as well as studies), and getting along with others. In family, leisure, school, and work the fine calculation of the relation of means to ends is emphasized, and this gives rise to the pattern of utilitarian individualism which we described in *Habits of the Heart*, a pattern moderated only partly by the attention to human relations—expressive individualism—for the emphasis here, too, is heavily strategic.

Life in this paradigm is a competitive race to acquire the objective markers (College Boards, admission to the right school, GPA, LSAT, advanced degree, entry into the right organization, promotion to higher-echelon positions) that give access to all the good things that make life worthwhile (attractiveness to a desirable mate, purchase of an appropriate home, American Express Gold Card, vacations in Europe).[13] But what this form of life minimizes, if it does not neglect it altogether, is any larger moral meaning, any contribution to the common good, that might help it to make sense. So while there are many rules, and the rules operate so as to put great pressure on us to conform to them, there are few reasons. In short, it is not just the "big institutions" that don't make sense but our own lives. Beyond following the rules that tell us how to get ahead, we have trouble making moral sense of our immediate actions.

From the individual point of view, the educational and occupational systems appear to have an objective givenness that puts them beyond question. Failure or refusal to adapt to them has the inevitable consequence of depriving a person of access to precisely the rewards that in this paradigm make life worthwhile. The presence of large numbers of people in our society who have failed in these regards serves as an admonition to make sure one does not join them, but it also, even if subliminally, raises questions about the legitimacy of the whole pattern. Part of the problem is that we do not bring the sense of institutional meaning that we intuitively have about baseball to bear on the educational, economic, and administrative institutions that demand so much from us. We think what is required here is only a high level of competence, of expertise, of "professionalism," not the moral wisdom that should be at the basis of any good institution. And when things go wrong, we tend to blame individuals, we decry their lack of "ethics," but we don't question the morality of the institutions themselves.

After four years in an excellent university, a recent Harvard undergraduate said in his graduation oration: "Among my classmates, however, I believe that there is one idea, one sentiment, which we have all acquired at some point in our Harvard careers; and that, ladies and gentlemen, is, in a word, confusion." The graduate-student orator the same year said, "They tell us that it is heresy to suggest the superiority of some value, fantasy to believe in moral argument, slavery to submit to a judgment sounder than your own. The freedom of our day is the freedom to devote ourselves to any values we please, on the mere condition that we do not believe them to be true."

Ironically, the confusion and nihilism that threaten these fine students is related to the commitment to reason, knowledge, and education that has always been central to American success. This country has rightly celebrated the intelligence of an educated citizenry, the common sense of the merchant or tinkerer, and, more recently, the scientific and technical knowledge that has made our nation an economic and technological leader. But just at the point when our citizens depend more and more on knowledge, we face a crisis about the purposes and meaning of that knowledge. This is the difficulty that created the poignancy of Bud Chapin's dilemmas in using sophisticated economic techniques in order to protect public safety: we have concentrated more on the technical effectiveness of knowledge than on its moral purpose.

There is a profound gap in our culture between technical reason, the knowledge with which we design computers or analyze the structure of DNA, and practical or moral reason, the ways we understand how we should live. We often hear that only technical reason can really be taught, and our educational commitments from primary school to university seem to embody that belief. But technical reason alone, as we have seen, is insufficient to manage our social difficulties or make sense of our lives. What we need to know is not simply how to build a powerful computer or how to redesign DNA but precisely and above all what to do with that knowledge. As the power of our ability to manipulate the world grows, the poverty of our understanding of what to do with that knowledge becomes more apparent. Even when we see that the solution must have something to do with institutions, we once again look for a technical solution in some kind of "management science" rather than in trying to understand the inherently moral nature of institutions themselves.

It is not only students who find themselves confused and without a moral compass. Marian Metzger, Bud Chapin, and many other highly successful Americans lack the moral reason, embedded in institutions, that would give clearer guidance to their lives. If it were only our experience in educational and occupational institutions that was problematic, and if our lives at home and in the family—which most Americans continue to think is the most important arena of happiness and fulfillment—were unproblematic, then we could feel that amidst all the uncertainty there is at least one central sphere in which we can feel secure. But there is no such comfort.

VIII. TROUBLE IN THE FAMILY

Even though most of us think we know what we mean when we use the word "family"—using it frequently, as we suggested, as a metaphor for other institutional contexts that we understand less well— the family as Americans have taken it for granted for generations is no longer certain. The family is in flux, and signs of trouble are widespread. Expectations remain high, but realities are disturbing. The great suburban expansion of the 1950s was focused on the family: you don't live in a suburban house *alone*. Yet divorce rates continue to rise, and the very meaning of the family as we have known it has become problematic. The poignant predicaments of the contemporary family are in large part the most immediate result of the changes and tensions in our larger society we have been discussing, of the fact that we no longer understand the moral meaning of our institutions.

Since at least the eighteenth century the nuclear family has been understood as an institution combining three elements: the emotional intimacy of a heterosexual couple, their sexual life, and the nurture and socialization of their children.[14] The viability of the institution was supported by local communities, extended kin groups, and religious organizations, as well as by many economic, legal, and political functions and constraints. The ideal of the nuclear family, while subject to a recent increase of vigorous criticism and competing conceptions, continues to enjoy the allegiance of a large majority of the population. But creating such a family and keeping it intact have become increasingly difficult; the communities of support for the family have weakened, and many family functions have been taken over by the economy and the state. As a result, the component parts of the nuclear family ideal have begun to drift apart: emotional intimacy, sexuality, and the raising of children do not necessarily form a "standard package" but are carried on in different contexts and with different partners, or sometimes, in the case of raising children, with no partners at all. While there are practical and sometimes moral reasons for this decomposition of the family, it coincides neither with what most people in our society say they desire nor, especially in the case of children, with their best interests.

It is both factually wrong and morally insensitive to blame these changes in family life on "women's liberation," even though increasing equality in the rights of women and their growing participation in the work force have been part of the picture. Improvements in the rights of women and the opening of the job market to them have certainly not made women "antifamily," since most women continue to want husbands and children. Returning women to a situation where they lack legal rights, cannot own property if they are married, and have no higher education so as to "save the family" would be not only repugnant to women but wholly incompatible with our current understanding of the dignity befitting any human being. Yet there is a small grain of truth in relating "women's liberation" to the decline of the nuclear family, and it has to do with the fact that in recent decades individual fulfillment has ranked ever higher as a central cultural value (a point we analyzed extensively in *Habits of the Heart*).[15] However, as the feminist social critic Barbara Ehrenreich and others have convincingly argued, men more than women have used this ideology of individual self-fulfillment to shirk the responsibilities of family life.[16]

One way of putting the change that is producing what the family sociologist David Popenoe calls "the postnuclear family trend"[17] is to say that we are shifting from a child-centered family to an adult-centered family. Or to put it even more strongly, as a French jurist has written, "Instead of the individual 'belonging' to the family, it is the family which is coming to be at the service of the individual."[18] This is a vivid way of saying that we no longer understand the institutional logic of family life. The most obvious result of the growing emphasis on the primacy of personal satisfaction in family life is the rising rate of divorce. Since few of us want to return to a situation where individuals are condemned to spend their lives in unhappy or even abusive marriages, we have hesitated to discuss the cost of the rise in divorce to children and to the whole society. The psychologist Judith Wallerstein, however, in her study of the long-term consequences of divorce for children, has recently drawn a picture that should give us pause:

> Divorce has ripple effects that touch not just the family involved, but our entire society. As the writer Pat Conroy observed when his own marriage broke up, "Each divorce is the death of a small civilization." When one family divorces, that divorce affects relatives, friends, neighbors, employers, teachers, clergy, and scores of strangers. Although more people stay married than get divorced, divorce is not a *them* versus

us problem; everyone, in one way or another, has been touched by it. Today, all relationships between men and women are profoundly influenced by the high incidence of divorce. Teachers from all over the country tell me that their students come to school wide-eyed with fear, saying that their parents quarreled the night before and asking in terror, "Does that mean that they are going to divorce?" Radical changes in family life affect all families, homes, parents, children, courtships, and marriages, silently altering the social fabric of the entire society.[19]

Yet even in our current extremity it is important not to forget the long-term endurance of the family through history and its capacity to adapt to new conditions. Mary Ann Glendon, a Harvard Law School professor specializing in family law, gives us a poignant description of our present situation:

However frail and faltering they may currently seem to be, families remain, for most of us, the only theater in which we can realize our full capacity for good or evil, joy or suffering. By attaching us to beings and feelings that are perishable, families expose us to conflict, pain, and loss. They give rise to tension between love and duty, reason and passion, immediate and long-range objectives, egoism and altruism. But relationships between husbands and wives, parents and children, can also provide frameworks for resolving such tensions. Even though, after the loosening of legal and economic ties . . . the principal bonds which remain to unite the family may be the ties of human affection, we can perhaps—if we are hopeful—recognize in those fragile connections analogies for the Love that invites a response from all men and women of good will. A note sounded by a player on one instrument may draw forth a corresponding note from another; a child, hearing an accordion outside the window, may begin to sing and dance.[20]

We do not argue that the modern nuclear family, which combines the emotional intimacy and sexuality of the parents with the nurture of children, is the only possible or morally respectable form of the family; but because of its importance in bringing children into the world and raising them, it has a kind of centrality and value that we cannot afford to ignore. We need to consider how changes in our society have made that kind of family less and less attainable and what we might do to alter the current trend. Pressures impinge directly on the family from the economy and the state, and the surrounding, supporting community is weakening, also largely because of pressures upon it from the economy and the state.

The sociologist Arlie Hochschild, in an important study of two-earner families, puts the issue bluntly:

> For all the talk about the importance of children, the cultural climate
> has become subtly less hospitable to parents who put children first.
> This is not because parents love children less, but because a "job culture"
> has expanded at the expense of a "family culture." . . . Corporations
> have done little to accommodate the needs of working parents, and the
> government has done little to prod them. The nuclear family is still the
> overwhelming choice as a setting in which to rear children. Yet we have
> not invented the outside supports the nuclear family will need to do
> this job well.[21]

Hochschild suggests various policy changes, some well established in other advanced industrial countries, such as family leaves, flex time, job sharing, and nonexploitative part-time work. But whether these are the policies Americans should adopt can become clear only after an extended national discussion of what we expect from the family and how we might better achieve those expectations. In the meantime, the pressures to make ends meet that have driven more Americans than ever into the work force, and into working longer hours as well, cannot but be profoundly destructive to family life.

Mary Ann Glendon has pointed out that family law has probably gone further than the public ever intended in instituting "reforms" that have had highly individualistic consequences, as well as negative consequences for the economic condition of divorced women and their children (a situation documented in detail by the sociologist Lenore Weitzman).[22] These changes have been ironically described as the "deregulation of the family." But Glendon sees a need not only for reforms in divorce law that will be more supportive of the family (reforms that have already begun in some states) but for what she describes as the modern equivalent to the prefaces to the laws in Plato's *Laws*: that is, laws that would educate us to see marriage and the family as solidary communities in which one finds one's identity, rather than laws that educate us to think of them as disposable resources for individual fulfillment. Such a teaching would help us to see more clearly that when marriage is a choice rather than a necessity, a choice between two people with a good deal of autonomy and independence, it is still a choice we want to make, an obligation we want to assume, a commitment we want to keep, because loyalty is a virtue essential to our sense of a genuine self. Such a teaching would remind us that the family is the first, and in some respects the most important, learning community. In turning the great society into a good society, a reinvigorated family is a critically important resource, in that it would teach, as Tocqueville believed, all its members, not only the female ones, unselfish concern for others. We need not to "return to the traditional family" but to understand what the family as a vital institution today would really be like.

IX. TRANSFORMING INSTITUTIONS

How do we Americans really enjoy our lives? It may be that we are not as privatized and cynical as we think. Psychological research has discovered some surprising things about us: for instance, that we are happier at work than at leisure, that we actually enjoy the challenges of dealing with serious problems more than we enjoy taking it easy. It is less surprising, but still encouraging, that we are happier with our family and friends than alone. Remarkably, we are not happy when we are watching television, even though most of us spend many hours a week doing so, because we feel we are "on hold" rather than really living during that time. We are happiest when we are success-fully meeting challenges at work, in our private lives, and in our communities.[23]

Why, then, representing only 5 percent of the world's population, do we consume more than 50 percent of the world's drugs? Why do we spend $160 billion a year on entertainment, an industry of which television is a major element, which diverts but on the whole does not challenge? It would seem that the way we live creates so much anxiety that we spend enormous amounts of money and time, often at great expense to body and spirit, to drown out that anxiety, rather than focusing on the activities that allow us to be the active, happy, responsible people we really want to be.

It is easy to see this as a personal problem, to say that Americans have become selfish, self-indulgent, spoiled by affluence and readily available consumer goods; or as a cultural problem, to say that we have lost the work ethic and have come to believe that the good life is a life of hedonism and comfort. But we want to argue that it is also, and perhaps primarily, an institutional problem. Our institutions to-day—from the family to the school to the corporation to the public arena—do not challenge us to use all our capacities so that we have a sense of enjoyable achievement and of contributing to the welfare of others. At moments they do (and some do this better than others); if they did not, we would be much worse off than we are. But we tend to accept our institutions as they come, passively, and we do not see clearly enough how some of them operate to encourage that passivity. In the case of dysfunctional institutions, we have simply tried to escape from them and have allowed them to fall apart rather than reform and revitalize them. In the case of coercive institutions, we have submitted to them as though they were unchangeable natural forces. And the malaise is palpable: a loss of meaning in family and job, a distrust of politics, a disillusion with organized religion.

American culture has focused relentlessly on the idea that individuals are self-interest maximizers and that private accumulation and private pleasures are the only measurable public goods. We have been blind to the way that institutions enable or cripple our capacity to be the persons we most want to be. We need to understand historically how we came to think that individual freedom is the highest good, that institutions stand in the way of our freedom. We need to understand how we failed to see that the virtue in autonomy, in the sense of personal freedom, can be realized only along with other virtues, such as care and responsibility. Our present problems are the result of historical conditions, not of some inevitable historical law. They are the result of actual choices that people have made in history, choices made without awareness of what the consequences would be if everyone made similar choices. A better understanding of the larger forces at work in the modern world could allow us to make different choices, with different consequences for us all.

We can see among us examples of institutions that are functioning well, that give the individuals within them a purpose and an identity, not through molding them into conformity but through challenging them to become active, innovative, responsible, and thus happy persons because they understand what they are doing and why it is important. Technological development and affluence, which are related to our deepest problems, can also, if used rightly, enlarge the possibilities for our fulfillment in work and as citizens, for democratic participation and committed family lives, even for the space to develop genuine spirituality. These are the things most of us really want, though we fear they are beyond our reach.

We now turn to our past the better to understand the institutions we have inherited and the ways we can change them so as to create the good society, which may be, after all, almost within our grasp. From 1914 to 1989 the world was engaged in what may be called the Seventy-five Years' War of the Twentieth Century. If 1989 was the last year of that great war, the possibilities for dealing with our problems are enormously brighter. The vast resources that for decades went into utter waste or, worse, horrifying destruction may now be available for solving the accumulating ecological, economic, and social problems of our battered globe. Institutions that were forged in an atmosphere of numbing paranoia brought on by continuous war or threat of war must be fundamentally restructured. Accepting the tragedies of the twentieth century and the toll they took on all the world's peoples is the beginning of wisdom. Paradise on this earth, we have learned, is beyond our capacities. But we can, if we are modest and hopeful, possibly establish a reasonably livable purgatory and escape the inferno.[24] Even attaining that modest goal will require that we achieve a dramatically new level of democratic institutionalization not only in America but in the world.

The Rise and Fall of the
American Century

I. PROPHECY FULFILLED: LIVING "FUTURAMA"

Had any of the five million visitors to General Motors' "Futurama" at the New York World's Fair in 1939 been able to travel ahead in time, the actual panorama of the United States twenty years later would have revealed the fair's vision of the future as amazingly prescient. The breathtaking vision of superhighways, high-technology farms, and skyscraper cities that Futurama spread before its visitors had become decidedly familiar to Americans by 1959. At the end of the depressed and fractious 1930s, such a future must have seemed deeply appealing but very distant. Yet in only two decades the American landscape was in the process of being rebuilt by the automobile, the interstate highway system, suburban housing developments, and the shopping mall. These physical transformations were both manifestations of and an impetus for equally sweeping changes in the social and working lives of Americans.

Futurama proudly showed its visitors cities transformed into skyscrapered metropolises and opened out by freeways that led on to a countryside of bucolic promise. During the postwar decades the proliferation of automobile ownership, along with vast government programs such as the homeowner loans of the Federal Housing Administration and the slum clearance of Urban Renewal, helped to move the white middle class and many blue-collar families out of the cities into the suburbs. But as millions of whites moved out, millions of black migrants, newly displaced from southern farms by mechanization, moved into central cities just as the highway projects emptied them of industry and blue-collar jobs. In 1939 the message of the Fair had been that the car and the highway would realize for everyone the American dream of mobility and provide an escape from the social conflicts and poverty of the Great Depression. Ironically, the very process that speeded movement out of the crowded cities generated within the new regional metropolises more racial and economic separation, and greater economic inequality, than had been the case in the more compact, variegated old industrial cities.

By 1959 the real income of most of the working population had doubled since 1940. Thanks to government support, many more Americans were going to college. The United States had taken its first steps toward racial integration. Simultaneous "booms" in economic growth, in suburban and new city housing development, and in the sheer number of babies born made the prospects for family life, after the discouraging conditions of economic depression and total war, appear more secure and hopeful than ever before. The promise of Futurama—a life that "would demand our best energies, our most fruitful imagination" and provide "greater opportunities for all"— seemed at the point of fulfillment.[1]

It is not surprising that so many Americans of the 1930s joined General Motors in looking forward to the realization of the highly mobile automotive utopia of Futurama. Their dominant cultural beliefs had long promoted the expectation that the future would be better than the past. American history had seemed exceptionally fortunate, with territorial expansion and economic development going hand in hand to provide a historically unequaled standard of material life. That hope for indefinite economic progress seemed to be coming true.

It is consequently understandable, though still surprising, to find Americans today modifying their habitual progressive optimism as they look wistfully back to those postwar years as a golden age of affluence and hope that seems unlikely to return. The irony is that a major cause of our present national difficulties is precisely the influence that institutional patterns and habits of mind acquired during the years 1945 to 1968 continue to hold over our notions of what "normal" life should be, and so, over our ability to confront a very different present and future.

II. THE CONFIDENCE OF DEMOCRATIC AFFLUENCE: POSTWAR AMERICA

Long-standing American dreams, particularly for achieving economic success and social respect, came true for many Americans in the two decades after World War II. In a sense more social and cultural than precisely economic, most Americans finally became middle-class. By 1960, for the first time in history, the majority of Americans owned their own homes, along with cars and an increasing array of labor-saving home appliances.

This home was for many the focus of care and family responsibility, and it became a symbol of aspiration. For those Americans who were still excluded from full participation in national life, especially the large black minority, it was also a focus of grievance and resentment. Typically, this home was a single-family, free-standing house with a yard around it, a garage, and plenty of privacy. It was a public state-ment of individual and family achievement, a proof of social worthi-ness and economic well-being, a "castle" and refuge. It came to symbolize the comfort, security, and respectability of being middle-class.

The dream house of the 1950s and 60s summed up the buoyant sense of possibility abroad in the land. Men and women were marrying earlier and in greater numbers, and giving birth to more children than at any other time in the twentieth century. A rare sense of stability surrounded these rapidly growing families. Divorce rates, which had been rising for decades, held constant; child health and nutrition im-proved, thanks in part to expanding employment and wages doubling from prewar levels. War-fed technological advances meant that each hour of work earned more real purchasing power each year. In an expanding economic climate, labor unions represented about one-quarter of American workers—the highest percentage in our history—and helped to ensure both job security and rising wages.

The image of the happy, stable family of the 1950s as popularized in the advertisements and media of the time, comprised a breadwinner husband, his homemaker wife, and three thriving children being raised in the clean, healthful, crime-free surroundings of a well-groomed suburb. The memory that such families could, and often did, expe-rience each coming year as better than the last raises strong gusts of nostalgia for many of us today, but it is important to understand that the era was exceptional in our history, and why.

Americans in the postwar years saw the prospect of affluence and respectability, the opportunity embodied in the suburban ideal, as a birthright. In their most generous moods, they believed that middle-class status could—or should—be attainable by all, regardless of re-ligion or race. And the most difficult, but noblest, effort they made was the great struggle to open opportunity to those Americans to whom it had so long been closed. Beneath the idealism of the battle for civil rights was a powerful awareness of the nation's extraordinary material abundance and a widespread moral consensus as to what full participation in American life meant: to be middle-class.

When Americans looked beyond North America in 1945, they understood that their nation bulked very large in the world. Immediately after 1945, much of Europe and Asia seemed to be no longer there, so terrible had been the destructiveness of the war, although Stalin's Russia was rising from the ashes to be our only serious challenger. Nearly half of everything manufactured anywhere on the planet was made in the United States, and virtually every country in the world outside the Soviet Union looked to America for support, guidance, and even survival. No wonder it seemed to some the beginning of the "American Century." To others it seemed an occasion to be generous to defeated foes and friends alike, imagining a global New Deal, a "Century of the Common Man." Everyone agreed that the future would be dominated by American power and American ideals.

The regime of democratic affluence became for many the meaning of the American way of life. Shortly after the war one of the popular heroes of the new democracy of opportunity, the housing developer William Levitt, invented the highly successful idea of mass-produced suburban housing, thereby making home ownership realistic for millions, with help from the Veterans and Federal Housing Administrations. Levitt was not above promoting his invention by noting the contribution it could make in the battle against communism. "No man who owns his own house and lot," he quipped, "can be a Communist. He has too much to do."[2] And the 1950s did turn out to be a politically and socially subdued time, as critics never ceased to remind the apparently satisfied—or exhausted—nation of homeowners.

John F. Kennedy's eventual call to arms of the New Frontier of 1960 was predicated upon the belief that America's democratic affluence was a social ideal that could win over the "hearts and minds" of the postcolonial states of Asia, Africa, and Latin America. These nations were to be allied with the United States "for progress." Of course, the reality of postwar international life was hardly uniformly benign, as the government's much-publicized encouragement of citizens to build "shelters" against nuclear devastation made chillingly apparent. But Americans seemed to know who they were and where they wanted to go, and the nation's institutions appeared fully able to take them there.

Contemporary nostalgia for the quiet 1950s should not blind us to the complex and deeply contradictory features in their apparent stability. Much like that other return to "normalcy" that followed victory in World War I, the 1950s masked profound economic and social developments whose force and momentum guaranteed that the era of democratic affluence, like the Roaring Twenties, would last far less than a century.

Even then critics complained about the shallowness of the dominant middle-class form of life. Lewis Mumford, writing in the early 1960s, attacked the "mass movement into suburban areas" as a caricature of "both the historic city and the archetypal suburban refuge" which was producing "a lowgrade uniform environment from which escape is impossible."[3] A decade earlier the sociologist David Riesman had worried about the dangers in the tendency to orient so much behavior and aspiration toward social acceptance.[4] Similar fears ran through William H. Whyte's critical study of aspiring managers and professionals in *The Organization Man* (1956),[5] while in *White Collar* (1951), C. Wright Mills pictured society as "a great salesroom, an enormous file, an incorporated brain, a new universe of management and manipulation."[6]

The critics ignored or downplayed the opportunities that postwar economic growth afforded for easing the invidious class distinctions that previous investigators of American society, such as Robert and Helen Lynd, had found so powerful before the war.[7] Yet they did catch something of what was new and distinctive about the world of democratic affluence. The leveling features of new middle-class patterns of work, consumption, and family life were real enough, if less widespread than Americans believed; but the apparent security they symbolized concealed vast changes that were remaking society and the world. Technological innovations were, in complex ways, setting in motion long-term processes affecting work, economic life, and the nation's institutional structure as a whole.

On one level, the postwar years were highly conservative, though far from static. As World War II ended, President Harry Truman declared, "I don't want any experiments—the American people have been through a lot of experiments, and they want a rest." The New Deal and the international crisis that had precipitated the war were behind us. Americans were again to be free to seek their happiness through economic competition in the free market, without the pressures of ideological or military mobilization, while they retained the considerable benefits of the New Deal's interventions to soften the harshness of the business cycle.

Reality turned out differently. To sustain the nation's intense new rivalry with the Soviet Union, manpower and industry had to be continuously mobilized through the draft and defense contracting, thereby nullifying market competition for an important sector of the economy. The public had to be ideologically united and activated as well. The intense hysteria of anti-Communist McCarthyism was not a wholly unnatural outgrowth, given the general atmosphere. Yet the overall progress of democratic affluence at home seemed a great relief from conflict and change. Because of the country's unique position of economic and military preeminence, Americans could, for a time, engage with the world collectively yet ignore it individually in the benign dream of "Futurama" realized.

III. FAMILY, JOB, NATION

Long before the 1950s the Jeffersonian ideal of the independent household and the self-governing township were overtaken by the ascendancy of Wall Street over Main Street and the lure of economic opportunity in the principal urban centers of commerce and industry. The economic pull of the national market drew the majority of Americans away from the old centers of life—the farm, workshop, or small enterprise—and into the large corporations that still dominate our economy.

Reconciling these actual conditions with the desire for memory and continuity in the family and local community was difficult. As the historian Frederick Siegel described the situation: "The man who moved from blue- to white-collar work also moved into a new social world where his old ways of living were no longer acceptable. Where he once bowled and played canasta, now he had to play bridge and golf. His wife had to raise the kids without the support of the parents and sisters and aunts who had usually done so much to make the task of caring for young children bearable." The novelist Saul Bellow captured the unexpected stresses of the new cultural freedom brought by economic affluence: "Nobody truly occupies a station in life any more. There are displaced persons everywhere."[8]

Yet because the ideal of the family was so powerful and effective, its gradual decline left many Americans deeply confused about the moral meaning of their lives. That erosion process was internal and external, proceeding both from moral questioning of the old ideal from within and from massive changes in the American economic and political order.

Internally, the inevitability and even the moral validity of the postwar family form has been challenged repeatedly since the 1960s, both by competing forms of social life and by the principled criticism of feminists. And, very importantly, the increasingly persuasive arguments of the civil rights movement challenged the exclusion of non-whites from the middle-class ideal. At the same time, the external conditions that made the typical division of labor between spouses and children plausible and possible steadily eroded. What were these external conditions?

The achievements of democratic affluence and middle-class serenity did not come about by accident. Historical currents pushed the United States into an extraordinarily favored world position, and conscious human effort greatly aided the postwar efflorescence. As with the building of the automobile suburbs and the sunbelt cities, only the cooperation of organized business interests and political decisions could have produced such consistent results. This is not to say that a mastermind was at work, for the institutional framework of economic and social order developed as quite disparate interests came together and accommodated themselves to each other.

Like the interstate highway grid, this institutional framework gave great scope to individual initiative while guiding that energy along carefully laid-out pathways. Postwar society encouraged Americans to define their own and others' lives in certain characteristic ways and to experience them accordingly. Central to this process was the habit of perceiving and evaluating life in terms of economic advance and the sense of personal well-being. The overall effect was to underwrite forms of family life and social participation thought worthy of a nation conscious of its exemplary status.

The framework of democratic affluence, then, was in part a designed social and political artifact. Like artistic designs, social designs always create more than aesthetic values. A design gestures toward a future even as it dramatizes a desirable identity. This is true even when the design is only partially a conscious one, created largely for and not by those who identify with its evocations. In the 1950s Americans created a design that no one specifically had intended, yet it was accepted as "natural" without being subjected to a serious public debate. Our future had already been anticipated by Futurama, conceived more as the inevitable product of "science and industry" than of public deliberation and moral choice. By the end of the war Americans were bursting with a desire to get on with "normal life" as their inherited culture had defined it and as modern industry promised it would be. And the leaders of both parties, President Truman, and Congress were doubly determined that the country emerge from the Great Depression and the war a prosperous, middle-class nation.

The result was a conscious policy of planned conversion of the world's greatest economic machinery to peacetime purposes. All were agreed that price and investment decisions should be returned to the invisible hand of the marketplace, yet it was also clear that a more visible hand of managerial planning would be required.

Three aspects of the postwar design gave it strength. The first was specific governmental intervention into the country's economic life, whether in the form of subsidies or of regulation. The second was a new accommodation between business and labor. And the third, perhaps in the long run the most significant, was the federal government's guidance of the economy as a whole.

The ascent of millions of families into the middle class was directly aided by subsidies, guaranteed loans, and tax breaks, as were the college educations of returning veterans after both VJ Day and Korea. Later, the children of these veterans continued to swell the ranks of the college-educated in unheard-of numbers, thanks to government-subsidized loans. Social Security gradually expanded beyond its modest New Deal coverage and aided new families by making the care of the aging less burdensome.

The centerpiece of the whole design was American business itself. Justly a source of national pride, American industry was the world model of efficiency. The cheap energy produced by the regulated oil and power industries enabled manufacturers to mechanize on a large scale, making each worker more productive. This boosted overall productivity at the same time that it made more goods available more cheaply. And, of course, low-cost fuel enabled regulated railroads and truckers to move those goods easily to growing markets. The expansion of market demand was itself underwritten by the rising real wages of the growing work force which it, reciprocally, helped to create. As President Kennedy remarked, "A rising tide lifts all boats."

Finally, a good job, especially in the "white collar" occupations, the burgeoning professional and managerial ranks, had the potential for career advancement through promotion. In the stable world of democratic affluence, workers could count on a predictable course of life. They could expect their income to increase fairly steadily and, along with it, social respectability and financial security for themselves and their children.

Many Americans preferred these benefits of the new order to the risks of prewar capitalism. As a veteran said upon graduating from college: "I know AT&T may not be very exciting, but there will always be an AT&T."[9] Still imagining itself a nation of rugged "independent citizens," America had become in fact a society in which nine out of ten workers labored for some entity other than themselves.

To the traditional responsibility of government to provide for the common defense, the era of democratic affluence added another. Government now had to see to it that this system of orderly growth did not falter. Citizens learned from the new television news broadcasts to base their judgments of political candidates and parties on how they supposedly influenced the economic climate of the nation, at least those aspects of the economy that affected people like themselves. Citizenship came to be defined, like work, as a means toward securing the basic elements of the good life. But that life itself was most often pictured on television as lived out not at work or in the public forum but in the private hours of home life and "leisure." Americans were only half-aware that the happiness of their private lives had come to depend on the massive postwar role of government as the funder, underwriter, and regulator of the national economy.

IV. INSTITUTIONS AND MORES

The institutional arrangements that made all this possible were typically justified simply as ways to get things done. That is to say, the postwar institutional framework was thought of as existing for instrumental purposes: to forestall a depression, to raise the standard of living, to benefit stockholders, to educate the work force, to assist the aged and indigent, and so on. But institutions, especially those which so deeply affect the life of an entire society, are never simply instruments. Besides getting results and making things happen, institutions also condition the behavior and thinking of those who participate in them or feel their effects.

Institutions always become in part ends as well as means. They shape identity and purpose. It is not only that welfare institutions shape the character of the poor, as we have lately been told. Institutions powerfully shaped the character and understanding of the middle class during the time of the great postwar boom and subsequently.

If the ideal of a universal middle-class prosperity was the moral center, the institutions designed for realizing that goal came to shape the nature of the ideal itself. Good jobs, a family wage, colleges available for everyone, home ownership supported by government aid and powered by an organized economy—these were the institutional conditions. Over time, by providing a distinctive experience of life, they came to shape expectations and virtues—the "mores"—of middle-class citizens. These mores resonated with a public philosophy of progress that put great faith in managerial expertise.

Everyday practices of work, school, and politics trained Americans to think and act in terms of individual competitive success. Life off the job or out of school came to focus around personal wants and their satisfaction. To contemporary social observers this seemed the logical effect of the emphasis on a standard of living measured by consumer goods. David Riesman commented that children seemed like nothing so much as "consumer trainees." This tendency was partially offset by institutions, especially family and church, whose practices emphasized the search for what is good for all. But while the logic of the common good remained alive in many domestic and religious contexts, it found little resonance in the public sphere. Unlike other democratic nations, the United States consistently defined Social Security as a system of individual insurance rather than as common provision. Postwar Americans tended to regard public concerns much as they did economic interests: in terms of pursuing their advantage, if need be, by striking advantageous bargains with others. Citizenship in practice exhibited the qualities typical of marketing and exchange. Furthermore, as government resources were put to ever new uses, Americans increasingly defined citizenship in terms of the claims they could legitimately argue they had, as individuals or as members of a special category, to some of those resources. Claimant politics began to overshadow civic politics.

In the private realm, it was believed, the highest of life's goods were to be realized. Here intimacy, solidarity, and voluntary accomplishments in sport, art, or craft flourished, crowned life, and made it whole. Public life became whatever happened beyond the sphere of family and friends—work, buying and selling, going to school, and having access to commercial and governmental services. These activities were all means to individual ends; the public sphere was perceived as instrumental. By contrast, the activities of the private sphere were seen as ends pursued for their own sake. This way of dividing up the social world seemed a great advance in freedom, opening up a realm of "value pluralism," as the theorists said, in which each person could pursue his or her own "life plan" with minimum interference from others.

But the regime of democratic affluence made it difficult in practice to subordinate the instrumental goods achieved in the "public" sphere to the intrinsic goods of "private" life. Instrumental goods such as monetary reward—or even increasing personal choices thanks to education—could overpower the appeal of the supposedly superior goods of dedication to family life. In the mid-1950s General Motors advertised the virtues of having a second car by showing a family barbecuing in front of two shiny autos. The caption read: "Going Our Separate Ways We've Never Been So Close." Perhaps not, but the theme of affluence-promoted mobility created severe strains when what had once been reserved as purely utilitarian public activity began to invade and undermine the supposedly sacred sphere of private life. The slogan of the 1960s came to be that "the personal is political!"

The severe criticisms of democratic affluence made by the massive social movements of the 1960s and 1970s, particularly the civil rights and women's movements, brought moral conceptions at variance with the postwar consensus into public view. The demand for racial equality and the criticisms of segregation were framed in explicitly moral, frequently religious terms. These criticisms presumed a public order sustained by more than instrumental and individual involvements. And while figures like Norman Vincent Peale had redefined biblical religion for the affluent as "positive thinking," for Martin Luther King, Jr., religious belief compelled major reform of the public order itself. Forging a national consensus on civil rights was a long and difficult struggle, despite public response to the historic resonances of the movement's republican and biblical language. What the civil rights movement put in question was the central tenet of democratic affluence—namely, that individual effort alone was sufficient to attain the good life.

The relative novelty of the feminist criticism of gender roles was all the more striking because feminists were pushing their attack into the private sphere itself. Since most Americans understood the private world as the unassailable source of intrinsic value, to question its ordering in public seemed to leave no moral place to stand. When the "private" problems of child raising, divorce, and the division of household labor spilled out in public, the capacity of American public discourse to make sense of these matters was tried and found wanting. As the separation of public from private proved experientially unrealistic, their moral separation became untenable.

V. A CRISIS OF MORAL ORDER AS FAILURE
OF PUBLIC PHILOSOPHY

The spirit of the postwar order had been most clearly enunciated during the Kennedy administration in 1961–63. The affluent society, which the historian Daniel Boorstin called "the republic of technology," setting the standard for the world to emulate, was based upon confidence in technological and managerial expertise. According to President Kennedy, the key issue for America's future was "the practical management of a modern economy. What we need is not labels and clichés but more basic discussion of the sophisticated and technical questions involved in keeping a great economic machinery moving ahead." The need, he thought, was for "technical answers, not political answers."[10]

At the same time the socialist Michael Harrington and the economist John Kenneth Galbraith demanded that a national effort be made to eradicate poverty, a problem that could be interpreted as a previously missed technical flaw in the system. The logical response, of course, would have been to apply the techniques of economic management and resource allocation that had been developed since the New Deal and the war. President Johnson's Great Society legislation was largely conceived in this spirit. An adviser recalls that the Great Society was intended to complete the "second stage" of America's growth. The first stage had built a massive and productive economic system. The second, starting at the beginning of the twentieth century, "put controls on the flourishing economic system in order to increase the standard of living and opportunities of the lower- and middle-income population." It was logical to complete that process by bringing the materially disadvantaged, especially black Americans, into the system. This achievement would lay the groundwork for a new stage in which concern with the quality of life would replace economic concerns in shaping the nation's agenda.[11] Events, however, failed to confirm this well-intentioned and optimistic expectation.

1968 was the watershed year. Politically, it was bloodied by the nationally traumatic assassinations of Martin Luther King and Robert Kennedy. It also saw a great breakup of the sense of cohesive purpose that the nation had sustained since World War II. That sense of cohesion had shown its dark underside in the McCarthy years, but it had survived the divisiveness of that time and even the Korean War. It had reached its apogee in the passage of the 1964 Civil Rights Act, when it seemed that the nation was finally righting an ancient and deeply troubling wrong. But it did not survive the war in Vietnam. By 1968 the hopes of the civil rights movement and the War on Poverty had been dashed by the warfare shaking the nation's cities. Working-class and lower-middle-class whites in the cities, tenuously grasping for middle-class respectability themselves, recoiled from the riots and activism in the black ghettos, whose inhabitants were angered by the slow pace of progress toward racial equality.

All this coincided with sharp reverses in the nation's international position. Major doubts developed about the viability of the very economic and political framework that had seemed at the point of triumphant fruition a few years before. Military spending for the undeclared war in Vietnam began to fuel inflation and seriously unbalance trade. It was proving impossible to wrest a victory in Vietnam, and the nation seemed to be dissolving within.

The first response to problems in the 1960s was to define them in ways that would make it possible to continue the basic patterns of postwar life. But during the 1970s the nation seemed to waver. Some pushed ahead with exploring the new possibilities of personal freedom and self-realization that had opened up. Others, styling themselves "conservatives" or "neoconservatives," tried to hold to the old moral center of "family values." Yet the world was changing in spite of what either side said. To take just one example, changes in the economy forced most households to have two breadwinners, regardless of whether they believed in women working or not, and job polarization in the workplace made entry into middle-class status more difficult. The mutual reinforcement between economic trends and middle-class life was no longer obvious, and that dissociation marked the collapse of postwar assumptions about the boundaries of private and public, of instrumental and expressive goods.

In 1980 President Reagan promised to recover the happy conditions of the postwar social world. In practice, the Reagan administration was able to provide some elements of that old prosperity for a sizable, affluent segment of the populace, but only by saddling the country with unprecedented debt. The cost was very high. The gap between success and failure grew greatly, and the old consensus was not restored. By the end of the 1980s Americans once again feared that the social—and moral—fabric of their lives was being torn apart. Change seemed neither intelligible nor manageable. At this critical juncture, public discourse had no means to come to grips with the dimensions of the problem.

VI. EXHAUSTION OF A DESIGN?

It was emblematic that the United States began its official celebrations of the bicentennial of the Federal Constitution in 1987 not in Philadelphia but at the miniaturized scale replica of Independence Hall at the end of Disney World's Main Street. The two locales of the Magic Kingdom are the most popular vacation destinations in America: Disneyland in California and Disney World in Florida are promoted as family entertainment, and indeed the two theme parks have virtually created a genre, a new kind of destination for families on holiday. Since Disneyland opened its gates in former citrus land in Orange County in the mid-1950s, other theme parks have sprung up across the American landscape, orienting the dreams of youngsters by the tens of millions and helping to shape our imaginations and lives.

As virtually every child raised in the United States since the 1950s knows, the Magic Kingdom is organized around five zones, each offering visitors an exciting experience of a different space and time. Adventureland, Frontierland, Tomorrowland, and Fantasyland are all oriented along the central axis of Main Street USA, an evocative rendering of an idealized town of the last century, slightly miniaturized. The Disney park, like its imitators and competitors, is a carefully planned organization of space, structures, landscaping, and staff. "Children of all ages," who have included foreign visitors (even, almost, Nikita Khrushchev) as well as parents from Des Moines, can experience jungle rivers, simulated space travel, and Abraham Lincoln delivering the Gettysburg Address. All this is tied together by chuffing steam locomotives which exchange passengers with whooshing monorails.

Perhaps it is just this controlled diversity, with the beckoning of the technological future ballasted by the imagined securities of a past America, that brings the crowds back. Or maybe it's the exciting rides and the many opportunities for shopping. Theme parks are all in essence fantasylands, with high technology providing the enchantment. Still, there is something affecting about the juxtaposition of the dreams of future progress with the pieties embodied in the frontier, the town, and the nation's founding. These symbols provide reminders of secure roots. They evoke a moral grid that can imaginatively channel individual energy toward a general soundness of life. All these meanings are, of course, part of the design of the place.

The Disney parks were designed—planned to a most extraordinary degree. The clear and ingenious order, reproduced on the maps and diagrams assiduously studied by every visitor to the parks, captures the popular imagination. It stands out starkly against the often illegible patterns of the urban fields of Orlando or Orange County. Perhaps this contrast, too, contributes to their magnetism. The attraction here is not too distant from the appeal that the monumental designs of Old World capitals have for highbrow Americans accustomed to sniffing at Disneyland.

An observer trying to understand the whole thing might see the enthusiasm of the visitors for the Disney plan as a projection of America's collective unconscious set forth for all the world to see. He might detect that Main Street and Tomorrowland are tied together by desire, a desire for a future open to limitless material progress, but made secure by a fixed moral universe of the sort which Tocqueville thought had once anchored American confidence. The gleaming metallic future and the pastel past are connected by subterranean pathways of desire.

The central points of reference remain Main Street and Independence Hall. These embody the desire to keep the moral and social dimensions of American life constant despite the vast transformations of technology and the world of nations. It is a wish for continuity with the spirit of the old middle-class republic and its independent citizen, adventurous yet rooted in family, home, and community. Yet, as we have seen, it is just these basic, defining contours of American life that are becoming blurred. In our rapidly changing society, what constitutes a family, a home, a job, a community? These disturbing questions now brood over the tranquil order of the parks.

Our observer might well wonder if even Tomorrowland is really an image of a world to come. Does it not already evoke nostalgia for a dream slipping beyond our grasp, even as its after-image lingers on? Guidance for the future will not come from fantasies of the "world of tomorrow," which is already our collective past. It also cannot come from the older familiar social design. We need to recover the capacity for common discussion and public invention that those in the postwar era who opted for purely "technical answers" thought we could do without.

VII. THE CHARISMA OF PROGRESS

At its birth the United States was endowed with the charisma of progress. 1776 was the date not only of the nation's independence but of an intellectual revolution ignited by Adam Smith's *Wealth of Nations*. The new federal government ordained by the freshly ratified Constitution came into being in the same year that the Old Regime fell in France, signaling the beginning of a new era. Americans have long been accustomed to thinking of themselves as the most modern of peoples, the smiling prophets of progress around the world.

The core of America's self-confidence has been its innovative and immensely productive economy. We have been the people of Futurama realized. We are the people who invented the computer and first sent a manned space flight to the moon. Little wonder, then, that the economic difficulty of the past two decades has given rise to profound and persistent anxiety. It is all the more important to emphasize that, despite the extraordinarily favorable circumstances that attended us historically, our economic progress did not just happen. Nor was progress imagined as a purely instrumental or technical project. Progress was a moral ideal.

The United States was planned for progress. It was a commonplace among the country's eighteenth-century founders that economic life was not simply a neutral fact of nature, that political economy was a branch of political ethics and its practice an exercise in public morality. The primary teacher of that public morality was John Locke.[12] It is remarkable how much of our current understanding of social reality flows from the original institutionalization at the end of the eighteenth century (the "founding") and how much of that was dependent on the thought of Locke. His teaching is one of the most powerful ideologies ever invented, if not the most powerful. It promised an unheard-of degree of individual freedom, an unlimited opportunity to compete for material well-being, and an unprecedented limitation on the arbitrary powers of government to interfere with individual initiative. In all these ways it expressed a modern liberal ideal that contrasted with the hierarchical domination and exclusiveness of most of the human past.

In its original context, as the historian John Dunn has forcibly argued, Locke's thought was inseparable from his theology and from his stern Calvinist sense of obligation.[13] But by the mid-eighteenth century the secular aspects of his teaching had been detached from his overall vision. What his American followers emphasized was that the right to life, liberty, and the pursuit of happiness is exemplified by the solitary individual's appropriation of property from the state of nature. Government is then instituted for the protection of that property. Once men agree to accept money as the medium of exchange, the accumulation of property is in principle without any moral limit. All limits on the freedom and autonomy of the individual, other than those he freely consents to in entering the (quite limited) social contract, are rejected. Locke attacked the patriarchal family, which had been used as a model for absolute monarchy, arguing implicitly for the rights of women and explicitly for the freedom of children from obligation to parents.[14] Limited government, in the Lockean view, exists to provide a minimum of order for individuals to accumulate property. All traditional restraints are rejected, and nothing is taken for granted that has not been voluntarily agreed to on the basis of reason.

That is an overly condensed but not unfair statement of Locke's position, or at least how it came to be understood in late-eighteenth-century America. Locke expected his social contract to produce benign results because he presumed that the "natural harmony of interests" (an assumption not shared by Locke's predecessor Hobbes) led to the creation of a free and tolerant good society. It is probable that Locke thought of his teaching primarily as a protest against the social and cultural constrictions of the past, and that he did not imagine any nation would put the whole conception into practice at one swoop, certainly not without the religious constraints that were basic to his thought.

The most forceful architect of the political economy expressed in the Constitution, Alexander Hamilton, was a Lockean who, like Locke himself, viewed this teaching as tempered by an older notion of moral order, one requiring not simply the free play of individual action but the deliberate direction of able leaders. For Hamilton, progress was a highly charged moral idea. But progress had to be institutionalized, to be given public standing and recognition in order to be an effective force in human affairs. Not for Hamilton the confidence of the moral philosopher Adam Smith that human nature "if left to itself, will naturally find its way to the most useful and profitable employment."

From the early 1790s on, Thomas Jefferson and James Madison challenged Hamilton's vision in public debate. Like Hamilton, these men also believed fervently in moral advance through economic progress; all three sought ways to combine the promises of Enlightenment liberalism with the older republican notion that the public realm alone could realize certain essential goods, principally security, justice, and fellowship. However, Jefferson and Madison differed profoundly with Hamilton on the question of how to promote individual liberty and at the same time serve the public good. For Hamilton, progress was a spirit human society had to learn and, once it was learned, carefully propagate by educating its members to it. The institutions of Hamilton's model of political economy—from the money supply and national bank to publicly chartered organizations for the promotion of enterprise to the laws of contract and obligation—were pedagogical devices. Their aim was the moral transformation and improvement of human beings.

Hamilton argued that the end of this institutionalized public pedagogy was "to cherish and stimulate the activity of the human mind"— the enlargement of human capacities and the consequent enrichment of the common life. Hamilton spoke of "the spirit of enterprise," because, for him, enterprise was indeed a spiritual matter. Enterprise, "useful and prolific as it is, must necessarily be contracted or expanded in proportion to the simplicity or variety of the occupations and productions, which are to be found in a Society." Here, agreeing with Smith on the advantages of the expanding division of labor that the market economy brings about, Hamilton drew the lesson for the spiritual wealth of a society: "It must be less in a nation of mere cultivators, than in a nation of cultivators and merchants; less in a nation of cultivators and merchants than in a nation of cultivators, artificers and merchants."[15]

It was not accidental, given this understanding of the significance of political economy, that Hamilton was also the great proponent of national unification. A strong new nation would be created by a national commercial and financial elite, not a loose alliance of local gentry. Through becoming an active and industrious people, the Americans would come to take their place in the world of nations. Such was Hamilton's vision of world progress through economic development.

Perhaps it was also no accident that Hamilton was an immigrant, an outsider to the gentry worlds of most of the other national founders. Hamilton distrusted Thomas Jefferson's praise for settled agriculture. He expected instead that a strong central government and a market economy would continually challenge and stimulate the naturally talented to rise to positions of prominence and leadership. The revolution had done this for Hamilton. Could not a growing economy do the same for many others?

In this Hamiltonian vision, the realm of private market exchange, with its attendant institutions, was to be established and chartered by the popular will acting through the national government. The workings of the market in turn would teach the virtues of mind and spirit that the eighteenth-century Enlightenment called "manners." So educated, the citizenry would form a free sphere of public opinion. This opinion, when organized through associations, would shape the popular will that government served. Thus Hamilton conceived political economy as making possible a cycle, or spiral, of human progress, not just in commerce and technique but in morals as well.

Jefferson and Madison worried that Hamilton's plans would, in the end, establish an economic aristocracy privileged by the national state. They feared that the national institutions Hamilton favored—the national bank, vigorous federal support for economic development—would become corrupt, tyrannical, perhaps would even reinstate a monarchy. Jefferson, slaveholder and aristocrat though he was, expressed an essential faith in democracy, in the initiative of ordinary people, that in the long run was more deeply expressive of the American ethos than Hamilton's ideas ever were. He followed Locke in believing that private property and contracts were prior to government, and could thereby be thought of as by nature private matters; government should protect private contracts and property but not attempt to interfere with them or shape them toward common ends. The purpose of social life, in this liberal vision of natural right, was identified primarily with protecting the liberties of individuals. It was for this reason that Jefferson urged his fellow citizens to remain politically active as citizens of a democratic republic. For Jefferson, even more than for Hamilton, an educated citizenry, forming a public ever watchful of the actions of government, was an essential precondition of a free society.

By the early nineteenth century it seemed as though the Jeffersonians had won a conclusive victory. America in 1800 was perhaps the most egalitarian society the world has ever seen, at least since the hunter-gatherers—and this even though Indians, blacks, and women were excluded from citizenship. Jefferson was a pacifist in the White House, and it was indeed a Lockean world. Enterprise was free, government was weak, and law was more concerned with "releasing energy" than with restraining it. In many ways this early-nineteenth-century world remains the self-image of "America," a land where essentially equal individuals can make their way unencumbered by ancient traditions or large institutions.

Since then, the ancient traditions have not fared so well, but the large institutions have grown immensely. However much we wish otherwise, the America of the late twentieth century is far from that world of independent citizens living in small towns. What happened? Why did America fail to become the Lockean paradise that the founders envisioned?

VIII. THE RISE OF THE CORPORATION

The Lockean notion of endless accumulation proved to be a social force with extraordinary, unexpected consequences. Already in the 1830s manufacturing enterprises of considerable size had appeared. The business world had ceased to be entirely one of enterprising individuals competing with each other, as Adam Smith largely conceived it. By the last decades of the nineteenth century business firms of massive size were employing ever larger proportions of the work force. Although the new corporate world celebrated the ideology of individualism more than ever, large structures were emerging that the sociologist Philip Selznick called "private government." These private governments did not govern with the consent of the governed, and it has been impossible, in spite of a long history of efforts to do so, to integrate them effectively into a democratic polity. Competitive advantage rapidly swung against the individual farmer, mechanic, or merchant and in favor of larger and larger combinations of investors organized under law as "corporations." The economic and legal doctrines of the free market no longer seemed unproblematic. The very term "corporation" had undergone a fateful transformation.

As Hamilton and Jefferson knew them, corporations—a term borrowed from English law—referred to exceptional "bodies," as the word suggests, chartered by the state to perform certain functions. The primary instances were municipalities, churches, colleges, and the like. When, as Hamilton conceived them, private groups did organize for economic purposes, such as companies to build roads or canals, corporate charters were negotiated with state legislatures that specified the new body's rights and extraordinary—usually monopoly—status, and also the obligations it had to assume for the public benefit in exchange for this concession of special standing.

In the nineteenth century all this changed dramatically. The corporation lost its public character at law, largely because of the fear of special privilege. Legislatures passed bills permitting "free" or general chartering of business corporations simply on the payment of fees and in compliance with certain organizational regulations. The courts in turn ruled in favor of treating the corporation as a private economic actor which could then for all intents and purposes compete as freely as individuals, but with the advantage of much greater economic resources and, as critics noted, with much less responsibility than that required of individuals. By late in the century, corporations were regarded at law as having the natural rights of persons. Such corporate "persons," the Supreme Court ruled, had to be left free to enter into contracts, including labor contracts, on whatever terms the market allowed. The state could not interfere.[16]

This turn of economic events confounded the hopes of both Hamilton and Jefferson. The theory that the corporation was legally a "private" citizen was now used to justify precisely the "economic royalists" that the Jeffersonians had feared and the "private governments" they would have feared even more, while the organizing and civilizing institutions that Hamilton favored had never been put in place. Something had clearly gone wrong with the civic pedagogy of the political economy; its results were contradicting its purposes. A constitutional order designed for one kind of political economy was trying to cope with a very different economic system that the older order had disconcertingly given rise to. The victory of the Jeffersonians and their even more populist successors the Jacksonians had become the basis for the centralizing economy which they most feared. Where wealth had once meant tangible goods such as land, ships, houses, and artifacts, it had come to mean above all negotiable instruments such as cash, stocks, and bonds. But there had been no accompanying institutional reconstruction of the public realm. On the contrary, the legislatures and the courts seemed intent on forcing the new wine into the old skins.

The corporations and the world economic system in which they were enmeshed grew up "over the heads," so to speak, of the people and even of their leaders. Misunderstanding these new institutions, and insisting on speaking of them in the older Lockean language, Americans failed to make sense of them and, even more than the citizens of most other modern nations, allowed them to produce whatever unintended consequences they would, some of which were serious indeed.

IX. THE ECONOMY AND THE STATE

The rapid growth of industry, railroad transportation, and centralized banking in the nineteenth century created entirely new problems of large-scale economic organization, problems that often caused severe instability and cyclic recurrences of boom and depression. Like their counterparts in Europe and Japan, American industrial firms organized to gain some control over their markets. In other countries, traditions of governmental oversight of the political economy permitted the organization of industries into cartels, and the recognition of labor unions as analogous groupings. In the United States, however, both political tradition and the legal order worked against such a legalized, quasi-public organization of large industry. Still, the question of the role of government in economic life took on a salience that continued to grow throughout the twentieth century. The terms of the debate about the relation of the economy and the state changed, but the debate itself would not cease.

American firms had long been used to protecting themselves against foreign competitors through the political device of having Congress impose high tariffs on imported goods. In the huge domestic market that the railroad and telegraph made possible, the competitive advantage went to big firms, which were by necessity increasingly joint-stock corporations rather than family or partnership enterprises. But now, in the expanded and more complex market, these heavily capitalized firms were vulnerable to all kinds of financial fluctuations for which the most attractive remedy was to create some form of monopoly.

The American belief in opportunity for the small producer in the free market triumphed, however, in form if not in substance, in the Sherman Antitrust Act of 1890. From then on, the consolidation of the industrial system proceeded fitfully, through various devices such as mergers and acquisitions of the kind the house of Morgan made huge sums from engineering. The process of reorganizing the nation's resources and productive arrangements would go on, but it proceeded in the realm denoted by law as "private."

Still, the American public had long been deeply fearful of the power of "monopolists," especially what Jacksonians had liked to call "the moneyed interest." By this they did not mean the rich per se, since many Americans aspired to improve their financial condition. Instead the target was those who, by dealing in assets and credit, could hope to get suddenly rich by no toil of their own, and those who could make decisions with consequences for thousands of their employees, suppliers, and customers on the basis solely of their own economic interest. Such worries animated agrarian movements for government control of railroads and banks. Some of these features of the new economy were hard to reconcile with the nation's Protestant religious heritage, still influential among the middle class at the beginning of the new century.

Controversy over the form of large economic organizations grew so intense that many feared that economic progress could be endangered. J. P. Morgan claimed that popular resistance to what he considered the efficient and therefore rational restructuring of the economic order threatened the changes necessary to progress. Socialists such as Eugene Debs thought Morgan and others like him were proof that the capitalist system of private financial organization was curtailing progress by a tyrannical concentration of wealth and power. Middle-class reformers felt that their own best ideals of self-reliance, industry, and generosity were being rendered meaningless by the new era of giant institutions.

The notion of progress had given meaning to individual lives and struggles. Economic improvement, education, providing a better life for one's children: these were deeply held purposes. They were communicable to new immigrants, to blacks suffering under racial oppression, to nearly all Americans. But the family and household economic team was manifestly no longer the vehicle of material progress, even if it retained its central position in the moral firmament. Changing technology and the division of labor were disconcertingly moving beyond the producer-household. The market, which now included very centrally the labor market, seemed to impinge ever more intrusively on the conduct of daily life.

"The job" became separated from family and kin, neighborhood, and church. More rather than fewer Americans were working not for themselves but for someone else, or something else. Some, like many farmers, fought the power of the market and its manipulation by the railroads and corporations. Others, like Morgan and like Debs—though on very different grounds—claimed that the growth of economic organization was inevitable. But most citizens vacillated, trying to keep things going while vaguely scanning the horizon for harbingers of new possibilities which could continue the old faith but adapt it to the new world. Such people in those years sometimes found themselves gravitating toward the cause of "reform."

In 1909 those devoted to reform were galvanized by a new book written by a previously unknown author, Herbert Croly's *The Promise of American Life*. Croly's book helped to focus a new debate on the direction of American life and institutions. In an important sense, that debate has continued throughout this century. His vision, and the reactions it occasioned, began to compete for attention with the familiar private conception of the political economy which the first hundred and fifty years of American history had bequeathed.

Croly accepted the superior efficiency of the modern division of labor and the large economic organization. But he also advocated a more positive role for governmental institutions and public forethought in national affairs. In this he was doing more than offering a new design for the national society: he was also creating a new context for political and economic argument. What had Croly seen in advance of most of his countrymen? As he put it, "the traditional American optimistic fatalism," the belief that the "Promise of American Life" would be inevitably realized, was no longer adequate. "The automatic fulfillment of the American national Promise is to be abandoned," he wrote, "precisely because the traditional American confidence in individual freedom has resulted in a morally and socially undesirable distribution of wealth."[17] What many in that day termed "the social problem"—poverty and oppression amid the new technological abundance—would have to be addressed by conscious, deliberate organization.

The old, passive Promise needed to be transformed into an active "national purpose" if the United States was to live up to its high ideals of equality and freedom. And "no voluntary association of individuals, resourceful and disinterested though they be, is competent to assume the responsibility," Croly argued. "The problem belongs to the American national democracy, and its solution must be attempted chiefly by means of official national action."[18] Vast concentrations of private power only revealed the limitations of "an excessively individualized democracy." The solution seemed inescapable to Croly and those who felt the power of his interpretation: because "a democratic ideal makes the social problem inevitable and its attempted solution indispensable," the country needed to reform its institutions in the direction of "a more highly socialized democracy."[19]

What Croly had discovered, then, was, as he himself admitted, the great fact about the modern industrial world that British and European political thinkers had been discussing for some time: the growing world market and advancing technology were creating a new environment of interconnection and interdependence utterly unlike the isolated, slow-moving conditions of previous ages, and the existing structures of democratic decision making could neither understand nor control it. The British political theorist Graham Wallas, as we have noted, called this new international network of interdependence "the Great Society."[20] Croly was the first to show its reality in American life. He also showed how the disconcerting new conditions had developed, even in a United States virtually separate from the rest of the world for nearly a century, from the very workings of the pioneer economy.

The American nineteenth century of nostalgic dream had been, said Croly, "essentially transient. It contained within itself the seeds of its own dissolution and transformation; and this transformation made headway just as soon as, and just as far as, economic conditions began to prefer the man who was capable of specializing his work, and of organizing it with the work of his fellows."[21] Thus Croly described the new division of labor in which specialization made for greater precision and efficiency. He then argued that the new integration this situation required could be thought out in the active processes of popular democracy and institutionalized in a more expansive public realm. Government, in other words, could become the instrument of a "national democracy."

It was a long time, however, before Croly's vision gained significant public support. Under the pressures of mobilization during World War I, some of the government initiatives that reformers like Croly advocated were indeed attempted, but so resistant were the leaders of American business, even to Woodrow Wilson's highly voluntaristic policy of national coordination during the war, that the apparatus of coordination (and public spending) was dismantled immediately after the armistice. Within months, the nation swung from boom to depression. America's spirited but brief and tentative flirtation with Progressive reform ended, with few permanent institutional changes to show for it.

Yet, in spite of all the obstacles, a skeletal regulatory state, designed to bring some public standards into the operation of the now largely corporate economy, had been growing for some time. The Interstate Commerce Commission predated the Progressive movement. Agencies such as the Federal Trade Commission, the Food and Drug Administration, and the Federal Reserve System and a national graduated income tax had been established. A host of other regulatory agencies had been established at the state and municipal levels, where the Progressives were more successful than in the federal government. Nonetheless, what these institutions amounted to by 1920 was a set of agencies run by experts in a weakened polity where the will to take vigorous policy initiatives had largely expired. This continued to be the case during the 1920s, when the corporate economy was developing significant innovations in mass production, vertically integrated production systems, and the organization of consumer credit. But the economic collapse of 1929 shifted the emphasis once again toward governmental responsibility.

In response to the Great Depression and World War II, the American political economy developed around major initiatives of the national government. The argument about the relation between the economy and the state, though still muted, moved forward significantly in the Roosevelt years. As compared with the role of government in the political economies of Europe and Japan, that role here, it is true, remained relatively limited and diffuse; but it was still on a notably different scale from what had been the case before the New Deal. Even so, the programs that Progressives such as Croly had argued for were implemented only partially and hesitantly. The growth of a national state occurred more under the impetus of war and cold war than as a response to needs for greater democratization of society—and this had significant consequences for the kind of state that emerged.

The debate over corporate responsibility and the role of administration and law in economic life was conducted with great vigor in the 1930s. Walter Lippmann's *The Good Society* was one of the more thoughtful contributions to it. But no intellectual consensus was reached, and public policy veered pragmatically in response to what various constituencies demanded or would accept. Well before any coherent solution was attained, the whole debate was ended by the specter and actuality of United States involvement in World War II. Thus, to an opaque, misunderstood economy going on "over the heads" of the citizens was added the apparatus of a national defense state, even more insulated from normal democratic review and decision.

X. WAR AND THE STATE

The final phase of the Roosevelt years powerfully influenced the shape of American institutions for decades. Wartime mobilization spawned a new set of coordinating agencies, frequently headed by veterans of Wilson's mobilization (FDR himself being one), and staffed by New Dealers assisted by a crop of fresh young talents eager for public service. These cadres were to play a huge part in building the postwar order. The War Production Board, the Office of Price Administration, the Office of Science and Technology, and the continuing Reconstruction Finance Corporation all suggest simply by their names the extent of the national government's involvement in activities once judged to be matters for the private economy. While many of these were dismantled after VJ Day, the chilling of relations with the Soviet Union and the decision to assist Europe in reconstruction through the Marshall Plan ensured that there would be no return to the world before the New Deal.

The cold war was the dominant preoccupation of the executive branch of government during the Truman administration and justified a new level of centralized state power. The armed forces were now placed under the unified command of the Department of Defense. The Central Intelligence Agency (CIA) was created initially to coordinate information from various existing agencies but soon became a vehicle for planning and carrying out secret initiatives abroad (even in some cases at home), with very little accountability to anyone except, officially, the President. The National Security Council, headed by a national security advisor, created only a little later, extended the direct initiative of the President in foreign policy over the heads even of the secretaries of state and defense. A report written in 1950 by a committee headed by Paul Nitze for the National Security Council (NSC 68)[22] became a kind of blueprint justifying the emergence of a national defense state within a state. Nitze's logic was that America had to use Soviet means to counteract the Soviet threat. The ironic consequence was to create a powerful apparatus of centralized authority outside the normal constitutional structures of democratic accountability that mirrored the Stalinist state itself. Up until at least 1990, virtually all congressional and public efforts to control this structure were successfully resisted in the name of a constitutionally dubious claim that the President had "sole power" over foreign affairs. America had known something close to national mobilization in both World War I and World War II, and indeed Lincoln had assumed extraordinary powers during the Civil War; but only now did such a centrally mobilized power as the national security state continue decade after decade to exert powerful influence over every aspect of American society, not least its economic life.

The federal government now assumed, as we have seen, three key roles in the national economy: funder, underwriter, and regulator. As often as not—as with the vast federal interstate highway program and the expansion of federal subsidies for education during the Eisenhower years—these functions were justified on the basis of national defense. For decades much of the government's new spending went for military purposes. Huge amounts of money expended at the Pentagon, with their influence on monetary and fiscal policies, had a major impact on all levels of corporate investment and employment, and the national security argument trumped any repetition of arguments from the 1930s about the impropriety of this scale of government intervention into the market. The continuation, decade after decade, of very high levels of military spending created something that has been called Pentagon socialism in a large sector of the American economy. Just as in the Soviet Union, bureaucratic inefficiency and incredible waste proliferated in companies that had to meet no competition, for whom cost was never an issue, and whose profits were assured no matter how inefficient they were.

Military spending was heavily concentrated in certain new industries and geographic regions. The airplane industry, and later the aerospace, electronics, and atomic-energy industries, absorbed enormous amounts of resources and newly trained personnel: the sunbelt enjoyed a boom at the expense of established industries in other regions. The American political economy entered an era of planning, but it was one guided largely by political entrepreneurship in the name of national defense.

For a long time the accepted goal of containing the communist world made it virtually impossible to question the validity of this government by fiat in the name of national defense. In the name of the defense of democracy effective democracy could be subverted. With living standards continuously rising, Americans were ready to believe that the vast economic and administrative structures being erected "over their heads" could be managed by experts, that technology rather than politics was all that was needed. But the Great Society that Lyndon Johnson hailed (without understanding what the term originally meant) continued to generate profoundly disorienting consequences for ordinary Americans. With the collapse of much of the communist world at the end of the 1980s, the possibility arises for a democratic discussion of and intervention into the conditions that have produced such dismaying problems. Perhaps only now is it possible for Americans too to dismantle the quasi-Stalinist structures of the national security state that have exercised such largely unanswerable power over our lives for decades.

XI. THE PRESENT IMPASSE

One way of summing up the difficulty Americans have in understanding the fundamental roots of their problems is to say that they still have a Lockean political culture, emphasizing individual freedom and the pursuit of individual affluence (the American dream) in a society with a most un-Lockean economy and government. We have the illusion that we can control our fate because individual economic opportunity is indeed considerable, especially if one starts with middle-class advantages; and our political life is formally free. Yet powerful forces affecting the lives of all of us are not operating under the norm of democratic consent. In particular, the private governments of the great corporations make decisions on the basis of their own advantage, not of the public good; and even the government agencies that are supposed to regulate them are usually ineffective or in collusion with those they are supposed to regulate. The federal government has enormously increased its power, especially in the form of the military-industrial complex, in ways that are almost invulnerable to citizen knowledge, much less control, on the grounds of national defense. We have gotten the strong state that the Jeffersonians opposed on the basis not of Hamiltonian design but of national security. The private rewards and the formal freedoms have obscured from us how much we have lost in genuine democratic control of the society we live in.

It is important to remember that when un-Lockean institutions were growing beyond the control of ordinary citizens, the dynamic impetus of the Lockean paradigm at its best did not weaken. The significant achievements of the civil rights and women's movements should not be underestimated, but their successes were attained largely in terms of the established order whose tenets they originally challenged. Women, blacks, and other minorities were given enforceable legal rights that made it possible for them as individuals to compete in the public sphere as workers and consumers, always provided that they had the competence to take advantage of those rights; but middle-class white men, who now had to move over and allow others into their once exclusive club (albeit with continuing legal pressure), nevertheless set the terms for the newly arrived. The key was individual competition for property and the private enjoyment of its acquisition.

Government became ever more important because it provided the context in which individual competition could effectively take place, by supporting the educational institutions and the vibrant economy that allowed individual achievers to get ahead. But governmental initiatives to deal with the structural problems that prevented some Americans from ever entering the competitive race in the first place were fitful, inadequate, and never wholly legitimate. The public debate that had begun in the early twentieth century with the Progressives was never fully revived. John Kennedy's notion that our problems are technical and not political prevailed. In this atmosphere emphasis on individual freedom and achievement went hand in hand with turning over public decisions to managers and experts. The ever-reiterated praise of "free enterprise" obscured the degree to which the federal government had become the funder, underwriter, and regulator of the national economy, and prevented a critical appraisal of how and for whose benefit it was carrying out those responsibilities.

Public and private managers have soothed us into believing that they know what they are doing, and their successes have been tangible. Yet the administered society that we have gradually become is showing signs of severe strain, so that it is time to ask the question not just whether we need a different management team, but whether we need a new level of democratic institutionalization. For, as we have seen, it is not only those left out of the American dream who have suffered under the present institutional arrangements: the coherence and meaning of life have become endangered for every social group. An obsessive pursuit of private ends has resulted in more problems than solutions in both public and private life. Futurama and Tomorrowland have come and gone; but the public and private happiness that the millennial idea of Progress, conceived in exclusively technological and economic terms, had promised seems more elusive than ever. It re-

mains to be seen whether moral and democratic progress, based on a
deeper understanding of public and private happiness, is still possible.

The question for the responsible citizen today is, Are we responsible
only for our own good or also for the common good? Even a benevolent
tyranny can permit us the former; only a genuine democracy can make
possible the latter. As long as we thought that the freedom of private
life required only a technically competent organization of the economy
and the state, we opted, in a strange perversion of the original Lockean
teaching, for benevolent tyranny, for the administered society we have
largely become. To make the democratic alternative possible again,
we would have to think seriously about the nature of our institutions
and what they are doing to us. With Herbert Croly, we would have
to return to the Hamiltonian institutional project, but with a Jeffersonian intent. For historical and cultural reasons, that seems extraordinarily difficult for us to do. But it may be our only option.

The citizens of the ancient Greek city-states were determined to
govern themselves rather than submit to an oligarchy, a tradition
revived and continued to the verge of modern times by some of the
medieval cities of Europe. The founders of the American republic
established a regime that guarded individual rights while ensuring that
citizens could choose their own representative rulers—a project that,
in spite of progress, is still not completed. Today the question is
whether we can go beyond the earlier democratic projects and subject
the structures that have grown up since the eighteenth century, the
modern economy and the administrative state, to genuine democratic
control. If not, as Tocqueville warned, even though we may maintain
the forms of democratic rule, our government will become precisely
the administrative despotism to which Americans in principle are most
opposed. We need today what the political scientist Robert Dahl has
recently called the third democratic transformation: this would move
us beyond the stages of the ancient city-state and the eighteenth-
century regime of individual rights and representative government,
while preserving and advancing their gains.[23]

In the next two chapters we shall attempt to envision what that
third transformation might look like in our economic and political life.

3

The Political Economy:
Market and Work

I. "TAKE A WALK ON THE BOARDWALK"

Most Americans know Monopoly as a game: Parker Brothers' famous entertainment has been a continuous favorite since the Great Depression. The very name Monopoly is likely to conjure memories of sociable hours spent taking turns moving counters around a board bordered with brightly colored squares connoting real estate properties. Some properties are empty; others are dotted with small green houses and larger red hotels. The properties bear the names of streets of Atlantic City in the early twentieth century: Park Place, Marvin Gardens, the Boardwalk. It is not today's East Coast Las Vegas of casinos but the stylish resort of Dos Passos's *Manhattan Transfer*.

The game combines skill with a heavy dose of chance through dice and situation cards. These can suddenly propel players into lucrative ventures by sending them racing ahead of the pack to buy high-value properties such as the Boardwalk, or on a similarly enriching "ride on the Reading [Railroad]." Less pleasantly, "Chance" can send the hapless to jail—without collecting the customary two-hundred-dollar windfall when passing "Go." The object of the game is to bankrupt your opponents by buying up so much real estate that they have literally no place to rest that does not require payments to you, now the holder of property all around the board: the monopolist. For a few hours anyone can taste the excitement, risks, and rewards of life as a would-be business tycoon. The game gives many children their first sense of the free market.

Oversimplified as games always are, Monopoly presents a compelling and curious picture of life in a market society like ours. At the end of a game, any player, even one of quite tender age, is likely to assert the importance of taking chances, balanced, as the player becomes more seasoned, with prudence about what properties to save up for and where to invest in improvements to enhance their value. An experienced player is also likely to emphasize the quiet but indispensable function of the "bank" as supplier of funds and credit. Most of all, the players are likely to recall the thrill and agony of competition. Winning at Monopoly requires sticking at it through adverse turns of play. And it requires playing by the rules, which the players mutually enforce.

For winners lucky enough to land on and buy properties like the Boardwalk, on which everyone else will have to pay, the rules are rarely a matter of scrutiny. But when you are losing, it is a different story. Losing players not infrequently rail that "it's not fair" to have to fork over so much carefully hoarded cash to an opponent just because the winner was lucky enough to land early—and flush—on lucrative properties (an argument, by the way, that would have made perfect sense to John Locke). Yet Parker Brothers offers no means by which players can discuss and modify the rules.

From the player's point of view, Monopoly is a free market situation in which no one compels the actions of another. But once begun, the game proceeds according to a relentless logic that is no longer subject to the wills of the players either individually or collectively. In this game, as in the world of Thomas Hobbes, "there is no other goal, no other garland, than being foremost," and the rules are as immutable as laws of nature.

In its strict separation of collective discussion and rule-making from competitive play, Monopoly embodies the economic viewpoint known as laissez-faire. The game separates the market from the polity, the sphere of economics from that of politics. It presents as common sense what is actually a historically rare notion: that the market is a self-regulating device whose rules exist independent of common agreements about the conduct of social life.

In another way, too, Monopoly is a poignant commentary on a market society like ours. A game that begins with equality of resources among all players ends with only one winner and all the rest dispossessed. Adam Smith's notion that in the market all players win because the vigor of exchange and the efficiency of production increase the common store of wealth has somehow been contradicted. Of course, with the game you can always play again, and if you lost before you may be the monopolist next time. Still, Monopoly is a far from reassuring metaphor for a market economy, and it is worth remembering that the monopolies, and the corporations that created them, were passionately resisted when they emerged a century ago precisely because it was believed that they threatened the very foundations of our society, based as it was on the consent of free and equal citizens. Yet, as the game subtly suggests, the shift from a situation of free and equal players to one in which there is one monopolist and all the rest are paupers has occurred as the result of the inexorable rules of the market game itself.

In the nineteenth century, laissez-faire theory led some thinkers to conclude that one could not intrude upon the workings of the market. If competition produced monopoly, even general misery, so be it. Any attempt to interfere would be to go against nature herself, with even more catastrophic results. What proponents of the free market rarely noted was that the rules governing market behavior were not "natural" but had been gradually introduced over the course of several centuries in Europe and North America.

Old-fashioned laissez-faire in its pure form has fewer proponents today, but it is still conventional, among experts as well as in common discourse, to speak of "the economy" as an entity as though it were quite separate from government and society. Instead of these familiar but, we think, misleading distinctions, in this book we shall use the older, more accurate term "political economy." This term implies that, whatever Parker Brothers may have thought, economic activity is part of a larger social whole; the economy can be completely isolated from politics only in a game.

The root of the word "political" is the Greek word for city or, more accurately, self-governing community: *polis*. The word "economy" is also derived from Greek. In its origins, it meant management of the household, particularly as this was concerned with production and provision for the household's members. Political economy, then, refers literally to "the management of the public household";[1] it suggests that the functions of household management are embedded in the structure of the larger community life and are framed by institutions grounded in law and the mores; and the phrase further implies that the rules governing production and provision ought to reflect the moral claims of justice that order the polity as a whole. Political economy is thus a moral and institutional as well as a technical term.

Political economy has an honorable lineage in modern thought. The term was made famous by Adam Smith, whose treatise *The Wealth of Nations* of 1776 is usually taken as the foundation of modern economics.[2] Actually, economics in the narrow, modern sense was not separated off from the discipline of political economy until late in the nineteenth century. Today the older, broader term seems especially useful as Americans, like the citizens of all modern nations, have come to understand better the importance of governmental and social activity in the economic realm.

There *is* a kernel of truth in the notion, popularized by laissez-faire, that economic competition is governed by rules outside human control. Once market exchange has organized the various components of a society's efforts at production and provision, the processes of market competition draw all resources in their train, including people and their talents. The market system has become the sea in which all modern societies must navigate. This historical process was greeted with joy by Adam Smith, who believed that the division of labor generally increased society's wealth and tended to level the disparity between rich and poor. As the industrial era arrived, Karl Marx viewed market processes with dismay. For Marx the end of competition was, as in the game, the monopolistic domination of the many by the few.

In our own century it has become clear that the market, left to itself, does not automatically result in human well-being. The outcomes of market processes, even the rules according to which the market operates, are in important respects the result of human activity, in some cases even of design; and we now know that law, government, and the world system of nations are central to economic life. The focus of public deliberation must accordingly be broadened to take in the political economy and how it is institutionalized—an insight, as we have seen, already advanced by Croly and others decades ago, but one that we need to appropriate again.

We have briefly surveyed the history that teaches us how our institutions developed and why they remain so mysterious to us. Now we need to imagine how we can use this better understanding of our historical reality to enhance our capacities to reflect, debate, and act together, so that we can reform the institutions that we have come to take for granted but that no longer are working very well.

II. LIVING OUT THE LOCKEAN PARADIGM

In our great desire to free the individual for happiness, we Americans have tried to make a social world that would serve the self. But things have not gone quite according to plan. We have made instead a world that dwarfs the self it was meant to serve. Especially in the economic realm Americans find themselves under the pressure of market forces to which the only response seems submission. This is the ironic result of trying to live by the Lockean language of individualism in an institutional world it can no longer describe, and yet the Lockean language still seduces us at every turn. We have no chance of seeing things more accurately unless we can explain why the Lockean view is still persuasive though fatally flawed. The key to this enigma is the appealing but treacherous notion that we can create a good life simply by striving for individual comfort and security, and that by so doing we are indirectly enriching the lives of those around us.

The great gift of civilization, Lewis Mumford wrote, is twofold: a cultural tradition to locate ourselves in and a vision of renewal that lures us forward. Without an orientation to past and future, Mumford argued, identity and meaning are not possible, and even purely personal freedom and pleasure are diminished.[3] The eddies of change that ceaselessly swirl through the global great society of modernity have made these gifts precarious. But the ability to preserve them realistically yet hopefully distinguishes those societies that have created a livable modernity from those that have foundered in the seas of uncomprehended change. By contrast, in America, Lockeanism's lack of historical sense together with the passive economic metaphors of Monopoly have impaired recognition of the civilizing gift of historical orientation. Yet we need it badly at this critical juncture of worldwide economic restructuring.

The founders of our republic imagined that the civilizing tasks of creating a democratic society and opening up unheard-of economic opportunities could go hand in hand. But it has become apparent through much of our history that the two do not always go together. In 1985 Robert Dahl posed the alternatives in stark form:

> We Americans have always been torn between two conflicting visions of what American society is and ought to be. To summarize them oversimply, one is a vision of the world's first and grandest attempt to realize democracy, political equality, and political liberty on a continental scale. The other is a vision of a country where unrestricted liberty to acquire unlimited wealth would produce the world's most prosperous society. In the first, American ideals are realized by the achievement of democracy, political equality, and the fundamental rights of all citizens in a country of vast size and diversity. In the second, American ideals are realized by the protection of property and of opportunities to prosper materially and to grow wealthy. In the first view, the right to self-government is among the most fundamental of all human rights, and, should they conflict, is superior to the right to property. In the second, property is the superior, self-government the subordinate right.[4]

It is possible to interpret the fundamental commitments contained in the Declaration of Independence—all men are created equal; they are endowed by their creator with the right to life, liberty, and the pursuit of happiness—in either way. A comment of President Reagan's is telling with respect to how we have been interpreting these words of late: "What I want to see above all is that this country remains a country where someone can always get rich. That's the one thing we have and that must be preserved."[5] Most Americans know that this is a one-sided interpretation of our tradition, but it still has extraordinary resonance. Even people who know that their chance of getting rich is only as great as their chance of winning the lottery still want to live in a country where *someone* can always get rich. And even if not wealth, a degree of autonomy is available to a significant number of people. That autonomy is closely related to owning property, especially a home, perhaps an RV, often a gun. And people who have something—and most of us have *something*—want it protected. That is what the social contract is all about. So they want a "strong defense." And they want more jails for the criminals, and they want the death penalty. Economic opportunity is not necessarily, but is easily, equated with blaming the losers—it's their own fault if they don't have a job, money, and property.

The sociologist Herbert Gans, in his important book *Middle American Individualism*,[6] reminds us that Middle Americans (whom he defines as the middle 40 percent of the income distribution, people who describe themselves as "working people"—sociologically they are working-class or lower-middle-class; educationally they are high-school graduates or have one or two years of college) want above all to live their lives in their own way. They see work as fundamentally unpleasant but an essential means to paying for the house, car, etc., that allow them the freedom their parents, or certainly their grand-parents, did not have. They want as little to do with large organizations of any kind as possible. Gans believes this is intelligible and even admirable for descendants of generations of peasants and laborers who could never call their lives their own. Middle Americans want what upper-middle- and upper-class people have always had—some control over their own lives—and why not? It is one of the successes of the postwar "American Century" that economic opportunity became a reality for most Americans. Home ownership, that most intensely personal form of private property, reinforces the equation of the good life with individual security and private happiness. Yet in exchange for the real freedoms they have attained, these Middle Americans have

implicitly accepted a degree of social and economic precariousness
that is unacceptable in most other advanced industrial societies.

As long as most Americans lacked property or opportunities, New
Deal liberals, drawing as almost all of us do from our Lockean heritage,
appealed to workers and farmers with the argument that the interests
of the numerical majority were equivalent to equal justice for all. This
simple equation seems far less obvious now. The success of the New
Deal and the "American Century" have so changed majority perceptions that many of the former bulwarks of the old liberal coalition—
farmers, labor union members, and urban ethnic voters—can be persuaded to align their interests with those of the affluent rather than
with those at the bottom of the heap. It is harder and harder to get
those in the middle ranges of our society to identify with the plight
of the truly deprived, even though their own situation relative to the
rich continues to worsen.[7]

It may be that the source of Americans' declining interest in democratic participation and social justice is not their affluence but their
new sense of its fragility; for quite some time the material situation
of many middle Americans has either stagnated or declined. Benjamin
Friedman has suggested that as long as our income doubled every
generation, we could afford to concern ourselves with those who had
not yet come to share in the general affluence.[8] Once that is no longer
the case, we resent the use of public funds for common provision.

In spite of a long history of governmental measures taken to alleviate
the harshest consequences of rapid industrialization (measures we will
consider in more detail in the next chapter), compared with most other
advanced industrial nations, the United States has emphasized economic opportunity for individuals (and corporate "individuals") at the
expense of public amenities. Indeed, the sociologist David Popenoe,
in a book comparing the United States with Sweden and England,
says that, relatively speaking, "Americans live in an environment of
private affluence and public squalor," where a "very high standard of
private consumption represents a trade-off with public services." Since
we have much lower levels of taxation than Western Europeans, we
can use our "saved taxes" to purchase more consumer goods than
Englishmen or Swedes of comparable gross income, but we do so at
considerable cost:

> The environmental squalor of American metropolitan communities
> stems in part from their dispersed character and the associated domi-
> nance of the automobile. But the relative lack of public funding dooms
> public services of all kinds—parks and playgrounds, public housing,

public transportation—to a level of quality that is meager at best by European standards. The poor quality of older communities, for example the inner-city slums in most older American cities of even modest size, also results from the lack of publicly financed planning efforts to direct urban growth and renew town centers.

Popenoe recognizes that most Americans aren't too distressed about this trade-off of public services for private consumption. We like our spacious homes and our automobiles, and we don't like taxes. Yet for all but the strongest, our way of doing things makes us extremely vulnerable:

At least as compared with life in European societies (and Japan) American life is also marked by a high degree of economic insecurity. American society has the character of a gambler's society: You may hit the jackpot and become really rich (something that is extremely difficult today, for example, in Sweden), but you can also with relative ease find yourself "out on the street." American employment policies are much less geared to job stability than are European policies. Many health care costs require private payments to the extent that a serious medical problem can be financially disastrous to the individual. And the pressures for ever-expanding personal consumption can quickly lead to indebtedness and even bankruptcy, to cite but a few examples.

Differences between income brackets are much greater in the United States than in Britain or Sweden. Whereas Americans in the top-5-percent income bracket earn thirteen times as much as those in the bottom 5 percent, the difference in Britain is a factor of six, and in Sweden merely three. Yet, as Popenoe points out, even this disparity is not the whole story, for the poor in America can count on much less community support than in Europe. In short, economic life in America turns out to bear an uncomfortable resemblance to the game of Monopoly after all: "Thus to be reasonably well-off in the United States with job stability and economic security in old age, is to have a life of great personal freedom and affluence. But to be poor, or even economically marginal, is to be a second class citizen in a way that is not found to be acceptable by the English or Swedish societies."[9]

But there is also a problem with the assumption that all is well with those who have continued to experience economic betterment even if the system as a whole does not work very well for those at the bottom. Many Americans suspect, but are afraid to admit, that they are not nearly so "free" as they think they are. First of all, they must submit to the discipline of an educational system that operates with ever-increasing severity. There is evidence that the anxiety level of college freshmen has been rising steadily for at least two decades. These anxieties only take on new forms in professional schools, in probationary first jobs, and indeed throughout the whole of life for those who are socialized to expect high achievement.

Secondly, as we described in detail in *Habits of the Heart*, the way of life of affluent members of our society is so oriented to outcomes and achievements that the very question of a good form of life is occluded. In principle, as liberal political theory has always held, our enhanced freedom should allow us to choose whatever form of life we feel would be most fulfilling. In fact, the relentless emphasis on freedom combined with the draconian conditions for its attainment empty out the very notion of a form of life. Our institutions continue to enhance our range of "consumer preferences" at the same time that they undermine our capacity to sustain forms of character and community that would give choice substantive meaning.

Success in a culture of economic opportunity is anxious and problematic, but failure is devastating. If one believes that "in America you can do anything you want," as almost all Americans of whatever class and race do, and then you find yourself at the bottom of the heap, out of work, or with a miserable job, living in unpleasant or dangerous surroundings, it is natural to think you have no one to blame but yourself. Hopelessness and despair can be profoundly self-destructive (drugs, alcohol, suicide), profoundly antisocial (vandalism, crime), or both. To have a hostile and disaffected minority is not a happy situation for any society. Yet it is precisely our Lockean individualism that has tempted the United States, more than most advanced industrial societies, to abandon concern for those unable to take advantage of economic opportunity.

III. THE TYRANNY OF THE MARKET

During the 1980s Americans gambled their future on wish rather than sober reflection. Three times in national elections we voted for a simulacrum of the "American Century," for a candidate who projected a sense of American superiority in the world and ethically untroubled affluence at home, willingly suspending disbelief in the possibility of such a restoration. Belief in the free market was revived; the premise of the game of Monopoly was offered with messianic expectations such as have seldom been heard since the nineteenth century. In a situation where further advances in democratic affluence seemed unexpectedly problematic, the market metaphor took on singular power. Disillusionment with the welfare state, combined with the weakening of the languages of biblical religion and civic republicanism that traditionally moderated Lockean individualism,[10] led many to take the market maximizer as the paradigm of the human person.

One powerful version of the market paradigm derives from the teachings of Milton Friedman and the school of economics he founded. In the view of Friedman and his successors, human beings are exclusively self-interest maximizers, and the primary measure of self-interest is money. Economics becomes a total science that explains everything. As so-called "rational choice theory," it has invaded all the social sciences—especially political science and sociology. Alan Wolfe, in his book *Whose Keeper?*, describes how this so-called Chicago school of economics is attempting to become our new moral philosophy or even our new religion:

> When neither religion, tradition, nor literature is capable of serving as a common moral language, it may be that the one moral code all modern people can understand is self-interest. If social scientists are secular priests, Chicago school economists have become missionaries. They have an idea about how the world works. This idea seems to apply in some areas of life. It therefore follows, they believe, that it ought to apply in all. . . .
>
> Chicago school theorists insist that the tools of economic analysis can be used not just to decide whether production should be increased or wages decreased, but in every kind of decision-making situation. Thus we have been told . . . that marriage is not so much about love as about supply and demand as regulated through markets for spouses; . . . and a man commits suicide "when the total discounted lifetime utility remaining to him reaches zero." From the perspective of the Chicago school, there is no behavior that is *not* interpretable as economic, however altruistic, emotional, disinterested, and compassionate it may seem to others. . . .

Wolfe cites an extreme example of two economists of this school who argue that a free market in babies would solve many current problems having to do with unwanted pregnancies, surrogate mothers, etc. They hold that women should be allowed to sell their babies on the open market and suggest that the situation would improve if "baby prices were quoted as soybean future prices were quoted."[11] We should not perhaps be surprised that the French speak of American capitalism as *le capitalisme sauvage*—"savage capitalism."

This savagery was not part of the intention of the nation's founders.

The American commercial republic, as we have seen, was conceived as an institutional design that would stir the self-interest of individuals to produce not brutal competition but civilized emulation, uplifting the people's material and moral standards of life. Like Adam Smith, Hamilton and Jefferson believed in the providential design of nature and in the possibilities of a self-regulating political economy that included not only market and government but an active public life as well. Although many of his latter-day prophets ignore this, Smith taught that the social benefit of the free market would be realized only in the wider public sphere, with the populace actively debating matters of common concern and expressing its will through the state. Opinion circulating among members of a myriad of voluntary associations would produce a collectively prudent public. This public would expand in social inclusiveness as its ethical level rose, gradually elevating the minds of commercial men toward the standard of judgment summed up in Smith's idea of the "Impartial Spectator," the quintessentially public citizen.[12]

The failure of the American political economy to develop spontaneously along the lines prophesied by Adam Smith has made regulation of the political economy, especially the protection of social life from undue market pressure, a challenge for each generation. On balance, the American polity has succeeded, though never very well and never without struggle, in developing institutions that stimulate yet channel market forces and promote, or at least preserve, the space of society and public life. But the achievements of the Progressive and liberal movements of the past are now called into question by the general obsolescence and breakdown of the arrangements that were made during the New Deal and postwar years.

Today, we must rise to a new level of economic sophistication and creative institutional imagination. To advance Adam Smith's hopes for a free society growing progressively more cooperative and inclusive, we must make more conscious efforts to redesign markets for public aims. For market forces are rapidly invading every sphere of society—even the family, that traditional bastion of refuge from the "heartless world." Due to its dogmatic belief that individuals develop independently of the web of institutional life, our Lockeanism makes this hard for us to grasp. It thereby blinds us to that great promise of modern civilization: the mutual emergence of individuality and solidarity in a plurality of activities fostered in a genuine public sphere.

The economist Robert Heilbroner, writing of "the implosion of capitalism," has suggested how the market is invading our private lives:

From this point of view, "economic growth" means the introduction of capitalist social relations into new social terrain. . . . For example, the enlargement of the proportion of the population engaged in wage labor, dramatically evidenced in the case of women in all capitalist nations, testifies to the implosion of capitalism, just as the imperialist extension of power during the late nineteenth century testified to its explosion. No less important is the "commodification" of life, the extension of commodity production to areas previously outside the ambit of the market. The rise of prepared foods, laundry services, home entertainment, and the pharmaceutical industry are instances of how the accumulation implodes capitalist relations. . . .[13]

As an example of what Heilbroner is talking about, a recent poll showed that the one thing affluent Americans said they could least do without was, not their BMWs or their vacations in Europe, but their microwave ovens. We know that more and more American families never have a meal together. One by one, family members drift into the kitchen and stick something in the microwave. Then it's "So long, I gotta go," as each one departs on his or her separate pursuits. The family meal was once a primary family sacrament, where children learned the terms of civil discourse. What happens to the family when commodification reaches this extent?

Or what happens when parents decide to buy a home in an outlying suburb that will be safer than the city streets and have better schools "for the children," and then have such long commutes to work that they have very little time with their children? The impingement of the market and the job culture on the family makes it hard for family members to take responsibility for a shared form of life that each person can affirm as his or her own. Developing the capacity to cultivate a shared form of life may make the difference between a personal life rich in connection and meaning and one bereft of lasting satisfaction. Opportunities for taking a responsible part in a shared life sustain the life not only of families but of schools, communities, religious organizations, business enterprises, nations, and even, we are now coming to see, a habitable planetary ecosphere.

No sphere is immune to market pressures. We shall see in a later chapter how the market mentality is penetrating our educational institutions. The following example of religious commodification is taken from a suburban newspaper in the San Francisco Bay area:

The members of St. John's Lutheran Church have a money-back guarantee.
They can donate to the church for 90 days, then if they think they

made a mistake, or did not receive a blessing, they can have their money back.

The program is called "God's Guarantee" and the pastor is confident it will work.

"We trust God to keep his promises so much that we are offering this money back policy," the pastor said. . . .

The program is modeled on a similar program at Skyline Wesleyan Church in San Diego.

Economic ideology that turns human beings into relentless market maximizers undermines commitments to family, to church, to neighborhood, to school, and to the larger national and global societies. In *Habits of the Heart* we documented what this kind of thinking does to our capacity to sustain relationships in every sphere, private as well as public. But the final irony is that this apparently economic conception of human life turns out to be profoundly destructive to our economy itself. If thinking of ourselves as members of a community made us poorer, there would still be many reasons to advocate it; but the fact is that commitment to a community turns out to be a much stronger basis for an effective economy than the individualistic pursuit of self-interest. We have only to look at the case of Japan to see that.

Let us illustrate the point by an example that applies to our high-tech industries. Here, shocking as it may seem to "common sense," the old neoclassical categories of capital and labor no longer apply. The productivity of a high-tech company resides in the quality of its work force, in the competence and responsibility of individuals, but also, critically, in the trust they have in each other to nurture creativity and innovation. These companies need not "hands," labor in the old sense of routine manual performance, and not just brains, but persons, persons who trust each other and genuinely enjoy working together. A company with people who work well together will outperform, many times over, a company with the same amount of capital and the same physical equipment where the workers are not responsible and where no one trusts anyone or is willing to take any risks.[14]

What is happening to such companies under the logic of interest maximization? We have over the last ten years seen an advance of what is called the commodification of the corporation. Any effective company will be looked at hungrily by people who want to make a profit by buying it, stripping it of its assets, firing managers and employees, and reorganizing it for immediate gain. Indeed, that is just the situation facing Marian Metzger, the fired manager of Persis Paints whom we met in Chapter 1. Persis Paints was a candidate for takeover not because it was inefficient and losing money but just because of its success and high morale. The commodification of the corporation, as we saw in the case of Persis Paints, destroys the corporation as a community. The prospect of such takeovers creates an atmosphere in which everyone is suspicious, ready to bail out, looking out for number one, trying to make the next quarterly statement look good at whatever long-term cost so as to advance the prospects of getting another job. By strip-mining our most valuable economic asset—namely, the creative interaction of people who have grown to understand and trust each other—we sink our long-term economic viability, while we appoint another commission on "competitiveness."

The principle of immediate interest maximization that cripples our economy weakens every other aspect of our lives together. People in our big cities are worried about the high cost of housing and the problem of clogged transportation arteries. But when every affluent person simply wants to buy the best possible house for his or her family with no concern for the provision of low- and middle-income housing in the community, then the cost of housing rises beyond their means, and even the affluent become indentured servants of their mortgages, while those in need of low-cost housing go homeless. When we think only of our own convenience in driving individual cars to work, then we spend ever more time on the freeway breathing the foul air our cars are polluting, but we could be working for better public transportation that would serve everyone, not just us. Again, one response to problems such as these is the polarization of our society, with the rich creating private enclaves, protected by private guards, where they live removed as far as possible from ecological blight and social breakdown. This feudal or Third World solution is unworthy of the tradition of American democracy, of the spirit of a society based on the belief that all men are created equal.

Our individualistic heritage taught us that there is no such thing as the common good but only the sum of individual goods. But in our complex, interdependent world, the sum of individual goods, organized only under the tyranny of the market, often produces a common bad that eventually erodes our personal satisfactions as well.

IV. LIVING OFF OUR CAPITAL

It is very likely that this same symbiosis between Lockean ideas and un-Lockean institutions is in part responsible for our structural problems at the national level. Having substituted consumer sovereignty for democratic control, the consumer-voter for a democratic citizen, we have oriented the nation toward immediate or short-term payoffs that have dangerous structural consequences.

What is true for individual consumers is also true of our corporations. An emphasis on short-term payoff—what the quarterly earnings are—has skewed our corporate economy toward financial considerations instead of production, at least in comparison with our chief economic rivals. In the American economy energy and prestige are accorded to buyouts and takeovers, to the highest yield rather than to the steadiest productivity. As a result, other possible, and liberating, economic developments are inhibited. An increase in investment and in productivity, thanks to advances in automation and robotization, for example, would release time for creating a good form of life, for family activities, and for participating in our own self-government. But these advantages will occur only if we curtail immediate consumption and short-term profits. We have to acknowledge that individual, private consumption is dependent finally on our common endowment—the natural, technological, social, and moral infrastructure of our daily lives. Unfortunately, Americans show little aptitude for this kind of realism.

We discussed in the last chapter the ways that the economy and the state have become deeply intertwined over the course of this century, and how the federal government is the funder, underwriter, and regulator of the national economy. But unfortunately our political life shows the same shortsightedness as our economics. Our politicians operate under the constant threat of the question put to the voters, "Are you better off now than you were four years ago?" So it is little wonder that long-range planning is not their strong suit. Early in the Bush administration a Democratic senator, not unfriendly to the President, was asked whether Bush had finally gotten "the vision thing," and he replied, "In this town, if you can see six months ahead, you've got vision."

The exceptional shortsightedness of American economic and political life is an expression of the symbiotic relation between our Lockean ideology and our un-Lockean institutions. It is as though the undemocratic accumulation of power in the hands of corporate and administrative bureaucracies were bought at the price of indulging some of our citizens in immediate rewards. This is our version of what the Romans called bread and circuses: a situation that simultaneously creates disabled institutions and corrupted citizens.

It would be troubling enough if the price were merely the indulgence of our citizens, especially the most affluent, best organized, and most vocal of them. But this pattern of indulgence puts at risk not only the future of our present adult population but, even more seriously, the lives of our children and the as yet unborn. This is evident in our stunning failure to care for and well educate our most vulnerable citizens, those born into poverty and insecurity—a failure that has social and even economic costs we are only beginning to recognize. It is also evident in our weak and vacillating efforts to control environmental pollution. Today, Jefferson's famous words "The earth belongs to the living and not to the dead" have a hollow ring. We are missing any concern for the future when the world is devoted to individual happiness, defined in terms of consumer prosperity. The earth may not belong to the dead, but that hardly excuses its thoughtless exploitation at the expense of future generations.

The massive accumulation of environmental problems—air pollution, acid rain, the greenhouse effect, ozone depletion—suggests that few of our citizens and virtually none of our politicians have seriously considered that the very meaning of progress in the future must be different. A proliferation of consumer goods can no longer be the chief definition of progress. Genuine progress today still requires technological advance, but advance by means of appropriate, nonpolluting technology, and, even more, progress in the learning capacity of our citizens, in what Robert Dahl, following a long tradition, calls "enlightened understanding."[15] Only progress of this kind enables us to discern a common good, which is clearly not the same as the sum of individual goods. Fortunately history has given us some extraordinary opportunities, and it is to be hoped that we have the wisdom to take advantage of them. Such wisdom would require self-disciplined and thoughtful citizens able to participate consciously and democratically in reforming our economic and administrative institutions so that they serve the common good of those living and those yet to be born.

V. CHANGING ECONOMIC FOCUS

In the last chapter we described the gradual growth of the American political economy and the institutional matrix for democratic affluence in the postwar era. Despite the undeniable achievements of that time, one of its principal legacies has been a massively false idea: the idea that society, or at least that portion of it we call "the economy," is an automatic mechanism whose motive force is the self-interested action of millions of unrelated individuals. According to this presumption, it does not much matter whether individuals understand the structure and operation of the social whole, nor is it particularly important or desirable that they should concern themselves with it. Simple strategic action is all that is required; the larger order will take care of itself.

This is the familiar but misleading perspective we noted at the core of the game of Monopoly. It is as though the economy were a vast circulation of traffic in which each driver has only to concentrate singlemindedly on grasping any available opportunity to get ahead of the other drivers, and not to seize each opening as it appears in the line of vision is to get pushed onto the shoulder, which harms both the individual driver and the overall flow. Such drivers happily or necessarily leave the regulation of the pattern—the construction of traffic signals, safety regulations, and so forth—to the engineers and experts who are supposed to know about such things. Or they do so until unpleasant consequences of their aggregated individual decisions begin to cause serious inconvenience: it takes gridlock or its equivalent to raise serious questions about the design of the system. But at that point, it quickly becomes obvious that the system has done little to educate the drivers to perform more active and cooperative tasks. In the new world economic situation the singleminded rush for short-term expediency stands revealed as crackpot "realism" indeed.

For most of its history, the American political economy was, by geography and design, relatively insulated from the vagaries of world trade. It is like a vast highway system that now finds itself intermeshed with other systems with different kinds of vehicles and traffic flows. For American drivers accustomed to speedy and uninterrupted passage, it is no longer enough simply to drive faster and more aggressively. The basic arrangement of the system can no longer self-evidently deliver on its former promises. Even more unsettling, it is likely that its very design may have contributed significantly to the present congestion. With unprecedented change, the end of which is visible nowhere on the horizon, there is suddenly a premium on understanding the new situation and making appropriate responses to it.

To a degree unique in the industrial world, the United States placed its faith in the capacities of the market system to promote the general welfare. However, as we saw in the previous chapter, we had to construct institutional devices to channel the market's floods of "creative destruction" away from human habitation—or at least the habitations of those economically and politically powerful enough to make the decisions. The law has been the primary means for this regulation and control of the market's operations, and the primary institutional creation of American economic law has been the business corporation.

The history of the American economy is in large measure the story of the corporation, which has evolved characteristics of private governments. Today some of our largest corporations are multinational, with incomes larger than the tax revenues of many nations.

It was a long-standing principle of the civic republican tradition that power follows wealth; and for that reason a rough equality of property was assumed to be one of the prerequisites of a democratic republic. Alexis de Tocqueville, discerning the first beginnings of large-scale industry in the 1830s, warned that this development might lead to the creation of a new aristocracy, to a new kind of feudalism fundamentally incompatible with democratic equality.[16] Fears of "economic royalism" were endemic in America from the late nineteenth century through the New Deal. It was clear that business corporations exercised inordinate power at federal, state, and local levels.[17] Nonetheless, ever since World War II, with the exception of a brief flurry of concern in the 1960s and early 1970s, we have taken the corporation for granted as a natural feature of our society—subject to regulation, to be sure, but not seriously scrutinized as to its fundamental terms of institutionalization. In large measure this was because the corporation was apparently stable and effective as the provider of technological and economic progress.

Now, however, even at a time of widespread neoconservative and neo-laissez-faire sentiment, serious doubts are being raised about the adaptive and innovative capacities of corporations. Much ink has been spilled to discuss the problems of corporate finance and management in the changing world market. And even more profound questions have been raised as to the legitimacy of the public chartering of a private power that is oriented to private gain and has few public responsibilities. These doubts have always been the foundation of democratic criticism of the corporation.

In designing economic institutions and laws in the postwar era, the United States turned away from many of the active social-justice aspects of the New Deal and toward a system of private consumption and corporate organization that characterized the American Century. We are now at another point of major institutional decision. It is not at all clear that those postwar priorities and institutional arrangements are any longer worth the price they exact. At least some of our citizens have come to see that the present organization of our economic life, including the corporation, threatens not only our democratic government, because of its inordinate political influence, but also our national character and form of life, because of its propagation of the idea of wealth as merely the accumulation of consumer goods. This

criticism is only heightened when the corporate economy shows serious signs of malfunctioning even on its own self-defined terms.

VI. THE WORLD OF WORK: A MOMENT OF OPPORTUNITY

Many analysts have pointed out the new circumstances that are changing familiar patterns of industrial and office work. Changes in the
technology of production emphasize worker participation and blur the
boundary between worker and supervisor, and this has enormously
positive possibilities; the new information technologies increasingly
require workers and not only managers to innovate, cooperate, and
take responsibility for the directions of work. But these developments
are themselves deeply ambiguous. Some observers of the American
economy, such as David Noble,[18] Harley Shaiken,[19] and Robert Howard,[20] also note that the potentials of the new technologies may remain
untapped because of American management's traditional fear of
worker autonomy. Others, such as Robert Reich,[21] Michael Piore and
Charles Sabel,[22] and Shoshana Zuboff,[23] believe that the need for
well-trained, highly skilled workers using new "smart machines" offers
opportunities for major reform in the structure of American corporate
management, particularly under pressure to match similar advances
abroad. Joseph Pratt and Louis Galambos,[24] pessimistic about the
record of American management, maintain that only increased corporate democracy will enable American business to break out of the
stagnant productivity that has plagued the economy for decades.

In order to increase the learning capacity and flexibility of American
corporations, reform would have to move in the direction of more
collaboration and sharing of authority and responsibility among (increasingly well-educated) workers and managers, thereby reversing
the previously dominant twentieth-century pattern of "scientific management." The business ethicist Charles Strain concludes that the
outcome is not predetermined, that "the evolution of the corporation
into a democratic learning community" will not happen simply by
the pressure of technological change or "the assertion of moral will
alone": "It will require structures of democratic learning within the
workplace and structures which check and balance the tendency of
any human organization to develop factions which hoard power. If
we accept Jefferson's argument, as I do, that the lack of forms of
democratic governance within the economic sphere inevitably corrupts
the forms of democratic governance in the political sphere, the choice

that we make at this technological divide will affect far more than our individual workplaces."[25]

The Cuomo Commission Report, surveying the demands of the global economy, argues in remarkably similar terms.[26] The recovery of a high rate of productivity necessarily requires various forms of worker participation—whether in involvement in decisions about what happens on the work floor, or in ownership of shares in the company, or in bonuses for increased profitability, or in actual worker ownership and election of the corporate board of directors. Are such arrangements genuinely democratic, or do they only involve forms of co-optation without effective participation in corporate power? The latter possibility is a part of the present crisis.

We would do well to remember Hamilton's notion that economic institutions teach and form us as effectively as schools and families do, if not more so. Any institutional arrangement of the market or corporation effectively makes some kinds of experience available to its participants and renders other experiences impossible. In the American political economy, the competitive, individualistic form that sanctions of success or failure take exerts great pressure. There is an unmistakable Darwinian ground bass playing under the Lockean melody sung by the contemporary sirens of the market. The effect is to make people anxious about defending their perilously fragile dignity, and it encourages a short-term focus on narrow self-interest. The way the work world educates us limits our capacity to acknowledge our real dependence on the work and resources of others, including other nations and the natural environment itself—even the common inheritance of the family.[27]

In short, the experiences of daily work often screen out those very considerations we most need to take into account when developing the potentials of the new technologies for more craftlike work and responding effectively to the new imperatives. When fear of "losing" freezes the adaptive intelligence of a people, it is obvious that we must change the nature of "business as usual."

VII. THE CORPORATION AND THE MARKET:
A NEW DEMOCRACY

Big corporations and small, like individuals, finally respond to the way the market is organized and the sanctions institutionalized in prevailing commercial practice and business law. Here again, the root problem is the folly of trying to operate with Lockean principles in an un-Lockean world. In conditions of general instability, it is dangerous for economic actors, either individual or corporate, to rely nearly exclusively on the short-term strategic logic of a narrowly interpreted self-interest. As the institutional pressures of the economy change, alternative behaviors will supplant this shortsightedness, but this will not happen without a political and legal restructuring of the corporation's place in the society.

The economic historian Jeffrey Lustig has well summarized the issues: "What is necessary is not an impossible attempt to separate the corporation from its social integument, but to acknowledge their mutual dependence and to ensure that the corporations become socially accountable. The point is not to try an impossible divorce of corporation from politics, but to assure that its politics are consistent with democratic practices. . . ." He goes on to suggest that there is currently a "crisis of membership" in the corporation. When capital and labor, as categories, no longer make as much sense as they once did, it is not clear who in a corporation should have more power than others. Ownership and decision-making power must be shared more equitably in an enterprise that depends on the intelligence and initiative of all its members, not just the "entrepreneur." The corporation must also be held accountable to larger constituencies—the communities that have given it tax advantages and public facilities, suppliers and customers, a general public that expects from it ecological responsibility, ethical practice, and fair dealing in return for its exceptional powers.[28]

What critics are arguing for is, essentially, to bring the corporation into full democratic accounting with respect to its own claim to be a "citizen." The legal scholar James Boyd White has argued, "The corporation is and always has been a collective citizen," which "should be spoken of as having both the responsibilities and the benefits of that status." To argue that the corporation's defining objective is "enhancing corporate profit and shareholder gain" leads, in his opinion, to unacceptable conclusions: "To say that a corporation's only goal is to make money would be to define the business corporation—for the first time in American or English law as I understand it—as a kind of shark that lives off of the community rather than as an important agency in the construction, maintenance, and transformation of our shared lives."[29]

White argues that American corporate law has considerable resources to give us for thinking about the corporation as citizen, resources that are endangered when we define the corporation exclusively in terms of economic gain. The issue is not whether corporations, as much present literature has it, develop better "corporate cultures," or promote more ethical leaders—both of which would be good things in themselves. When any corporation may suffer a hostile takeover at the hands of other business interests that want to exploit its resources for short-term gain, the issue is not just culture or leadership but legal norms, the institutional structure within which corporations can operate. The market could be structured to favor long-term, productive investment over speculative profit, but it is not so ordered, for good Lockean reasons that are now increasingly dysfunctional. We agree with those who believe that only a significant change in the present pattern of institutionalization will enable corporations to be the good citizens that most business people sincerely wish them to be.

To restructure the incentives of the market so as to favor long-term investment over short-term consumption, or to change the institutionalization of the corporation to accountable democratic citizenship, does not at all mean to centralize industry under a government ministry. Neither we nor those we have quoted are advocates of a command or state socialist economy. Still, it is worth remembering that there exists in America a very powerful form of command economy: a large and powerful sector of American business (by some estimates up to one-fifth) is effectively removed from the strictures of the market economy since it does most of its business "on command" with the military branches of the American government. This "Pentagon socialism" not only has all the disadvantages of command economies anywhere but corrupts the American political process. Few congressional districts do not have plants and workers dependent on the defense establishment, which leads to the strange situation where Congress votes to fund fighter planes or missiles that even the Pentagon doesn't want, because otherwise there would be a loss of profits and jobs in districts represented by powerful legislators.

The new international situation after the cold war offers unparalleled opportunities to redirect the present level of defense spending to other uses. Given the sad state of our highways, public transportation systems, and other material infrastructure, as well as the severe needs of our educational system, increased government spending in these areas could take up the slack in declining defense expenditures while contributing enormously to the potential productivity of the United States. But to do something about this requires that we face government's economic responsibilities directly rather than cloaking them in the guise of national defense.

VIII. THE MORAL CONTEXT OF WORK

The most fundamental reform to bring about economic democracy is not in the realm of government spending, important as that continues to be. An increasingly social ownership of corporate wealth is quite different from government ownership. We have in mind not only the kinds of thing that Lustig has proposed, but something like the Meidener plan, proposed in Sweden, in which the general populace participates in the increase in wealth, to which all contribute; a certain proportion of new stock offerings go to the government not for government use but as a source of dividends for the public, at first limited, but eventually providing the protection against complete impoverishment that those with independent incomes have always had. This arrangement would give everyone a stake in the increase of productivity in the economy. Proposals for a guaranteed minimum income or a social wage would accomplish the same thing by different means.[30]

The Lockean ideology and the way our economy has worked up till now have obscured the truth about work: namely, that we are not isolated individuals picking fruit or making money; we are all profoundly dependent on the work of others. The sociologist James Stockinger, in his critique of Locke, puts it eloquently:

> It is not at first with our own hands that we pick the acorns and apples from the commonwealth of nature to nourish our own bodies. It is the hands of other people that supply the needs of our bodies, both in our infancy and beyond.
> For each of us lives in and through an immense movement of the hands of other people. The hands of other people lift us from the womb. The hands of other people grow the food we eat, weave the clothes we wear and build the shelters we inhabit. The hands of other people give pleasure to our bodies in moments of passion and aid and comfort in times of affliction and distress. It is in and through the hands of other people that the commonwealth of nature is appropriated and accommodated to the needs and pleasures of our separate, individual lives, and, at the end, it is the hands of other people that lower us into the earth.[31]

Today people know that this is true, but they don't see it in the economy. They see it in private life—it is one reason the family is still so important, if not as a fact then as an ideal—and they see it in charitable acts. In a democratized economy it should be much clearer that the work each of us does is something we do *together* and *for each other* as much as by and for ourselves. As we have already noted, studies have shown that even now, when many workers feel they are constrained at work and their real lives are lived off the job, they are actually happier at work than at leisure. Doing work that is challenging and cooperative seems to fulfill a deep human need. If people felt that the workplace as well as the home really belonged to them and contributed to the good of all, the lingering resentment might lessen.

A more democratic economy cannot represent moral progress unless it also helps eliminate what has come to be called the underclass. The doctrine of individualistic equal opportunity has often divided communities between those who succeed and those who don't;[32] worse, the success of some actually *causes* the situation to worsen for others, as for example when middle-class blacks move out of neighborhoods that then have only a more hopeless, more isolated underclass left behind. With a much higher level of public commitment to institution building, family support, quality education, and self-respecting work, and a concerted effort to involve skilled volunteers in the tasks of community building,[33] presently impoverished people would be empowered to become stakeholders in the democratic economy and society and thus increase their participation as citizens. People like Ed Loring and Murphy Davis, with their Open Door Community (which we described in Chapter 1), would be invaluable, not just holding up a candle against the dark but contributing an immediate human quality to a much larger, and in part necessarily bureaucratic, effort. Some such policy is essential to keep the ghettos from turning into the police states they are beginning to resemble.

There is some reason to believe that Americans may be readier for a major reform in our economic institutions than is sometimes imagined. Many people would prefer a better "quality of life" to a simple increase in personal income. What "quality of life" really means and what a person would agree to in a political situation where one can have little trust that one will be fairly treated are of course open questions. Yet the old-fashioned notion of "a sufficiency"—a secure, modest income, rather than a potentially exorbitant but insecure one,[34] that allows one to form attachments, make commitments, and engage in activities that are good in themselves—is very attractive to many Americans.

The present heavy emphasis on economic opportunity puts a terrific burden on winners as well as losers; for there is the ever-present fear that one misstep will have you tumbling down the ladder. This fear will only increase as one comes to realize that for whatever reasons,

there are "limits to growth." It is idle to talk of "a sufficiency" as
though it were a static reality. As technology changes, sufficiency
changes as well. But in a world of tightening competition, organizing
American society around an ever more intense competition for affluence—more Hobbesian than Lockean—is not the only institutional
possibility. A democratic economy, in which appropriate technology
is combined with high productivity and therefore with the possibility
of increased leisure, is not utopian in terms of present possibilities.

A highly individuated self is an essential product of a truly modern
society. Yet the changes we suggest could go far to relieve the competitive, anxious self-assertiveness of this individuated self, for they
would encourage other virtues and competences. For example, feminist critics suggest that women have social and emotional competences
that help to cushion the demands and anxieties of the precarious
achieving self.[35] In short, we are not arguing for an end to competition
and achievement, any more than for an end to the market economy.
What we seek is a more socially grounded person in a more democratic
economy.

The United States until now has had an extremely unequal distribution of income as compared with other capitalist countries, as we
noted in the comparison with England and Sweden, and even more
inequality with regard to property. The American Catholic bishops
have pointed out that this is morally intolerable.[36] But the reforms
we advocate here do not involve simply a better distribution of income,
making the poor richer. We advocate, as the bishops do, a great
increase in the participation of everyone in the vitality of a healthy
economy. True, this participation would enable us to rebuild the
institutions of the underclass, not just allow individuals to escape it;
but most important, it would mean a richer public life, making a
satisfactory life for all of us, including the high achievers, dependent
less on our own success and more on a healthy society.

Above all, this means a change in the meaning of work, a lessening
of its pure utilitarianism, a recovery of the idea of work as a calling.
Interesting work, work that we know contributes to others, is its own
reward. It would be utopian to try to disentangle achievement and
material reward altogether, but some weakening of the connection is
the only way we can introduce an alternative to the Lockean pattern.
As Christopher Jencks has said, we must reduce the "punishments of
failure and the rewards of success."[37] We know that this cannot be
done without a great deal of conflict. Yet the reason for doing it would
not be just to help the deprived, or any "class." The change we favor
would help the successful as much as anyone, giving them what is

presently slipping beyond everyone's grasp, a form of life that is intrinsically meaningful and valuable. It will, of course, take an extraordinary exercise of political will to achieve so major a transformation in our ideology and our institutions.

Whatever the specific reforms—and we would expect a period of experiment to see what forms are most effective—the major benefit in the democratization of the economy would be to limit the harshness of the labor market, to give everyone who works a stake in the enterprise they work in and even in the economy at large, thus reducing both the anxiety and the cynicism that are rampant in our present economic life.[38] To be truly beneficial these changes would go hand in hand with increasing productivity and declining work hours, reversing recent trends, so that family, community, and civic concerns might flourish. Genuine democracy has always required a degree of leisure. A democratized and productive economy might at last give some genuine leisure to the demos itself. These considerations point toward the second major area of this third transformation toward greater democracy: the development of a democratic administrative state able to support and extend a vital public sphere, rather than supplant it.

IX. STEPS TOWARD ECONOMIC DEMOCRACY

At this point it would be good to summarize our argument and specify some of the changes we envision.

(1) In a democracy, as Václav Havel and the peaceful revolutions of Central Europe have eloquently reminded us, consciousness precedes being:[39] raising consciousness is the premise for institutional reform. The nature of our Lockean presumptions and the way they fail to capture our present reality need to be better understood. Our first step, therefore, must be more of the kind of discussion that this and the previous chapter have tried to advance. The goal must be nothing less than a shift from radical individualism to a notion of citizenship based on a more complex understanding of individual and social happiness.

(2) A more active citizenship is not a matter of consciousness alone. The new democratic transformation also requires the public will to reshape institutions. We are all—corporations, workers, consumers—citizens in our economic life. We need to make our economic institutions more responsive to this truth as well as to our capacities, as citizens, to take responsibility for developing our economy with the

common good in mind. Our swift historical review has suggested that the economy and the polity were always mutually involved; it is clear that few if any economic decisions are merely private in their consequences. Even consumer preference—the very quintessence of private action in the Lockean scheme—is itself a political decision. It is no longer the case, if it ever was, that if each economic actor pursues immediate self-interest, the result will be public benefit. We need institutional arrangements that enable the relevant publics to recognize the indirect consequences of private economic activities and empower them to regulate these activities for the common benefit. To achieve this end will require legal as well as economic reform.

(3) Corporations are and always have been legal entities. As James Boyd White has shown, they have never been radically "deregulated," for their very existence depends on legal rules. Our economy today requires not more or less regulation but a different kind of regulation, one that limits irresponsible and destructive activities (toward workers, toward the environment, toward productivity itself) while enhancing and encouraging others (greater worker participation, ecological responsibility, and effective growth in productivity). But again, to shift the corporation's legal institutionalization depends on a much more sustained and substantive public discussion of our present mode of economic organization and its costs.

(4) An increase in economic citizenship in the workplace is not only imperative for the third democratic transformation but necessary for increased productivity. We all know that effective companies today require the knowledgeable participation of everyone, from assemblers to the CEO. And this participation must be more than cosmetic. "No participation without representation" would be an apt slogan. For maximum productivity as well as maximum job satisfaction, full participation by all in the corporation as a learning community is essential.

(5) We need an entirely new level of understanding of what might be called consumer citizenship. Our culture has encouraged people to think of consumer choice as entirely individual. Indeed, "free to choose" has come to mean freedom to select the product of one's choice almost more than the freedom to choose one's elected representatives, or, even worse, to mean that the grounds for the choice of a candidate are identical with the grounds for the choice of a product, which is to say immediate private satisfaction. We need a much higher level of consumer intelligence, responsibility, and self-discipline. We have come to see in the case of tobacco that public pressure on individual choice through education, taxation, and restrictions on areas of use is appropriate for the common good. It will be much harder for Amer-

icans to see that the automobile is another consumer product that requires similar controls. As in the case of tobacco, we must obviously balance individual freedom with the common good, but there is nothing in our entire pattern of consumption that does not require careful scrutiny and citizen responsibility at the present time.

(6) Finally, there is the issue of economic justice, where economic citizenship merges with and depends upon political citizenship in the broad sense. Here the massive changes in the world economy present the most troubling problems. The long-term effects of America's push for individual advancement have been to shift concern from public to private well-being, and the abandonment of the urban underclass is simply the most glaring—and threatening—symptom of this. This trend is likely to be accentuated by the internationalization of economic growth in the world market system. Increased demand for the skills of salaried technical and professional workers will enhance their economic position, while unskilled workers of all types face more competition from lower-wage countries abroad. The market will be working against rather than for a decent society.

However, as James Fallows has reminded us, "People don't live in markets, they live in societies, and the question is whether our society can tolerate the even greater extremes [of wealth and power] that full internationalization would bring. Manhattan is the closest thing to a test case."[40] The challenge is to devise ways to make civic equality real. That means that the possibility of meaningful work and genuine participation in public life must become real for all members of American society—an impossibility unless we translate into political will the realization that democracy, the involvement of all citizens in a common civic as well as economic life, is the chief national goal and the best means toward redeeming the promise of American life.

X. ECONOMIC DEMOCRACY AND POLITICAL DEMOCRACY

Today an educated and engaged work force is no longer simply a moral desideratum. It has become a hardheaded, pragmatic necessity imposed by the spread of new technologies in the global market system. But it is similarly true, if less obvious to many, that reflective, flexible, and resourceful participation by citizens in the public realm is equally necessary for a decent and just society. The institutional order of the past half-century has depended too much upon apparently expert, technical management, particularly in our private corporations and in government regulation. It has complacently trusted the short-term logic of economic growth, led by private consumption, to bring about a good society. But the evident depletion of so much of our natural, physical, and moral endowment now reveals how unrealistic that alleged "realism" has been. To search for ways to structure interdependent lives more responsibly is no longer, if it ever was, mere idealism. It has become the fundamental need we all share. Yet in politics and law, as in the economy, Americans seem caught in a conundrum: many realize that the old institutions and ways are working badly, but our inherited pattern is so powerful that it inhibits the quest for a new paradigm that would respond to present realities.

4

Government, Law, and Politics

I. THE AMERICAN POLITY TODAY

The game of Monopoly gave us a metaphor for the way Americans think about their economy—one that is rather terrifying, but revealing about much of our received ways of thinking. Is there any comparable metaphor that might help us understand how we conceptualize our political situation? A report from the pollster Geoffrey Garin in spring 1990 gives us an account that, if not a metaphor, has a representative significance: "When we bring up the cost of the savings and loans bailout [the need to repay hundreds of billions of dollars in federally insured accounts in failed savings and loan institutions], we often hear people say, 'Why do the taxpayers have to come up with the money? Why can't the government?' " This anecdote discloses a basic line of tension in our thinking, a deep misunderstanding of democracy—as though government could operate without taxpayers! Americans, who are, compared with other nations, very patriotic, are at the same time very skeptical about government. We want very much to be "strong" abroad, but we want the government "off our backs" at home.

But even the way we talk about the role of government domestically is contradictory. Some of our rhetoric would make it seem that we are still wedded to the idea of the "night watchman state," with the government having as few functions as possible; at the same time, every disparate interest group in the country wants drastic and immediate governmental action on its behalf—and people expect the government to solve the problem of bankrupt savings and loan institutions on its own. Although we seem able to put up with a remarkable decline in the quality of many of our public goods, we are ready instantly to blame the government for any big difficulty, such as a recession. Since politicians in the executive and legislative branches, especially at the federal level but also to a degree at the state and local levels, are concerned more with monitoring public opinion with a view to reelection than with educating it with a view to solving problems, a discouraging gridlock seems to affect both the administration in power and the legislative opposition alike. It is not that the government does nothing—its numerous balkanized and poorly coordinated agencies do a great deal—but that it does it in a sort of holding pattern, often with reduced resources and with no vision of how to respond to new conditions and new challenges.

The public is not quiet. The last twenty years have seen an enormous growth in national voluntary associations, many focusing on single issues, that put intense pressures on both the administration and the Congress. But they do not stimulate debate about the major issues before us. And our political parties are presently more concerned with organizing and placating as many special interests and single-issue constituencies as possible to their own electoral advantage than with encouraging a serious debate among them. Similarly, the courts are not lacking in cases that raise important issues affecting our common life. Indeed, the courts have often given us the kind of sustained deliberation about important issues that the rest of our political system has failed to, but since the very jurisdictional limits of the kind of case with which courts can deal largely confine them to issues of individual rights, our major concerns can be only partially addressed in this forum. And the quality of the legal debate itself falters when judges are appointed or elected more for ideological reasons than for judicial distinction.

The task of replacing Lockean individualism in our economy is daunting, but a significant improvement in knowledgeable democratic participation seems even more difficult. Yet, as many Americans realize, the cost of the present drift is high. In the polity as in the economy, Americans have imagined that they can behave as autonomous individuals pursuing their own interests and that somehow the democratic process will produce an equitable compromise where interests clash, though they tend to believe that the market probably operates more fairly than government in this regard. But the illusion that we are autonomous is becoming increasingly implausible as we experience more directly our dependence on collective forces. For better or worse, we have developed an activist state, which in its own confused, fragmented way not only provides for the welfare of individual citizens but manages the national economy—setting interest rates, guaranteeing bank deposits, bailing out failing corporations, regulating the stock market. Its activities are central to the agendas pursued by virtually every social group. The government provides or guarantees medical coverage and income in old age, unemployment insurance, and protection against job discrimination; it subsidizes college education for the middle class, guarantees home loans for veterans, and underwrites much of the research and technological innovation that fuels the national economy. We depend on collective resources even to maintain the middle-class way of life that makes us feel that only our private concerns are significant.

This expansion of the responsibilities of government is part of the modern expansion of the public sphere, of the arena in which problems are defined as public and political rather than purely private. We expect government to protect children against abusive parents, wives against battering husbands, and employees against sexual harassment by their bosses. More and more we think of problems that government cannot or will not solve—infant mortality in poor communities, the AIDS epidemic, rising drug use—as public problems for which government is responsible. And this expansion of public responsibility leads us to experience an interdependence that we both recognize and resent.[1] Very little in our social world remains "private" in any meaningful sense. The building of a dam or the start-up of a nuclear power plant has effects on a ramified ecology of animal, plant, and human life, effects of which our institutional order—including our legal system, our politics, and our changing intellectual assumptions—now make us increasingly aware. From every side the day-to-day realities of our life as a people force us to think about our society as a whole in ways to which we are little accustomed. The interdependence of modern society is particularly problematic for Americans. A political tradition that enshrines individual liberty as its highest ideal leaves us ill prepared to think about ways of managing a modern economy or developing broad social policies to meet the needs of society as a whole. Yet it is more and more difficult to avoid a consciousness of "society as a whole"—and, indeed, of the world as a whole.

As a national state shapes and manages so much in day-to-day life, the possibility, and sometimes the necessity, of collective choices arises where none appeared to exist before. We have turned to administrative regulation and the judicial process to resolve social problems, yet in so doing we have only created more problems that seem even harder to resolve. As government pays for or underwrites health care, for example, its policy planners also begin to ask questions such as whether it is reasonable to fund ever more expensive medical technologies that will be used primarily for the aged, or whether the percentage of social spending spent on medical care makes sense in the light of other social needs.[2] In a world whose dominant institution is the market, such decisions are not even perceived as decisions: those who can afford expensive medical treatments get them and the poor do not. But new levels of government responsibility render visible what under the rule of the market remained invisible, and in so doing strain our institutional and cultural capacities for defining the common good.[3]

For all these reasons we need an extended period of serious and sustained national discussion: first, to learn why our ideology of Lockean individualism is inadequate for our new level of interdependence; and then to discuss alternatives that will safeguard our traditional concern for individual liberty and also more effectively conceptualize issues of the common good. Leadership for such a discussion might well be provided in the White House or the Congress, but we have elected officials who offer only directionless reticence in the presidency and timidity if not cowardice in the Congress. Without this public debate the actual administrators of policy must make do with the best they have at hand. All too often that is nowhere near enough.

II. DILEMMAS OF THE REGULATORY STATE

In the regulatory state, the interdependence of economic decisions, social choices, and human well-being becomes the direct focus of policy deliberation, and the dilemmas of interdependence emerge with special acuteness. Government administrators are responsible for thinking about the effects of public programs on all citizens, and they are forced to make difficult choices: money spent on advanced medical technology is unavailable for preventive health care; removing pollutants from the air may mean burying them in the ground or dumping them in the water; reducing sulfur emissions will reduce industry profits and perhaps cost some people their jobs. Here we can see the fundamental cultural limitations of our thinking about our common life, and we can begin to explore ways of thinking about a good society that do not reduce every issue to one of forced trade-offs between desirable goods.

In the thinking of government regulators, as in American culture as a whole, two kinds of individualism vie for dominance: one is moral, ultimately grounded in religion, according to which life is sacred and each person is unique, irreplaceable, and priceless;[4] the other is rational and utilitarian, in which the social good is whatever best satisfies the preferences of individual actors.

Talking to government regulators about their work—in agencies that deal with human health and welfare (the Environmental Protection Agency, the Occupational Safety and Health Administration, the Health Care Finance Administration [HCFA]) or agencies like the Congressional Budget Office [CBO] and the Office of Management and Budget [OMB]—one finds that they are often puzzled by the contradictions between the techniques they work with and their own moral intuitions. Neither traditional moral individualism nor utilitarian individualism produces an understanding of the common good. And in the absence of moral leadership from the executive and legislative branches to stimulate public discussion about the common good and move toward a more effective formulation of social priorities, they are left, by default, with only these contradictory traditions.

All too often, for reasons that should not surprise us, it is to the language of economics that administrators turn in order to talk "rationally" about the interrelatedness of the choices they face. The economists' ways of approaching these issues have made increasing headway in the federal government since cost-benefit analysis and zero-based budgeting were introduced in the 1960s; their current vogue is also a by-product of Reagan's and Bush's efforts to cut domestic programs and lift the "regulatory burden" on industry. This is the source of Executive Order 12291, for example, which has required every administrative regulation proposed by a federal agency to be reviewed by the Office of Management and Budget in cost-benefit terms (taking into account costs imposed on industry as well as direct government costs) before it goes into effect. The executive order was actually the brainchild of James Miller, a Carter appointee, and the vision of increased economic rationalization of government decision making was widely shared by high officials of both parties. Various versions of cost-benefit analysis have influenced policy makers because they seem to offer the only apparently rational, systematic way of making decisions that reconcile competing claims; in the absence of serious, sustained public or legislative deliberation about the common good, one can understand why this approach is so attractive.[5] Cost-benefit analysis has the apparent virtue of allowing a purely neutral weighing of advantages and disadvantages of any given policy in monetary terms, though its critics argue that it systematically overlooks important public concerns that cannot be quantified.

The deeper appeal of cost-benefit analysis is that it holds out the possibility, however visionary, of an integrated approach to policy, of doing what is really important rather than whatever happens to be politically popular. Its most fallacious, but equally appealing, claim is that it offers a set of neutral rules, a methodology, for arriving at just decisions.[6] If, as we believe, justice depends on forms of deliberation and judgment that cannot be reduced to rules or derived from a neutral methodology, but must always result from substantive considerations about the common good along with universal concerns about human dignity, then cost-benefit analysis cannot substitute for judgment in the choice of ends, though it can sometimes be a useful tool in choosing among alternative means. Our interviews suggest that even devotees of cost-benefit analysis find themselves baffled when they come up against fundamental questions about our common life.

Even though he said he "isn't thinking about that" now, Ed Sanders, a senior EPA regulatory analyst, described his sense of the irrationality of current decision priorities: "There have been some fairly crude studies along these lines, and they show what you would expect: people are doing crazy things. People have tried to compute the cost per life saved for a whole variety of programs, and it looks like a scatter diagram. And no rational person would choose to have it so. You would go after the ones where the cost per life saved was low first, and then you would go after the ones a little more expensive than that, and so forth." He also made clear how frustrating he found the political process by which such priorities were set: "This agency is not spending money on the Superfund [to clean up toxic wastes] because it wants to. It's been told to do so, and it's been told to do so by Congress; and Congress is worried about it because the folks back home are worried about it."

Cost-benefit analysis thus is powerfully appealing as an image of how government (or an individual) might integrate its decisions—across risk factors in the lives of individuals (stopping smoking will extend your life three years on average; the Superfund might extend it a few minutes), across decisions within an agency (should the EPA concentrate on removing lead from the air, which directly affects infant health and IQ, or clean up toxic dump sites?), and across decisions made by different agencies.[7] As committed cost-benefit analysts see it, one must be able to estimate how much a life is worth to decide rationally where government should intervene to save lives. To outsiders this enterprise may seem macabre, but to them it is a rational, indeed a *moral* and democratic, way to assess government policies.

How can the "value" of a life be established?[8] For cost-benefit economists today, the value of a life is not a person's *social* value— lifetime earnings less cost of maintenance—or even the value of the services or emotional gratifications a person might give to others. Rather, the value of life is what individuals themselves would be willing to pay to avoid risks of dying. As they see it, an individual's "willingness to pay" to live longer should determine how much of his tax money government spends to help him do so. Researchers gather data on this willingness to pay by measuring pay differentials between risky and less risky jobs, by measuring expenditures on safety devices (seat belts and smoke detectors), and by surveying people to find out how much money they would require as an inducement to undergo specific risks (riding in a plane with a one-in-ten-thousand chance of crashing).

All these approaches to valuing life have fundamental features in common. First, they define the value of life abstracted from any particular life. In doing this they ignore an essential meaning of life as we commonly understand it—that each life is unique and irreplaceable. The accumulated moral, religious, and social meanings associated with the value of life—not just an individual human life but life itself—make no sense from this point of view. An economist at the Environmental Protection Agency, when asked "What about the theory that human life is priceless?" answered, "We have no data to support that."

A number of the regulators we talked to took care to stress that they were discussing the value of a "statistical life." One can calculate the costs of saving lives, but no one can know which particular life will be saved. They regard it as a defect in the studies that have been made of actual social willingness to save certain lives (the amount spent to rescue workers in a mine disaster or a child trapped in an abandoned well, for example) that expensive rescue efforts involve particular, identifiable individuals. As one authority notes: "The coal mine operators know exactly who is trapped in the tunnel. Very large amounts are often spent to rescue the identified miners. However, these outpourings of effort and resources do not transfer to saving statistical lives, or we would not observe such large numbers of traffic fatalities."[9]

Second, the regulators abstract the issue of saving lives from the specific situations within which lives may be saved or lost. While they acknowledge that people mind some risks of dying more than others—being more willing, for example, to tolerate voluntarily assumed risks than those imposed by others—they lack the means to calibrate variations in the meaningfulness of dying (dying fighting for one's country vs. being killed by the wanton indifference of one's employer, for example), or of living, for that matter.

Third, they conceive "value" as aggregated "preferences"—preferences that themselves are arbitrary products of autonomous individual choices. Lives thus have no value beyond the value their possessors give them measured in market terms.[10]

Preferences, conceived as individual desires that are the source of all value, are both the foundation on which these government regulators rest their thinking and a source of their frequent confusion and bewilderment. The EPA economist spoke with contempt of arguments grounded in popular sentiment, such as those that politicians use when they criticize the economists' practice of discounting the value of benefits occurring far in the future: "Do you mean to tell me that our grandchildren's lives are worth less than ours?" He sees this reformulation of the issue in concrete, personal (but also culturally resonant) terms as a manipulative distortion of "true" preferences—those discernible in the way people actually behave (about smoking, for example, discounting the long-term risk of dying from lung cancer). For him individual preferences are sovereign, but the moral intuitions or cultural traditions on which they rest are suspect.

Many popular preferences seem irrational in this world view. Ed Sanders noted: "People's risk perceptions are so far off base, even with the best information government can give them. The people of the U.S. have voted for a $9 billion Superfund [to clean up toxic wastes where the immediate risks are small], and we spend much less for air pollution [where the risk to health is great]." Preferences are sovereign, yet "people behave irrationally with respect to risk." He concludes that "maybe we just don't understand what people want." Since for him there is no larger framework of meanings that justifies these preferences, he cannot defend his own intuitions about which preferences are "rational" and which make no sense.

The idea that government should be guided by the sum of what individuals want weighs only the preferences of citizens present right now. Without a larger moral theory, there is no sense of responsibility for others unknown or unborn. It distresses the EPA analyst that in "the case of stratospheric ozone depletion, the costs [of regulation] are all today: the benefits don't even begin to start occurring for twenty years—there is no real benefit for fifty years. We are doing all this for generations down the pike." Deciding what is good for society as a whole by assessing an aggregate of autonomous, individual preferences sharply constricts the definition of what that whole is; and current generations, who are considered to be obligated only to maximize their own welfare, are cut off from a sense of responsibility to the future.

Such calculations also take no account of the possibility that the preferences are linked and interrelated, making them more than idiosyncratic personal opinions. Asked about the possibility that loss of stratospheric ozone might proceed so quickly that it would destroy life on earth, Ed Sanders avoided the substantive question by treating it as an issue of individuals' preferences to worry or not worry about this likelihood: "If you're worried about an irreversible catastrophe, okay, fine, you do it. But we shouldn't let one person decide. People want many things. What we're talking about are people's preferences. That's where it is."

As he sees it, cost-benefit analysis, weighing what individuals apparently want, is democratic; the only alternative would be imposing one preference over others. He does not even imagine the possibility of substantive democratic debate. Asked whether the current generation has the right to spend up all the world's resources, leaving nothing for future generations, even though the members of future generations have no vote in current assessments of individual preferences, he again evaded the question by talking instead about variations in the preferences of the living: "But everyone doesn't want to spend. Some people want to spend now and some people want to save. If they didn't, there wouldn't be any savings. And to decide that balance between spending now and saving for the future, it's better to let people's preferences determine it, rather than having one person impose his view."

The value of lives of people who have no say in American politics, although they may be profoundly affected by American policy choices—other nationalities as well as generations yet unborn—cannot be accommodated in this system of calculating costs and benefits. To aggregate measurable individual preferences is to undermine larger conceptions of the common good, conceptions that start by recognizing the profound interdependences that characterize our world. To substitute this way of thinking for an informed public discussion is to abdicate political responsibility; despite surface appearances, it is undemocratic, for it does not allow a genuine democratic consensus to emerge but depends instead on an uninformed and undebated plebiscite of transitory and unexamined desires. It is an example of the fundamental error of replacing a genuinely democratic process with a consumer market choice model.

III. THE LIMITS OF MORAL INDIVIDUALISM

In general, opponents of this approach to public policy invoke embedded cultural traditions, a sense of moral and religious absolutes, which themselves derive from America's individualist tradition of political discourse. The atomistic, Lockean liberal vision of cost-benefit analysis is countered with a deeply rooted moral individualism that respects the dignity of persons, but has largely lost the social context of the older traditions. This has little to offer in dealing with the complexly interrelated choices a modern society must make, and therefore is not an effective alternative to cost-benefit logic. Cost-benefit arguments can be resisted on a case-by-case basis, but they continue to dominate policy discourse in the heart of government, where crucial questions about our shared future are decided.[11]

Even people who are profoundly committed to the economic approach sometimes find that other aspects of their experience conflict with their professional training. Bud Chapin, the regulatory analyst we met in Chapter 1, trained as an economist and now evaluating regulations for the Occupational Safety and Health Administration, made clear his basic commitment to cost-benefit analysis: "Do I think regulatory analysis should be held to a cost-benefit standard? Absolutely yes. It's a handy-dandy way. Against the costs, what are the benefits? Cost them both and identify benefits as accurately as possible." But he broke with other economists over the issue of "discounting" future costs and benefits. His resistance came partly from his thinking in more concrete terms than the abstract logic of economics usually allows about the actual circumstances of people affected by the OSHA's regulations. Consider the small-businessmen whose future costs are discounted "by the amount you will have made by putting that dollar you have in your pocket into a bank": "Absolute rubbish, I say. Because it doesn't make sense to me. Most medium- and small-time guys don't have it in their pocket. It's not out there accumulating dollars to be offset against the picture five years from now."

He is also troubled by the underlying moral logic of discounting future costs and benefits. "Discounting became popular in the 1970s. In the 1980s OMB had the bright idea of also discounting benefits. Then they got to the absolutely absurd notion of . . . discounting lives . . . with latency periods of diseases, discounting the value of that [life] over the latency period of the disease. Absolutely incred-

ible!" Discounting at, say, 10 percent a year over the twenty years a
disease caused by asbestos or benzine may take to develop, and starting
with an estimate of $5–7 million for a life, would leave so little "benefit"
from regulation that government would "do nothing" to control dangerous substances in the workplace.[12] But his objections go deeper,
to his substantive sense of the nature of human life:

> You see, I think I could argue that there's *appreciation* in the value
> of people. Given enough time, and given the right moral philosophy,
> logic, and sociological-anthropological considerations thrown in, the
> human person, the individual today, is on these three ranking
> schemes worth more than their father and their fathers and mothers
> before them.
>
> Q. Because they have more human capital?
> A. That's one approach.
> Q. I thought you were going to say that as you get older you have
>   more people who care about you, greater wisdom. . . .
> A. Yes. We've argued all of those approaches. Why not? Is there some-
>   body out there who says that there's no basis for that at all?

Bud Chapin's dissatisfaction with standard economic approaches
has grown more urgent the longer he has spent at his job. There is
simply something about human lives that cannot, and should not, be
evaluated in economic terms: "When I first came into this job, someone
said a human life is worth $3.5 million. There was nothing, no re-
sponse that I had to that intelligence. So I just didn't say anything—
didn't for two years. Now I'm just saying that I don't get it. There's
something missing." Convinced that putting a money value on lives
is "nuts—it's wrong, totally wrong," he nonetheless has little to fall
back on in trying to rethink how to make policy choices. Instead, he
continues to accept the basic outlines of cost-benefit analysis as a way
of aggregating individual goods into a collective good, but maintains
a conflicting set of personal values based, ultimately, on a bedrock
conviction that there is something sacred about individual lives that
can never be measured in money: "You're dealing now with that which
is outside the traditional cost-benefit framework, and it goes to my
own conscience—conscious, subconscious—and my background,
training, and my perception of what people are . . . that they stand
outside of the basic kinds of valuation systems that characterize market
economies. People are different from supply-and-demand transactions. That's just rudimentary. I can't go much further than that,
other than that's evident. . . . If you try to relate these [economic]
formulas to a head price on people, to my mind it's absurd. You can't

do it. You shouldn't do it. . . . Why? I don't know why. That's just the way I feel."

This vivid sense of individual human lives, a kind of reminder of the texture of lived experience, is important to many who resist utilitarian ways of thinking about political and social choices. Sam Gallardo, a long-term congressional staff member who is responsible for formulating environmental legislation, passionately objects to cost-benefit analysis, which he believes underestimates risks (and thus also the benefits of improvements in environmental health and safety) because it ignores whatever risks can't be measured. Using a recent EPA analysis of the dangers of lead as an example of "the best cost-benefit analysis that has ever been done," he cites the many kinds of damage it misses, contrasting its cost-benefit logic with vivid images of the unique value of concrete, individual lives: "It ignores, does not even attempt to assign a value to, an 8 percent intelligence loss that deprives you of an Einstein or a Newton. . . . They'll only tighten [lead standards] to the degree that it's warranted by dollars and cents. I think it's worth having an Einstein. I think it's a great loss to the human race to lose an Einstein."

He also thinks economists fail to think about the world's interdependent ecology, whether natural or social. Speaking of problems such as the greenhouse effect, he says: "You better worry about what the two most powerful nations on earth will do when they're both confronting famines because their bread baskets have turned into dust bowls. . . . There is no question about that—that the earth has gotten, is getting, and will get warmer. Of the last five years in the Southern Hemisphere, three have been the warmest on record. . . . That's a case in point. These [cost-benefit] people don't have any understanding of basic biological systems. What happens if you change a fundamental parameter like that is the system collapses. People won't even be around. They have absolutely no idea what they're talking about, economists."

Gallardo criticizes economic analyses in terms both political and moral; yet his politics, like his morality, are cast in traditional individualist terms. He has a populist suspicion of the interested motives of those who resist government regulation, and an even greater suspicion of their capacity for empathy: "I'm not saying that all of the economists who advocate cost-benefit analysis . . . have a hidden agenda, but . . . the hidden agenda is to shift the cost of their actions to the public so they can declare dividends for their shareholders. . . . The other thing is, frankly—now this is a personal value judgment—I find that . . . nineteen out of twenty of the people who end up being my adversaries on this issue . . . have not at any point really suffered in their lives, and they don't have any . . . fundamental understanding of human suffering and pain and therefore are able to dismiss death and pain and suffering, to say, 'Well, if you don't die of that you'll die of something else.'

"I don't think I'm dealing with people who've ever lived, who've ever earned an hourly wage, who've ever gotten up in the morning and not had a dollar in their pocket. Have you ever not had, literally, a penny? Nor have any of these people."

This man's populist, even alarmist, sense of tragedy also finally rests on a sense that political choices matter for their symbolic resonance within a cultural tradition. In his view it is wrong for society to say that it will trade lives for dollars in any circumstances, wrong because of the set of meanings we attach to human lives: "You can't say he's going to endanger a child because it costs him too much to avoid endangering that child. If you were to ask the average Joe whether a company has a right to endanger a child because it costs too much . . . I know what the average person would say: 'No.' "

From his deeply felt sense of commitment to individual human lives, this politically passionate staffer has developed a critique that moves beyond individualist moral repugnance. For him, what is ultimately wrong with economizing logics is that they erode the moral understandings that bind a society together, that make even suffering and inequality bearable.[13] "The kinds of values that economists seek to monetize, and thus have traded, they're the glue, the intangibles that make this country stick together. We've terribly oppressed a lot of minorities in this country, and we've gotten away with it for years and years, I think largely because we hold out a lot of intangibles, a lot of beliefs in opportunities, whether they're real or not, and if you throw those away I think the inevitable result would be a change of society." For him a central aim of social policy must be to preserve the integrity of the moral understandings central to our society, to preserve a heritage of cultural values. Policies, he says, may be "irrational in the economic sense, but not irrational in a societal sense." "What is the difference between this country and the Third Reich?" he asks. "Isn't it those sets of moral principles and values? What is the difference between this country before *Brown* v. *Board of Education* and this country after *Brown* v. *Board of Education*? Isn't it a commitment to a set of values and principles? There are some things that are more important than money."

There is a paradox at the heart of this hard-won insight into the essentially social nature of the values that policy might realize. Gallardo has distinguished between policies that maximize the aggregate fulfillment of individual desires and those that, even at great cost to the fulfillment of individual aspirations, preserve the integrity of a social community. But on what values does the integrity of a social community depend? For him, as for most Americans, the idea of a common good is still built around the ideals of an overly abstract individualism. The rights and capacities of individuals, which must be protected from the economic rationalizers, are still abstracted from the social contexts that influence and even constitute individual lives.

IV. THE TURN TO THE LAW

There is one arena in the American political order where deeper conceptions of the nature of our life in common are debated. This is in the courts, under the rule of law. Principled debate about legal rights are a counterweight to both the play of interests in the market and the sway of power in the political sphere, although the courts are not immune to economic and political pressures.[14]

Some of the most significant institutional and cultural efforts to deal with the social changes of the contemporary period have come from the courts. Many of them have tried to take account of increased social interdependence. Thus when the courts briefly, in the 1960s, gave legal standing to environmental organizations and other concerned groups to challenge government projects in which they had no direct economic stake, they were acknowledging broad social interests outside the narrow interests of the immediate parties, a position the Supreme Court severely restricted in the early 1970s. Pressure for expanded public provision, such as claims for equal schooling, demands for public funding of abortions, efforts to expand welfare, has been focused on the courts, with mixed results. More importantly, the courts have been the forum for debate concerning fundamental social and moral questions about the nature of a good society.

How does law—both as a set of social institutions and as a body of cultural traditions—approach the interdependence of modern society? American courts have done so largely by extending the notion of individual "rights." This occurs in two ways: first, by expanding the negative rights people are understood to enjoy against arbitrary government (such as broader interpretations of the constitutional guarantees of free speech, freedom from unwarranted search and seizure, right to a jury trial); and second, by expanding, unevenly and uncertainly, positive rights to equal treatment in welfare, housing, medical care, schooling, and employment.[15] This extension of rights recognizes that people are not simply autonomous actors who should pursue their interests without interference from public authorities. The courts have largely accepted the idea that in a world of mandatory schooling, large bureaucratic employers, and government-funded health and welfare programs, people are dependent for their security, for their autonomy, and for their well-being on the claims they have on such organizations. As Charles Reich argued in his classic paper "The New Property," those claims now constitute a fundamental part of the "property" that law must protect in order to make citizens secure against arbitrary infringements on their autonomy.[16] Welfare has become a right, and the courts block efforts to deny benefits or restrict coverage without due process. Since the Supreme Court's 1954 *Brown* v. *Board of Education* decision, the courts have moved aggressively not only to insist on a wide range of remedies for segregation but to raise the issue of inequities in school financing created by differences in local property taxes, so far without much practical effect. They have protected employees' stake in their jobs and pensions and prohibited dismissals based on age, sex, and gender discrimination. All these are ways of recognizing that an interdependent national society has replaced the moral fiction of a world of independent individuals linked only by market exchange.

A second way the legal order has recognized interdependence is by protecting people against threats posed directly or indirectly by the actions of others. A manufacturer's decision to use dangerous chemicals in the workplace can be challenged by employees whose health it threatens. A developer's decision to dam up a stream for recreational purposes can be challenged because it threatens survival of an endangered species. The law thus both recognizes and makes real forms of interdependence that were previously invisible and unacknowledged.

As people sense that they are surrounded by risks from the activities of legions of unknown others—polluters, drunken drivers, farmers who use pesticides on their crops, government authorities responsible for regulating airlines or drugs or consumer products—they tend to panic. Here again, the search for remedies through the courts—the explosion of litigation[17]—is both a cause and an expression of the underlying change in public perceptions. People try to find particular solutions—suing the manufacturer of a drug that caused an unnecessary death; demanding restitution for job discrimination; suing a school district that has failed to educate a student—for problems of interdependence that are fundamentally public and collective in nature. And still there is no overall sense that public debate and decision making have defined a common good.

Lawrence Friedman has described the aspiration for "total justice," based on an assumption that people have a right to live out their lives in reasonable security from personal and social catastrophe and that they should be compensated for any calamity. This presumption contrasts sharply with what life was like, for example, in the nineteenth century, when "there was of course no such thing as unemployment insurance. There were no pensions, public or private, and no social insurance to speak of."[18] Many formerly "private" ills are now seen as public problems, and people see public, social causes for private ills—the failure of industries to maintain safe workplaces, for example, and ultimately the failure of government to set the standards and enforce the policies that would make them do so. Even where the causes of distress are still private—drug and alcohol abuse or family violence, say—the remedies looked for are usually collective ones. The presumption of a right to certainty and security increases the demands on the public sphere, even if they take the form of individual claims for protection or compensation in the courts.

What are the virtues and the limitations of law as a way of understanding interdependence? The great virtue of the law is that it creates an arena of public debate where current problems can be addressed in light of a body of established principles. As Philip Selznick has noted, such debate involves both reason and tradition. Legal principles "should be capable of reasoned elaboration; yet, they should also be founded in propositions that define the historic commitments of the political community." Through legal debate, Americans explore how their fundamental principles can guide them in new circumstances. These principles emerge out of the life people lead together and the traditions they share, Selznick notes. "If the social world is itself 'absurd,' if there are not touchstones of shared tradition and common fate, then legal principles are hard to come by."[19]

These shared legal traditions are of mixed help in grappling with interdependence, in discovering the common good. Central here is the reliance of our legal tradition on protecting and extending "rights." First, recognizing and responding to increased social interdependence by protecting individual rights systematically distorts the solutions to social difficulties. For example, requiring due process before a worker can be fired may protect a person's claim to a specific job, but it does nothing about workers' wider dependence on economic forces outside their control. Policies to deal with jobs threatened by technological innovation or foreign competition, to retrain workers, or to guarantee employment go beyond the legal remedies available to combat instances of injustice to particular persons.

Our legal tradition has rich resources for dealing with the negative side of social interdependence—at least offering limited remedies when a factory's wastes pollute someone's backyard or when a hospital's negligence leads to a patient's death. But the emphasis on protecting individual claims to equal treatment, rights against harm from others, and rights to due process is of only limited help in developing new conceptions of the common good. For example, in dealing with poverty and welfare, the courts have extended social provision by limiting the power of government arbitrarily to deny benefits or coverage. But thinking of welfare as "a right, not a privilege" does nothing to rethink the whole relationship of the privileged and the unprivileged, to acknowledge that we all inhabit the same social world and that the entire community has a stake in the well-being of all its members. The welfare rights movement may have succeeded, at least symbolically, in moving welfare recipients one step closer to the American ideal of an autonomous individual in possession of a full complement of rights,[20] but it has been unable to provide grounds for the fuller dignity that adequate levels of support (public support for the community infrastructure—hospitals, day-care centers, schools, parks, prenatal clinics, youth centers—and direct income support to individuals and families) and full inclusion in the community would assure. The legal order sustains a moral commitment to righting particular injustices, but it does not encourage consideration of the common good or of justice in more general terms.

Legal debate as a way of addressing broad social questions has a second disadvantage. To cast a social question in terms of rights tends to make the answer to it an all-or-nothing affair, and to prevent precisely the consideration of how one choice is interdependent with other choices. A revealing example is the issue of "bilingual education" in public schools. Representatives of ethnic minority students argued in court that non-English-speaking students had a "right" to bilingual education because being forced to attend school in a language they did not understand deprived them of the constitutionally protected right to an equal education. When this issue is thus cast in rights language, the range of remedies is restricted. Broader policy issues about the adequacy of the education offered to minority students, about programs for new immigrants in school or out, or about the question whether students learn English better in bilingual classrooms or in intensive English-language lessons, cannot be explored. A right is absolute, and once legally established, must be assured regardless of cost or consequences. Thus, important questions are not addressed: the need to hire minority teachers, to devise better ways to integrate new immigrants, to consider the social value of retaining distinctive cultural heritages, including languages. Instead, the courts required school districts in California to hire bilingual teachers in each of the many languages spoken by the students. This was an extraordinarily expensive and administratively cumbersome solution that did not solve most of the important underlying problems.

Rights language is appealing, of course, precisely because it is absolute. In the American legal tradition, rights are those absolute immunities that prevent tyranny by the majority. But the notion of rights has been extended to include positive claims upon others—claims for equal treatment and claims for such fundamental goods as health care, housing, and food. But casting complex moral or social questions in rights language—how minorities will achieve equality, what are the just ways of distributing income or guaranteeing employment, how we understand the relation between our plural cultural traditions and our identity as Americans—restricts our understanding of them. Rather than debating the kind of cultural unity and diversity Americans want, the kinds of policies that might reincorporate the desperately poor into the social community, or how Americans will understand economic justice in a centralized, rapidly changing economy, we end up with rigid protections of a limited number of social goods that are understood as inviolable individual rights, with no way to attend to broader questions about our common future.

The third difficulty with the rights language is its abstractness. Rights language is, for Americans, a morally powerful way to understand injustice. Indeed, the movement for economic and civil incorporation of African-Americans into full citizenship was called the civil *rights* movement. Problems must be cast formally as matters of abstract, procedural justice in order to expand rights under the Constitution, such as rights to equal treatment or due process, while issues of substantive justice appear secondary. The most troubling problem with "rights" is that everyone can be said to have them, and when rights conflict, the rights language itself offers no way to evaluate competing claims. As rights crowd each other out, the rights language seems inadequate for dealing with major social dilemmas.

The discomforts, double-talk, and moral confusion Americans display about "affirmative action" programs, for example, which are justified as a remedy for specific acts of discrimination even when such justification makes little sense, might be resolved if more substantive debate over historical responsibility and social justice complemented the discourse about "rights."[21] But because they rely exclusively on a rights language that cuts both ways—as charges of reverse discrimination show—affirmative action programs are legally precarious and of uncertain legitimacy. An individualistic language of "rights" and "equality" was important in galvanizing Americans to confront social injustice; but the desire to right historical wrongs lay behind affirmative action, and the attempt to justify it in the abstract language of equal rights often makes it seem illegitimate, even to its supporters.

In a powerful analysis of American abortion law, Mary Ann Glendon has made a similar point about the way rights language has stunted the American abortion debate.[22] Comparing the laws about abortion in twenty Western democracies, Glendon points out that the United States is anomalous in both its policies and the way it frames the issue. Only in the United States are the laws framed with abortion seen as a matter of rights—the abstract rights of the fetus versus the right of a woman to control her own body. This formulation, Glendon argues, has led to an all-or-nothing approach: either the fetus is a person, whose right to life is absolute (except when the life of the mother is directly threatened), or the fetus is not a person, in which case the woman's right to an abortion is absolute and not subject to social intervention. In many European societies, Glendon notes, the laws acknowledge the fetus as a life that deserves social protection, but this does not endow the fetus with an absolute "right" to be born. Instead, the government's general obligation to protect life first requires positive social policies that allow women to afford to bear and rear children; second, courts and other government agencies can balance the life of the unborn child against the needs of the mother and other social goods (the dangers of unwanted children, battered children, or illegal abortions). In such societies abortions are legal, but the decision to abort is not the woman's absolute right. There is respect for the value of a woman's being able to choose parenthood rather than having it forced upon her, but society also has an interest in a woman's abortion decision. It is often required that she participate in counseling; she is encouraged to consider the significance of her decision, and she must offer substantial reasons why the potential life of the fetus must be sacrificed and why bearing a child would do her real harm.

American feminists may bristle at the thought of a woman having to justify her decision about abortion to anyone else, but the European systems Glendon describes have many virtues. First, as American women have begun to find out, rights language is only a fragile protection against state interference in the abortion decision. If a majority on the Supreme Court decides that the fetus is a person with a "right" to life, then abortion may be banned just as absolutely, and with just as little recognition of the social and moral complexity of the issue, as women's right to abortion was established by the landmark Supreme Court decision legalizing abortion in *Roe* v. *Wade*.

More central to our argument, to frame the abortion debate only in terms of rights has been to inhibit realistic, morally engaged social debate about the nature of abortion.[23] For example, what does it do to a society's social and moral fabric to require women to bear children? What does it do to a society's respect for life in general to deny that the fetus is a potential life? In what sense does society bear a general responsibility for the well-being of mothers and children? As Glendon makes us aware, the language of rights cuts off debate, polarizing society politically between those who support the absolute rights of adult women and those who insist on the absolute rights of the "unborn." We cannot then deal realistically with the conditions that lead to abortions on the one hand and the moral complexities of abortion decisions on the other.

Because the courts sustain debate about fundamental principles of how Americans live their lives in common, they are an arena where we can address central social questions—of racial justice, gender equality, or environmental devastation—that the political system shies away from. As the legal scholar Michael Perry has put it, the courts are a forum for a deliberative and transformative politics, which our society so desperately needs, when elsewhere such forums have been lacking.[24] But the courts as an institutional system have grave weaknesses in this regard: they have no independent fact-gathering ability; they adjudicate only particular cases rather than formulating general social policy; and they respond to the adversaries in cases brought before them rather than framing a debate about what is best for the common good.[25] The individualistic language of rights at the heart of the American legal tradition is a way of talking about the common good that inadequately addresses the kind of interdependence that is crucial in modern society.

V. THE POSSIBILITIES OF POLITICS

The obvious counterbalance to a regulatory state devoted to aggregating preferences and a legal order preoccupied with defending rights is a vibrant, democratic politics in which competing interests not only press their own demands but come forward with general programs for the common good. But it is precisely the institutional and cultural failures of American politics that have made the regulatory state and the courts so prominent in our political system.

Some of the difficulties in our political life go back very far. It has been argued that because the United States became a mass democracy before it had developed an autonomous civil service, American political parties came to rely on patronage rather than on appeals to broad social groups.[26] Politicians got ahead by offering benefits to specific individuals and groups rather than by developing programs that promised to advance the common good. Thus politics easily became an extension of the Lockean system in which individuals as well as industries, localities, and other interests ask of their representatives only: "What have you done for us lately?"

The reforms of the Progressive era reduced the direct role of patronage in American politics, particularly in city politics. But the ironic effect was to cut off working-class access to political and social benefits, especially for African Americans who were arriving in northern cities just as the urban machines that had fostered the mobility of earlier immigrant groups were being dismantled, while leaving intact patronage for larger and better organized interests—business corporations, labor unions, farmers, etc.[27]

As government and politics have become central in American life, the political arena has not effectively formulated a vision of a common good. Rather, the political arena has become dominated by a congeries of private interests (best symbolized, perhaps, by the increasing significance of single-issue Political Action Committees), which fight it out without regard to how the outcome affects the good of the community as a whole. And the political parties, within which comprehensive views about the social good might be formulated and debated, have weakened dramatically and are now little more than holding companies for agglomerations of specialized interests, while the influence of industry lobbies, single-issue organizations, PACs, and similar groups has grown enormously. Thus our institutional resources for forming a common political understanding of the good society have weakened, just as our expectations of government and the direct demands particular interests make upon it have grown.[28]

Much has been written about Americans' increasing disaffection from politics. Rates of voting, never high compared with those of other nations, have fallen sharply in the past few decades. Despite lowered barriers to voting for southern blacks and rising educational levels, 64 percent of those eligible voted in the 1964 presidential election, for example, while only 53 percent did so in 1984 and 50 percent in 1988. Attachment to political parties, traditionally the major way Americans have integrated themselves into national politics, has declined even more dramatically. Since the New Deal Americans have lost interest in and commitment to parties.[29] "Independents" now constitute some 40 percent of the electorate, and even those with nominal party affiliations are less and less influenced by the party ticket when they vote. The already weak institutional structure that once organized American political life is weaker than ever.

There is also dramatic evidence that Americans have lost confidence in government as they have in most major institutions such as business and labor. In 1980 only one-quarter of Americans reported a high degree of trust in the federal government, compared with three-quarters in 1958. Similarly, most Americans polled since 1970 have expressed doubt that public opinion makes much difference to government policy.[30]

This apparent alienation and withdrawal of Americans from the public arena is only half the story. As the sociologists Ronald Jepperson and David Kamens have emphasized, Americans' *interest* in politics has remained consistently high, as has their sense that it is a "citizen's duty" to vote. The public's belief that it understands politics and can influence politics in other ways than voting has also increased; there has been a remarkable growth in collectively organized political participation in forms other than voting and party activity: social movements and protest politics; single-issue organizational activism; class-action litigation to challenge government policy and laws; and collective efforts to lobby and negotiate with administrative and legislative bodies and officials. The enormous growth of registered lobbyists and of organizations headquartered in Washington signals the vast increase of the federal government's centrality in American life.[31]

As Jepperson and Kamens argue, while the American state has moved only partway toward the European model of a centralized welfare state, the American "polity"—the mobilization of people and resources in the national arena—has grown enormously. Mobilized around particular issues, interests, and causes, various groups in American life—women, minorities, the elderly, veterans, the disabled, homosexuals, those opposed to or in favor of abortion, the religious right, and many others—have become participants in the national arena. Thus government is more things to more people, and, indeed, more people increasingly expect more things from government. But there is no natural arena in which these competing claims on public resources, let alone those of the traditional private interests that want to receive benefits from or avoid regulation by the state or both, can be adjudicated. American politics is an arena of power, in which competing interests battle without responsibility for or a conception of a common good.

Thus American politics is paradigmatic of the dilemma that, we have argued, plagues our common life in diverse spheres. We make greater demands on institutions for private satisfactions, while depleting the institutional infrastructure upon which any common good (or even the ability of the system to continue to produce individual goods) depends. The currently popular demand to lower taxes while maintaining middle-class benefits, for example, can be fulfilled only by further reducing support for the already desperately poor and continuing neglect of our already weakened social infrastructure.

VI. TRANSFORMING THE PUBLIC SPHERE

Americans fool themselves when they think they can strengthen democracy by weakening government. They correctly see the danger in an administrative state preempting democratic decision-making, and overburdened courts that cannot solve all the problems they are asked to deal with. But only an institutionally strengthened politics can renew real democracy.

What would it mean to increase our public institutional capacities? To renew the endowment of our political institutions we must simultaneously reinvigorate an active citizenry and develop organizational forms in which their participation can be meaningful. Within the American presidential system, the innovations required are daunting yet essential. As in all modern democracies, the public's capacity to participate in politics has depended upon vigorous political parties; where they are active and effective, citizen participation and levels of information and involvement are high.

The patronage system today operates largely through the favors politicians procure for special interests in return for ever-more-necessary campaign contributions, without the major involvement of political parties. The public votes (when it votes) largely for political personalities as they display themselves through managed, handled, and "massaged" campaign appearances and the thirty-second "image bytes" produced for television by advertising agencies. It is no wonder that Americans feel disaffected from politics, for they have no way to link candidates to coherent programs and no way to hold them responsible after they are elected.

To strengthen political parties (and, not incidentally, political participation), we must shift the balance of power from the candidate to the party, so that candidates would really need party support and would have to demonstrate loyalty to party principles in order to attain it. Then it would make sense for voters to vote a "party line," and parties would once again be important brokers of political influence. But how would strengthened political parties, as opposed to attractive individual candidates, attempt to woo and win voters?

Because candidates rely so much on media advertising and images to get elected, they are driven to the corrupting, exhausting quest for campaign money, which puts them ever more under the control of particularized interests, and they can get elected only by making promises unrelated to the real difficulties of governing. We need to reduce the power of special interests to buy elections, and encourage candidates and parties to rely on grass-roots organization on the one hand and appeals to general political principles on the other to build a secure political base. Changes in the laws governing campaign financing are obviously an institutional mechanism essential to realizing these reforms. So far, efforts to make these changes have been sabotaged by the interests whose power would be diminished by them. Only a major public campaign for such changes that would simultaneously raise public consciousness about the state of our democratic politics is likely to effect more than cosmetic reforms.

If individual candidates were not able to win (or buy) elections through advertising, and if parties could consistently influence blocks of voters, politicians would be more responsive to the positions their parties developed. It would be in their interest to support long-term and general party programs rather than appeal to short-term interests or make unkeepable promises. Competing interests would then have to formulate their aspirations in terms that could win wide and principled backing, and local interests would have to express their aims in general terms useful for party programs.

Of course, in our presidential system, parties are not directly responsible for making government policy, as they are in parliamentary systems, and thus it is difficult to hold them responsible for what government actually does. We must break the influence that campaign contributors have over politicians and we must replace it with other devices to make representatives responsible to their constituents and raise their constituents' public consciousness.

Finally, parties might be more responsible if they had more resources with which to address public issues. We should consider public subsidy, not simply for campaign funds but also for party policy institutes with the intellectual and technical resources to develop programs for American society and make them realistic. If parties were more than simply arenas for brokering interests, if within them one could go beyond the usual zero-sum logic of American political debate, then they might genuinely inspire voter loyalty.

These proposals for strengthening parties may not be sufficient, and we would welcome debate about other ways to endow political parties with greater capacities to articulate visions of the public good. But we would insist that one essential stimulus of reinvigorated citizen participation in a democracy is vigorous competition among parties that articulate public programs through which democratic choice can become meaningful.

A renewal of American political institutions must go beyond the revitalization and transformation of political parties. Partly because the web of interdependence in our society is so complex, many citizens (and many politicians as well) have difficulty grasping the problems we face and the choices we must make. Genuine democratic participation today, when the administrative state looms large, requires the administrative state itself to be opened to democratic participation.[32]

To some degree this has already occurred, as when public projects are required to solicit public comment and sometimes to set up public advocacy groups. But we must go further. One model might be the land-use agencies set up in several East Coast states.[33] These agencies engage ordinary citizens and stakeholders in a complex planning process in which they take responsibility for the difficult decisions involved in examining the opportunities for government action. They have the advantage of expert analyses, including cost-benefit calculations where appropriate, and they are in a position to appreciate that any choice in one area (not to allow development, for example) will have consequences in others (decreasing the supply of housing, raising housing prices, or limiting new jobs). But research suggests that when citizens are engaged in thinking about the whole, they find their conceptions of their interests broadened, and their commitment to the search for a common good deepens.

Programs of widened citizen participation in actual policy planning and decision making complement another principle we consider crucial in dealing with the scale and complexity of a modern society—the principle of "subsidiarity."[34] According to this principle, power should devolve on the lowest, most local level at which decisions can reasonably be made, with the function of the larger unit being to support and assist the local body in carrying out its tasks. But it cannot mean simply enlarging the number of potential groups that have a veto over decisions. This kind of participation without responsibility accentuates a not-in-my-backyard mentality and impairs the capacity to recognize interdependence. New forms of participation have to make citizens responsible for solutions for the whole rather than involving them simply as interested parties who, in classical pluralist style, enter the public arena only when their private interests are threatened.

The most obvious example of subsidiarity in the American political system is federalism, and the way in which individual states have often pioneered new programs is a significant source of creativity and strength. Unfortunately, the states, which have resisted the pull toward centralization by the federal government, have themselves not always understood the meaning of subsidiarity with respect to the units beneath them. State governments now carry out more and more of the functions that might usefully be handled by county, city, and town governments.

At every level, new forms of citizen involvement should transform the very conception of interests. The fundamental flaw in the notion that government exists to maximize the satisfaction of individual interests is that what people value is itself shaped by their institutional experience. Thus our public institutions shape the very possibility of public values.

Even economists who think primarily in cost-benefit terms are sometimes forced to recognize (though they may not be able to account for) the emergence of genuinely public values. One economist we talked to, working in the Congressional Budget Office, holds to the general theory that government is a mechanism for satisfying private wants. A specialist in natural resources, he is frustrated by economic irrationalities. Speaking of recreational uses of public lands, for example, he argues that the function of government is to "overcome barriers to [people's] preferences being expressed," to "aggregate the demand itself. Now if you could better and better price these services, there would in the extreme be no need for the government to provide them."

In accounting for the preferences that government serves, however, this resource specialist is forced to acknowledge values that depend on public life itself. He notes first that "there is a value attached, by the American public, to having lands held by the government. It's a trust . . . there's a sense that the government will take better care of the land than if you leave it to the market—that the market forces aren't there to protect it." He notes that the preference for public ownership is not swayed by arguments that private landowners would have incentives to preserve and beautify the land. "People say no, the public ought to own this. The history of public lands management in this country shows the evolution of shifts toward this preference that exists today. . . . There is just a deep-seated sense that people trust the government to take the appropriate care of these resources."

This analyst points out that economists can identify a whole range of *new* values the public holds about natural resources, which they can measure and give monetary weight to: "An economist might formalize it by saying that it appears that government is responding to values such as option values and existence values—things economists like to associate with these resources. Option value is [expressed] when an individual says, 'I don't want, need to use this now, but I want to reserve the ability to use it sometime in the future, and I'll pay to reserve it.' Existence value is somewhat broader than that. It means, 'I have no interest ever in using this resource, but I will pay something in order to have it exist.' People give money to save whales. They're never going to go out and see a whale, but they think it important that there be a whale, and condors."

Here the economists' logic of trying to satisfy individual preferences gives way before a fundamentally different, more social, more institutional understanding of the common good. The new values of which the economic analyst spoke are not autonomous, individual preferences but arise out of public discussion and public institutions that evolve their mandates over time. It is the long *institutional* history of public resource agencies—the National Park System, the Forest Service, the Bureau of Land Management—that has allowed these new values to emerge. As this CBO economist himself notes, the value the public places on government ownership of parks and wilderness derives from its experience of public ownership. The "deep-seated sense that people trust the government to take care of these resources" is based on experience. "America's public lands agencies, with few exceptions, have done a good job. [We have] an awesome national parks system in comparison to virtually any others in the world. It appears not [to be] a misplaced trust." Thus the values people are willing to pay for are not inexplicable, arbitrary preferences but themselves evolve from public engagement with institutions that embody public purposes and engender public trust; these in turn depend on an ongoing public discussion and argument about their importance.

Law and the legal order also continue to be crucial in the vitality of American democracy. The function of the nation's highest courts has become that of reasserting the Constitution's principles, which define our national tradition, when politics or the play of power and interest obscure them. Thus the courts have often reasserted claims of equality, justice, and due process when these have been threatened.

But we need to think about how the legal system can maintain this commitment to principle and this role as a corrective to excesses of politics and administration. The problems of the law are as much intellectual as practical ones. The deep intellectual rethinking required in contemporary law is less about individual rights than about how to sustain an order of institutions with public and social responsibilities.[35]

It is ultimately through the legal order, where political concerns may be reframed as matters of enduring principle, that Americans can address questions about the institutional structure of the corporation, the proper forms in which public participation in government might occur, the possibilities and limits of other institutions (a redefinition of what marriage and family are, preserving core principles while incorporating new social realities; redefinition of educational, health care, and financial institutions). Such deepening and broadening of the social bases of institutions must, of course, be initiated by the legislature as lawgiver, not just as interest compromiser. But when new institutional experiments are mounted—such as public-private governing boards mandated by federal health-care regulators—it is crucial that the courts actively define the principles that can sustain and nourish effective institutional life.

VII. A RENEWED PUBLIC

Politically as well as economically, ours is a new historical moment. Without romanticizing it, we can recognize the tremendous accomplishments of the "American Century" now past. We can also acknowledge its large limitations. But we think the gravest threat to our collective ability to seize the opportunities before us lies not in our knowledge but in our understanding. It is odd that in what many conceive as the world's greatest democracy, a vigorous democratic politics is absent from our public life; it is in this realm that we must innovate. If taxpayers don't know that government has no money that doesn't come from them, it is hardly surprising that a vigorous life of public debate and decision has languished, leaving our balkanized bureaucracies and our overburdened courts to manage as best they can to give us direction. No institutional innovations, however ingenious, can rescue us without an intelligent and responsible public life. Our primary task is to recover a public capable of understanding and so of enacting a genuinely democratic form of government.

A mass of claimants organized into various pressure groups is not a public. There is nothing wrong with interests and nothing wrong with having them represented. But democratic government is more than the compromising of conflicting interests, important though that is and important as it is at present in America that the interests of more of our citizens attain effective representation. Compromise, the art of the possible, is not enough. There are major problems to be solved and great ends to be pursued. The eighteenth-century idea of a public was not just a congeries of interest groups but a discursive community capable of thinking about the common good, of taking the point of view of Adam Smith's Impartial Spectator.[36] Many of our problems are truly common. We all breathe the same air. We all are vulnerable to the same lethal rays of the sun coming through an ozone-depleted atmosphere. It is not only the poor inhabitants of decayed inner cities who suffer from their civic decline but the inhabitants of expensive town houses and suburban homes when no one dares to go out on the street at night or even feels safe in his own home. A work force with a large proportion of functional illiterates is a problem for all who are dependent on a productive economy.

Often our politicians and political parties debase the public by playing on its desires and fears: desire for private benefits at the expense of public provision; fear of just those most in need of public provision. What we need is precisely the opposite: a vision of how we are indeed dependent on and jointly responsible for a common life. Perhaps we need to learn from the Eastern Europeans. Václav Havel, president of Czechoslovakia, said:

> Let us teach both ourselves and others that politics ought to be a reflection of the aspiration to contribute to the happiness of the community and not of the need to deceive or pillage the community. Let us teach both ourselves and others that politics does not have to be the art of the possible, especially if this means the art of speculating, calculating, secret agreements, and pragmatic maneuvering, but that it also can be the art of the impossible, that is the art of making both ourselves and the world better.[37]

The place to begin political reform is within each of us, Havel also said: we get better politics only when we become better citizens.

John Dewey's conception of politics, from which we still have much to learn, is not by any means an "interest group" theory. Dewey did not subsume the citizen under the category of the consumer of political goods. "Public" for Dewey refers to common goods, not the mere addition of private ones:

We say in a country like our own that legislators and executives are elected by the public. The phrase might appear to indicate that the Public acts. But, after all, individual men and women exercise the franchise; the public here is a collective name for a multitude of persons each voting as an anonymous unit. As a citizen-voter each one of these persons is, however, an officer of the public. He expresses his will as a representative of the public interest as much so as does a senator or sheriff. His vote may express his hope to profit in private purse by the election of some man or the ratification of some proposed law. He may fail, in other words, in the effort to represent the interest entrusted to him. But in this respect he does not differ from those explicitly designated public officials who have also been known to betray the interest committed to them instead of faithfully representing it.[38]

Dewey's goal was "liberation of the potentialities of members of a group in harmony with the interests and goods which are common." Why, however, in a day where pluralism and diversity seem to have obscured the notion of "a good shared by all," should we think that public discourse about issues such as day care and family support, or managers and workers, or the practices of corporate finance, will promote mutual understanding? Why not, in such a pluralistic society, think rather that increased public participation will only exacerbate conflict and proliferate hostilities? There are two reasons for cautious optimism. First, our diverse society (and let us remember that we have been a very diverse society for a long time) is in fact increasingly bound together in an interdependent life, so that objectively our problems are common and our solutions must become common. As Dewey insisted, "The clear consciousness of a communal life, in all its implications, constitutes the idea of democracy."

The second reason for believing that we can renew common conversation about our collective life is that despite diversity Americans still share a set of overlapping cultural traditions. We cannot nor would we want simply to restore received traditions; but it is through the reinterpretation and renegotiation of shared traditions, even argument and conflict concerning them, that we discover how our society is still constituted by significantly shared meanings.

Public argument would not eliminate interests, coalitions, or factions. Rather, it would revive James Madison's approach: he attempted to reduce the zero-sum quality of politics by structuring a forum in which more people could coherently deliberate. And here we arrive at the heart of the intermeshed institutional and cultural innovation we require. Meaning comes from practices, especially those embedded in institutions. Our forms of life are woven through by languages, or more aptly, texts, that embody meaning. Like musical scores, these provide what coherence individual or collective life may achieve. But the texts, the scores, must be interpreted and brought alive in specific contexts and situations. Public discourse, like the forms of the law and public life, is of a similar constitution. This is a vital fact for our era, though the dominance of Lockean individualism has tended to obscure it in our tradition. We badly need to enrich the way we understand our public institutions and comport ourselves regarding them, particularly by attending to how they affect or even create our identities as selves and as citizens. In an age of cynicism and privatized withdrawal, it may seem quixotic to call for a reinvigoration of an enlightened public. But we believe this reinvigoration is not an idealistic whim but the only realistic basis on which we can move ahead as a free people.

So far we have been outlining a new politics so at odds with current American reality that it would be easy to dismiss our argument as "idealistic." The present mood of American voters would seem to be that of consumers out to protect their own interests, hardly capable of understanding what John Dewey thought the responsibility of a citizen is, and attentive to neither general nor particular issues that do not appear to have an immediate effect on their personal lives. Commenting on a similar mood in British politics, Ronald Dworkin has recently called attention to the startling consequences of the spread of democratic affluence, leading to self-centered and short-term political thinking, in ways that bear directly on the United States:

> . . . It has proved enormously difficult to persuade successful workers, struggling to improve their living standards, to reach their culture's definition of a good life, to *vote* to keep less of what they earn. The greatest barrier to equality, in prosperous Western democracies, is the otherwise happy fact that many more voters now lose through genuine egalitarian programs than gain; even suggesting tax rises is now thought to be political suicide in America. Economic disaster could reverse that situation. But the dismal axiom all this suggests—that equality can be a workable political principle only in very bad times—will not be displaced until some way is found to detach politics from self-interest and persuade a democratic society to take its own injustice seriously.[39]

Dworkin later speaks of replacing a politics of self-interest with a politics of principle, but he does not make clear how we can surmount the hold which the Lockean notion of self-interest has maintained in our public life. But unless we can overcome its tendency to inhibit a broader understanding of self and a longer-term sense of interests, the invocation of principle will remain hollow.[40] What Americans need to understand is that creeping disaster is already occurring, that we are already severely depleting the life chances of our children and grandchildren. Without waiting for the apocalypse, we need to change our hearts, enlarge our sympathies, and reform our institutions.

VIII. REVIVING DEMOCRATIC CITIZENSHIP

The creation of a genuinely democratic public is a daunting enterprise, and we can make only modest suggestions concerning it. Perhaps it is useful to indicate the direction in which our argument might lead us by offering some specific suggestions.

(1) We need to pay serious attention to the institutional development of political parties—making them better able to articulate meaningful national programs, and making it more possible for voters to engage in politics by seeing their votes as affecting important positions as the parties articulate them. Among these institution-building devices might be the creation of policy institutes, or think tanks, perhaps with public funding, which would help parties formulate national platforms with the intellectual breadth and technical sophistication necessary for governing a modern state. An essential change would involve election-funding reforms that would increase party influence over campaign financing while reducing the direct ways organized interests finance individual candidates. While parties have a bad name in America due to their history of patronage politics, we know both from our own historical experience and from comparison with other modern democracies that vigorous party competition is the major stimulus to active voter participation.

(2) The level of national political debate has degenerated into enormously expensive media wars with little sustained intellectual content. Without willing it, we have in fact created the most influential of contemporary political institutions, the media-managed candidacy, which corrupts both candidates and publics and makes getting elected almost incompatible with governing once in office. To cut to the heart of this corrupting institution, the antithesis of real politics, we suggest radical surgery: outlaw campaign advertising on radio and television. This would at one fell swoop eliminate the single biggest need for political candidates to raise campaign funds, with all the potentialities for corruption and illicit influence that go with it. It would also help to reduce the debasement of public discourse, for there would be no

more thirty-second commercials composed of vivid images stimulating fear or desire but inhibiting thought. Rather than limiting free speech, such a prohibition would enhance free speech through encouraging, as a meaningful substitute for shallow image-manipulation, the broadcast of candidates' campaign speeches and of debates between them— genuine debates rather than the sanitized media-monitored question-and-answer shows that have substituted for them in recent years. Candidates, who could no longer rely on media blitzes, would be encouraged to engage in substantive debate and, at the same time, to rely more on the continuity of party programs and party performances to win elections.

(3) With parties playing a stronger, more educative role in defining our national commitments, the national government must actively strengthen federalism and local responsibility that are part of the American political tradition. The federal government needs to encourage new institutional arrangements that engage individual citizens and organized groups to become active participants in planning and administration. In working for major structural changes, preliminary changes at the state and local level can be extremely helpful and instructive. Conversely, the national government should lead in strengthening supranational institutions concerned with trade, world economic justice, military security, and human rights—including the United Nations and the World Court but also many other formal and informal arrangements—and creating new ones where needed. These supranational institutions need not infringe on appropriately national responsibilities, but they ought to give force to the growing world understanding that nations are no longer the ultimate arbiters, and the fate of both biological and human community can no longer be left to nation-states alone.

(4) Perhaps most important, the focus of public debate must move away from a concern for maximizing private interests, as encouraged by the Lockean understanding of individual and society, toward the central problems of a sustainable future in our own society and in the world. The focus must be on justice in the broadest sense—that is, giving what is due to both persons and the natural environment. Without a healthy social and natural ecology, we put at risk everything we have received from our ancestors and threaten to leave nothing but violence and decay as the inheritance of our children and grandchildren. These are not matters of charity, of the rich giving to the poor, but of solidarity and hope for the whole human species in relation to the whole natural world.

(5) The entire process of democratic participation is educative in

the broadest sense, yet education for citizenship is a responsibility of all our institutions—economic institutions, as we saw in the last chapter, but also families, churches, and certainly schools. Indeed, our educational system must transmit an understanding of what democracy really means to all of our citizens if we are to make the changes advocated here.

IX. POWER AND MEANING

In the last two chapters we have been talking about the institutions that have the greatest power and control over our lives: the economy and the government. We have been concerned with ways in which these powerful institutions have become distorted, have not done their jobs well, and have influenced other sectors of our lives in unhealthy ways. We must now turn to the institutions that focus mainly on meaning: education and religion. We know we have experienced an erosion in our capacity to deal with the world economically and politically, but we must consider whether a comparable erosion has occurred in our educational and religious institutions. It would be unlikely if such were not the case. Yet education and religion draw on deep cultural resources that can put our present difficulties in new perspectives. There is at least the possibility—and the hope—that out of these institutions can come some new initiatives for the institutional transformation of our common life.

5

Education: Technical and Moral

I. EDUCATION FOR LIFE

It is part of our classical heritage to see education at the center of our common life. This is an understanding going back to Plato and to Aristotle, who concluded both his *Ethics* and his *Politics* with discussions of education as a central concern of the *polis*—a term that is usually translated as "city-state" but that includes the idea of society or community as well.

For Aristotle, "education" had a considerably broader meaning than we usually give the term. It was indeed the primary function of the *polis* to provide those laws, written and unwritten, that would educate citizens into a life of virtue, for only such citizens would make a good *polis* possible.[1] So it was not schools that Aristotle was thinking of in the first instance when he discussed education, but the laws and the mores of the whole community. These are what educate people, both as children and as adults. And so for Plato and Aristotle the great educators were, above all, the great lawgivers. It was the responsibility of citizens, however, as those who ruled and were ruled in turn, to deliberate about the laws and to concern themselves with the common good. The Greeks invented not only political philosophy as an aid to practical reason (*phronesis*) in reflecting about these matters, but also rhetoric, the use of persuasive speech in public deliberation. While there was an argument about the legitimacy of rhetoric from the beginning, it had an honored place in the educational curriculum for millennia and was closely associated with the search for the common good in republican and democratic societies.

These Greek ideas were intelligible to Jews and Christians of later eras, for whom communal practices, focused on the injunctions contained in their sacred texts, were the primary source of the education of the faithful. And the letters of Saint Paul show that Greek rhetoric was already in his time in use for sermonizing about the common problems of the new churches. It was not that schools were not important in the classical and biblical traditions, but that they were only part, and perhaps not the essential part, of what was meant by education.

For Americans today education means, above all, schools, and we have elevated schools into something of a secular religion. As the historian Daniel Boorstin puts it: "If there was to be a new American religion of education, the universities were its cathedrals, just as the high schools later would become its parish churches. It was no accident that American universities adopted the architecture of the great age of European cathedral building. Collegiate Gothic naturally became standard for institutions that could afford it. Just as the great cathedrals overshadowed the parish churches, so too the universities would overshadow the high schools."[2] Today educational institutions—universities and high schools, and a bewildering variety of other schools for all ages and almost all purposes—are central institutions in our society. In them most of us spend many years of childhood, adolescence, and early adulthood, and we return to them with increasing frequency throughout our lives. It is worth remembering that this vast expansion of educational institutions took place mostly in the last hundred years. In 1890 only 7 percent of the relevant age group went to high school and only 1 percent to college. By 1970 90 percent of Americans aged fourteen to seventeen were in high school, and by the 1980s a majority of Americans of college age were receiving some higher education.

Yet we should not presume that in the nineteenth century most Americans were uneducated. Reading was often learned at home or at a local parish church rather than in a formal school. Free public "common schools," available for most of the population, provided a basic grammar-school education. Indeed, free public schools that taught at least basic literacy were to be found in some of the New England colonies almost from the beginning. In seventeenth-century Massachusetts adult male literacy was about 80 percent, twice the rate for adult males in England at the time, and adult females had a literacy rate of 60 percent. Thousands of books were imported into the colonies, and many more were published here. Thomas Paine's *Common Sense* sold more than four hundred thousand copies after its publication in 1776 (one hundred thousand in the first three months)—the equivalent of twenty-four million copies in today's population. So we were a literate people, capable of reading and conversing about complex issues of religion and politics. Yet schools, except for the tiny minority preparing for the learned professions, particularly the ministry, were not a major part of the lives of most people.[3]

Under these conditions, education in America was closer to what Aristotle imagined than what we have today. It was the whole community that educated: the home, the church, the voluntary association, and local politics had an educative function at least as important as that of the school. And yet, while such "island communities," as the relatively isolated towns and villages of the day have been called, carried the main burden of education, many Americans—even in the colonial period and certainly by the nineteenth century—were subjected to educational influences that far transcended their localities. Newspapers, however limited in size and information and however opinionated their views, had begun to circulate; books, and especially pamphlets, were widely read. Visiting ministers, lecturers, and politicians were listened to, admired, sometimes heckled. Horace Mann, the great Massachusetts educator, as early as the 1830s led a national effort to create a system of common schools that would give all citizens, rich and poor, basic cognitive skills and training in character and citizenship. European examples stimulated the American effort; but, unlike that in Europe, the initiative in America did not come from the federal government but from citizens acting at the local and state levels, even though stimulated by the national movement. The ideal of citizens who could debate the great issues of the day and believers who could read the Scripture and understand even the fine points of its exposition was realized in America more than in most of the European countries from which the American population had come.

Until late in the nineteenth century formal education beyond basic literacy was not essential to prepare for an occupation. Even among the clergy, for whom formal preparation was traditionally most expected, seminary training was not required in the fastest-growing Protestant denominations, the Baptists and the Methodists. Doctors and lawyers learned their professions by entering the offices of an established practitioner as apprentices rather than by going to medical or law school, though in the second half of the nineteenth century such schools were growing in numbers and prestige. Apprenticeship was the time-honored way to learn a trade, too—for example, printing or carpentry. In the new factories, apprenticeship was not essential, for the skills required were simple and took little time to learn; what was important was the discipline of punctuality and application over extended periods of time to tasks that were often boring and sometimes physically demanding. A great deal of education was occurring in the workplace, but it was "on-the-job training" that did not require much formal schooling. Thrift, honesty, and the habits of hard work were instilled at home, in church and at school, and these fitted well with the expectations of the workplace, where most Americans could look forward to earning a "competence," particularly through self-employment, that would allow them to play out the role of "independent citizens," the character that best expressed the American culture of the day.

If we compare this mid-nineteenth-century backdrop with our present situation, we can discern stunning transformations in our system of education that parallel the changes in our economic and political institutions which we discussed in earlier chapters. We have already mentioned the enormous growth in the number and types of schools and in the years of our lives we devote to them, and we will have much more to say about that later in this chapter. But the whole mix of educational influences has altered dramatically. The earliest educational experiences still occur at home with a child's parents, but as day care becomes ever more common, these take place in extrafamilial contexts as well. And if home and local community were ever "islands," they are certainly less so today: although books, newspapers, and pamphlets were read in American homes from the earliest settlement, these printed materials can hardly be said to have created an environment that competed with familial and neighborhood life. Today, in contrast, it is hard to find an American family that does not have a radio and a television set, and indeed most families have several; children are exposed to these media from birth and spend many more hours with them than they do in school.

One of the things radio and television do—as do also America's brightly illustrated and attractively designed newspapers and magazines—is to expose children and adults alike to a variety of experiences from all over the world as they are happening or soon after. Before the invention and spread of the telegraph in the mid–nineteenth century, news could take weeks or, in the case of events in Europe, months to arrive in American towns and villages, if it was attended to at all. Today we are bombarded with a continuous flood of images and information about all sorts of things from all parts of the world, much of it uninterpreted or presented in such detail as to be overwhelming. If one tried to read the *New York Times* from beginning to end every day, one would have time for little else. While it is still true that discussion about what is happening helps to make sense of the vast array of information—at the family dinner table in those families that still have meals together, in the local congregation for those families that regularly attend church or synagogue, in political groups for those who are active in them, and in the schools for those who are attending them—it is often hard for us to see the flood of events as anything more than transient images on the screen, mildly exhilarating or vaguely disturbing but hardly calling for responsible action or even judgment.

But it is not only the mass media that have given us this evanescent sense of a global technological society. Many small events in our daily routines remind us, however subconsciously, that we are part of a worldwide system of economic and technological relationships, a great society on which we depend but which we do not understand in its vast, invisible interconnectedness. Making the fire in the kitchen stove is no longer a daily ritual that involves all members of the family in a familiar routine of tasks: chopping the wood, carrying it in, lighting the fire, coming down to finish dressing in the only warmth the house is able to supply. Instead we turn up the thermostat and turn on the gas or electric kitchen range. Rather than going to the well to fetch water and perhaps chatting with others doing the same, or going to the local bathhouse to bathe, as most mid-nineteenth-century urban Americans did (three pennies for the common bath with members of one's own sex, six pennies for a bath to oneself), we now turn on the hot and cold running water in our private kitchens or bathrooms. These amenities tie us into ever-larger structures of public provision at the same time that they isolate us from our neighbors and enhance the illusion of our autonomy. The automobile, bus, and subway immensely expand the possible distance between the place where we live and the places where we work or go to school or play. But they also confront us with overcrowded freeways, scarce urban parking facilities, and inadequate systems of public transportation. All these experiences educate us, in that they constitute a world for us that affects how we think and feel.

We sometimes feel isolated and threatened in hostile urban environments (women kept late at work who must walk through darkened streets or parking lots to find their cars), or frustrated when the public amenities we count on suddenly fail to function (sitting in an immobilized subway car under San Francisco Bay because the computers are down); but we nonetheless respect and count on many aspects of public life. Americans still, as they did in Tocqueville's day, sit on juries and do so with a surprising amount of goodwill and civic responsibility. The law, as in ancient Athens, is still our teacher, even if we are somewhat confused about what it is teaching. And the classic lawgivers, the founders of our republic and the drafters of our Constitution, if not exactly folk heroes, are still widely admired. (A fourth-grade child of Vietnamese refugees, in a Denver public school, points to a picture of George Washington on the classroom wall and tells the visiting professor of education with pride that "that is the father of our country.")

We have come to take for granted (until they break down) the great labor-saving public services (running water, electricity, central heating, etc.) and the public conveniences of transportation and communication (most of us can hardly function for an hour without a telephone). And we are reminded with great insistence about other things we can buy that, it is alleged, will make our lives even easier and that we really need. But advertising in anything like its modern form is only a century old, and as late as 1920 almost everything one bought in a grocery store was sold in bulk (one asked for a pound of salt from the bin; one didn't take a box of salt off the self-service shelf). The world of packaging, name brands, and a multitude of items (in the catalogs that weigh down our mailboxes, for example) is a world that only decades ago even most futurologists could hardly imagine. Whether or not the enormous proliferation of consumer goods has really made our lives better is not the issue here. Our point is that this continuous surround of items of consumption and their images is both an educational influence and an educational challenge. How can we begin intelligently to manage the array of choices that some defenders of free enterprise take to be the essence of our freedom?

Indeed, the broader questions we have to ask are, What are the educational implications of our whole form of life? Is the confusion about "values" and the absence of larger meanings that seem to characterize many Americans the result of life contexts that produce more confusion than clarity? If the answer is yes, then there is a reciprocity between the reforms we have suggested in our economic and political life and education. Education for life is, then, both the cause and the effect of needed institutional changes in our society.

II. EDUCATION IN THE PROGRESSIVE ERA

By the last decades of the nineteenth century it was clear that America's educational institutions were going to expand and change radically in response to the social, economic, and technological changes that were already everywhere in evidence. John Dewey was one of those most sensitive to the challenge of not only educating citizens for a free society in the classic sense but also making education responsive to the unprecedented conditions of modernity. In 1899, in a book that remained influential for decades, *The School and Society*, he addressed both these issues. He expressed his appreciation of the educative vitality of the older forms of life that were then being replaced:

> Back of the factory system lies the household and neighborhood system. Those of us who are here today need go back only one, two or at most three generations to find a time when the household was practically the center in which were carried on, or about which were clustered, all the typical forms of industrial occupation. . . . Instead of pressing a button and flooding the house with electric light, the whole process of getting illumination was followed in its toilsome length from the killing of the animal and the trying of fat to the making of wicks and dipping of candles. . . . The children, as they gained in strength and capacity, were gradually initiated into the mysteries of the several processes. . . . In all this there was continual training of observation, of ingenuity, constructive imagination, of logical thought, and of the sense of reality acquired through first-hand contact with actualities.[4]

While extolling the educational qualities of everyday life in the preindustrial epoch, Dewey excoriated the limited nature of formal education and argued that its heritage had largely to be overcome if education was to respond effectively to the new social reality:

> If we go back a few centuries, we find a practical monopoly of learning. . . . A high priesthood of learning, which guarded the treasury of truth and which doled it out to the masses under severe restrictions, was the inevitable expression of these conditions. But, as a direct result of the industrial revolution of which we have been speaking, this has been changed. . . . The result has been an intellectual revolution. Learning has been put into circulation. . . . Knowledge is no longer an immobile solid; it has been liquefied. It is actively moving in all the currents of society itself.[5]

The very complexity of this new world, which made knowledge so much more readily available, required a drastically different model of schooling than the drill and memorization of the traditional classroom. Since life itself no longer supplied an intelligible environment— Dewey in his description of the household and neighborhood system could be describing his own Vermont boyhood—the school must innovate. It must make the great society as intelligible as the little society once was. All his life Dewey was concerned with this problem. Here is how he saw it in *The School and Society*: "The obvious fact is that our social life has undergone a thorough and radical change. If our education is to have any meaning for life, it must pass through an equally complete transformation. . . . When the school introduces and trains each child of society into membership within such a little community, saturating him with the spirit of service, and providing him with the instruments of effective self-direction, we shall have the deepest and best guaranty of a larger society which is worthy, lovely and harmonious."[6]

For America's most influential—and in the eyes of many, its greatest—philosopher, education was not a side issue or an "applied" field. However "modern" Dewey insisted on being, he showed his classical philosophical roots when he wrote in 1916: "If we are willing to conceive education as the process of forming fundamental dispositions, intellectual and emotional, toward nature and fellow men, philosophy may even be defined *as the general theory of education*."[7]

Jane Addams, Dewey's friend and in some respects his teacher, had founded Hull House, the famous model settlement house in the Chicago slums, in 1889. She believed that one of its chief functions was to offer community education, to make the world of the chaotic American metropolis intelligible to its least favored and most disadvantaged citizens. Such an education would allow a degree of participation not otherwise possible, and Addams believed such participation essential in a good society: "We have learned to say that the good must be extended to all of society before it can be held secure by any one person or any one class; but we have not yet learned to add to that statement, that unless all men and all classes contribute to a good, we cannot even be sure that it is worth having."[8]

Before Dewey had fully formed his own educational ideas, Addams was already speaking of the settlement as "an institution attempting to learn from life itself."[9] Lawrence Cremin describes her educational method: "In the case of young men and women about to go to work, it meant a concerted effort to give them some sense of the history and nature of a modern urban, industrial society, so that, wherever they ended up as workers, they would have a conception of the whole and of their own particular parts in it—she gave much of *The Spirit of Youth and the City Streets* (1909), which she always claimed was her favorite book, to this need for workers to have a sense of context that would give meaning to their lives."[10]

In her work at Hull House, Addams found that university lecturers were not always the most effective teachers and that the people among whom she worked were capable of conducting vital discussions among themselves. "A settlement soon discovers that simple people are interested in large and vital subjects," she wrote. In *Twenty Years at Hull House* she remarked that "simple people did not want to hear about simple things; they wanted to hear about great things, simply told."[11] To give her people not only a sense of the larger society of which they were a part but pride in themselves and their background, she developed a Labor Museum at Hull House that dignified the daily occupations of the working class. She also encouraged classes in the languages and literatures of the immigrants themselves, believing that "Americanization" should never obliterate ethnic memory.

While Dewey and Addams in their different ways were trying to re-create under modern conditions forms of education that would involve the whole community in the creation of responsible citizens in a good society, the very complexity of those modern conditions made their efforts increasingly difficult. The difficulty was evident even at the pinnacle of the educational establishment, the universities, which Boorstin called the cathedrals of the new religion of education.

III. FROM COLLEGE TO RESEARCH UNIVERSITY

Liberal arts colleges in America before the Civil War were too small to be divided into departments. As late as 1869 there were only twenty-three members of the Harvard faculty, and they mostly taught the traditional liberal arts subjects of classical languages and mathematics. Language, spoken and written, was at the heart of the college education, whose students were destined mainly for the ministry, law, and public service. College education, then, was largely rhetorical (we must remember that "rhetoric" has become a pejorative term only recently) rather than philosophical or scientific. Before the Civil War there was not a single course in experimental science in an American college. Science in America (as in Europe and England) was still pursued largely outside the university context.

In the later nineteenth century this traditional form of college education came under increasing attack as "old-fashioned" and "impractical." In terms of the society for which it had been designed, it was, of course, neither. Its function was to build character and citizenship among future leaders, for whom the use of language would be their most essential skill. But in the urban industrial society America was becoming, such an education was considered anachronistic. The sudden appearance of the research university in America in the last decades of the nineteenth century can only be understood as a response to the emergence of the cultural paradigm of scientific knowledge, put forward most evidently in the universities of Germany, and the new relationship between science and industry. It was the research university that would become Boorstin's cathedral. Some of these were new institutions, privately founded, like Johns Hopkins and Chicago. Others, like Harvard and Columbia, were older institutions transformed by dynamic new leadership. And new state universities, such as Michigan and Wisconsin, quickly attained high levels of excellence.

There are great ironies about the emergence of the research university. From one point of view it was to be an institution that would perform for higher education what Dewey's new vision of the public school would do at the elementary and secondary levels—namely, educate for full participation in the modern world, not abandoning but broadening the older educational ideals of character and citizenship. The first decade of the University of Chicago, which opened in 1892, appeared to embody this promise. Its president, William Rainey Harper, previously a professor of Old Testament studies, saw the new university very much in the context of public service to the city of Chicago and to the world. He had the good sense to see that John Dewey could make an enormous contribution to his ideal, and in 1894 he brought him from the University of Michigan, where he had first been employed, to the University of Chicago. Dewey himself embodied the integration that, in one understanding of the new university, represented the ideal. He became head of the department of philosophy, which at that time included psychology and pedagogy, and also head of the separate department of education when that was formed. The "Chicago school,"[12] loosely formed around Dewey, had a broad impact on the life of the whole university, especially the social sciences. George Herbert Mead, for example, one of Dewey's closest associates in the department of philosophy, long taught a course on social psychology that gave the Chicago sociology department some of its special quality. Not only was there an unusual degree of communication across departmental lines, but many Chicago faculty members, none more than Dewey himself, were deeply involved in community affairs. Dewey was on the board of Hull House and was much concerned with the settlement house movement. He was also influential in the Chicago public school system. Other professors were active in social welfare and reform politics. In Harper's and Dewey's eyes the new research university was a powerful force for the democratization of education. Not only would its doors swing open to students of merit of whatever background, but all the subjects of concern to the modern world, not just the classical concerns of the old liberal arts curriculum, would be taught there.

The tensions involved in these complex aspirations soon proved unbearable. After Dewey's departure for Columbia in 1904 the sense of a "Chicago school" rapidly gave ground to the increasing specialization and departmentalization that characterized all the research universities. The faculty's community involvements, while not ceasing, seemed to take lower priority in the face of the pressures of professionalization. As Harper added more and more departments and professional schools to the rapidly growing university, Chicago came to be known familiarly as "Harper's bazaar."

Within less than two decades of its founding the effort to create an integrated, democratic higher education had degenerated into an early form of what we have come to know as the multiversity cafeteria. The research university, the cathedral of learning, rather than interpreting and integrating the larger society, came more and more to mirror it. Far from becoming a new community that would bring coherence out of chaos, it became instead a congeries of faculty and students, each pursuing their own ends, integrated not by any shared vision but only by the bureaucratic procedures of the "administration." It would be unfair not to note that the University of Chicago has never wholly succumbed to these disintegrative pressures. Its president Robert Maynard Hutchins, with controversial results to be sure, in the 1930s and 1940s brought a new integrative vision to the university. Even today, more of the older search for coherence survives at Chicago than at most other research universities, and should not be underestimated.

In one undeniable sense the research university and its many spin-offs in the twentieth century brought democratization. Though the full promise did not begin to be fulfilled until after World War II, from the very beginning there was the idea of institutions open to a much wider spectrum of the society than the old colleges had ever been. And the new university, rather than providing the final polish to an already established upper class, would itself be an avenue toward advancement in the world.[13] The chancellor of the University of Kansas, Francis H. Snow, in his inaugural address of 1890 put it as plainly as it has ever been put: "Let it be everywhere made known that at the University of the State, every son and daughter of the state may receive the special training that makes chemists, naturalists, entomologists, electricians, engineers, lawyers, musicians, pharmacists

and artists, or the broader and more symmetrical culture which pre-
pares those who receive it for that general, well-rounded efficiency
which makes the educated man a success in any line of intellectual
activity, ten years earlier in life than the uneducated man."[14] The
hope that a university education would bring success not only sooner
but at a higher level motivated millions of Americans to aspire to
attain it, if not for themselves then at least for their children. In itself
that is a thoroughly intelligible, indeed admirable aim, close to one
very concrete meaning of "the American dream." But to focus exclusively on education as a means to advancement in an ever more complex occupational system, itself a function of an ever more complex
industrial and postindustrial division of labor, is to leave many other
questions unanswered.

IV. THE UNCERTAIN PLACE OF MORAL EDUCATION

There has long been a tension over the balance in primary and secondary education between indoctrination, the "inculcation of values"
that the Supreme Court says is a function of education at those levels,
and the transmission of methods of free inquiry, value-neutral in their
implications. When education was embedded in family, church, and
neighborhood and formal schooling seldom went beyond the fifth
grade, there was no such problem. In the nineteenth century Mc-
Guffey's Readers, perhaps the most popular series of textbooks ever
published, combined an American patriotism with a vague Protestant
piety that, for much of the population at least, meant that the school
largely reinforced the teachings of the family and church. We have
long since been unable to ensure that textbooks will not be offensive
to some families and some believers. And though some "community
standards" still apply in local school districts, they have had less and
less claim at the level of higher education since the emergence of the
research university. The university may not have developed the integrative democratic vision that John Dewey projected for it, but it
does indeed communicate value judgments, especially in its relentless
insistence that its only norm is free inquiry. Most university students
learn something different at college from what they learned at home
or at church; and the better the college, the greater the difference.

For most college teachers this situation is an unalloyed good. Isn't
it the function of the university, after all, to sweep away the cobwebs
of tradition and superstition and give its students the tools of clear
critical inquiry? The fact that most of our students have no intention

of devoting themselves to clear critical inquiry but are concerned primarily with pursuing economic advancement is seldom taken into account by the professors, or if it is, they still assume that critical, value-free citizens are the best guarantee of our freedoms. It is worth considering whether the academic warriors in this *Kulturkampf*, this cultural war, that has divided our society, if not as flamboyantly, at least as deeply, as it has other modern societies in the last century, have all the truth on their own side.

Perhaps the most dramatic event in the American *Kulturkampf* was the trial in 1925 of John Thomas Scopes, a teacher who had violated the Tennessee state law against the teaching of evolution. The confrontation between William Jennings Bryan and Clarence Darrow is one of the epic moments in our cultural history. The trial, which received enormous publicity, largely drowned the fundamentalist opposition to Darwinian evolution theory in a sea of derision. But most of the modernists who held these religious conservatives in contempt failed to realize that they themselves were indulging in the same kind of stereotyping and prejudices which in other instances their own liberal consciences deplored. Reinhold Niebuhr, with his unusually developed sense of irony, saw the confrontation as something more than simply one between the forces of superstition and the forces of enlightenment. He wrote in *Leaves from the Notebook of a Tamed Cynic* in 1929: "If we must choose between types of fanaticism, is there any particular reason why we should prefer the fanatics who destroy a vital culture in the name of freedom and reason to those who try to strangle a new culture at birth in the name of authority and dogma? The latter type of fanaticism is bound to end in futility. The growth of reason cannot be stopped by dogma. But the former type is dangerous because it easily enervates a rational culture with ennui and despair."[15]

What added poignancy to this cultural conflict is that the fundamentalists, in their effort to defend what Niebuhr called "a vital culture," had already submitted to a version of the very position they were opposing. Fundamentalism is a twentieth-century movement that could only have appeared in a culture where the scientific paradigm of knowledge was already gaining hegemony. The fundamentalists shared with their opponents a notion of a purely cognitive truth resting solely on objective evidence. They were willing to stake the cognitive claims of the Bible against the cognitive claims of science. They were thus engaging in a battle they could not win, because they had already conceded what was essential before the issue was joined.

In order to understand how education has changed in our recent history, we will have to look more closely at this fundamental shift in our culture toward an exclusively scientific paradigm of knowledge, and at some of its accompanying features. It is characteristic of that older form of knowing which Dewey located in the household and the neighborhood that one learns, not through accumulating tested propositions about the objective world, but through participation in social practices, by assuming social roles, by becoming familiar with exemplary narratives and with typical characters who illustrate a variety of patterns of behavior. One does not feel like an autonomous subject learning specific facts about an objective world out there. One becomes what one knows. That is how one learns in the family, on the job, and, largely, in church. Religion is learned through worship, prayer, hymnody, familiar narratives recounted at appointed times of the year, far more than from a propositional theology, or certainly from any empirically testable claims of such a theology.

V. FROM RHETORIC TO SCIENCE AS THE BASIC PARADIGM

Of course the scientific paradigm had been prominent in Anglo-American culture since the seventeenth century, and the predominant Scottish common sense philosophy of early-nineteenth-century America had an objectivist cast. Yet until the last decades of the century, when writing became ever more central to business and administration, much of the culture was still oral, and thus based on a communicative and interactionist paradigm, to a degree we can now hardly imagine. Eloquence in preachers and politicians was revered, and Shakespeare was popular entertainment, not yet elevated to the hushed reverence of "high culture." America's greatest mid-century teacher was Emerson, almost all of whose "essays" were originally lectures, delivered in cities and towns all over the country. Emerson's lectures were still organized like a tapestry, with figural references to the classics, the Bible, Shakespeare, and indeed to many of the narrative and literary traditions of the world. They did not take the form of either empirical or deductive expositions of objective truths. And Emerson's own writings on "eloquence" showed that he had a sense of the communal, communicative nature of speech and the discovery of truth through the democratic exchange of speech.[16]

Actually, rhetoric was well established in the eighteenth century at the time of the founding of the American republic. The rhetorical tradition was central in the revolutionary period, because rhetoric was at the heart of the notion of a public and the public sphere that is essential for genuine democracy. The idea of the public and the idea of publicity, in the sense of that which is expressed in speech or writing in public, are closely related.[17] Consequently when, in the twentieth century, the links between rhetoric, the public, and democracy began to come apart, the result was not merely the downgrading of the once respectable field of rhetoric but a threat to the functioning of a vital democracy itself.

As we have already seen, the oral emphasis in American culture up to the end of the nineteenth century was not characteristic only of "popular culture." (Actually, even the distinction between popular culture and high culture itself was a late-nineteenth-century product.)[18] Not only in families and in neighborhoods was eloquence admired. Rhetoric was central to college education as well. This is not the place to rehearse the long history of conflict between rhetoric on the one hand and philosophy or logic or science on the other as the basic orientation for higher education, a conflict that goes back to the fourth century B.C.[19] Suffice it to say that the conflict was latent in American colleges in the nineteenth century, and was evident more in the loss of coherence in the rhetorical pattern than in its replacement by the scientific paradigm, which was still largely excluded from the college curriculum up until the Civil War.

The last uncompromising restatement of the classical rhetorical tradition as exemplified by Cicero and Quintilian was contained in John Quincy Adams's *Lectures on Rhetoric and Oratory*, delivered at Harvard in 1806 and 1809, when Adams held the title of Boylston Professor of Rhetoric, and published in 1810. Though Adams was exemplary in combining a scholarly interest in rhetoric with the active role of a statesman, the impact of his lectures was minimal because of the predominance in American higher education at the time of the eighteenth-century British rhetorical tradition, with its strong emphasis on empirical description. Yet even within this tradition important elements of the classical rhetorical position survived. Most significantly, early-nineteenth-century rhetoric still united an orientation to cognitive truth, the effort to attain aesthetic beauty, and the search for ethical and moral insight. For it, as for classical rhetoric, persuasion was the highest element in rhetoric.

The tradition of rhetoric as the focus of higher education came to an effective end in the closing decades of the nineteenth century, and the way it ended is emblematic of the new idea of education, which was to reign with little challenge in the twentieth century. We have already noticed that a shift from an emphasis on speaking to an emphasis on writing had been going on since the eighteenth century. By the end of the nineteenth century the required course on writing was the last remnant of the old curriculum, and an emasculated remnant it was. Persuasion, if it had a place at all, was relegated to the department of speech. Aesthetic considerations, what were classically called poetics, were relegated to literature departments. The study of ethics and morality now belonged to the philosophy department. Yet the new managerial and technological occupations for which students were being trained, as well as the scientific disciplines within the university, required that students write serviceable expository prose, and it was that function that was now the almost exclusive purpose of the writing course. By the 1890s at Harvard the composition class was the sole course required of all students in an otherwise elective curriculum. Other universities followed suit more or less rapidly.

The required writing course, with its necessarily large staff, became something of a stepchild in the newly departmentalized university. Tenured professors of English turned their attention to courses on literature and preferred not to teach writing. The result was a kind of proletarianization of the writing faculty, which came to be made up of graduate students and temporary or part-time teachers. Yet in many ways the writing course, even in its emasculated condition, continued to carry a central if unrecognized educational mission. As the historian of rhetoric James Berlin has eloquently put it:

> When we teach students to write we are teaching more than an instrumental skill. We are teaching a mode of conduct, a way of responding to experience. . . .
> The way we teach writing behavior, whether we will it or not, causes reverberations in all features of a student's private and social behavior. One obvious reason is that the freshman writing course, despite its low status, is the last vestige of the nineteenth-century collegiate way, almost the only place in a large university where first year students are more than numbers. Beyond that, regardless of one's approach to writing instruction, it is impossible to deny that in teaching students about the way they ought to use language we are teaching them something about how to conduct their lives.[20]

Unfortunately the type of conduct encouraged by the new "practical" approach to writing, which came to exclude all the functions of classical rhetoric except objective exposition, and which relentlessly emphasized superficial correctness as the "most significant measure of accomplished prose," had limitations as well as advantages. As Berlin puts it: "This very exclusion, meanwhile, encourages a mode of behavior that helps students in their move up the corporate ladder—correctness in usage, grammar, clothing, thought, and a certain sterile objectivity and disinterestedness."[21]

These reflections on the nineteenth-century change in the cultural paradigm of knowledge bring us back to the correlative changes in the economy and society. The scientific paradigm as popularly understood, the increasing rationalization of the economy and administrative bureaucracy which was opening up many new technical and managerial middle-class occupations, and the aspirations of students to acquire the skills that would allow them to enter those occupations—all combined to reinforce the pattern that in *Habits of the Heart* we called utilitarian individualism. In many respects the school system in general and the university in particular were among the primary institutional embodiments of utilitarian individualism.

The utilitarian individualist pattern took a certain understanding of scientific cognition as its focus, an understanding that we shall see is subject to serious question. It was the great prestige of the natural sciences in the new university that reinforced this pattern. The story of the social sciences, a largely new set of disciplines emerging only at the end of the nineteenth century, is complex and instructive. The main tendency, the effort to develop the social sciences on the model of natural science, had implications for our common culture that we will need to consider. In the reigning conception, science holds its centrality in our intellectual life because of its capacity to produce valid knowledge that is entirely independent of values, but upon which our progress in controlling the conditions of our existence depends. The social sciences, seen in this light, are not continuous with the long-standing discussion about the nature of the good life and the means to attain it but are, rather, a new form of objective cognition that properly qualified experts might indeed put to use. Yet in spite of the power of the scientific paradigm, the social sciences never entirely lost their connection to the reformism from which they emerged, so that their practical, moral, and political intent was not entirely abandoned. Even more significantly, in the early moments when social science and philosophy had not yet entirely severed their connections, a fundamentally different cognitive pattern tentatively emerged, one that has managed to survive only precariously in the face of the dominant metaphors of objectivity, control, and utility.

The humanities, the backbone of traditional higher education for a thousand years, were also forced into a radical reorganization. To some extent the essential notion of the humanities crumbled when they no longer meant exclusively the study of the Greek and Latin classics. So-called "modern humanities," introducing the study of modern languages and literatures on equal terms with the classics, had significant cultural consequences. The modern preoccupation with an emotive self, characteristic of romanticism and of modern literature in general, allowed the humanities to develop a counter-paradigm to the scientific one—namely, the paradigm of expressive individualism, whose metaphors are drawn largely from the rich interior realm of human subjectivity. Unfortunately this paradigm operated less to challenge the dominant one than to complement it. The humanities were assigned the subjective realm, now that the objective world was the province of science alone. And also, the scientific paradigm found its way into the heart of the humanities themselves, especially in philology and history; it was sure that the humanities would not be the source of a counter-paradigm that would effectively challenge the dominant scientific one.

Whereas in Europe a general notion of "the human studies" kept the social sciences and the humanities together well into the twentieth century, in some respects even up to the present, the social sciences in America, especially economics, sociology, and psychology, declared their independence of the humanities by committing themselves to the task of becoming sciences. Consequently, they adopted the fundamental assumptions of positivism, reductionism, relativism, and determinism, all of which were aspects of what the social scientists thought the scientific enterprise entailed. Positivism required a methodology that would be as close to the assumed objectivism of natural science as possible. In psychology this meant the use of experiments; in economics and sociology it meant the quantification of data and its statistical manipulation wherever possible. Reductionism is the tendency to explain the complex in terms of the simple and to find behind complex cultural forms biological, psychological, or sociological drives, needs, and interests. Relativism, following naturally from positivism and reductionism, assumes that matters of morality and religion, being explicable by particular constellations of psychological and sociological conditions, cannot be judged true or false, valid or invalid, but will vary with persons, cultures, and societies. Determinism, intrinsic to this conception of science, assumes that human actions can be explained in terms of "variables" that will account for them.

While social scientists were exhilarated by their newly won independence and the prospective status of their disciplines as true sciences, they in fact recapitulated to a remarkable extent certain assumptions—empiricist, reductionist, and relativistic—that were already present in the seventeenth century with Thomas Hobbes. The tendency of what we have called Lockeanism to think of human beings as atomistic self-interest maximizers made the teachings of the "new" social sciences quite comfortably familiar. Among educated and ever more secularized Americans, the social sciences reinforced the language of utilitarian individualism, and its assumption that social problems are primarily technical rather than moral or political. But self-confidence in the "objectivity" of the new social sciences, and the relegation of the humanities to the status of specialized disciplines within a curriculum dominated by the model of natural science, exacted a high price. A central part of our cultural endowment was severely diminished. Ethical reflection about the good life and the good society, drawing on the religious, philosophical, and literary heritage of the West, was no longer at the center of higher education. Indeed, it survived only precariously in the interstices of the research university conceived as a collection of specialized disciplines.

VI. THE MEDIATING ROLE OF CLASSICAL AMERICAN PHILOSOPHY

At the very time when older forms of communicative deliberation contained in the oral culture, the academic tradition of rhetoric, and associated religious and political practices were being rapidly replaced, a remarkable development occurred. A new communicative understanding of science itself appeared in philosophical circles closest to the social sciences, first of all in the university, but with effects throughout American society, and it had deep implications for our conceptions of mind, self, and society.

It was the philosopher Charles Peirce who argued that science is not an enterprise in which isolated individual minds try to construct intellectually coherent ideas of objects in the "real world," testing those ideas by experiments, but is, rather, a social enterprise carried on by a community of inquirers, whose ideas develop in constant conversation with each other as to what the questions are and what the experimental results mean. An isolated investigator unable to influence the consensus of inquirers might as well not exist. Sometimes forgotten discoveries are rediscovered, not infrequently by a number of people apparently working independently. This happens because the scientific community has now understood the background and context for the forgotten discovery and is prepared to assimilate it.

Unfortunately, scientists themselves often subscribe to the individualistic understanding of the scientific enterprise, and so dispute bitterly over priority of discovery in what is fundamentally a collective achievement. The sociologist Robert Merton has told this story in *On the Shoulders of Giants*, and the anthropologist Mary Douglas has recently (*How Do Institutions Think?*) used his findings to show the significance of science as a cultural institution.[22]

While Peirce himself, probably the most brilliant and original of American philosophers, never found a home in the new research university, his central insights were taken up and generalized by the Harvard philosopher Josiah Royce, who saw not only science but the whole moral life of mankind as necessarily carried on by what he called "a community of interpreters," reconsidering the heritage of the past in the light of present reality in a continuing conversation about spiritual truth and moral good.

William James stands apart from the other American philosophers of the classic period in emphasizing the individual more than society, in this way continuing the tradition of Emerson, against which most of the others were reacting. But he exemplified the group as a whole in his effort to mediate between the older, public culture and the newer, specialized academic culture. Along with John Dewey, he wrote and spoke to a large public on matters of importance to society at large. His sharp critique of the success ethic is well known, as is his famous effort to find a "moral equivalent to war,"[23] an idea whose influence can be felt in many programs (the Peace Corps is one) and whose relevance is as great today as when James first uttered it.

John Dewey and George Herbert Mead may have been indirectly influenced by Peirce (Mead had studied with Royce, but before Royce had worked out his idea of a community of interpreters), but they each to a considerable degree independently developed an interactive and communicative model of cognitive and moral reason. Mead's work on the social constitution of the self was fundamental, as the German philosopher Jürgen Habermas has recently emphasized.[24] Nothing could be more at variance with Locke's idea that human consciousness develops through the individual's economic interaction with the natural world than Mead's notion that cognitive and moral capacities develop in the growing child through a process of "taking the role of the other."

A social understanding of individual development and human action was central to John Dewey's entire project of educational and political reform. His version of pragmatism bolstered a concept of life that was continuous with older Puritan and republican ones even though based on new arguments.[25] He was always at odds with utilitarian individualism and positivist scientism, though his fondness for the notion of science as the quintessential form of community, his idea that the growth of scientific intelligence would solve all our problems, and even his proclivity for calling his philosophy "instrumentalism" tended to obscure his differences from the positivistic and technocratic ideas then in vogue. So while Peirce, Royce, and Mead were ignored and then forgotten (or in the case of Mead, misinterpreted in terms of the prevailing individualistic paradigm, first by the sociologist Herbert Blumer and then in more extreme form by the sociologist Erving Goffman), Dewey was influential but often misunderstood, until he, too, was largely forgotten. The tradition of antiutilitarian, antipositivistic social science never died out, however. The Harvard sociologist Talcott Parsons, with his voluntaristic theory of action (though owing more to Durkheim than to Mead), kept it influential in the decades after World War II, although Parsons had an influence at least as ambiguous as Dewey's, given the former's notion that he was creating a science.

Today, in an academic and social context that continues to be dominated by instrumental reason, the paradigm of communicative reason needs actively to be reappropriated—as a model for research and teaching in the university and as a support for nonutilitarian tendencies in the culture at large. Dewey was probably right in holding that only such an approach to truth is genuinely compatible with a democratic society. The efforts made by American philosophers of the classic period remain exemplary for us as we, too, try to keep communication open between the new specialized disciplines in the university and the larger concerns of the public.[26]

VII. SOME CONTEMPORARY VIEWS OF HIGHER EDUCATION

Before turning to former president Derek Bok of Harvard University for a representative view of higher education today, we may pause for a moment to consider the views of his mid-century predecessor James Bryant Conant, who in many ways set the course for Harvard as a research university of international reputation in the mid–twentieth century—or as some of its admirers like to put it, Harvard as the national university. Conant was an eminent chemist who applied his talents to military projects in both world wars: during World War I he worked on perfecting a formula for a new poison gas; during World War II he helped to direct the program that produced the atom bomb. He believed that science was the only reliable source of truth, yet he did not believe that science offered the values necessary for the survival of a free society—science would always be the province of an intellectually favored elite and had no answers outside the area of its own special competences. In the breach, so to speak, Conant sponsored the Harvard General Education Program, and similar programs designed for schools, which would teach in a secular mode the rudiments of a common culture that the generalized Christianity of the nineteenth century no longer could. For Conant, an ardent supporter of the cold war, education was a crucial ideological instrument to strengthen Americans for their long struggle with communism. But, as the historian Sam Bass Warner, Jr., points out, it seems doubtful that Conant believed the humanistic content of general education could stand up under the cold scrutiny of science.[27] With Conant it would seem that what Parsons later called the "cognitive complex" in higher education had indeed come loose from the "moral evaluative complex."[28] Without the integrative context that classical American philosophy might have provided, they have only become more disparate ever since.

Derek Bok has recently argued persuasively that the American university system is the most successful and adaptable system of higher education in the world.[29] Yet his criterion of success is largely limited to the production and dissemination of knowledge, and it implicitly accepts the conclusion of Conant and Parsons. He notes the increased specialization within already specialized disciplines, and the loss of the capacity of anyone to put the pieces together, but he views those developments complacently: among the multiplicity of knowledge there are riches for everyone. Integration, Bok argues, is no longer a possibility if we think in substantive terms: there is nothing, or there is far too much, for every educated person to know. He thus endorses the idea behind Harvard's Core Curriculum, which replaced Conant's General Education Program in the late 1970s, that what every student needs to learn are skills and methods in the natural and social sciences and in the humanities, relative to which substance is simply illustrative.

When Bok allowed himself to worry about the ethical content of university education, as he did only occasionally (and more in connection with professional than with undergraduate education), his suggestions only indicate how marginal the issue has become. With respect to undergraduates he sees the dimension of ethics and citizenship largely in extracurricular activities. Harvard students are supposed to learn about ethics by doing volunteer work in nursing homes or shelters for the homeless. Ethics courses may also be necessary, particularly in the professional schools, but they must be focused on methods of ethical analysis rather than matters of substance, so as to avoid the possibility of indoctrination.

Bok also views the enormous proliferation of student services, particularly psychological counseling, as a positive development. He does not ask himself the question how their college education actually affects late-adolescent students, living perhaps for the first time away from home and trying to make sense of the world. It does not seem to occur to him that a university proud of its ever more specialized departments offers an education that has little connection with the work students do as volunteers but may indeed have much to do with their need for psychological counseling. We have already heard in Chapter 1 Harvard students' graduation addresses claiming that the meaning of their education adds up to confusion and moral nihilism.

The very complacency of a Derek Bok perhaps explains the extraordinary popularity of Allan Bloom's bitter critique of our best universities in *The Closing of the American Mind*,[30] for much (though certainly not all) that Bloom wrote about undergraduate student culture and the soullessness, if not nihilism, of the education the students receive is accurate. But one must question sharply his account of where we have come from and how we got here, and thus of where we have to go. He painted a portrait of an idealized university that existed in the past—perhaps at the University of Chicago in the 1950s—which he leads us to believe was quite widespread until recently, a place where able students searched for truth in scientific laboratories and in the great texts of the Western tradition, nurtured by dedicated teachers, and at least partially insulated from harsh realities. But such a university has never existed, not at Chicago in the 1950s nor anywhere else. And the traditional university was almost never centered on "philosophy" as Bloom understands it, ignoring as he did the competing and usually dominant tradition of rhetoric. Even more important, the fact that the disinterested pursuit of truth has never had a particularly easy time in the modern research university, which after all arose in response to the needs of the modern economy and state, remained veiled in Bloom's account. Instead he developed a rather bizarre conspiracy theory to account for the relativism and nihilism inherent in so much of today's higher education. It all came from Nietzsche, he said, brought to these shores by German refugees in the 1930s and 1940s and purveyed largely through the essentially Nietzchean teachings of Max Weber and Sigmund Freud. This is to overlook the fact that the ethical relativism and nihilism Bloom abhors have been implicit in the Anglo-American intellectual world since Hobbes and were certainly present in American social science before the 1930s.

Even more bizarre was Bloom's bitter attack in the third section of his book on the student revolt of the 1960s as the cause of the "lowering of standards" in our best universities. Bok is surely more accurate when he notes that any "lowering of standards" was quickly repaired by the mid-1970s. But the more important point is that among the sometimes conflicting meanings of the student revolt of the 1960s was a demand for just the moral seriousness that Bloom believed lacking in today's university. Further, as we shall have occasion to note below, the 1960s saw the beginning of initiatives to recover a moral dimension in the university that had largely been obscured by the regnant utilitarian paradigm and its expressivist counterpart.

What we believe is the real source of the soullessness in American higher education Bloom alludes to only glancingly, if amusingly, when he wrote of the MBA program's influence on undergraduate education as "a great disaster. . . . Liberal education puts everything at risk and requires students who are able to risk everything. Otherwise it can only touch what is uncommitted in the essentially committed. The effect of the MBA is to corral a horde of students who want to get into business school and put the blinders on them, to legislate an illiberal, officially approved undergraduate program for them at the outset. . . . Getting into those elite professional schools is an obsessive concern that tethers the mind."[31] Whereas pre–medical school students learned to have a respect for biology and physics, he pointed out, prebusiness students not only ignored sociology, anthropology, and political science while concentrating on economics but did not even show interest in the discipline itself:

[The prebusiness student] is not motivated by love of the science of economics but by love of what it is concerned with—money. Economists' concern with wealth, an undeniably real and solid thing, gives them a certain impressive intellectual solidity not provided by, say, culture. One can be sure that they are not talking about nothing. But wealth, as opposed to the science of wealth, is not the noblest of motivations, and there is nothing else quite like this perfect coincidence between science and cupidity elsewhere in the university. The only parallel would be if there were a science of sexology, with earnest and truly scholarly professors, which would ensure its students lavish sexual satisfactions.[32]

Yet the notion of education as a means for the acquisition of wealth, the wedding of science and cupidity, was present from the beginning of the research university. Even more unfortunately, the trend that Bloom associated only with the influence of the MBA program is much more widespread. The research university has grown in tandem with the business corporation; yet for all the interpenetration, there has always been a difference in structure and a difference in aims. Now that difference itself is under attack. The prospectus of Stanford University's new Institute for Higher Education Research states: "Advances in economic theory and empirical analysis methods, developments in organizational behavior, and refinements of managerial technique have reached the point where we can hope to understand the complexities of non-profit institutions—including colleges and universities—to a degree approaching that for business firms."

William Massy, Stanford's vice-president for finance and a member of the School of Business, the chief instigator of this new institute and a professor in the School of Education as well, says, "Ever since I joined [Stanford's] central administration in the early '70s, I have become really fascinated with higher education as an industry where institutions with many interconnections interact in a kind of marketplace."

Massy's institute has placed high on its list of research questions "an examination of the productivity and cost effectiveness at universities. Are universities delivering the product that the public expects?" This is the central concern that also dominates much of Derek Bok's book: in Massy's words, "the effectiveness of teaching and learning. What is a good set of measures for each of those?" Much of the public, he recognizes, thinks of university education as primarily "job preparation," and he believes the university is obliged to meet that concern. For him the university is one more element in the market system:

It's hard to deny that when students come for a particular service, someone will supply it. Tastes have changed: people used to be interested in the classics; now they are interested in making money. In the end, we have fundamental and deep social changes—and they are what they are. I do believe in the market. If there is a demand, we have an obligation to meet it.

We need to provide an interesting menu at the university—a menu of where we think the world is going—but we can't dictate what people are going to want. If they don't like the menu, we have an obligation to change it—but not too quickly. We have to balance "leading" and "following."[33]

In Massy's view the education industry should be responsive to market demand: if people used to be interested in the classics but now are interested in making money, so be it. Not only does he implicitly reject Bloom's concept of liberal education, he rejects any notion of the university as a community of moral discourse. One can imagine that in his university the notion that higher education has anything to do with a coherent view of the world or the meaning of life would be absent—and one must hope that indeed student services and psychological counseling would be available. Unfortunately, given the culture of therapy today, the help the students get would be oriented to strengthening their autonomy in a difficult world, rather than to finding a larger meaning or a more socially viable context for their education. One can also be sure that during the critical transition from adolescence to young adulthood which most undergraduates are making when they are at college, extracurricular activities, not all of them ethically elevating, will to a considerable degree do the real teaching that their formal curriculum does not.

VIII. EDUCATION IN THE THIRD DEMOCRATIC TRANSFORMATION

The idea of an "education industry" that is simply responsive to market pressures is one more example of how a massive un-Lockean institution can encourage people to think of their lives in terms of purely individualistic aspirations. It is thus deeply inimical to the possibility of Dahl's "third democratic transformation," for it leaves the basic structure of the educational institution unexamined while it claims only to be responding to the already fixed "preferences" students bring with them.

The idea of an education that simply gives individuals the methods and skills they need to get ahead in the world is almost certainly inadequate, even as "job preparation," in an advanced technical economy, which requires morally and socially sensitive people capable of responsible interaction. It is even more inadequate in preparing citizens for active participation in a complex world. Fortunately, concepts of university life other than that of "the education industry" have been revived in the last two or three decades. Theirs is certainly an uphill battle, but alternative voices have not been lacking.

For example, in the marginalized and denigrated but still indispensable field of writing instruction, James Berlin discerns a renaissance of rhetoric in the period 1960–75, a rebirth whose repercussions continue to the present. It is entirely fitting that rhetoric, so closely associated with the first and second democratic transformations, should be reemerging now as a mode of discovery in the process of democratic deliberation.

Berlin defines the most important new tendency as "transactional rhetoric": "Transactional rhetoric does not locate reality in some empirically verifiable external phenomenon (sense impression or the quantifiable) or within some realm apart from the external (ideas or vision). It instead discovers reality in the interaction of the features of the rhetorical process itself—in the interaction of material reality, writer, audience, and language."[34] This rhetoric develops in part from the recent revival of interest in classical rhetoric and in part from new developments that Berlin describes with the help of the scholar of rhetoric Richard Ohmann:

> The old rhetoric emphasized persuasion, Ohmann explains, but modern rhetoric includes other forms: "communication, contemplation, inquiry, self-expression, and so on." The old was more aggressive in its design on the audience, whereas "modern rhetoric . . . lowers the barriers between speaker or writer and audience. It shifts the emphasis toward cooperation, mutuality, social harmony. Its dynamic is one of joint movement toward an end that both writer and audience accept, not one of an insistent force acting upon a stubborn object." The second characteristic of modern rhetoric is that it regards the discipline as "the *pursuit*—and not simply the transmission—of truth and right. . . ." Finally writing always takes place within a discourse community.[35]

In a college today, then, the teacher of writing is actually working with several discourse communities, all of which must be treated respectfully, at the same time that students must learn that mastering standard written English enables them to participate in a linguistic community of great importance in our culture. "The point is to enable the student to realize the diversity of world-views within our society— the different ways in which language is used to organize experience. The object, ultimately, is training for citizenship in a democracy: the student 'becomes a voting citizen of his world, rather than a bound vassal to an inherited ontology.' "[36]

Along with shifting the emphasis from objective expository writing to writing in the context of a discourse community has come a change in how the classroom is organized. Instead of a teacher using words as a conduit to convey the one correct way to use language and students passively receiving what comes through the conduit, the class is conceived as a collaborative activity in which students take responsibility for discovering how to use language effectively. This is an example of a more general phenomenon that the sociologist of education Zelda Gamson calls "learning communities" in colleges and universities.[37] As against the notion of the university as a cafeteria with different options for different students (Massy's market model), the learning community has a coherent curricular focus that connects the various courses into some kind of whole and allows students to understand education as a common enterprise. In contrast to the standard classroom as a locus for individualistic competition of students pitted against each other for high places on the grade curve, learning communities emphasize the cooperative and interactional nature of learning, and make the development of individual skills the responsibility of the community as a whole. In a curious way, this development is a rediscovery, conscious or not, of central features in John Dewey's much misunderstood notion of "progressive education."

If small liberal arts colleges are so minded, they can become learning communities. In large universities, learning communities have appeared when concerned faculty have taken the initiative to establish them, in special programs. It is significant that in both situations it is a precondition that the faculty itself become a learning community of mutually intelligible interpreters.

At the primary and secondary levels, the idea of a learning community is, if anything, even more valuable. In primary and secondary schools teachers who care both about the subject matter and about the students as individuals can have, we know, a life-changing impact. What is required is not just dedicated administrations and faculty but parents devoted to their children's education, and a community among them that can support both each other and the school. Bok has pointed to "the steady drop over the past twenty years in the academic qualifications of entering freshmen, a drop occasioned in part by the larger proportions of young people attending college in the 1960s, and in part by the effects of television, family disintegration, and the declining standards in many of our public schools."[38] It should be obvious that learning is never the result of the efforts of isolated, competitive individuals alone, and that the evident weakness in American schools has much to do with the weakening of their community context. The weakening of community and the erosion of the cultural endowment upon which a viable community is based go hand in hand.

Returning to higher education, we must not exaggerate the strength of the learning-community movement; but restlessness with the idea of purely instrumental education (or instrumental with a little expressivism thrown in) is widespread enough to lead many teachers, not just or only in ethics classrooms, to ask what the common enterprise of modern society means and how it can be evaluated.

One of the more interesting of such efforts comes from the humanities, remembering their original mission, and illuminating modernity in the light of what we have learned from nonmodern societies. The humanist Robert Proctor in his important book *Education's Great Amnesia*[39] traces the origin of the humanities to Petrarch's effort to recover the true human meaning of the classics, particularly Cicero. Proctor argues that in confrontation with the Greek and Latin classics we come in contact with a fundamentally different understanding of the self, one that is "extensive," in that it understands the self only in terms of its relation to others, as against our own intensive self, which searches ceaselessly for a "true self" entirely independent of anyone else. The educator David Hicks has shown a similar concern for the value of classical and Christian sources in education at the secondary school level in his fine book *Norms and Nobility*.[40] Both Proctor and Hicks make specific suggestions about curriculum.

We know more about different cultures from all of human history than we have ever known before, but only in a few places are traditional and non-Western cultures studied with the conscious intent of understanding our own situation better by grasping as deeply as possible cultures that are radically other. Certainly the crux of any proper higher education today must be the effort to make sense of our own uniquely modern form of culture and society, including the place in it of the natural sciences. The social sciences and the humanities cannot in this endeavor be confined to presenting the student with "basic skills" and "methods of thought and inquiry."[41] Even a "Great Books of Western Civilization" approach would be preferable, though the treatment of great texts as timeless and disembodied, speaking more or less in the same voice about common problems, is finally both precious and disorienting. It is precisely the way that Plato is different from Weber, Confucius from Freud, that is significant and that can teach students about the peculiarities of our own situation as well as about other cultures. And if we want to understand traditional cultures, we shall have to take seriously that religious concerns are central to most of them. The philosopher Thomas McCarthy has suggested, "We have things to learn from traditional cultures as well as they from us, not only what we have forgotten and repressed, but something about how we might put our fragmented world back together again. This is not a matter of regression, but of dialogue—dialogue that is critical to be sure, but not only on one side."[42]

The need to put our modern culture into perspective by considering very different forms of life is related to, but not identical with, much of the current concern for pluralism or diversity in higher education. This latter concern is misguided, we believe, when it identifies modern culture with a particular racial or ethnic tradition. The notion that the European classics are the special heritage of white American students is as fallacious as the notion that Asian-American students are familiar with Confucianism. The operative culture of most of our undergraduates is the monoculture of the tube: "L.A. Law" or "Miami Vice." Educational reform consisting largely in search-and-destroy missions to prove that previously canonical works promote racism, sexism, and class domination will not be of much help to students for whom those canonical works had no meaning in the first place. We are not likely to give up what some philosophers call the hermeneutics of suspicion—the tendency in the West since the Enlightenment to call all received traditions into question. But without a hermeneutics of recovery, through which we can understand what a living tradition is in the first place, a hermeneutics of suspicion is apt to be an exercise in nihilism, which, far from liberating students, merely disorients them. To have curricular reform break down into a turf war between ethnic studies, women's studies, and more established disciplines is unedifying and unhelpful. Only a much deeper awareness of the uniqueness of modernity and of the profoundly different worlds of nonmodern cultures will give us a model of curricular reform that combines intellectual seriousness with a genuine respect for human diversity.

No teacher with eyes to see, in school or university, has failed to notice those moments of joy that come when a student understands something important for the first time—not as a means to any end, but as an enlargement of his or her participation in reality. The moment of joy in education is not at odds with the moment of criticism. The delight in a good classroom, at any level, is not just the delight of understanding but also the delight of questioning and having one's question taken seriously. Ultimately the teacher must help the student become a part of a community of interpreters, to use Josiah Royce's phrase, or a community of inquirers, in terms closer to Peirce, which not only carries on the tradition, but constantly amends and expands it in active participation. That is the kind of education that Jane Addams and John Dewey were seeking to embody early in the twentieth century.

We have focused in this chapter on the research universities, the cathedrals of the religion of education, as Daniel Boorstin called them.

Since they set the tone for the whole educational system, there is some justification for our emphasis; but it would be against the spirit of Addams and Dewey to imagine that we can leave our concern for education at that level alone. The research universities are merely one expression of the ethos of our society and of the pedagogy that goes on throughout society. We stressed in earlier chapters the centrality of education for the kind of society America is becoming, particularly in its economic and political spheres. With a technologically advanced economy, a skilled and educated work force is essential. But in an enormously complex and interdependent world, an educated and informed citizenry is even more essential. On the whole Americans have done better in developing their educational resources for the transmission of specialized knowledge and skills than they have for citizenship. In this respect the research university reflects the general trend. Yet moral issues and social and ecological problems are considered at every level of educational life. Attentive publics are nurtured in schools and colleges and nourished by serious journals of opinion and commentary and (inadequately, to be sure) by other media as well, especially public radio and television.

Education at all levels is tied closely to the priorities set by the economy and the state. Those priorities obviously affect funding decisions that decide the fate of programs, curricula, and sometimes whole institutions. Still, in important ways our schools and our universities are free and are institutionally insulated from externally set agendas. Within the social sciences and the humanities teachers can still ask the central questions of social self-interpretation that are essential to citizens, and in our professional schools efforts are widespread to link professional expertise more explicitly to social responsibility and ethical sensitivity. The very diversity of American education allows a variety of forms that would link intellect with character and citizenship. For these to flourish we must make changes throughout our institutional life, particularly in our economic and governmental institutions, changes that would show that we understand education less obsessively in terms of "infrastructure for competition" and more as an invaluable resource in the search for the common good. Then we could realize how badly depleted our cultural endowment is throughout the educational process and cultivate again those resources without which reflection about a good society is impossible.

IX. LIFE-ENABLING EDUCATION

The philosopher Albert Borgmann has said that "to educate is to enable and disable for life." However pluralistic its forms, education can never merely be for the sake of individual self-enhancement. It pulls us into the common world or it fails altogether. Creating a "life-enabling" education is a public task of great difficulty, but it is essential. Here we may summarize some of our suggestions as to needed changes:

(1) Education has become something of a panacea for all social problems in the twentieth century. But instead of dumping our unsolved problems on our public schools or expecting our universities to come up with technical solutions to our difficulties, we should recover a more classical notion that it is the whole way of life that educates. Our jobs, our consumer marketplaces, our laws and our government agencies, our cities and neighborhoods, our homes and churches, all educate us and create the context in which our schools operate, supporting them or undermining them as the case may be. A genuine "education society" means something more than a society with good schools. It means a society with a healthy sense of the common good, with social morale and public spirit, and with a vivid memory of its own cultural past. Schools can contribute to that, but they cannot create it out of whole cloth and should not be expected to. Only a further democratic transformation of all our institutions will make possible a genuine "education society."

(2) Our entire educational system, in some ways like our economy and our government, has grown enormously in response to particular and often transient pressures so that larger coherence has suffered. Many parochial schools, we are told, since they have a good sense of their mission and the support of their constituencies, produce not only skilled but responsible citizens. The sociologist James Coleman's work on schools shows that they can succeed only when, first, the school itself, its principal and teachers, has a solidary concept of its mission; second, strong families are behind the children; and third, effective communities help to organize the families in support of the schools.[43] The experience of the parochial schools he studied cannot be easily generalized, and yet the principles seem clear, and we must invent ways to bring these same principles to bear on public education.

(3) Higher education has also expanded in ways that no individual can any longer understand. To overcome disciplinary specialization

so many interdisciplinary programs, projects, and institutes have been produced that they only increase the level of incoherence. Adding new entities to deal with every new problem is not the answer. We must give serious thought, particularly within the older established disciplines, to the meaning of the educational enterprise and its effect on students and faculty. In small institutions the community as a whole can sometimes do this. Large institutions often leave it to the initiative, and sometimes the entrepreneurship, of individuals, allowing enterprising students to discover teachers who can give them a sense of a quest for a larger vision, although some universities organize special seminar programs in an attempt to increase the coherence of the curriculum. Almost all university faculty members are more oriented to their disciplines than to the educational purposes of their institutions, and it will take extraordinary leadership to get them to think about the educational implications of what they are doing. A greater awareness of large educational issues among the faculty of our more prestigious institutions is probably a precondition for successful institutional innovation.

(4) We must recover an enlarged paradigm of knowledge, which recognizes the value of science but acknowledges that other ways of knowing have equal dignity. Practical reason, in its classical sense of moral reason, must regain its importance in our educational life. We must give more than a token bow to art and literature as mere vessels of expressive values, for they can often give us deep moral insight. Ethos is the very subject matter of the humanities and social sciences; ethics cannot possibly be merely one more specialty or a set of procedures that can simply be sprinkled on wherever needed. We must critically recover the project of the classic American philosophers, following them in their willingness to see science as a social process that cannot be divorced from moral learning and imagination without the impoverishment of every field. The enormous pressure in the university to come up with something new, to revise the inherited view, makes it perilously easy to forget that, as Randolph Bourne put it, "the past is not yet over," and that the critical assimilation of it is a central task of education.

(5) The idea of education for citizenship in a complex world is not some quaint leftover from a nineteenth-century curriculum. It is an essential task for a free society in the modern world. We must redefine our paradigm of knowledge to see why education for citizenship is not subsidiary to the dominant "cognitive complex" of higher education, and is not a decorative "general education" ideologically necessary but lacking cognitive validity. Indeed, cognitive competence is

essential for effective citizenship, in close interaction with moral sensitivity and imaginative insight. Perhaps specialization in (largely scientific) cognition, freed from older dogmatic and culturally parochial constraints, was an essential stage in the development of higher education; but now it is clearly time to reintegrate cognition with a more fully human understanding.

X. EDUCATION AND ULTIMATE MEANING

Genuine education knows no boundaries. As we have argued here, once one seriously begins to consider America's economic and political situation, one is led to think about the larger context in which economics and politics have meaning at all. A concern for understanding our own society inevitably raises the question of where we are in relation to all other human cultures, past as well as present. Today more than ever, we cannot think about the human species without thinking about the natural world that sustains it and whose viability we threaten. The more deeply we study, the closer we come to the fundamental questions of the meaning of life. While such questions are raised at many points in our schools and universities, in our kind of society it is in religious institutions that they are apt to receive the most sustained attention. It is not surprising that the difficulties we have been discovering in our economic, political, and educational institutions turn up in new forms in our churches and synagogues as well.

6

The Public Church

The very title of this chapter may strike some readers as peculiar. Doesn't our constitution insist on a separation of church and state in the United States, and isn't religion an essentially private matter? This way of thinking represents a continuing confusion over the word "public." Often in America when we distinguish between the "public sector" and the "private sector," we mean to distinguish what is governmental from what is nongovernmental. In this usage religion is indeed "private." But in two senses religion, at least biblical religion, which in a variety of forms constitutes the major religious tradition in America, cannot be private. Firstly, both Christians and Jews recognize a God who created heaven and earth, all that is, seen and unseen, whose dominion clearly transcends not only private life but the nations themselves. There is nothing in the private or public realm that cannot concern such a religious tradition.

Secondly, in one important respect "public" does not mean governmental but is a contrast term to it. In the second democratic transformation of the eighteenth century, "public" came to mean the citizenry who reflect on matters of common concern, engage in deliberation together, and choose their representatives to constitute the government, whose powers are limited by a constitution.[1] Religious bodies are very much part of *this* meaning of the public, not because they are governmentally "established" religions with legal privileges but because they enter into the common discussion about the public good. It is in this sense that one can legitimately speak of a "public church." Indeed, the "free exercise" clause of the First Amendment to the Constitution guarantees the right of religious bodies to public expression, just as much as the "no establishment" clause ensures that none will gain any favored governmental status.[2]

The founders of the American republic were quite clear on the public place of religion in this latter sense. They believed that religious belief made an essential contribution to the formation of a responsible citizenry capable of sustaining a democratic republic. John Adams said, in his first year as our first vice-president, "Our constitution was made only for a moral and a religious people. It is wholly inadequate to the government of any other."[3] John Locke, in spite of his individualism in other respects, was convinced that belief in God was essential for the existence of any society. In his *Letter Concerning Toleration* he wrote, "The taking away of God, though even in thought, dissolves all. . . ."[4] Both Locke and the founders knew that sectarian dispute could be politically dangerous; but they did not, on that account, underestimate the public importance of religion.

Historically, the clergy, religious bodies, and religious associations have been concerned with public issues in America from the earliest settlement. The clergy in most of the denominations supported the revolution itself and provided some of its ablest publicists. It was the Quakers who called for the abolition of slavery even before the revolution. Indeed, there has not been a major issue in the history of the United States on which religious bodies did not speak out, publicly and vociferously, and often, as in the case of the nineteenth-century struggle over slavery, on both sides.

Philosophical liberals have sometimes worried about the active participation of religious groups in public life. They have tended to define politics as narrowly concerned with procedural justice, with, as they put it, matters of the right rather than of the good. In this reading, religious groups, with their strong visions of the good, tend to disrupt democratic politics by bringing into public life matters that should remain essentially private. According to this point of view, each of us should be allowed, as individuals or in groups, to pursue private versions of the good life, under the common umbrella provided by a "thin" consensus concerning rights. But according to critics of philosophical liberalism, the liberals are only smuggling in their own version of a good society in the name of transcending others' versions, and have no special claim to precedence.[5]

Indeed, it could be argued that the greater public role of religion in the United States, compared with the situation in most European countries, for example, compensates for the narrow spectrum of our political parties, which often act as congeries of interest groups that seek the center for the sake of electoral victory. Frequently, issues that parties would not touch were raised first by religious groups and only after a long process of public debate and education taken seriously by the political parties. The Civil Rights Act of 1964, for example, cannot be understood as the result of political-party initiative except after a long period of public protest led largely by persons within religious communities.

As it turns out, both the liberals and their critics have had too strong a view of the amount of agreement within various religious and secular groups concerning the common good. We have more of an "overlapping consensus" among our diverse religious and secular con-stituencies than doctrinaire theorists realize.[6] Few if any issues in the history of the United States have pitted the churches against the secularists; usually we find different denominations on different sides, disagreement within denominations, and religious and secular people joined on one side or the other. Shared religious and political symbols allowed civil discussion to continue (with the one exception of the issue of slavery) even when disagreement and conflict were intense. Consensus about substance is ever fragile and changing, as in a free society it ought to be, and has not required people to pass religious or (except under aberrant conditions, such as the McCarthy period) political tests of orthodoxy. The importance of the discussion, and of the religious contribution to it, however, cannot be overestimated. The public church has almost never spoken with a single voice; that does not diminish its significance in our common life.

Some of the founders of the republic, deists themselves, may have had a rather utilitarian idea of biblical religion, affirming the value of religious bodies in inculcating morality even if they did not consider their doctrines to be true. Such a view is not unlike the modern sociological functionalism that attributes to religion the function of "social cement" without regard to the validity of its system of meaning. A simple functionalism, regarding religion only as a contribution to "social integration," is manifestly false, since religious groups have frequently voiced disruptive demands that polarized society and led to severe conflict (as in the case of the religious abolitionists). But even a subtler functionalism that evaluates religion only with regard to its contribution to the social good, whether integrative or disruptive, also distorts the deepest meaning of the religious life. In all the biblical religions, the ultimate loyalty is to God, in whose hands the nations are as but dust, and not to America. While not infrequently God and country are fused in a conventional piety, it is never forgotten that religious loyalty transcends the nation. So, unlike many other groups, religious communities are often concerned not only with the common good of the nation but also with the common good of all human beings and with our ultimate responsibility to a transcendent God. To forget that is to obscure perhaps the most important thing we need to understand about the role of religion in society.

While well over 90 percent of Americans continue to answer "yes" when they are asked in a poll if they believe in God, we know that the term has a broad variety of meanings for them. For many it means the God revealed in the Bible. For others, even some of those in the pews, it means a cosmic force or spiritual energy. Among affluent and well-educated people, nontraditional forms of spirituality have become widespread in some parts of the country. In the late 1960s and early 1970s we saw a massive upwelling of interest in alternative spiritualities, many of them of Asian origin, and they have not ceased since then to be important. This "New Age" consciousness, or simply new consciousness, embraces a wide spectrum of beliefs, from astrology to reincarnation to an ecological earth mysticism. We do not underestimate the importance of these developments, but we do not believe that they represent a schism in the American soul, any more than earlier radical religious changes did, as, for example, when the population was altered by large-scale Catholic immigration.[7] These groups, too, enter the overlapping consensus that has characterized American public life from the beginning.

In this chapter we shall look closely at one Protestant denomination in order to illustrate the current predicament of religious bodies in American life. We do this partly for the sake of manageability, but even more because we believe that the major tendencies and cleavages can be illustrated within, rather than between, every large religious group. Tensions over race and gender, conservatism and liberalism, fundamentalism and liberationism, are found in the major Protestant denominations, in the Catholic Church, and, to a modified degree, in the major divisions of Judaism as well. Our choice of the United Methodist Church is not only because it is, as the Catholic writer Michael Novak called it, a "middle-class heartland church"[8] but because it illustrates the issues with peculiar poignancy. We do not believe it is any more, but neither is it any less, representative than any other large religious body in the United States.

Devout, diligent, and popularly oriented, Methodism flourished in postrevolutionary America, becoming an independent church in 1784. Fired by revivalism in frontier camp meetings, it surged in size to become the nation's largest denomination, with more than a million members in 1844 and almost five million in 1890. Over the nineteenth century, Methodism led in forging a "common core Protestantism" around revivalism, perfectionist piety, and moral reform. Tied to popular ideals of democratic progress and America's manifest destiny, this Protestant consensus joined the denominations of British origin (Episcopal, Presbyterian, Congregationalist, and Baptist) into a cultural quasi-establishment of "mainline" churches which contained 80 percent of all American Protestants and more than half of all churched Americans by 1890. In its subsequent vicissitudes Methodism shares many of the problems of the other mainline churches. In this way Methodism exemplifies a group of churches that no longer are as central in American religious life as they once were but are by no means marginal.

Just as we have done in other spheres of public life, we shall look at institutional difficulties and institutional reforms. We shall be concerned with how the problems in other sectors of life spill over into religion, and also how religion might address them. Given the structural significance of organized religion in American life, we believe this discussion will be of interest to those who are not religious as well as to those who are.

The major religious bodies, certainly including the United Methodist Church, have for a long time been attempting to cope with the social problems generated by the emergence of a large-scale economy and an activist government. In the late nineteenth and the early twentieth century, the Social Gospel movement drew many Protestant churches, including a significant sector of Methodism, into a critique of economic individualism and a call for social reform based on an idea of the self as more social and interdependent with others than the dominant individualist ideology imagined. Social Christianity has been a vigorous force in American religion in a variety of forms throughout the twentieth century.

But religion did not just challenge the Lockean consensus that has exerted such a strong cultural influence in America; to some degree it has succumbed to it. Already in the nineteenth century the privatization and "feminization" of religion led to a religious expressive individualism that complemented rather than questioned the dominant utilitarian mood.[9] In the twentieth century, and especially since World War II, religion has been invaded by the market mentality, so that it has become in many instances another consumer good. "Consumer Christians" shop for the church that is most convenient for their needs and switch, as casually as they change brands of dishwasher detergent, if they think they can get a better package deal elsewhere.

The tension in American religion is not ultimately between local congregations and national organizations, though often it seems that way. The issue, both for the local parish and for the national or international church, is whether membership is accepted as having a formative claim on one's very sense of self, as involving a loyalty that can persist through difficulties, or whether membership is merely instrumental to individual self-fulfillment and, like some current conceptions of marriage, can be abandoned as soon as it "doesn't meet my needs." In the framework of *The Good Society* the question is whether organized religion can offer a genuine alternative to tendencies that we have argued are deeply destructive in our current pattern of institutions, or whether religious institutions are simply one more instance of the problem. As with education, where we faced a similar question, the answer is not simple.

II. GOD GOES TO WASHINGTON

One revealing place to begin this story is with the religious advocacy groups located in Washington. Linked to national denominations and interdenominational structures, these organizations aim to embody the public church in America. These groups want to bring religious faith and ethical insight to bear in defining America's vision of a good society and in making recommendations for public policy on specific issues. They try to educate their own members and those of related church organizations, to mobilize them as moral supporters and political constituents, and to influence the larger public through the mass media. They also advocate their policy views and moral values with legislators and administrators by testimony, persuasive research and argument, lobbying, negotiation, and court action.

Probably the most visible and best-known religious advocacy group in American politics during the 1980s was Moral Majority. But Moral Majority and its recent offspring on the "religious right" are only part of a much larger and longer story. Since 1945 some five hundred new national religious agencies, societies, and "special-purpose groups" have been founded, three hundred of them since 1960, compared with the total of four hundred in existence in 1945.[10] In the last fifteen years, these "para-church" groups have grown faster than the churches themselves, and most of them were not originated or sponsored by denominations.

By 1970 religious advocacy groups and movements dedicated to advancing theologically conservative views on issues such as creationism, school prayer, and abortion also began to appear. Their numbers and members grew steadily over the next decade at a pace strong enough to challenge their liberal counterparts. Compared with churches, these groups generally appeal to narrower segments of the population, whether measured by class, age, and race or by social values and attitudes. Some evidence indicates that the members of these groups divide into two contrasting clusters:[11] less educated religious and cultural "conservatives" fill the ranks of antiabortion, Bible study, evangelism, and healing or hunger ministries; more educated religious and cultural "liberals" belong to groups dedicated to nuclear disarmament and world peace, racial equality, and economic justice.

As we have argued in earlier chapters, the federal government's growth, fragmented centralization, and greater social responsibility have called forth increasingly organized responses from other institutions.[12] Local churches have become intricately connected to denominational bureaucracies and agencies, and more densely surrounded by interchurch and para-church groups that educate and mobilize citizens on specific social issues.[13] In short, American religion, like the rest of the postwar American polity, has grown morally conflicted, nationally integrated, and densely, formally organized in response to expanded state regulation. In mediating between the state and the churches, so as to preach religious visions of a good society from public pulpits and exert moral influence on the state, specialized para-church institutions may have the effect of making the churches more like the state and related political structures in their organization, moral ideas, and modes of discourse. How have such institutional changes affected the moral order of our public life and the place of religion within it? Striking answers to this question can be discerned in the interdenominational advocacy groups linked to America's mainline churches.

The Methodist director of one such group, the Ecumenical Alliance for Peace and Justice, sees us as living in a time of crisis: "There is a sickness setting in now in the mainline churches," says Mel Reese, an intense, resilient veteran of twenty years' work in national religious advocacy and organizing.[14] "It's as if people have lost a vision that stretches outward over the society. So now they're turning inward and tearing at each other, 'reorganizing' instead of getting on with the public business at hand. We have a lot of internal factional politics— fratricidal politics, really. You build a strong activist organization, get things done, and denominational leaders are scared you're not 'bringing everyone along in the churches.' "

Asked to weigh criticism from evangelicals that activists and bureaucrats alike within the mainline churches enjoy too free a rein and too big a budget, Reese replies, "That's total poppycock. There's no such thing as big budgets in 'the big church.' One good-sized metropolitan congregation raises and spends more money in a year than almost any national advocacy group or agency. But that's one reason people accept the monolith myth, because money is tight now in the mainline churches, and everyone's afraid it's going to be snatched away from *their* budget."

Evidence of declining financial support for interdenominational offices and agencies related to the mainline churches, and infighting over its control, can be found within the National Council of Churches, perhaps the most visible spire of the "big church." Many of the old denominations in turn are declining at the national level. National budget and staff reductions at the end of the 1980s occurred among Methodists, Presbyterians, Disciples, Baptists, Brethren, Lutherans, Congregationalists, and Unitarians. For example, the United Methodist General Board of Global Ministries suffered a $2 million deficit and cut seventeen staff members from its national division in 1988.[15]

If money is an index of declining commitment to mainline religious denominations and the sort of public church they have sought to be over the past generation, what are the underlying reasons for and social conditions of this decline? One observer of the National Council of Churches offers a nutshell summary of how its fortunes have shifted with the times since World War II; her comments may well apply to the health of its member churches, too. "Some would say that the 1950s were actually more of a culmination than a beginning of ecumenical enthusiasm and that since the 1960s, when it was a leader in the civil rights movement, the NCC has never again occupied a place of such importance in the culture. In the late 1960s, the NCC entered a new era of cultural transformation and began to experience the same questioning of institutions that typified the period generally. During the 1970s many of the council's denominational members became preoccupied with membership losses, as conservative and evangelical churches grew, and some of the disenchanted youth of the 1960s left the churches altogether."[16]

Between 1970 and 1986, among the old and well-established Protestant churches, the Presbyterians and Episcopalians lost more than one-fifth of their members and the Methodists and Lutherans more than one-tenth of theirs—losses that are proportionately larger when measured as a percentage of the expanding U.S. population. In a 1985 letter, a Membership Committee of United Methodist Bishops confessed, "We have not stopped the hemorrhaging of our membership. . . . Our troubles are systemic, and until we, as bishops of the church, become deadly serious about the well-being of the local church, all the reports, all the diagnostic articles, all the screams in the night will be to no avail."[17] Striking with generational abruptness, the exodus from the mainline churches has been led by educated young adults of the postwar generation who came of age and became unchurched beginning in the late 1960s. Meanwhile, theologically more conservative Protestant churches—notably evangelical, fundamentalist, and Pentecostal groups—expanded their membership by one-sixth or more, holding on to their postwar children and sustaining higher birth rates. Black Protestant churches and Roman Catholics have also grown by one-sixth in the same way. So the mainline churches have aged and lost more members than other denominations.[18]

Some observers have linked these dynamics of evangelical growth and mainline decline to the secularizing effects of higher education, which has grown enormously itself and has a greater impact on the mainline churches, since their members are usually more educated and of higher social status. Some saw the "cultural transformation" of the 1960s as similarly secularizing and selective in its impact. Increased college and graduate education, together with the outsized numbers and peculiar experience of the baby-boom cohort, created a cultural generation with weakened institutional loyalties to the mainline denominations *and* the major political parties. Educated, middle-class young adults who swelled the ranks of political "independents" (now 40 percent of the electorate) have also helped to triple the proportion of unchurched religious "independents" from 3 percent to roughly 10 percent of all adults while lowering levels of participation among nominal church members.[19] Taken together with the growing cultural centrality of Catholicism and the black churches, this adds up to a real loss of power among the old-line white Protestant institutions, say some critics, and they need "to ask what God is calling post-establishment churches to be about in a culture that no longer takes us as seriously as we take ourselves."[20]

One irony of playing the numbers game of proportionate growth and decline among different denominations is that it may ignore some larger truths. "Heartland" Protestants—Methodists, Lutherans, American Baptists, Disciples, and Reformed—still make up 24 percent of the American population. If one adds the more culturally elite Protestants—Congregationalists, Presbyterians, Episcopalians, and Unitarians—one comes to a total of 33 percent of the American population, more than twice the 15 percent of evangelical white Protestants (e.g., Southern Baptists and Pentecostals) and more than triple the 10 percent who are unchurched. Catholics meanwhile make up

26 percent of the population, having increased by about the same proportion, one-sixth, as Protestants have declined over the last thirty years. This growth can be accounted for by higher birthrates among Catholics; by immigration, especially from Latin America; and by the fact that defection rates are half those of mainline Protestant denominations.[21] Rising social status and cultural assimilation during this same period have brought Catholics closer to mainline Protestants in many respects: in their social attitudes, theological views, and political-party affiliations; in a somewhat lower birthrate (although still higher than Protestants); in their falling levels of church attendance, doctrinal orthodoxy, and doctrinal knowledge; and in new tensions. The desire among "Americanists" for greater freedom of conscience and belief than a strong doctrine of papal authority allows runs counter to calls from "traditionalists" for a reassertion of ex cathedra papal authority in faith and morals. And this conflict can be seen in issues from abortion, contraception, and divorce through women's ordination and clerical celibacy to liberationist political activism.

The crucial point in such trends is that the erosion of mainline religion's strength has been a matter more of ethos than of numbers. It remains numerically strong but with a growing consciousness of itself as a beleaguered cultural minority, caught between the widening freeways of the secular city and the rising bastions of the religious right, and divided from within by conflict between spirit-filled evangelicals and dispirited if still stubbornly principled liberals.

How does all this apply to the predicament of the public church experienced by liberal religious advocacy groups in Washington like the Ecumenical Alliance for Peace and Justice, which Methodist Mel Reese heads? "There's probably some truth to most of the big theories about the declining mainline, or the divided churches," he replies. "But I'm still not sure about what it all means, and what we should do to respond to it in any very practical way." Declining support for religious advocacy and action on behalf of social justice, economic equality, and the reduction of poverty is not simply a matter of smaller budgets and fewer members in the mainline denominations; and there is no problem of direct competition from evangelical para-church groups advocating causes like world evangelism and school prayer.[22] National surveys done during the 1980s show that mainline Protestants favor them little more than evangelical Protestants when they require increased government spending.[23]

Faced with this institutional problem, leaders of groups like Mel Reese's have mapped out strategies that include prudent efforts to broaden support from the denominations while seeking new sources of income from local churches, dioceses, foundations, and people who share their established policy goals for social welfare and economic justice. Prudence also recommends that close attention be paid to fitting the policy agendas of the para-church advocacy groups and the denominations' broad social commitments to the views of their members. Environmental issues, nuclear disarmament, a less aggressive foreign policy, direct relief aid, battling drugs, registering voters, and volunteerism are all worthy causes in their own right that enjoy strong support among liberal and moderate Protestants (who are, as we have said, predominantly members of the white middle and upper middle class) even as support for government intervention and social spending to help the poor and redistribute resources has ebbed. It is increasingly evident to church leaders, writes ecumenical activist Arthur Keys, that "we need to communicate in a way that encourages response and feedback. Local church members indicate they want the national bodies of the church to be active in public policy advocacy, but they want a style of advocacy that allows them also to be involved in the process so they can also take action as individuals."[24] One survey of Congregationalists' social concerns, for example, reported that they wanted greater communication with national church bodies.[25] If they are to be engaged with their own public without becoming driven as interest groups, the para-church advocacy groups must listen more closely to their local members and the people with whom they converse culturally beyond the pews. They need to talk with them more deeply and persuasively about the meaning of faith lived out in a good society. Plotting an astute organizational strategy is necessary, but it is no substitute for this conversation.

Mel Reese is troubled less by cultural conflicts between religious liberals and evangelicals than what seems to him a loss of vision and commitment to a good *society*, not just a strong local congregation or a caring local community. "Sure, I see a 'conservative backlash' in some of the big denominations," he acknowledges, "and I take it seriously." Nonetheless, he says, "I'm not so worried about fighting it out with the Evangelicals. I see a lot of them recognizing the positive role of the church in social action besides soup kitchens and shelters. They know about food stamps, too. They're for peace and civil rights. You can even hear that from top people in the Assemblies of God. You'd think they were Methodists," he laughs. "They're moving toward the center as they get smarter and better institutionalized."

Yet upward social mobility and cultural assimilation assisted by college education will not resolve the deeper problems Reese sees, since they are not simply a function of ideological differences grounded in class-bound social perceptions and interests. "There's a strong pull toward localism in all this. Maybe some of it *is* intended to tie down us loose cannons in Washington and keep us from veering to the left, but I think it runs deeper than that. Pulling back into the local church and prescribing 'community' for whatever ails us is giving up the hope that we really can make the whole society any better, any more just or caring."

Yet at the same time, American society, more complex and interconnected than ever, has problems that are nationwide, and so are the political and economic structures it has to address these problems. "We have a big state," says Reese, "but we don't have a big state church, and of course we don't want one. Still, I sometimes think we have the worst of both worlds: the churches are too decentralized and disorganized to make much of a dent in the state when it's set on its course, and we're so bureaucratized ourselves that it's hard for us to take strong stands or make big changes when we need to, like right now. Maybe we need a pope, you know, instead of a dozen general secretaries who can't even speak for their own boards and councils. It's as if Protestantism today has no leaders, almost by definition. The leaders it does have are all self-appointed, with this or that group behind them, maybe, but I don't see any Reinhold Niebuhrs out there among them." Faced with the choice between a pope of sorts and the "priesthood of all believers," Reese, like most American Protestants, would choose the latter principle, with the political ideal of participatory democracy it implies. He also appreciates the authority of "self-appointed leaders" such as Reinhold Niebuhr once was, which rests on the power of religious insight and moral persuasion instead of ecclesiastical or bureaucratic office. But what disturbs him is the absence of leaders with sufficient intrinsic moral authority to bring ideological factions and interest groups into coherent institutional action and debate.

Reese sees the localism that worries him as a reaction against the relationship that has developed between the mainline Protestant churches and the liberal democratic welfare state. "Gradually, over the nineteenth century, churches evolved denominational structures, with their mission societies and mission boards. Now it seems like we're losing the theological rationale for a church that goes beyond the local congregation. It's only grudgingly that people think about any larger church. Even in Methodism, people resent the apportionment [a levy apportioned to congregations and regional conferences], or they want to control it. Locally, the churches are very strong on providing food, health care, sheltering the homeless. But nationally they're not. It's an anomaly." Reese agrees that social class and economic inequality may have something to do with this, for a stress on localism weakens interest in the large issue of redistributing wealth at a time when economic inflation and recession make the middle class feel that "charity begins at home." Because their own slice of the pie has shrunk, middle-class people are less interested in cutting off a piece of it for have-nots across town or around the world.

The anomalous relationship between local churches and national denominations today, then, follows largely from the relationship between local communities and the national society that is favored in our present political discourse. It may also underscore the importance of religious and civic voluntarism in solving social problems, much as Presidents Reagan and Bush have pointed out.[26] Reese wonders whether it signals a failure on the part of the liberal welfare state and an error of the liberals within the churches in looking to the state for institutional answers to problems that were their own social responsibilities. Politically there are parallels between resentment of "big government" and resentment of "big religion," he notes, and movements favoring localism and decentralization have arisen in contemporary religion and politics alike. "We never learned how to deal with losing access to the White House," he says, "and not being able to get back in. And we never learned how to oppose Reagan. You may think it was a pipedream or actually terribly destructive, but at least Reagan did have a powerful vision—and we had no clear alternative."

Similar themes have been sounded throughout the mainline churches in recent years, notably in their ecumenical organizations. When Arie Brouwer, general secretary of the National Council of Churches, resigned under fire, he made an impassioned plea that the National Council recognize its failings instead of scapegoating his leadership. The beleaguered Brouwer recalled the Reagan years for "the devastation of those hardball politics practiced by a ruthless cabal who stripped this our native land of its capital, robbed our children of their inheritance, drove many thousands of people from their homes and crushed from them their hope . . . and yet, in the face of that terrible destruction, there were only a few lonely voices among the media and the politicians who did not bow their knees to the baals of photo opportunities, good stories, pork barrel contracts and other such false gods. And what of us? Sometimes we lifted our voices in protest and sometimes we marched in protest, and we did restrain a few demons. But mostly we shook our heads and wrung our hands."[27]

What, then, are the underlying reasons for the predicament of the public church in American religion today, and what is to be done about it? Reese reflects: "I think that the churches have lost their own sense of social mission, and it's hard to write a single prescription for the mainline churches to recover it. But at least we can be humble and realistic about what has happened. A bigger HEW Department is not the answer to all our problems, even if we could pay for it. We should be critical of the welfare state *as a system*—and I think we have been for the most part—just like all the churches, liberal and evangelical, should be critical of any given social and political system, in any given time. Because it's *not* the Kingdom of God. Political programs and policies don't add up to the holy commonwealth. The church's social role is not to design a perfect society. It's to make the existing society *more* Christian, whether the society's capitalist or socialist or whatever." Faithful Americans have to look at what the actual problems are in our society: jobs, schools, housing, health care. But, Reese stresses, "any programmatic agenda for national policy has to come out of a truly ecumenical theological vision, because it has to take care of the whole society, not only the members of one church or even all the churches put together."

This insight leads us from the realm of organizational strategies and structures to the moral and religious ideals that order institutions and define their ends.

III. THEOLOGY AND SOCIAL EXPERIENCE

What are the theological symptoms of the churches' loss of moral vision and sense of social mission? By way of response, a distinguished theologian recalls a recent visit he made to Washington to advise a group of church board members, agency staffers, and activists. "After I'd spent a while laying out lines of theological justification that bear on some of their major issues, one of the lobbyists raised his hand and asked, 'What's the point of this? We agree on the issues. The point now is to organize and get something done about them.' I turned to the director who had asked me down there, and said, 'I'm sorry if I'm wasting your time. Just say so, and I'll stop right now.' That's part of their problem, of course, particularly the poli-sci types. They're so theologically inarticulate that they can't persuade anybody in the churches who doesn't already agree with them, and even then they come across as political partisans, not as reflective Christians." And it is true that many advocates and activists cannot communicate to the faithful the truths and stories that inspire their efforts to "live out the gospel," or to argue the moral principles and imperatives that justify specific social actions. Perhaps in the process of learning the state's languages of legal rights, cost-benefit utilities, and justice as due process, they have forgotten the language of covenant and communion. In their preoccupation with developing the right strategy for dealing with the great society, they have allowed their unique endowment, their biblical and theological heritage, to suffer the same kind of erosion as our other fundamental resources. When they fail to cultivate that endowment, they live, like so many other sectors of our society, on borrowed time.

Situated within denominational bureaucracies or para-church offices structured very like state agencies or political lobbies, have these mainline church leaders lost the capacity to speak genuinely religious truth to modern political power? Do they merely echo the lawyers' and administrators' own secular ideas with less expertise and authority? "I have a personal concern that theology and practice come together in what we do and say in public dialogue," Mel Reese replies. "But the reality is that we don't think first 'theology,' then 'church mission,' then 'practical problem and solution,' then back to 'theological reflection.' I don't know who does. I hear preachers talk like that sometimes in the pulpit, but people in the pews don't think that way. They don't live that way. Most people in the mainline churches are theologically illiterate, but they're not morally bankrupt. They're morally rich. They're there in church because of some value base, some goodness in them. They don't get paid or forced to go to church. It's not a ticket to social advantage or respectability anymore, outside the South anyway. You don't go to church to make powerful friends or find somebody to marry."

If all this is true, then mainline Protestant theology fails to map a course for socially concerned Christians, to move them to follow it, and to guide them along it because it fails to ring true to their actual experience of social life. How has this faltering occurred? "What's wrong with mainline religion is not any lack of systematic theology," Reese argues. "There's plenty of that. It's that the theology has to come out of the life experience of the people and connect with what they go through in the world—and it doesn't. Professional theologians and intellectuals write books nobody can understand. That means politicians, policy practitioners, and ordinary people, too, are free to ignore the church's official message. They're entitled to." Reese believes that "the church has to be an actor on social issues *in order to educate*. Our approach to particular issues is to try to ask where the justice of it lies, which position on it makes for a more just society."

But if justice is the first virtue of our social institutions, we need to know what it means in practice and in the structural arrangement of institutions and relationships. We might wonder, too, if justice possesses peculiarly religious forms and reasons. Does religion have contributions to make to legal and political thought, let alone social action? "Justice means taking care of one another," answers Reese. "Parents need to care for their children, and people need to work to support themselves and take care of the community. The community needs to enable people to work and care for one another, to enter in and have a voice in public. It needs to care for the poor." American churches draw mainly on biblical sources for this vision of a just society defined by mutual care and responsibility, not simply by individual rights, fair contracts, and due process of law. For many church activists this vision is clearest in the prophetic literature of the Old Testament and in the Gospels' Great Commandments to love God and neighbor. "People in the churches can see how the parts of the society are accountable to one another, especially for bringing in the poor and the weak to be full partners," says Reese. "Look at Isaiah: seek justice, end oppression; defend the fatherless, plead for the widow. You find a society being measured in God's eyes by the justice and care it gives the homeless, the sick, the powerless and uneducated. You see God most active when things are most critical, on behalf of those who have the least. People have a sense of justice that is religiously inspired: God made us all, and we should love our neighbor and give our earthly treasure to help each other."

But this biblical vision does not alone define our practical sense of justice. That is also conditioned by our pragmatic "experience of how laws and power and money actually work out there in the world, and the ethics we think will work in relation to them," Reese observes. "You can stand against the tide of realpolitik, but you can't ignore its force. On the other side of the coin, when a society loses its way, realpolitik can't tell it which way to turn. It doesn't know anything about good ends or the right direction to go. That's where the public church has to step forward."

Does it step forward? Asked to diagnose the difficulties in doing so, Reese offers the example of recent efforts on behalf of reform in the Aid to Families with Dependent Children welfare programs, beginning with an attempt to say what is so profoundly wrong for Christians about the poverty of children in a society like ours. "We went in with Interfaith Action for Economic Justice and some other ecumenical and denominational agencies to put together a teaching document. We began with children becoming the poorest age group in the society just since 1974, especially since 1979, because of welfare cuts to families while Social Security went up with the cost of living and inflation went through the roof.[28] We didn't start with 'Covenant,' not because we're against it, but because we couldn't have started there. It had no context. We worked on that study for ten months. We struggled with it," Reese recalls. The working group finally consulted with an Old Testament professor. She helped them define how children are part of creation in a way they could grasp. Children are God's gift to a people, which they must "care for to carry out the Covenant of trust between them and God."

The finished document begins:

> Among God's promises to us was a promise of children—a promise of generations to inhabit and care for the earth. The promise was given at the time of creation and was repeated to Abraham and others through the Hebrew and Christian Scriptures. In making this promise, the Lord offered the gift of hope. . . .
>
> Children occupy central roles throughout the Scriptures. They are often described as one of the most important gifts that God can offer, or that a nation can offer to God. When God gave the *Torah* to Moses, for example, it was in exchange for a promise from the people of Israel that they would teach it faithfully to their children through the generations. . . . The innocence and vulnerability of children are recognized, as in the stories of Ishmael and Isaac, the story of Moses, the teachings of the Proverbs, and, in the Gospels, the stories of the little children following Jesus.
>
> Children are our gift of hope for a future time when our broken and injured world is healed and our relationship with God becomes whole and just. How do we nurture our children? What gifts do we give to them to enable them to survive in wholeness and justice?[29]

Several hundred thousand copies of this document went out to government officials and lawmakers, the mass media, and thousands of local churches. "That's a great example of how we communicate with our constituents, through denominational boards and agencies that run down through regional districts or dioceses to local churches and ecumenical groups," Reese explains. He adds that religious mobilization of broad popular support for this issue across class and race lines bolstered bipartisan legislative support for family welfare reform, which is particularly vital for black and Hispanic children and for women heading families.

Such examples of biblical insight into public issues, charging them with a sense of moral gravity and urgency, are immensely significant in themselves. But they are also significant by contrast with other cases of mainline church advocacy that were more remarkable for their partisan appeals or their naive confidence in technical, legal, or administrative solutions to the deep institutional and moral dilemmas. "Okay, maybe we're partly to blame there," admits Reese. "There's an ecumenical fear of talking too much about theology because it can be divisive or diversionary, and you wind up getting stymied or watering down your position on the issues, although in principle we can all agree that we need to know what divides the churches in order to unite them." Faced with the theologian's complaint about theologically inarticulate and impatient "poli-sci types" acting as religious lobbyists, Reese hesitates. "Maybe some of our problems with theology say as much about us as the world. There are only a few hundred professional staff persons working with the churches on public policy. Most of them didn't go to seminary, and almost none of those who did preach regularly or serve a church. Less than one in ten of our staff are ministers. They're personally religious, but they're politically oriented. The primary question for us is 'What are your political skills? What are your organizational skills? What can you *do*?' The people who do more, who are more effective, are considered better."

Asked how the churches should justify and inspire religious social action today, Reese throws up his hands and asks, in effect, for a division of ecclesiastical labor. "We can't do everything. We can't even try. Most of what you're asking about probably has to go on in the local churches, or it doesn't go on at all. As far as the local churches go, all I can say is that we need to appreciate the commitment that goes into soup kitchens, night shelters, and every other kind of local self-help. The same goes for things like Habitat for Humanity, outside local churches but with a local focus. That's all good in itself. Get people involved and working in the soup kitchen on Saturday. Give them a chance to see that the problems of food, shelter, and jobs are bigger than local churches can handle. So they need to support national advocacy, too. Habitat spends one hundred thousand dollars and builds houses for five or ten families. Spend that much to change HUD regulations, clean up HUD, fund it adequately, and you could house five thousand or five million families. You have to bring in the state." Reese pauses, then shakes his head. "As to how the churches can make for the kind of people who care enough about their hungry, homeless neighbors to do any of this in the first place—that's another matter."

Denominational offices, boards, agencies, and advocacy groups have been criticized more and more by their own church members and pastors, and notably by evangelicals, for ignoring their own church congregations, which do the job of nurturing good Christians and citizens. In turn, denominational leaders and activists like Reese have asked parish leaders and members to educate themselves, mobilize, and contribute financially to support the social efforts of the public church. What else can congregations do—and be—to make the national and global institutions of the public church not simply more effective but more faithful in living out their professed love of God and neighbor? "That's hard for me to say," Reese confesses, "in part because my generation, educated liberals in their forties, is gone from the churches I know best. They are not mad at the church, like some of my ex-Catholic friends. They're just gone, even though the liberal churches are the ones closest to us politically, culturally. Even for me, I'm not as active in a congregation as I used to be, as I would have been a generation ago. I don't find it as interesting or meaty, and I don't know exactly why." Others believe they do know why. We need to heed their voices, raised from other institutional and moral vantage points within the church.

IV. LOCAL CHURCH, BIG CHURCH

Evangelically oriented pastors in the mainline denominations often experience the sense of an eroded ethos, but they hold a different view of its causes and cure than do denominational leaders or para-church activists like Mel Reese. One such pastor, Robert Cooper, is remarkable for being deeply concerned about his denomination's declines and struggles yet largely unscarred by them. He heads one of the largest, fastest-growing Methodist congregations in the urban South. By turns folksy, funny, and dead serious, he can be disarmingly self-deprecating yet rock solid in testifying to his faith in the church he serves. "I've always been a local-church person," he explains. "I've never been primarily concerned with the denomination. I'm a narrow person, I suppose, and that's probably just as well. If I were elected pope of the Methodist Church, I'd kick butt. I'd clean house," he laughs. "But I do believe the denomination, like the local church, is actually the Body of Christ, just like Paul tells us. So it's a good thing we got liberals, because the body needs different members to be whole. They're a healthy irritant in my spirit and in my mind, just as I hope I am for them. I believe they are as sincere as I am, and they love God as much as I do. My main concern about the United Methodist Church and the other mainline denominations is not that they are in error or heresy, but that their priorities are wrong. We're straining at gnats and swallowing camels."

The churches should speak about political issues, a man like Cooper believes, because "Jesus is Lord of the whole of our lives" and politics is part of life. But the church doesn't begin and end with liberation theology or feminism or even civil rights; and resolution of such issues does not "bring the Kingdom of God any closer." Congregations are the center of the church; they are a practicing community of worship which shapes and saves souls, says Cooper, and denominational structures should serve them, not dominate them. "The denomination needs to debate ministers' pensions and boycotting Shell Oil, and that's what our General Conference and boards spend a lot of their time doing. But the central issues in Christ's church are, first of all, *worship*, praising God and joining together in God's love; second, *evangelism*, winning people to Jesus Christ, our Savior, in a personal relationship; third, having won them, *discipling* them in the faith, so they won't remain baby Christians, so they can grow in their understanding and give witness in the way they live their lives; and then, having been discipled, they become *apostles* and put into practice Christ's word and love in their home, in their neighborhood, in their job and school."

With this vision of the life of the church as expressed primarily in congregational worship, evangelism, and the pastoral care of souls shaping moral character, Cooper disagrees with liberal church leaders and scholars who explain mainline membership losses as due to the secularizing effects of higher education or the cultural transformations of the 1960s. "Even if all that were to be true," he asks, pragmatically as well as pastorally, "what could the church do about it?" Instead he stresses the weakened patterns of evangelism and formative "discipling" within the mainline churches in the postwar era. "Instead of repentance and raising up Christians through prayer meetings and Bible study in rooted churches, 'visitation evangelism' came in. You went around and rang doorbells and talked to people about their neighbors who attended, the music, and all the programs the church had for the children, the Sunday school, the sports teams. The idea used to be 'Get 'em involved,' " Cooper explains. "If we can get them involved in local church organizations, we won't lose them. Well, we raised a generation on that idea, and we did lose them, a lot of them. 'Get 'em in a choir, get 'em in a Sunday school class, get 'em on a committee.' There's some truth to that, but if that's all you do, it's like planting on fallow ground. They flourish for a time, but they don't endure." He nods. "I believe mainline church people today can look back and see we made a mistake with that approach. . . . The buzzword today is 'spiritual formation.' You hear that all over the Methodist Church: 'Let's get people studying the Bible on their own, praying with a small group, really being open in the body of the local church.' But very few churches are *doing* the work of evangelism. Why? Because it's hard work. It's confrontational and it's relational, and sometimes it cuts deep enough to hurt."

Evangelical weakness of will stems from roots deeper than simple laziness or love of leisure. Pastor Cooper sees its deeper causes evident in the reasons that impel those who leave churches like his. "It's not so much political or even theological as it is the *practice* of worship, and whether the living word of our authority in the Bible is dead or alive in church life." Like other Bible Belt pastors in the moderate denominations with congregations that span the broad middle class, Cooper's church loses more members switching "downward" to more emphatically evangelical "Word" churches than "upward" to more liberal churches or "outward" to the ranks of the unchurched.[30] He acknowledges that issues of demographics, social class, and regional culture are at play in these patterns of defection. But he stresses that he finds what people do and believe in the mainline churches wanting by comparison with their more evangelical counterparts. "For one thing, there's a lot of Bible authority in the pastors, plus a lot of 'praise,' a lot of joy and movement in the worship experience. The people we lose are good people—Sunday school teachers, tithers, committed workers. They come to me and say, 'We love you, we believe you love the Lord and you preach the Bible, but this worship service is so structured, it's so rigid and heavy!' Yet we work at it! We've probably got the lowest low-church worship service of any Methodist church in the greater metropolitan area. But that's their complaint. They don't leave because they're mad at some liberal de-nominational board or agency they hear about. Oh, occasionally, they may call me up and say, 'Do we give money to them?' and I'll say, 'Yeah,' and they'll say, 'I can't believe it, I can't believe it—I'm gonna quit giving money.' And I say, 'Well, I'm sorry about that. You know, that's just something where you're in a big denomination, you're gonna have some of that.' "

Whereas a liberal church activist like Mel Reese refers to the prophet Isaiah to underscore the Bible's injunctions for judging the justice of a social order and assessing public policy, Robert Cooper stresses the Bible's authority that flows from its pastoral power to touch people's everyday lives, pierce their pain, and shape their self-understanding, moods, and motives. "Most of our people don't want a pastor telling them what to do, but you can't just do without authority, either. I believe the church has weakened the bedrock of our authority in its approach to the Scriptures. We have met the enemy and it is us. The 'higher criticism' has missed the real issue. Who cares who wrote the Book of Hebrews? The real question is, 'What is the Book of Hebrews saying that actually makes a difference in my life, that's gonna help me in my marriage, that's gonna help me when I find out my sixteen-year-old daughter is doing drugs, when I find out that my company has just been bought out and the job I've had for twenty-five years has just been terminated?' Then who cares who wrote Hebrews? Nobody, that's who." He pauses for emphasis. "What matters is what Jesus Christ says—'I will never fail you or forsake you.' He died for us, outside the gates of the city, so we can bear our burden and follow him. 'For here we have no lasting city, but we seek the city which is to come' [Hebrews 13:5,15]."

By contrast to Pentecostals or fundamentalists, the mainline churches need "a balanced, biblical theology, not just emotions or authoritarianism," Cooper proposes. "John Wesley knew that. We try here to be very intentionally Bible-based." Some three out of four worshippers bring their Bibles to his church every Sunday, and Cooper asks them to refer to them several times during his sermon. "This Sunday I'm preaching on Jesus' words 'I thirst,' so I'll have them read John, then look back there to Psalm 69 and see that, and then Psalm 53. I want them to write and underline in their Bibles, then maybe at home they will read their Bibles and it will touch them: 'What shames us? What is it our souls thirst for? What does Jesus suffering share with us?' "

Since the 1960s analysts have depicted "a gathering storm in the churches" raging between "a new breed" of liberal activist clergy urging civil rights marches, anti-Vietnam sit-ins, and grape boycotts, and a more conservative laity. As was later acknowledged, the controversy did not rage between clergy and laity but between a coalition of college-educated laity and clergy supporting these causes, and less educated, often older lay people with more conservative political and cultural views.[31] Like many other evangelicals in the mainline churches, Pastor Cooper has gradually shifted his views on these conflicts over the past two decades, seeing them less as a battle waged between activist cosmopolitan elites and conservative locals and more as evidence of a gap between the national denomination itself and its local congregations. "I used to think the national boards and agencies were full of subversives. By now I've heard them enough to know they have a mentality which is very much like mine. They believe they must be right, and everybody else must be wrong. What the church really needs to be doing is getting the President and Congress straightened out. As long as we country-cousin, local-church folk pay our Conference askings [i.e., apportionment], that's all that matters, so they can keep doing the real work out there on the cutting edge. I doubt most Methodists think they *are* doing the real work of the church." Yet for the most part Methodist boards and agencies carry out the dictates of the denomination's General Conference. The trouble is, Cooper contends, that the General Conference is out of touch with the local churches and is unwilling to have a genuine dialogue about the moral issues that divide its congregants so deeply. "Most Methodists *could* be wrong," Cooper allows. "We don't run the church by majority rule, and we shouldn't. The world doesn't set the agenda for the church. God does, although God does it in the world."

All churches must take account of "the worldly wisdom" of the law, the market, and the social facts of contemporary life in their social ethics. Yet they must take their moral stands in forms that keep their conscience true to their traditions and scriptures even when they run counter to secular principles and rules. On abortion, for example, Cooper agrees with the Methodists' carefully measured acceptance of a woman choosing abortion as "the lesser of two evils."[32] But the church should spell out more clearly that abortion is essentially "a moral tragedy, not a moral right," he adds. "So many times we talk about our rights. I find that in the Constitution, but I can't find that in the Scriptures. I can't find that I have a right to my own body. I'm ready to be shown it if it's there, but what I find there is that my body belongs to God. It's a gift of grace; it's the temple of the Holy Spirit."

Neither historicist nor fundamentalist interpretations of the Bible will suffice to settle moral and political controversy over specific social issues, Pastor Cooper acknowledges, and majority rule will not suffice to order the church's polity. Instead, he comes back to the primacy of the Gospels' commandments to love God and neighbor and the primacy of the "Great Commission" to "make disciples of all nations" within the Church as Paul defined it: the body of Christ (Matthew 22:37–40; 28:19–20). "We can have some ideal that's not God-given," he concedes. "Then we find scriptures to back it. That's why loving God and your neighbor have to come first. If a person really has Jesus living in their life, and they are in a Christian fellowship growing in the Scriptures and learning what He is talking about; then eventually they are going to worry and be concerned about homeless people, pregnant teenagers, people who are addicted, people in minorities being persecuted and denied—women, blacks, poor people in the rest of the world. If Jesus is really in their life, and they read in there that God is no respecter of persons, that Jesus died for everybody, it's going to come out socially. Saving souls is not the whole gospel. That's just getting born." In short, the gospel and its ideal of a life worth living is contained in the injunction, "Love thy neighbor as thyself."

V. A CAUCUS CHURCH

Mainline Protestant leaders commonly describe conflicts in their churches as between "pastoral" and "prophetic" ideals of ministry. "Not being 'prophetic' enough isn't my problem," objects Robert Cooper. "It's having to be too much of a manager and getting distracted from the whole picture by all the administrative details. I think that's probably true for the denomination's would-be prophets, too. Frankly, they look more like managers to me. That relates to how they handle conflict, by playing with the rules and procedures instead of hearing what Jesus said to do when you are in conflict—you go to each other. Possibly you can do that in a local church in a way you can't in the denomination. Maybe that's just a fact of life. But I think we're giving up something if we try to take the church back from the lay people in the congregation."

The idea of a church as a congregational body bound in communion and conversation by an all-reconciling love goes back to the beginnings of Christian history. And pastoral concerns and institutional priorities such as Robert Cooper's reach back more than a century in the history of Protestantism in America. His populist claims have a place in the rhetoric of some evangelicals who call themselves members of a "moral majority." But lower-middle-class members of the mainline churches have also tended to be theologically conservative. Because they lacked education, however, they long had difficulty in articulating a response to the modernist theology and liberal cultural views of the educated upper-middle-class clergy and laity who have led these churches. But in the postwar era, expanding educational opportunities have dramatically raised the educational level of these traditionally conservative mainline Protestants and enabled them to gain a voice as considerable as that of their more liberal brothers and sisters.

One observer of these new trends, a thoughtful Methodist Church leader and theologian now in his sixties, Gene Sansom, offers his own picture of the cultural divisions within the mainline denominations.

They have led to what he calls "a caucus church." Soft-spoken and sympathetic, Sansom agrees that many, if not most, of the members of large moderate denominations like the Methodists have been more "evangelically oriented" than their denomination's leaders and intellectuals—that is, they have been more "orthodox" in their beliefs and more "devotional" in their religious practices and attitudes. "For them the church is the local church. It's about the family and home life more than the society at large or the government." He confirms Cooper's sense of the nonpolitical reasons for leaving the church: "If our churches have lost people over the past generation, it's not been because of politics. People have been disappointed that the church wasn't going along with whatever their particular political concerns were, but they didn't leave because of that. I suspect the reasons lie more in what people experience in their local churches, and what our theology means or fails to mean, in the middle of the culture we breathe like the air around us. During the 1960s and 1970s people in the mainline churches heard a good deal of theology urging them to get out of the pews and into the city.[33] That is not an easy call for most people to heed for very long. The congregation *is* the center of the church. If people are not nurtured and uplifted by it, there's not much out there in most churches to take its place. A few may get deeply involved in some special agency or cause—for example, the homeless— but that's a small minority."

No simple waning of evangelical fervor accounts for mainline church declines in Sansom's view. Rather, he thinks a growing "theological pluralism" began to spread in tandem, if not quite in step, with the beat of popular cultural changes, with mixed results for church morale and authority. "During the 1960s, 'death of God' theology and the like played a part in alienating more conservative biblical and evangelical Christians from the church leaders they heard actually apologizing for the blasphemers and trying to 'explain' what they meant. As a result, people just threw up their hands and decided the church leadership didn't know what it was talking about. It had lost hold of the reins. For some of them, that feeling has just grown stronger with the rise of black theology, feminism, liberation theology. Each of these voices is genuinely biblical and contributes something important to the church, I believe, but I don't know that we mainline theologians have done a very good job of making clear what that is or why it is."

In an effort to be more democratic and take account of "all the different voices" in each denomination, church leaders have presided over what Sansom calls a "deconfessionalizing" of what has become "essentially a caucus church," says Sansom. Deconfessionalizing means essentially a decline in doctrinal religious education in the churches, a de-emphasis on the central confessional beliefs.

In order to understand Methodism's central confessional beliefs we should consider its origin as an eighteenth-century revival movement in the Church of England. It aimed "to reform the nation, particularly the Church, and to spread scriptural holiness over the land," wrote its founder, John Wesley, an Oxford-educated Anglican clergyman whose heart was "strangely warmed" at a prayer meeting in Aldersgate Street, London, in 1738.[34] Methodism emphasized faith in God's grace, freely offered to all and equal to every human need. It fostered a morally rigorous ideal of "Christianity in earnest" in the practical discipline of devotional piety, evangelical preaching, and communal discipleship in flexibly organized yet strictly governed "societies" led by lay preachers. Methodists gathered weekly to nurture and strengthen each other by testimony, admonition, study, and prayer. By the late nineteenth century American Methodism grew more eclectic in outlook, even as a continuing stress on free will, infant baptism, and informal worship marked off Methodists from Presbyterians, Baptists, and Episcopalians, respectively. From the beginning of the twentieth century, a history of social benevolence, coupled with the waning force of Wesleyan doctrinal discipline, made Methodism fertile ground for modernist theologies and a Social Gospel calling for sweeping social reform. Since the 1960s some Methodist leaders have grown relatively receptive to liberationist, feminist, and black theologies. Currently the denomination is experiencing a reaffirmation of evangelical piety and a resurgence of concern for Wesleyan thought and classical Reformation theology in an effort to reassert its confessional heritage.

In the caucus churches of the mainline, says Sansom, "almost every cause and group has a voice now," and almost every view is represented by an interest group. Ever since the 1972 "Faith Statement" in United Methodism, for example, there has been an emphasis on "pluralism," on the pluralist church being an umbrella big enough to include evangelicals along with liberationists and feminists,[35] all these positions being "options in the belief that it takes all kinds of Christians to serve the Lord." In practice, however, Sansom observes, the principle of "one person, one vote in a big mainline denomination like Methodism means the will of the great middle class, whereas the denomination's formal organization since 1968 [has required that] you must have minority members and groups represented on every committee and commission: one black, one ethnic, at least one woman, one youth, and so on." As a result, minority representation in United Methodist church government is much higher than in the membership in general, which comes to less than 10 percent for blacks, for example. "That makes for resentment on the part of 'the silent majority,' " notes Sansom. "They feel special interests are using the church for their own ends and dragging them along in the process." Like many responsibly reformist yet moderate church leaders of his generation, Sansom is now dismayed by "orthodox reaction or rigidity that has set in to close off new possibilities for dialogue and rapprochement between the church and the modern world." But he also criticizes the debilitating effects of "a pluralism that has no center, in which there's no clear, common commitment to what unites us as a body."

Two related prospects seem likely from Sansom's standpoint. "Institutionally we seem to be moving toward more of a confederation model within our denomination[36] and across the Protestant churches generally," he observes. "Different groups with their own identities will sit down together in mutual recognition. They'll dialogue and cooperate as closely as they can, without denying the differences that continue to separate them. We'll continue to pay careful attention to democratic representation for different groups, especially minorities. We'll keep relying on constitutional sorts of rights to protect them from the tyranny of the majority."

At the same time, he thinks, "losing our easy association as mainly male, middle-aged members of the WASP middle class presents itself as an opportunity to rediscover what holds us together as a church that's not defined or limited by a dominant class or race. It can lead us back to our own denominational roots." Greater social diversity within each denomination mandates the effort to recover denominational doctrines, practices, and polity and to redefine them in forms fitted to the present moment. Sansom sees hope for the prospects. In Methodism twenty years ago, he recalls, "you couldn't get anyone to talk about Wesley. He'd been done in by theologians as diverse as Karl Barth and Dietrich Bonhoeffer as just a pietist sentimentalist who began and ended with the warmed heart. Today there's much greater recognition that Wesley understood that salvation and human destiny require the transformation of persons to overcome the effects of original sin, almost on the model of the Eastern Fathers; and that salvation requires social sanctification as well, in order to return us to the purposes for which we were created."

Within the confessional tradition of Methodism, then, grounds exist for embracing an evangelical emphasis on personal salvation through the spirit of Christ's love for every human being, while heeding no less strongly the imperatives of social Christianity to make the world a better place. "Christianity 'is essentially a social religion; and . . . to turn it into a solitary one is to destroy it,' " Sansom quotes John Wesley. "You must have a community for Christians to help one another to be recreated in God's image. That's what Methodist revivals, preaching, class meetings, and societies were all about. We don't live in the dark in our own little closets, communing with God and reading our Bibles alone. Like the Gospels' charge to be the salt of the earth and a light unto the world, God has put us here to touch others and heal society," Sansom concludes. "Think of H. Richard Niebuhr's ideal of 'Christ transforming society'[37]—not following it or standing against it or above it all. That has been a Wesleyan ideal ever since the beginning."

VI. A CHURCH RENEWED OR TRANSFORMED?

To the generation of church leaders, scholars, and teachers who came of age in the 1960s, the ideal of a transformative Christ applies as much to the church itself as to the larger society and culture. What is wrong with the mainline churches, in a nutshell, is that "they give out the worst schlock in the culture," charges Mary Hatch, a distinguished young theologian and outspoken churchwoman. "The preaching and teaching people actually get in the churches simply reify what people get from the newspaper and television. They tell people that what it means to be a good human being, a good Christian is to fit in as best they can, to put up with painful marriages and pointless work. Deal with the wasteful, unjust forms our society takes by writing a check or going downtown to an inner-city church twice a year and handing out baloney sandwiches or Christmas baskets." Most mainline churches bore their members, in short. They stifle their imagination and pacify their emotions in a surprising, unsettling world full of brokenness and joy, according to Mary Hatch, though the true church has a tradition to draw on and rework that is critical and pluralistic enough to wake us up to reality.

How did the mainline churches get into this fix? From the standpoint of Hatch's radical cultural critique, the answers lie deeper than membership losses, mergers, and political controversy. "A lot of it stems from assigning religion to the private realm," responds Mary Hatch, "along with art, sexuality, and every kind of moral feeling that can't be reduced to a rule or law. All of that gets made into the feminine realm, with secondary status because it's not 'real knowledge.' Real knowledge rests on facts, not feelings. It's scientific. It's public because it's 'objective data,' which yields real power to control things." This privatization and feminization skews the cultural constitution of American religion in the modern social world. "When modern Christianity decided that it couldn't say anything true in substance about the public or political world, it turned inward," Hatch goes on. Religion then becomes either deeply interior, precognitive and prelinguistic, or totally transcendent and "other." "In a way, once you make that move, you don't really need a church," says Hatch. "You find a church to go to in order to express yourself and find like-minded others. But the church doesn't incarnate religion. It's not really 'the Body of Christ,' nor is it part of the public world."

In quite distinct terms Hatch develops themes Pastor Cooper began and Dr. Sansom summed up under the rubric of "the caucus church." Factionalized interest groups within and around the mainline churches are "not the fault of women and blacks. They're the fault of the consensus model of democratic politics, [lacking] a normative culture of community to embrace genuinely different persons and groups in their differences. Once you lose that—skeptics say we never had it in America—and you have democratic principles, of course you're going to have caucus group politics. Because there has been real political progress in America for 'different' persons like women and blacks, and now it's harder to exclude them, even in the evangelical churches. No matter how much money and time and energy we spend trying, we're going to find out caucus group politics don't work in the churches." In this light the problems of mainline membership losses and the factional politics of the caucus church of national denominations are dual symptoms of a deeper loss of the church's own integrity as a moral community that 'conscientizes' its members' subjectivity and confronts the world with unconventional moral responsibilities.[38]

Although Mary Hatch describes the process of transforming the mainline churches in more radically open-ended and less doctrinal terms than Gene Sansom or Robert Cooper used to urge their revival, they all agree on key points. What ought the American churches to look like? Replies Hatch, "I guess if I had my way they would look more like—God, I hate to say this!—more like Wesley's cells! And more like basic Christian communities on the liberation model."[39] She believes the church should give more emphasis to forming and nurturing community, so that its members discover how to live together in a diverse, pluralistic world without being so determined by our sex, color, or class. "That means less emphasis on getting eight hundred people into a big hall for an hour or so one morning a week. It means searching for more compelling, complicating, intense ways to bring people together to know themselves through one another." The church ought to form its worship and liturgy around "waking people up and getting them moving in the spirit instead of putting them to sleep with a thirty-minute lecture. There the black church is our single best model, because it stirs the imagination aesthetically, and it moves the emotions in profoundly moral, joyous ways." Obviously there are many models of community, worship, and learning that churches can test and work with, each of them calling for critical change in self-understanding under new historical, social, and cultural conditions. "Look at the basic Christian communities in Latin America," Hatch proposes. "Look at the Alcoholics Anonymous model, which is closer to home. It's very good at breaking through psychological 'denial,' which is a massive problem in our society, even if AA doesn't say much about how to live constructively as a community, which the BCC [basic Christian community] model does, although in a very different kind of society from ours."

Cooper's language of evangelical revival and Sansom's rhetoric of reappropriation lead, in Hatch's voice, to a rhetoric of bold cultural experiment and subtle "blending" that rise phoenixlike from the critical fire of a "hermeneutic of suspicion."[40] Says Hatch, "We can try things out. You get people together in an adult education group in a local church or a seminary class, and you begin to go around the group, naming one's oppression, naming what one is suffering or struggling with. Students will talk about being the son of an alcoholic parent, about coming from a very poor, working-class family and being the first one to have gone to college and made it and thus belonging to neither world; or a woman will talk about being divorced, or returning to school in midlife and finding she and her husband don't know how to live inside their marriage anymore, being equalized yet not equal. Then you read some Scripture together, and talk about what that means in their situation; and they explore that together and look for the common ground of meaning that they share. That's a kind of 'basic Christian community' model."

Public confession and Bible study, seminar and psychodrama, moral conversation and social analysis: the intertwining of biblical, personal, and social texts offers a taste of religious community that is at once pastoral, prophetic, and sacramental. "It's shared confession, if you will, but also narrative ethics in the sense that one puts oneself in a broader context and comes to see how one is caught in a web that binds us all.[41] It names sin institutionally as well as personally, so we can resolve to change institutions and not just say, 'I'm guilty, forgive me, and next time I'll try to do a little better.' " Thus each person's story is part of "our story" told within a community. It is also a story of the social world we share, and the social institutions, relations, and practices that enable or frustrate our flourishing.

In this process of communal re-creation through public worship, prayer, confession, and storytelling, the Bible has a practical function closer to Pastor Cooper's evangelical inspiration than to Mel Reese's prophetic benchmark for a just society. Hatch offers an interpretation of the Bible's meaning enmeshed within the web of history and culture, not just Cooper's vision of "our bedrock." Yet she seeks to do so without diminishing its centrality or relativizing its moral authority for Christians. "The Bible is the collection of texts that Jews and Christians have used through history to make meaning. It's a working document. The texts don't create our world. But Christians in every age use it, together with the rest of their culture, to create images and discourses to know the world and act in it.

"So *use the Bible as a working document*. We can do that, too, because of the incredible pluralism within the Bible. Because there is no one meaning to the Bible, thank God. It is a rich text, like the Catholic theologian David Tracy says, full of the *different* stories that are the classics of our tradition.[42] On Sunday morning, then, don't just stand up and read it in a monotone. Sing it, chant it, act it out in a play. Go and find out what they do with it in a black Baptist church, or a Pentecostal church where you can feel the spirit moving, even if you don't agree with their theology. There's no reason we can't do that, and do it with a renewed Social Gospel flair." This stance does not really differ from the biblicism of an evangelical or fundamentalist, Hatch believes, so long as "they recognize that the Bible is just a book until it is infused with the Holy Spirit in a worshipping community," a view she argues is the theological truth of the Christian tradition, not a modern relativist one: "Augustine said it, Luther said it, Calvin said it. Unfortunately, not enough Christians say it today."

Calls for sweeping cultural and institutional transformation have to find support within the existing social and moral order, says Hatch; otherwise its advocates become utopian dreamers or "prisoners in the iron cage of a world where everything's wrong and there is nothing we can do about it." She sees the Social Gospel as a broad, uniquely American movement that included the "Christian realism" of the Niebuhrs and has been inherited by feminist and liberationist theology; she emphasizes the dialectically critical and syncretistic character of social Christianity.[43] It uses American democratic norms and prophetic Christian ideals to criticize both society and the church, including the undemocratic aspects of America's political economy and the privatism of bourgeois Christianity. Thus, for example, feminism has used democratic equal-rights ideas to criticize the male hierarchy in the churches, and now it is using Christian ideas of community and relational love to criticize the limited idea that simply gaining more rights and professional jobs for women will create a just society or a true church.

The American Social Gospel tradition as narrowly conceived was limited because it never figured out how to transform the inner self. It was basically aimed at institutional change. "It didn't hook up the powerful relationship between how institutions are formed, and how that forms our understanding and feelings," Hatch says. That is the particular contribution that black theology and feminist theology can make to social Christianity in America, because "blacks and women have to face that question in order to know themselves as fully human in a society whose structuring makes them feel incomplete." Knowing who we are as human beings internally, individually, is not somehow given to us a priori. It is constituted in history and through our experience of social life, not before it. Our individuality expresses the norms and metaphors of the society we live in, not only its structures. "Sexism and racism spring as much from the images and discourses we learn as children as they are imposed on us by biased laws or job discrimination. Feminism and black theology allow our eyes to see how that reality can be."

This vision of culture and community promises the church an institutional role of its own instead of asking it to imitate in vain the welfare state, the hospital, or the social club. "To name sin and announce grace is the mission of the church," Hatch declares. "It's very traditional, and it seems simple to say. But the mainline churches have done a lousy job in naming the suffering of middle-class existence in our time. We haven't told the truth about it. That's the church's greatest sin—not saying that the competitive, driven existence that divides what it is to be a man or woman, a white or black, is a form of human suffering. It narrows and binds the human spirit." The church's greatest challenge in America is "to enable middle-class folks to recognize that their nice consumerist existence is killing *them*, plus killing the Third World. We don't really have much of a commitment to the Third World, so those appeals for charity and inducements to guilt don't have much effect. What we do have is a fierce commitment to our own existence. If we see that our own existence is in danger, and in fact it is not good, even for us, then maybe we'll be moved to act."

Consumerism, in Hatch's view, denies the needs of the poor in the name of our own anxious desire. But, most of all, "consumerism kills the soul, as any good Augustinian can see, because it places things before the valuing of God and human community." It deadens our consciousness and thickens our senses. Drug and alcohol addiction are leading symptoms of this. The evangelicals cry out about this, but what do the mainline churches have to say? Almost nothing. "Why?" asks Hatch. "Because we have defined religion as a deeply interior or otherworldly reality prior to any kind of life practice. Once you do that, how you actually live every day doesn't affect it one way or the other."

Americans are facing a worldwide crisis about how we as persons and nations get and spend, how we divide up the spoils and dump the waste, how we bear arms and threaten to use them. "At the risk of being apocalyptic . . . ," testifies Hatch, "I believe our common survival and the fate of the planet depend on our facing up to this crisis. We need to make some major changes in our politics and economics, *and* we need to transform the ways we create community and discourse through how we act and think every day." By way of example, says Hatch, "the Catholic bishops' 'Letter on the Economy' called for a basic restructuring of our economic institutions from the outside in, *and* for changes in our own lives and thinking in local communities that would make economic practices and distribution fairer from the inside out. That's a good model. But the question is, Can we live it out in the flesh?" We must try, since in the long run simply making the modern state and economic systems work better by their own rules will not save us.

VII. THE EXAMPLE OF THE BLACK CHURCHES

Black church leaders are often careful to resist romanticization by their white counterparts of the black church as a positive role model for the moving power of its worship, its social solidarity and civic concern. "First of all, there are many different black churches, not one 'black church,' " observes Thomas Raskin, a thoughtful black Baptist churchman and theologian who teaches in a Methodist divinity school. "And let me assure you," he smiles, "some of them are every bit as boring and socially stifling as the most conventional white

church." While radical and liberation theologians make sweeping criticisms of American churches and culture for violating the truth of the
gospel, black church leaders are both forceful and measured. "I understand the kind of cultural alienation and political powerlessness
that gives moral force to that diagnosis," says Raskin, "but I have to
disagree with it. We can't just condemn the society we're actually
living in, and pretend we're not part of it. We have to look to the
church for the kinds of community that enable us to face up to our
society more honestly, and impel us to find a better way to be human.
I disagree, too, I suppose, simply because I love the church. I was
raised in it. It's my mother. It's my people, preaching and singing to
God, despite all its difficulties and compromises under duress."

To dismiss or indict existing churches across the board expresses
an anger and utopian idealism that only the affluent can afford, Raskin
believes. "Historically, the church has been an essential place of refuge
and empowerment for black people in America," Raskin observes,
"and that continues to be true. I don't find many of the goods it
nurtures—like caring for the needy and affirming their worth in the
goodness of God's creation—nurtured in very many other places in
our society. So I'm not ready to give up on the church as it stands
now, *before* the revolution. I also refuse to stop calling for revolutionary
action in places where the existing order of society stands in the way
of loving God and your neighbor because it's radically exclusive or
divisive. The black church has some common cause with revolutionary
liberation theology in Latin America or South Africa, for example.
But the church should not be ashamed to be a refuge for the poor *and*
a voice raised for justice in their name. Let's not lose our lives on the
battlefield trying to usher in the kingdom to come, without nurturing
one another, particularly 'the least of these,' here and now."

Churches still stand at the center of African-American communities.[44] But black churches bear the scars of racial exclusion and social
subordination; and they, too, face the temptations of an assimilated
ethic of middle-class success and respectability. Both these factors add
to the challenge posed to them by the increasing division of African-
Americans into two social worlds. A "coping" sector of middle-income
households makes up roughly two-thirds of black America, divided
between working-class and middle-class groups; another third consists
of a "crisis" sector, divided between working poor and jobless, welfare-
dependent poor.[45] These seriously deprived people have remained
behind in inner-city ghettos, increasingly isolated and socially stymied, as upwardly mobile blacks have migrated to more stable residential neighborhoods and new black suburbs. In Atlanta, for

example, nearly half the black population has left the central city for surrounding counties since the 1960s.[46]

The largest and oldest black denominations are composed mainly of middle-income people from the working class and middle class, backed by a small if intensely loyal slice of the poor, notably in the rural South. The poorest and most socially alienated blacks, meanwhile, seem to be slipping further away from these churches. Indeed, they seem to be slipping away from every kind of church, including the sects and storefronts, especially in inner-city areas outside the South, where seven of ten blacks are unchurched (the proportion is even higher among young men).

Reflecting on this unchurched black urban underclass and its growth in the past generation, Raskin warns: "We've got a generation out there on the street that is almost totally unaware of the governing symbols that shape African-American culture. We can no longer take for granted that everybody understands what exodus and exile mean for us, what crucifixion and resurrection mean. Twenty years ago a black preacher could take that for granted out in the neighborhood *and* in the pulpit. What we get now is the articulation of rage, from rap artists and from the gangs. Louis Farrakhan speaks that language, too, when he says, We have no investment here. We are a separate people. We have to do for ourselves. Even he pulls in a version of Dale Carnegie striving for success: 'Pull yourself up by your own bootstraps.' But he can say nothing about what it means to share space, and make a world where black and white can live together in justice. This is a kind of rage that doesn't trust anybody, that doesn't reach out any further than the other members of the gang. The crips and the bloods—that's my only family, that's my only community."

What should we do in response? Resolving the problems of a jobless, uneducated black underclass calls on the political will, educational institutions, and economic resources of the entire society. The black churches need to be realistic about what they can accomplish on their own, and all the more determined to engage the larger moral community. But it is also essential that socially mobile, educated blacks and their churches not abandon the inner-city underclass, who now number one in every five or six African-Americans, and good evidence suggests that they have not done so. Most black inner-city churches still stand where they were founded, and middle-income blacks who have moved to the suburbs still belong to them and commute regularly to participate in their services.

A few extraordinarily large black "megachurches" have reached across class lines and local neighborhoods to unify central-city communities and serve the black poor with educational, housing, sports, and welfare programs.[47] At the same time, as Raskin argues, the church must be a place where people learn "discipline through discipling," and where they strive not for individual achievement alone but out of love for God and neighbor. "Many small churches, including storefront churches, are doing this very basic kind of educating. . . . You can lose the discipline and love of a real community in seeking the strength of numbers that generate money, energy, and programs. Then you risk recapitulating the corporate world people live in all through the week. That's not ministry." By contrast, Raskin stresses, "We need to affirm the church that knows everybody's name, their kids' names, their birthdays. We need to join the church that can take in the needy or weak, the single parent who's been left to fend for herself, and say to her, 'We know who you are; you're important,' and show her we mean it by what we do."

In light of the black churches' dual responsibility to give prophetic voice and pastoral balm to the suffering of its people, Raskin welcomes changes in the churches some white observers decry. He acknowledges the painful and explosive effects of moral controversies, political conflicts, and the play of group interests within "caucus churches," yet he sees the turbulence as an inevitable condition of movement toward a more truly inclusive, genuinely catholic church, in which those who differ socially cannot easily be excluded or silenced.

"Many mainline churches are paying more attention now to the New Testament model of radical diversity within the 'body' of the early Christian community," Raskin notes. "Black churches have had to do that in the past in order to survive, because we were so divided and so weak. Church leaders today need to discover how conflict can lead to moral and spiritual growth and greater social openness, and how to be less threatened by its potential for power struggles and schism."

VIII. PARA-CHURCH GROUPS AND THEIR MORAL IMPLICATIONS

Socially active religious movements and groups have a long history in America, spreading through the benevolent empire of nineteenth-century voluntary societies for religious and social good works. Some critics of para-church groups today are bothered by the social divisions and cultural cleavages they represent and worry that they may deepen rather than heal these fault lines.[48] These fears usually occur when the movements are conceived as interest-based lobbies or pressure groups. But they are also contrasting visions of a good society, distinctively construed in terms of the moral traditions of American culture, and need not be feared.

Conservative evangelical public theologies underscore the idea of Americans' biblical origins as a people chosen to evangelize the world, and emphasize a duty to respect the authority of government, to work hard in a competitive economy, and to maintain a conscientious personal moral code. Sometimes they focus on issues such as abortion, promiscuity, and homosexuality, but they are also active in attempts to alleviate world hunger. Liberal Christians, by contrast, stress the special responsibilities that America's power and wealth place upon its citizens to bind up the wounds of the needy at home and abroad; they favor global reconciliation in the form of nuclear disarmament and world peace; and they work for civil rights, economic opportunities for all citizens, and ecological conservation.

Do these two visions, or something like them, represent a polarization of American civil religion or social ethics? We should remember several countervailing factors. First, American popular culture spans rather than separates many of the moral and social values emphasized in these two public theologies. For example, virtually all Americans are pleased with the easing of U.S.–Soviet tensions, favor a reduction or elimination of nuclear arms, and wish to see a decline in racial and religious prejudice, even if they doubt that existing policies and governments can fulfill all these hopes.[49] Second, as the evangelicals have grown in numbers they have become similar to liberal church members in education, occupation, and social outlook.[50] The possibility exists of rapprochement, rather than polarization, between religious liberals and conservatives, if one views them as social groups with moral ideas attuned to their different social circumstances. Third, perhaps most important, there is a cultural coherence underlying such moral disagreement that allows argument and even conflict to continue within enduring denominational structures.[51] If we see such disagreement simply as a tug-of-war of social interests, which prevents a uniform value consensus otherwise devoutly to be wished, then we will forever wish in vain.

The danger inherent in socially narrowed religious movements focusing on single issues is not so much that they will aggravate social-class cleavages but that they may set an example of religion in public life that shrinks the moral vision and shirks the moral responsibilities borne by mainline and evangelical churches alike. The churches reach across the full breadth of religious tradition and revelation to join specific moral positions and specific social actions to teaching and preaching incarnated in common worship, congregational life, and the care of souls. Individual salvation, prayer, evangelism, theological study, charitable works, and social reform are joined in one continuum. Para-church movements are a threat to religious self-understanding and public life only when they drift away from religiously motivated criticism and social action to manage public opinion, mobilize constituencies, and lobby the state along the morally instrumental and subjectivist lines of group-interest politics.

America's major denominations can no longer escape or insulate themselves by schism or segmentation from those who live and believe differently. They can no longer withdraw from public affairs in return for the state's mere tolerance. They are now enabled, and compelled, to sustain conciliar internal dialogue without schism, and to draw critically on related religious movements for their own reform. Now more than ever the churches can, and must, engage the larger public and the state in moral argument and education.[52]

IX. INSTITUTIONAL RELIGION

With their inveterate distaste for institutions in any form, many Americans use the term "institutional religion" with a negative connotation. They are apt to say, "I'm not religious, but I'm very spiritual."[53] Some of them may even find in this chapter confirmation of their prejudices. Mary Hatch may seem almost to agree with them when she says, "I don't really care if the mainline churches dissolve as we know them. . . . If the churches can be transformed, well and good. If the mainline institutions cannot change, then Christianity will continue outside them in other social forms." Yet for her, some social embodiment remains essential: "You have to have some place to stand, some structure to work through." And she is not prepared to dismiss the local church, "because then you have no institutions to debate and wrestle with."

Certainly "institutional religion" continues to be important in the lives of many Americans. As some of the people whose eloquent voices we heard in this chapter have put it, without institutions, however imperfect, religion tends to be vacuous, private and irrelevant. But like those who eschew institutional religion, these men and women are individuals, searching for meaning in their own lives, and uncertain about the capacity of existing churches to articulate that meaning in ways appropriate to themselves or their society. Still they have a notion of an ideal institution that carries out on this earth a transcendental task: actual religious organizations only approximate that institutional ideal and so are always in need of reform. In this they understand something about churches that we are arguing in this book is true for institutions generally.

Not that the church as an institutional ideal is simple and clear or that the only problem is how to embody it. Certain symbolic expressions came up repeatedly in our interviews—for example, the church as "the Body of Christ," or the notion of the church as united in *agape*, self-giving love. Christians of many different denominations who recite the Nicene Creed profess to believe in "one holy, catholic, and apostolic church." Yet each one of the voices we heard understands the church as an institution somewhat differently. Mel Reese's church is not the same as Robert Cooper's, and Gene Sansom's differs from both. Mary Hatch and Thomas Raskin might seem to be in essential agreement, but even they are at odds on some points. These disagreements are not so much a "failure of consensus" as they are evidence of the vigor of a debate over what the church, and ultimately religion, is all about in our society. In this vigorous debate we can discern a few conclusions about the role of religion in America today.

(1) For religious believers, religious loyalty transcends national loyalty. This does not mean that these loyalties necessarily must conflict; but when they do, the religious claim has priority. That they have indeed conflicted in America is evident from the history of conscientious objection and civil disobedience, but all the major religious communities have accepted the legitimacy of the American republic and have preferred deliberation to conflict, the latter being a last resort after witness and persuasion have failed. Believers have a qualified loyalty to the state but an unqualified loyalty to God, and this can on occasion move them to respond in love to human need beyond the relativistic play of interests of individuals, groups, or nations. In certain ways this gives them a larger opportunity to raise issues—about peace, about global ecology, about poverty in the Third World—than if their loyalties were purely national. Of course many secular people also have transnational loyalties and obligations, so this is not exclusively a religious prerogative, and it is one that many conventionally religious people do not exercise.

(2) People in organized religious congregations participate, in larger numbers and with greater generosity in time and money than any other groups in the United States, in communities that transcend the family and its informal circle of friends. For Mel Reese the localism of a congregation can be a problem, a kind of collective egoism, that

ignores the larger society. For Robert Cooper and for Thomas Raskin the parish may nurture not only believers but citizens better able to contribute to society than if they were isolated as individuals or families. Congregations often stand aloof from other congregations in their vicinity, and even from their own denominations; but where they come together they can make a significant difference in the quality of community life.

(3) Given the tension between local congregations and para-church organizations, which weakens the capacity of both of them to carry out their missions effectively, it is possible to imagine a set of intermediate institutions, crossing denominational lines, that would bring clergy and laity together to discuss the theological and social issues at the root of this tension. These institutions might be modeled on Europe's Evangelical Academies in that they would focus on education and discussion more than on direct action. They would promote theological and sociological sophistication, but their aim would be to enhance the life of worship and faith. Today divinity schools in various denominations attempt something of this sort in their outreach to the laity. But a stronger set of lay academies could do much to overcome the suspicion between congregations and denominational structures through renewing respect for the biblical and theological endowment that is their basic source. In this effort to recover and strengthen depleted resources, these academies could help provide a more educated and articulate voice for the public church. Such academies could also contribute to the essential dialogue between Christians and Jews and between the biblical religions and other faiths. Religious communities can contribute to the search for the common good only to the extent that they understand and respect different-faith communities in our pluralistic society and world.

(4) Many powerful institutions that influence our lives and consume much of our energies—economic, governmental, educational—pull us apart; they seem to pressure us to compete for individual advantage rather than to combine for the common welfare, and they empty out meaning from our lives when they structure our existence as a competitive race for money, power, prestige, or the consumer goods that symbolize them. Religious communities do not simply give us membership and recognition—qualities in short supply in America (remember Raskin's example of the storefront church whose members can say to the single parent, "We know who you are; you're important"). They also help us grapple with the ultimate problem of meaning, of trying to find a way to live that is based on something more than cost-benefit calculation or desire; of whether we have a place in

the universe at all and any abiding purpose to pursue here. Mary Hatch's sense of the Bible is that it is a *working document* that doesn't give us pat answers but helps us struggle to make sense of the abyss that so often seems to be opening up around us. For her, the Bible can speak to us today only if we do the hard work of making sense of it and seeing how it applies to our current situation. Without that continued effort religion slowly evaporates into pious phrases that no one understands anymore. What is so moving about Mary Hatch (and the other voices in this chapter) is that her search for meaning is not a lonely existentialist quest but comes out of a deep engagement with other people, with a moral world. The symbols and stories of the Bible give her a sense of a resonance not only with ultimate reality but with suffering and celebrating humanity everywhere. They orient the quest to create a world community in which individual dignity can be realized and not crushed by military, political, or market forces. Biblical religion is not our only resource in this quest for meaning and moral purpose. But we would fail to see what is going on around us if we did not see how deeply engaged it still is in that search.

7

America in the World

The ideological collapse of communism and the gradual transformation of once Communist societies in ways that are still not clear, but are at the moment militarily less threatening, present the United States with a radically new situation. Our reaction to this extraordinary unexpected change, the sudden collapse of the adversary that has dominated our imagination for forty-five years, has been at best hesitant. Triumphalism—We have won the cold war! There is a McDonald's on Pushkin Square in Moscow!—has not been lacking, but it has been remarkably muted, given the magnitude of the change. There is no nostalgia for the cold war. Along the entire political spectrum the chief response has been relief, particularly about the greatly lessened threat of nuclear war with the Soviet Union. But in contrast to the euphoria of VJ Day, for example, after less than four years of involvement in World War II, the lack of anything comparable after the end of this titanic struggle is amazing.

Perhaps the reason is that in spite of our bravado, America is far less self-confident at the end of the cold war than it was at its beginning. Well before the collapse of communism doubts about our economic competitiveness and our political influence in the world had been growing. Perhaps the end of the cold war has removed one more of our presumptions about ourselves in the world and we have not found a new understanding to take its place. We will not gain such a new understanding until we come to terms with our recent history in a more realistic and less ideological manner.

One way to put our central self-doubt has been to ask whether the

American empire is in decline. Since the publication of Paul Kennedy's *The Rise and Fall of the Great Powers*,[1] in 1988, this question has been the subject of national debate. The debate is less about the facts than about conceptions of America's identity. Although the facts are complicated, the basic political and economic situation seems clear enough. The United States still remains the strongest military power in the world, and its economy one of the richest, but it is no longer able decisively to control the flow of economic and political history in the world. Political scientists speak of this set of circumstances as a "decline in American hegemony."[2]

This decline is not primarily due to internal weakness. In many ways it is actually the product of our strength. After all, it was partially through our efforts that Western Europe and Japan were able to recover economically after World War II. In the past generation our economy has not declined in absolute terms, but theirs have risen to our level. Meanwhile, "newly industrializing countries" like South Korea, Taiwan, Hong Kong, and Singapore, which got started on the path to development with a great deal of American help, have been successful enough to give us stiff competition in the global marketplace. We have not gotten poorer, but other nations have gotten rich enough to claim a larger share of the world's resources.

At the same time, in large part due to our own efforts, the world has become more interdependent. The vast global market is increasingly dominated by huge multinational corporations. The growth in the interconnection of the United States with this market has been especially dramatic during the past generation. Economic initiatives taken outside our borders by economic actors not under our control quickly have repercussions in our own economy. In the first two decades after World War II, the other nations in what we called the free world were much more dependent economically on us than we were on them. Now the dependence is more nearly mutual. We have, for example, become deeply dependent upon Japan to finance our huge budget deficits, even as Japan depends on us for a market for its products.[3]

World economic interdependence also places more of the fate of the world's poorest nations into our hands—and generates fierce resentments in the Third World at the injustice of it all. The world financial system, for instance, helps to protect the richest countries like the United States while placing heavy burdens on the poorest. A purely "rational" international market system would require that when faced with competition from societies where workers are paid low wages and have few social welfare benefits, societies where wages and welfare benefits are high would have to either reduce their wages and welfare or stop competing in the world market. Yet powerful nations like the United States can, within limits, avoid doing this by manipulating the values of their currencies so that their goods are still competitively priced abroad. Weak and poor governments, like many of those in Latin America and Africa, however, have no such luxury. To make their export goods internationally competitive and to receive loans from international banks, they have to adopt "austerity programs" that decrease wage and price inflation by allowing high levels of unemployment and decreasing social welfare benefits. The resultant poverty and resentment constitute potent fuel for violent conflict.

Our armed forces are in a poor position to contain such conflicts. Militarily, we are still the strongest nation in the world, but the limitations on any use of military power have become increasingly apparent. Our nuclear weapons are an expensive, dangerous burden to us, a necessary evil at the very best, but useless for imposing our political will on others. As far as conventional forces are concerned, the Vietnam War (and for the Soviet Union, the Afghanistan war) dramatically demonstrated how difficult it is, even with vastly superior firepower, to win a "limited war" on an opponent's own territory. And modern warfare, even when victorious, stirs up malignant political forces that can create long-term instability. We can no longer unilaterally impose a Pax Americana on the world. The achievement of peace requires a great deal of international cooperation.

Finally, worldwide economic development has produced new global problems, like the greenhouse effect, that are beyond the capacity of any single nation to solve. For all its strength, the United States can address these problems only through cooperation with other nations. The United States has by no means become weak, but it has lost some of its independence.

To a culture so deeply devoted to independence, this loss gives rise to profound anxieties. Some people insist that it is unpatriotic to say that America is no longer Number One; the whole idea smacks of defeatism and breeds a lack of confidence unworthy of a great nation. Others say that we need to face the facts about our slippage of economic and political predominance in order to construct a new grand strategy for regaining our position as Number One. But few people ask, What does it mean to be Number One in an interdependent world? And what would be the moral purpose of being Number One?

II. THE FREE WORLD

The architects of America's postwar foreign policy didn't talk about being Number One; the very phrase might have sounded crass to their well-educated ears. For the most part born into affluence, the "wise men" of the American foreign policy establishment had been educated in exclusive prep schools and elite universities, where they had been trained to give at least lip service and often more than that to the moral obligations attendant upon wealth and power.[4] They knew that the United States was the wealthiest and most powerful nation on earth. They thought that it needed to become even more wealthy and powerful. But as they expressed it, wealth and power were not ends in themselves but means to larger, more transcendent purposes. The United States was to create a new, morally superior world order. Our fundamental goal was to "assure the integrity and vitality of our free society, which is founded upon the dignity and worth of the individual."[5]

Thus stated NSC (National Security Council) 68, the comprehensive statement of "United States Objectives and Programs for National Security" drafted by a special State and Defense Department study group under the leadership of Paul Nitze in early 1950. NSC 68 was drafted in an atmosphere of crisis. Within the previous six months, the Chinese civil war had been won by the Communists, Germany had been split into two parts, tensions in the Korean peninsula were building toward a breaking point—and, most terrifying of all, the Soviet Union had successfully tested its first atomic bomb. NSC 68 undertook a comprehensive review of the world situation and recommended a grand strategy for confronting it. "The issues that face us," it said, "are momentous, involving the fulfillment or destruction not only of this Republic but of civilization itself. . . . With conscience and resolution this Government and the people it represents must now take new and fateful decisions."[6]

NSC 68 was a document of far-reaching historical significance. A blueprint for the cold war, it provided the rationale for the greatest peacetime military buildup the world had ever known and for corresponding transformations in American economic, political, and educational institutions. The rationale had a rhetorical eloquence and philosophical subtlety that we no longer expect from documents produced by government bureaucrats. And one reason is that the very institutions so eloquently and imaginatively proposed by NSC 68 have gradually smothered the sparks of eloquence and imagination in our public life.

NSC 68 argued that the United States had to make itself powerful in order to defend the cause of freedom in the world. Today such talk seems excessively idealistic. Realists in and outside of government are more wont to talk about regaining our competitive edge, keeping on top, staying on as Number One. The drafters of NSC 68 predicted that the American people might have to accept a large measure of sacrifice and discipline to defend freedom; and Americans were generally willing to accept such sacrifice. As long as citizens could believe that they were really defending the cause of freedom, it seemed worthwhile. Now economists and politicians are saying that Americans will have to accept a large measure of sacrifice and discipline to remain Number One. Will they? And why should they? Answering such questions requires us seriously to reflect on the relation of our traditional moral ideals to our new situation in the world. We need to have a deeper understanding of freedom in order adequately to affirm our international interdependence instead of merely celebrating our independence.

For a democracy, a soberly realistic stance toward the world paradoxically requires high ideals. Relationships with a complicated, dangerous world require sacrifices, and free citizens must be given valid reasons for making those sacrifices. But it is part of the human condition that high ideals are often undercut by the means required to pursue them. Our ideals must be deeply enough grounded and richly enough formulated to sustain the arduous debates necessary to determine means acceptable to pursue them, and resilient enough to undergo renewal after their inevitable corruption. The architects of American foreign policy in the post–World War II world rooted that policy deeply in American ideals of freedom and responsibility. However, their formulations were not profound enough to prevent the eventual resort to means that would undermine them. They are perhaps resilient enough to undergo renewal. As they are renewed, they will have to be reformulated.

At the philosophical core of NSC 68's vision was the familiar American idea of "freedom under a government of laws": "The free society values the individual as an end in himself, requiring of him only that measure of self discipline and self restraint which make the rights of each individual compatible with the rights of every other individual. The freedom of the individual has as its counterpart, therefore, the negative responsibility of the individual not to exercise his freedom in ways inconsistent with the freedom of other individuals and the positive responsibility to make constructive use of his freedom in the building of a just society."[7] If it had emphasized the negative responsibility of this idea of freedom over the positive, the document might have called upon Americans to mind their own business, keep down the size of their government, stay away from entangling alliances with other nations. Such isolationist sentiments run deep in the American tradition. Indeed, no more than a decade before, most Americans had expressed a desire to stay out of the war started by Germany in Europe. But NSC 68 was stressing the positive responsibilities of freedom, of course. America had to "take up the responsibility of world leadership."

For freedom was threatened. The idea of freedom was locked in mortal combat with the "idea of slavery under the grim oligarchy of the Kremlin. . . . For the breath of freedom cannot be tolerated in a society which has come under the domination of an individual or a group of individuals with a will to absolute power. . . . The system becomes God, and submission to the will of God becomes submission to the will of the system."[8]

To stave off the threat of slavery under the will to absolute power posed by the Soviet Union, free peoples had to forsake some of the cozy pleasures of private life. They had to emphasize the positive responsibilities of freedom to create a global good society. "The assault on free institutions is world-wide now, and in the context of the present polarization of power a defeat of free institutions anywhere is a defeat everywhere." To meet this challenge, America had to "make the attempt, and accept the risks inherent in it, to bring about order and justice by means consistent with the principles of freedom and democracy." We had to "seek to create a world society based on the principle of consent."[9]

How were we to do this? NSC 68 was candid about some of the contradictions between its ends and its means. It recognized that "in relations between nations, the prime reliance of the free society is on the strength and appeal of its idea, and it feels no compulsion sooner or later to bring all societies into conformity with it." Although it declared confidently that "the idea of freedom is the most contagious idea in history, more contagious than the idea of submission to authority," the whole purpose of the document was to warn that by "every consideration of devotion to our fundamental values and to our national security," we had to safeguard freedom and democracy "by the strategy of the cold war." To carry out their ideals, the authors of NSC 68 were proposing the creation of a massive military establishment. This would require a "large measure of sacrifice and discipline . . . of the American people. They will be asked to give up some of the benefits which they have come to associate with their freedoms."[10]

How could the vast military power envisioned by NSC 68 be prevented from growing into absolute power—one that would demand that citizens serve the national security system as if serving the will of God? The authors affirmed the crucial importance of an informed public opinion in this regard. "Nothing could be more important than that [the American public] fully understand the reasons"[11] for the cold war, they stressed. Yet NSC 68 itself was classified Top Secret (it was declassified in 1975).

NSC 68 betrayed other concerns that militated against the public discussion it recognized as vital to a free society. The Kremlin, it believed, was seeking to bring the free world under its domination by infiltration and subversion as well as by overt aggression. "The doubts and diversities that in terms of our values are part of the merit of a free system . . . are but all opportunities for the Kremlin to do its evil work. Every advantage is taken of the fact that our means of prevention and retaliation are limited by these principles and scruples which are precisely the ones that give our freedom and democracy its meaning for us."[12] Even as the authors of NSC 68 sat down at their desks in Foggy Bottom in February 1950 to draft their document, the public consequences of this mood of paranoia were becoming ironically apparent. On February 9, Senator Joseph McCarthy stood up in Wheeling, West Virginia, to allege that 250 Communists held high, influential positions in the State Department.

In contrast to McCarthy, the authors of NSC 68 had a keen sense of the need to balance concern about Communist subversion with a commitment to free institutions. They recognized that "the free society is limited in its choice of means to achieve its ends. . . . The resort to force, to compulsion, to the imposition of its will is therefore a difficult and dangerous act for a free society, which is warranted only in the face of even greater dangers. The necessity of the act must be clear and compelling; the act must commend itself to the overwhelming majority as an inescapable exception to the basic idea of freedom; or the regenerative capacity of free men after the act has been performed will be endangered."[13]

"None of our scruples," as NSC 68 put it, "deter those whose only code is, 'morality is that which serves the revolution.' "[14] In the face of such a perceived threat, were America's "scruples" about freedom and democracy sufficient to combat the paranoid desire to destroy our free institutions for the sake of defending them?

The vision of NSC 68 flowed from a quintessentially American combination of virtues and vices. It was bold and generous in its conception of ultimate goals. Not afraid to reach for high ideals, it dared to commit itself uncompromisingly to the defense of the dignity of each individual human person in the world. It was generous in its inclusivity: every individual had dignity, and people everywhere were responsible for creating conditions that would guarantee the dignity of all.

But NSC 68 was also reckless and naïve. First, it was recklessly simplistic in its characterization of "free society" as anything outside the Soviet system. Granted that the Stalinist regime in the Soviet Union was brutal and tyrannical, an enemy of human freedom and dignity, and with its military might, augmented now by possession of the atomic bomb, a threat to our vital interests. But there were still many other threats to freedom and dignity in the world, arising not from the Kremlin but from hatreds produced by class inequalities, racism, radical nationalism. It was empirically false, strategically foolish, and morally wrong to make the Kremlin the root of all threats to freedom and dignity in the world and to suggest that simply by containing and rolling back Soviet communism, freedom and dignity would be preserved. NSC 68 was also naively optimistic in its conception of possible bases of world order in the "free world." It aimed to create a "world society based on the principle of consent." Given the differences in culture, history, and economic interest of the many communities into which the world was divided, it was utopian to imagine that these might someday all cooperate together in an orderly fashion—and in a way that meshed with American self-interest— simply on the basis of voluntary consent.

Both these virtues and these vices stemmed from the American individualist tradition. By attributing to the individual a sacredness, a dignity, stemming from each person's fundamental capacity for free choice, individualism morally impelled Americans toward universal concerns for the welfare of people everywhere. Most other empires in world history had made systematic distinctions between superior and inferior races, allowing the former to control the latter in the name of a "civilizing mission." Individualism has certainly not made America immune from racism, but it has offered a powerful basis for making racism illegitimate. Its predominance in the language of public discourse made it virtually impossible for our national leaders to base a foreign policy on any explicit discrimination against race, religion, or creed—unless, of course, that creed was communism.

But the moral thinness of individualism encouraged recklessness and naïveté in our foreign policy. Individualism privatizes, while world leadership demands a robust conception of public involvement. What else could motivate public involvement but a sense of clear and present danger, an all-encompassing dramatic threat to freedom everywhere? Under the logic of individualism would it have been possible to have a Pax Americana without a cold war?

The intellectual thinness of individualism, moreover, was at the root of the naïve hopes for a good "world society based on consent." Lockean individualism is a cultural tradition that assumes that culture, community, and history do not matter much in the long run. What matters is individuals' perceptions of their self-interest. A good society is a free society, or a free world, in which relationships are based not on coercion but on agreements—contracts—voluntarily entered into because all parties consider them to be in their interest. But suppose, because of cultural prejudices or memories of a long history of bad relations, some nations or societies refuse to cooperate, even though to an outside observer such cooperation might seem to be in the interest of most of their citizens. How could a peaceful world order based on consent be maintained then? In the early 1950s, Americans tended to hope that with proper enlightenment, most people would come to think of themselves as many Americans do, that is, as individuals pragmatically concerned with their (basically economic) interests, rather than as members of a community bound together by a shared sense of national pride and a shared history of hostility and resentment toward other nations.[15]

But, even supposing that the citizens of "modern societies" did end up thinking like this, what would happen if the differences between rich and poor societies were so great that it was clearly against the economic self-interest of the poor to cooperate with the rich? What if the poor societies were motivated to fight against the world economic system by the idea that the system was unjust? Americans tended to assume that economic development would be so expansive and so widely shared that the system would seem just and even poor countries would find it rationally in their self-interest to cooperate with it. These assumptions were ethnocentric and naïve, and the hopes expressed in NSC 68 were unrealistically utopian.

The problem with the utopianism of NSC 68 was that there could be no coherent relationship between the idealistic goals and the realistic means chosen to pursue them. It was not simply a matter of setting goals so high that they could only partially be attained. It was also a matter of the goals being just as easily subverted as pursued through the chosen means. For instance, a vast military mobilization carried out for the sake of preserving freedom and dignity might actually destroy freedom, since a massive military establishment can smother the rest of society and sow the seeds of paranoia among the citizens. If a nation—because of the proclivities of its cultural traditions, or because of the legacy of old hatreds, or because of the attractions of nationalism—would not cooperate with what to the United States seemed to be reasonable initiatives, the American government was stymied: Should it declare the country Communist and use military force against it? Covertly manipulate its politics through the CIA? Would such measures really enhance the cause of freedom?

Such questions easily occur to us now, in the light of the mistakes we have made in the forty years since NSC 68 was written. The questions occurred less easily in 1950, because our enormous wealth and power, our unchallenged political and economic dominance over the non-Communist world, encouraged a messianic self-confidence about our role in history. We had, many of us thought, now entered the American Century.

III. THE AMERICAN CENTURY AGAIN

The idea of the American Century was mythic, its language religious. Vividly expressing a widely shared faith and hope, it gave Americans a dramatic image of their identity and destiny and helped inspire the society to live out that identity and follow that destiny. The term "American Century" was coined by Henry Luce in a famous editorial in *Life* magazine, published in February of 1941, just ten months before Pearl Harbor. Luce was trying to rouse Americans out of their isolationism.

> The other day Herbert Hoover said that America was fast becoming the sanctuary of the ideals of civilization. For the moment it may be enough to be the sanctuary of these ideals. But not for long. It now becomes our time to be the powerhouse from which the ideals spread throughout the world and do their work of lifting the life of mankind from the level of the beasts to what the Psalmist called a little lower than the angels. [We are coming to a] great test . . . and in this moment of testing there may come clear at last the vision which will guide us to the authentic creation of the 20th Century—our Century.[16]

By 1945, we had reason to think that we had passed the test.

The myth of the American Century was a millennial myth, which suggested that America's history was bringing it to a time when the human division between spirit and flesh, means and ends, morality and power, was coming to an end. Luce had written: "America as the dynamic center of ever-widening spheres of enterprise, America as the training center of the skilled servants of mankind, America as the Good Samaritan, really believing again that it is more blessed to give than to receive, and America as the powerhouse of the ideals of Freedom and Justice—out of these elements surely can be fashioned a vision of the 20th Century." Wasn't our decisive victory in World War II a proof of the universal validity of our ideals? Now we were shouldering the task of creating a new world order. Our ideals were so powerful that that order could be based not mainly on the use of force but on the strength of our moral inspiration and our economic creativity. Unlike earlier empires, which had controlled unwilling subjects over the surface of the globe, American influence would now permeate the fabric of time itself.

There were resources within our culture to warn us against this millennialism. No one drew on those resources more eloquently than Reinhold Niebuhr. In 1946 he warned explicitly about the "egoistic corruption" mixed within this "dangerous hope not only for a reign of peace but also for an 'American Century.' "[17] His concerns were most brilliantly summarized in his 1952 book *The Irony of American History*. At that time, Niebuhr was by no means opposed to the cold war. His moral realism told him that it was sometimes tragically necessary for societies to confront one another forcefully in a sinful world; and, sharing the assumptions of his times, his book is suffused with a brittle anticommunism that seems paranoid today. Yet, remarkably, the book is at the same time a profound critique of America and a severe warning to America at the peak of its power. By "irony" Niebuhr meant to point out the deep connection between our achievements and our failures, to which we remain blind as long as we do not see ourselves as sinners—something that Americans, whether they go to church or not, are loath to do. Far from asserting American virtue, *The Irony of American History* calls for repentance:

> We cannot expect even the wisest of nations to escape every peril of moral and spiritual complacency; for nations have always been constitutionally self-righteous. But it will make a difference whether the culture in which the policies of nations are formed is only as deep and as high as the nation's ideals; or whether there is a dimension in the culture from the standpoint of which the element of vanity in all human ambitions and achievements is discerned. But this is the height which can

be grasped only by faith. . . . The faith which appropriates the meaning in the mystery inevitably involves an experience of repentance for the false meanings which the pride of nations and cultures introduces into the pattern. Such repentance is the true source of charity; and we are more desperately in need of genuine charity than of more technocratic skills.[18]

In closing, Niebuhr reminded us that if we should perish, the primary cause would be not "the ruthlessness of the foe" but "that the strength of a giant nation was directed by eyes too blind to see all the hazards of the struggle; and the blindness would be induced not by some accident of nature or history but by hatred and vainglory."

Many of the architects of America's postwar foreign policy did indeed consider such warnings. In 1949 Niebuhr himself consulted with the State Department's Policy and Planning Staff, on which the principal authors of NSC 68 served.[19] One finds echoes of Niebuhr's concerns especially in the passages that stress that the "resort to force, to compulsion, to the imposition of its will, is a difficult and dangerous act for a free society which is warranted only in the face of even greater dangers."

Niebuhr wanted Americans to maintain a heroic moral balancing act: they were to aspire to great things, to dare to use their power as constructively as they could in the world, yet to be constantly willing to measure themselves by transcendent standards, lest they lose perspective. A surprising number of Americans from all walks of life tried to do just that. Perhaps it was easier in the 1950s; the tightrope was not so thin. Defense spending stimulated enormous economic prosperity; the Korean War contained the advance of communism in Asia for the time being; Western Europe and Japan began to regain their prosperity. One needed to take the warnings of prophetic figures like Niebuhr to heart, but one could allow oneself a small cushion of complacency. Without succumbing to a millenarian conception of America, one could with some reason think that the nation might at least be sprinkled, if not fully anointed, with the charisma of progress. The tension between the exuberant boosterism of a Henry Luce and the stern prophecy of a Reinhold Niebuhr defined a cautious hope: though there were enormous challenges to be faced—ethical as well as political and economic—reasonably intelligent, morally serious Americans could meet those challenges and create a better world.

By the mid-sixties, though, that faith had begun to falter. The resulting confusion, as we have been arguing throughout this book, was a symptom of a general institutional failure. The institutions

Americans had constructed to allow for meaningful relationships with
the rest of the world now created experiences filled with contradiction.
At the beginning of the 1950s many well-meaning Americans might
have wondered whether they were personally up to the task of seeking
the good in a dangerous, complicated, but possibly perfectible world;
by the end of the 1960s they had difficulty knowing what it could
mean for anybody to seek the good.

We can get a sense of this by listening carefully to how people who
have been devoted to improving the world describe their lives at
different periods in the past forty years.

IV. "MODERNIZATION" AS POLICY AND THEORY

Frank Sutton, recently retired after spending thirty years on the staff
of the Ford Foundation, evokes a sense of the prevalent mood in the
1950s. "On the whole, the kind of people I have known at the Ford
Foundation have been very typical Americans," he says. "This place
has never been cynical. People here were very positive. They had a
faith that if things were managed right, things would go right. . . .
The idea was that if you've got a problem, there's an answer to it."

Throughout the postwar era, the big foundations—philanthropic
organizations like the Ford Foundation, the Rockefeller Foundation,
and the Luce Foundation—have played a major role in shaping American efforts to create a stable, just, and peaceful world order. The
Ford Foundation alone has spent more than $2 billion on international
activities: it virtually created the academic discipline of "area studies,"
sponsored a vast variety of other academic studies in international
relations, supported economic development projects in poor nations,
and funded meetings where leaders from around the world could
become acquainted and share ideas.

In the 1950s, the Ford Foundation gave high priority to this last
activity for reasons characteristic of the thinking of the time. "The
idea was," remembers Sutton, "that if people got to know one another
and understand one another we wouldn't have conflict. Matters of
contention between nations could be handled with common sense and
more information about one another. For instance, at that time great
emphasis was put on the science of public administration. The idea
was to train people in a general kind of scientific skill in administration
that would serve over a vast range of affairs to administer all sorts of
people—in corporations and governments. This view had something
to do with the nature of American society, its optimism and its dem-

ocratic faith in the ability and potential of certain kinds of people. There was the idea that no one was fixed in a particular position in life by rigid class barriers. And therefore, with the right information and the right encouragement, individuals would decide to put aside past prejudices and cooperate happily with one another.

"We felt," said Sutton, summarizing the Ford Foundation's vision in those days, "that we had something to give to the rest of the world: modernization, education, bringing people out of age-old prejudices. We had a moral obligation to do something about these. In the old days, giving religion to people like the Chinese was enough. Now we were believers in the development ideology—we all believed that if we could only transmit to other societies the ideology that had made us rich and great, poor societies would be able to develop themselves also. It was assumed that there were two classes of society—those relatively well off, which shared a sort of common ideology stressing the importance of economic development and various kinds of free institutions, and those that were not."

This vision of worldwide progress through scientific enlightenment, personal liberation, and voluntary cooperation based on mutually perceived self-interests was consistent with the theories about modernization being developed by American social scientists at that time. (It is tempting to say that it was derived from those theories. But in fact foundations like Ford financed much of the research that developed the theories, even as the foundations drew upon the theories to guide their practical work. The links between theory and practice were mutual.) Modernization, according to most mainline social scientific theories, was equivalent to what Max Weber had called "rationalization," a process of systematically organizing all social relations so as to make them the most efficient possible means to maximizing wealth and/or power. Its characteristic institutions were the self-regulating market and the bureaucratic state.

Modernization had its origins in the West but was fated to spread over the entire world. No society could escape its requirements. Some non-Western societies, like Japan, had cultures—"value systems"— that enabled them to adapt relatively smoothly to the requirements of modernization. Other societies found modernization a traumatic process. In societies like China, this trauma engendered irrational, revolutionary movements, which led to the tragic mistake of accepting Marxist-Leninist rather than American models of economic and political development. The best way to avoid such upheavals was to educate "modernizing elites" in Western values, including respect for efficiency, the impartial observance of procedural law, and a com-

mitment to continuous technological progress.[20] Such were the teachings of modernization theory.

Generally, the social scientists projected thoroughly secular visions
of modernization—attempts to use science to supplant religion in solving social problems. The professionals who staffed the great foundations advocated practical measures to establish a peaceful, free, and
just world order that were also self-consciously secular, though they
were happy to cooperate with religious believers. "The Ford Foundation," as Sutton put it, "has always been . . . very careful to avoid
involvement with religious people. This is not to say that we had
nothing at all to do with them. If you could make a program ecumenical enough, and keep it away from the God question, you could
get it funded."

Yet these secular, social-scientific visions had subtle connections
with at least one religious vision—that of mainline American Protestantism. Consider the memories of Don MacInnis, a Methodist minister who served as a missionary in China during the late 1940s and
in Taiwan during the 1950s. He first traveled to Asia as a delegate
from UCLA to a student conference in 1940, and ended up living for
a while in Shanghai with an American missionary who was operating
the Christian Herald Industrial Orphanage for Boys. His "missionary
vocation," he says, "was born at that time." During World War II,
he served in the U.S. Army, "and I asked to be sent back to China
because I was hooked on China. . . . I think it was a very romantic
kind of involvement at that point. In wartime China, the hero is
Chinese, the victim of the Japanese invasion." After the war he went
back to China as a missionary, but he had to leave in a year and a
half, after the Communist takeover. After further study at Yale Divinity School, he and his wife went as missionaries to Taiwan in 1953.

He had two main priorities for his work in Taiwan. "One was
ecumenical cooperation . . . and the second was that I was committed
to projects beyond evangelism and the local church. Not that I didn't
agree with [evangelism and church building], but I felt that as Methodists we had a lot of experience elsewhere [with] . . . vocational
training and vocational handiworks projects to help these people survive. And I also built a local housing project, 110 houses and a factory.
. . . We developed a high-school vocational training center. . . . I
always felt this was something we should be doing because . . . this
was part of Christian mission."

It is easy to see the similarities between this religiously inspired
vision and the secular visions of the professionals in the Ford Foundation. America had a moral obligation to share its blessings with the

rest of the world. For the mainline Protestant missionary, the Christian faith was the chief of these blessings, but it was a faith fulfilled through tolerance toward all, even nonbelievers. If secular foundation executives were willing to cooperate with religious believers so long as they didn't push their beliefs onto others, Christian church people were willing to cooperate "ecumenically" with secularists so long as they didn't push their nonbelief onto others. They would cooperate in bringing "development" to less fortunate societies: helping people help themselves by providing education, jobs, ("vocational") training, management skills. Even when it didn't lead to religious conversion, this social development was considered part of the Christian mission.

These mainstream religious and secular approaches to improving the world shared common origins: university communities like Yale, Harvard, Princeton, Chicago, Columbia, where faculty and students from divinity schools, professional schools, and social science departments cross-fertilized each other, were the kinds of institutions that had produced the authors of NSC 68, that had trained and often provided an intellectual home for public philosophers like Lippmann, Niebuhr, and Dewey. Americans educated at such institutions tended to share common enemies: fundamentalists educated at small bible colleges; and, as the memory of World War II faded, perhaps also soldiers from the military academies—that is, people who they thought were intolerant of intellectual diversity and who were prone to emphasize coercive rather than cooperative solutions to world problems.

V. THE CRISIS OF THE 1960S

"It is difficult to explain," writes Marilyn Young, a history professor at New York University who now proudly considers herself a left-wing critic of American foreign policy, "what graduate school was like in the late fifties, particularly at a place like Harvard. There was a sense of certainty about everything, at least among the people I knew. Few of us doubted the legitimacy of what we were doing, the splendors of the institution to which we were attached, the heady feeling of being at the heart of the matter."[21]

By the early 1960s, of course, that certainty was disappearing. As Marilyn remembers it, "Harvard looked less good to me, its standards and values not merely open to doubt but shoddy, hypocritical, even murderous." Similar confusion appeared in the new university graduates who were coming into the Ford Foundation. "A phrase you heard a lot of from the new people coming into the foundation in the sixties," remembers Frank Sutton, "was 'state your values.' They wanted to challenge values. Before that it was all assumed. You didn't have to discuss your values. What you discussed was what was practical within generally agreed-upon principles."

What was the cause of the new generation's doubts? Their education and their work were engaging them in an ever wider range of conflicts in the "free world," while making it increasingly difficult morally to understand such conflicts. Consider, for example, the experience of Franklin Woo, who went to Hong Kong in 1960 as a Presbyterian missionary, with the assignment of helping student refugees from China. He became a minister and a missionary because "there was a vision and a hope there. Making something out of your life—you know, 'You are the salt of the earth'—that's what the ministers I was in contact with were telling me. Do some good, identify yourself with a big cause." He became "involved in many discussions with Asian students coming out of colonialism, trying to express their sense of selfhood, dignity. . . . It took me a long time to understand the importance and the validity of this desire of the Asians to throw off the shackles of imperialism and colonialism. Around 1964 I was in the Philippines and I went to visit a prison there. I ended up talking to a man in prison who had been a Huk—a member of a Marxist revolutionary movement. 'Hey, pastor,' he said to me, 'we're here because we're political prisoners.' I ended up corresponding with him. He wrote to me about anti-imperialism. This was before [America's major involvement in] the Vietnam War and before an awareness of anti-imperialism among Americans of my generation."

In the American Century, the free world, under the leadership of America, was supposed to become progressively more peaceful and prosperous, and people everywhere would gladly cooperate with the system established by Americans. To many Americans traveling abroad in the early 1960s, the progress seemed less certain. Throughout much of the Third World, intelligent, patriotic people were complaining bitterly about economic injustice and political oppression in a system dominated by the United States. It was not plausible to attribute their discontents to the evil influences of the "slave masters of the Kremlin."

Some scholars added new wrinkles to modernization theory in order to explain the anomalies. One should not expect political and economic modernization to proceed together linearly, some said. There were stages; and at some stages authoritarian governments were necessary to enforce the discipline required to modernize.[22] But what about people whose cries for freedom during the early stages were stifled by dictators sponsored by the United States? How was this to be reconciled with America's promise to promote the cause of "freedom under a government of laws"? Many peoples—even outside the Communist bloc (which was appearing much less monolithic)—did not seem eager to cooperate with the United States, even when they understood Americans well. Understanding Americans only made them realize more clearly how their interests diverged. How were Americans to deal with such people?

Universities were of less and less help in answering such questions. They had become larger and more complicated: massive arrays of specialties and subspecialties were held together by ramifying administrative bureaucracies, awash in information churned out by new research centers—Russian Research, European Research, Asian Research, International Relations, Strategic Studies—funded by foundations and the government. Never before had there been publicly available to Americans so many books, articles, news reports, statistical data about so many places around the world. Yet at the same time, it seemed harder and harder to interpret the information—to evaluate it, synthesize it, place it in perspective, understand its moral implications. Sometimes, mastery of the facts seemed to have no relation to an ability to comprehend their moral meaning. Nowhere was this clearer than in discussions of Vietnam.

"It was one thing to argue about Vietnam with Foreign Service officers," Marilyn Young remembers. "It was quite another to discover indifference—or worse—among professors and fellow graduate students. I remember one argument in particular. It was 1963; in my professor's tidy living room over tea . . . a superstar graduate student told me that the United States must send a million men to Vietnam, occupy the place, and 'reform' it." Eventually, "Vietnam and the black liberation struggle in America changed the shape of my moral world. Professors, no matter how loved, who could not understand the meaning of these events, who could not bring themselves to protest—loudly, boldly—I found such professors difficult to listen to on any issue. Such men (and they were all men) began to seem crippled to me—morally lame, grotesquely blind to the real world."[23]

Already in the micro-confrontation over tea Marilyn Young could sense the social issues that were at the heart of the macro-confrontations of that time. The university was supposed to be a place where different generations of citizens engaged in civil argument about the past, present, and future of society. The confrontation described by Young followed the form of such an argument—a passionate but, we may presume, polite disagreement (so as not to disturb the decorum

of afternoon tea) among well-informed people—but its substance un-
dermined future prospects of civil debate. Between the superstar graduate student's cool, self-confident assertion that military intervention
in Vietnam was technically required and Marilyn's moral conster-
nation there was a chasm; they shared no common ground. By then
the universities were creating such gaps even as they papered them
over with a thin layer of gentility. As U.S. involvement in Vietnam
escalated and at the same time seemed more and more futile, the gaps
became gulfs. By 1969 there were no more polite conversations about
Vietnam over tea. Those wholeheartedly in favor of military solutions
to the war would talk to one another behind the walls of their research
institutes, and those opposed would assemble in demonstrations outside, demanding the overthrow of the university administration for
complicity in American monopoly-capitalistic imperialism.

Other confrontations took place in the great foundations. According
to Frank Sutton, "a lot of the new staff members in the sixties, graduates of social-science programs at major universities, saw themselves
as members of the new left. They wore long hair, while people like
me wouldn't take my tie off. There was criticism of the fact that these
headquarters were located in this building in midtown Manhattan
. . . In those days the new-left people would have criticized us for
spending too much money, not giving enough to the poor."

Similar confrontations occurred in the mainline churches. By 1969,
for instance, Don MacInnis, by then director of the China Program
for the National Council of Churches, was harshly criticized by some
younger clergy for not recognizing the moral goodness of Maoist
China. The churches were torn apart by the same institutional forces
that were tearing apart the universities, for they, like the universities, served people who worked in the burgeoning bureaucracies of
what Dwight Eisenhower a decade earlier had labeled the "military-
industrial complex." But they also served the children of these people,
many of whom were deeply troubled about a society that would send
them to die in a pointless war in Vietnam. In an earlier era, public
theologians like Reinhold Niebuhr, and political leaders too, might
have expressed those elements of the biblical tradition that would
demonstrate the common ground these different constituencies shared.
But seminaries didn't produce figures like Niebuhr. Liberal seminary
curricula were following the standards set by the universities: more
specialized courses, producing more scientifically structured knowledge about a world that seemed more confusing and more fragmented.
Clergy either followed the logic of such an education and became

bureaucrats or ivory-tower academics, or followed their hearts into the passionate social movements of the times.

It was a sign of the changing times that the confrontations divided the Jewish and Catholic communities as well. America's postwar expansion in educational opportunities had given Jews and Catholics opportunities to participate in the central institutions of public life— government, education, the media—that WASPs had hitherto restricted mostly to themselves. The contradictions within those communities helped to produce Jewish and Catholic confrontations like those that divided the Protestant churches. It seemed as if the more fully a community participated in America's central institutions, the more internally divided it became.

What gave those institutions the power to confuse and divide was the contradiction between the goals they embodied and the way of life they promoted. This contradiction was especially pronounced in American government and education; both made people act in ways that the institutions themselves proclaimed to be wrong. The American government was supposed to make the United States the leader of the free world, protector of the "dignity and worth of the individual"; but it made us fight a savage war that in the end mocked our ideals about personal dignity and worth. Our schools proclaimed that along with promoting scientific and technological knowledge, they were helping us develop the humane and cosmopolitan wisdom to use that knowledge well; but some of the "best and brightest" products of our education helped to plan and wage the Vietnam War.

VI. IMPERIALISM AS THEORY AND EXPLANATION

The Vietnam tragedy made these contradictions painfully clear, but it did not plainly reveal their source or their resolution. Understandably, those Americans who rejected the government's foreign policy often did not have a realistic alternative. Take, for example, the accusation by many in the antiwar movement that the United States was imperialist. One of the chief proponents of this view was the Committee of Concerned Asian Scholars (CCAS). Founded in 1968, "CCAS was post–Port Huron, post-SDS [Students for a Democratic Society, whose first important statement was the Port Huron Manifesto of 1962]," says Marilyn Young, an early active member and eventually an editor of its *Bulletin*. "SDS was basically focused on American domestic issues; CCAS was concerned with anti-imperialism."

For Marilyn Young and many of the "concerned scholars" of her generation, American history since World War II was not a story of the worldwide defense of freedom and dignity but a narrative of relentless, oppressive, imperialist expansion around the world, for the sake of enhancing American interests at the expense of poorer, weaker societies. "Imperialism," Marilyn Young wrote in the *Bulletin*, "was a total system—economic, political, social, and cultural—and its component parts were intimately related."[24] To expose these institutional connections the CCAS *Bulletin* published detailed reports about how the Asian studies profession had been created by funds from the American government and the foundations, especially the Ford Foundation, and how leaders of the profession had been eager to coordinate their research with needs expressed by the government. Senior members of the profession like John K. Fairbank, the distinguished historian of China who taught at Harvard, seemed to view these ostensibly incendiary revelations as statements of obvious facts: of course the foundations and the government funded research about Asia—where else would the money have come from? And of course Asian scholars had tried to do research that would assist American foreign policy—wasn't that the role of responsible scholars?

"When I wrote that American approaches to Asia were imperialistic," Marilyn Young recalls, "Fairbank's response was that I had discovered original sin." Like most serious intellectuals of the generation for which Niebuhr had been a moral spokesman, Fairbank took it for granted that the United States as a great power was closely involved in the affairs of nations around the world, and that its actions would be, as Niebuhr explained the Christian doctrine of sin, as ambiguous and imperfect as human action always is, especially in large organizations. American involvement was inevitable, part of "the history," Fairbank wrote, "that largely dominates us." Throughout history, "intervention by the advanced countries has been part and parcel of their growth process. As growth continues (can we stop it?) we must try to mitigate its increasingly bad effects. We need action on two levels, distinguishing between them. The first level is intellectual, to identify, diagnose, and describe these effects and the processes involved. . . . The second level is practical and political, to criticize public policy, formulate improvements in it and seek better action accordingly."

Fairbank, the senior professor who had made Harvard's Chinese studies program so prominent, seemed to be saying that the university should simply recover its older sense of purpose—to combine analysis of the structures of U.S. power with rational reflection on its moral responsibilities. Marilyn Young and many insurgent scholars like her seemed to be saying that this sense of purpose was beyond recovery, perhaps because it had been a hypocritical sham to begin with. A morally concerned scholarship should, in the words of James Peck, another leader of the CCAS in those days, "commit itself to service of the oppressed."[25]

But there was no realistic sense of how this was to be done. If key American institutions like the government and the university were irredeemably corrupt, where could one find the energy to replace them? To counter America's mighty power for evil, one had to find a vast power for good, a power representing the general will of the oppressed. One needed what Marilyn Young called a "redeemer revolution." For many American scholars in the antiwar movement, the redeemer revolution was China's "Great Proletarian Cultural Revolution." The North Vietnamese and other peoples around the world who copied it believed the Cultural Revolution would lead the way to a new, egalitarian, progressive world in which politics, as Mao Zedong had said, would truly "serve the people." There seemed to be a profound impulse to idealize China. But when the horrors of the Cultural Revolution finally became known in the West, many anti-imperialist American scholars were left without an ideological anchor. "China," Marilyn Young now says ruefully, "was the last revolutionary redeemer state that I'm going to back. The problem, though, is how to find a way to curb American nationalism. An alienated cosmopolitan is just what I want to be."

VII. AMERICAN MESSIANISM

There was something profoundly, idealistically American in the way Marilyn Young, and many other antiwar activists like her, radically rejected their country's foreign policy and embraced as a "revolutionary redeemer" the state that many of their fellow citizens feared as their worst enemy. They drew sustenance from the same messianic imagination that had produced Henry Luce's vision of the American Century. From the beginning of their history, many Americans have understood their society as part of God's plan for the end of time. The American experiment was directed toward the fulfillment of hopes for the redemption of all the people of the world. We were to be "as a city on a hill," preached John Winthrop, the first governor of the Massachusetts Bay Colony in 1630. We were the *novus ordo seclorum*, the new order of the ages, said our founders, inscribing this motto on the Great Seal of the United States in 1782. What else but such great hopes could have led the first Americans to leave the lands of their ancestors and journey on a new Exodus into a dangerous wilderness to settle a new land? What else could have emboldened the founders of our republic to risk their lives to gain independence from the British Empire?

The great danger in such talk, of course, has always been that we take it too literally. Taking themselves too seriously, Americans have been tempted to confuse their language of faith with their language of nation. From the beginning our great ideals were meant to inspire humility rather than triumphalism. That certainly was how Winthrop used his image of the city on a hill. God was making a covenant with the American settlers, Winthrop was saying, as He had with Israel after its exodus from slavery in Egypt. As written in Deuteronomy, this covenant not only promised blessings but threatened curses: "For we must consider that we shall be as a city upon a hill, the eyes of all people are upon us; so that if we shall deal falsely with our God in this work we have undertaken and so cause him to withdraw his present help from us, we shall shame the faces of many of God's worthy servants, and cause their prayers to be turned into curses upon us till we be consumed out of the good land whither we are going. . . ."

But already Winthrop was confusing the language of faith with the language of nation, for when he talked of the city on a hill it was not just the church of Jesus Christ but the plantation of New England he was referring to. His contemporary Roger Williams worried about this. He admonished Winthrop and his colleagues not to identify Massachusetts with the Kingdom of God, since "America (as Europe and all nations) lies dead in sin." Almost alone among his fellow settlers of New England, Williams argued that they had no right to take the land of others by force and that the American Indians were as much children of God as the English. Such warnings were frequently reiterated but not frequently heeded in our subsequent history.

Like many proud Americans before him, Henry Luce believed that America not merely had to measure itself with humility by the high standards of its messianic ideals but actually was "the sanctuary" of those ideals and could be "the powerhouse from which the ideals spread throughout the world and do their work of lifting the life of mankind from the level of the beasts to what the Psalmist called a little lower than the angels." Like Luce, many young antiwar activists in the 1960s believed that the American ideals of freedom and justice were universally applicable and could be embodied in an actual human polity. When confronted with America's failure to live up to its ideals, they assumed that there must indeed be a redeemer nation that was now the new sanctuary of those ideals. They fixed their hopes on China because its radical revolutionism seemed so different from the United States and because its self-destructive cruelties were for the time being hidden from outside view.

A Reinhold Niebuhr in his prime might have told them differently. By then he was old, ill, and approaching death; he died in 1971. Niebuhr would have echoed Roger Williams's insistence that redemption comes not from national politics but from God, and that all nations, including America and China, lie dead in sin. Nonetheless, he would have insisted that Americans, like all peoples, stand under the judgment of great ideals—freedom, justice, human dignity—and that the pursuit of these ideals is what gives meaning to life; that they should not give up, even though they would inevitably fail. But such wisdom was not readily available to Americans then. The institutional environment did not encourage the production or maintenance of the kind of moral balance that he had advocated.

Our universities, our government and corporate bureaucracies, our mass media, all tended to flatten out our understanding of what were our ideals. Freedom was interpreted as merely the ability to pursue private ends through the acquisition of the goods technology could produce and money could buy. Justice was equal opportunity for everyone to pursue these private ends as far as they could, so long as they did not hurt anyone else. There was little place left in our universities, bureaucracies, or media for people who questioned this understanding of freedom and justice; indeed, it was embodied in the very institutions that had given America its great wealth and power. But there was no way for Americans with this view to comprehend the international predicament they now found themselves in.

VIII. THE GLOBAL PREDICAMENT

In a far-off corner of the world, a small, economically backward, technologically primitive society was resisting the will of the United States. We presented it with a combination of carrots and sticks that should have made any reasonable society come into line: cooperate with us and we will eventually offer you generous economic assistance to rebuild your country, we said; defy us and we will unleash all the power of our technology against you—demolish your industries, lay waste to your cities, make life a living hell for your people. An aggregate of rational individuals should have quickly cooperated with us. But they did not. And when we savagely bombed them, they dug in their heels and became even more defiant, out of some collective sense of national anger and pride.

Our citizens, on the other hand, objected to the high costs of punishing this faraway enemy. The government tried to justify the war with the claim that our very security as a nation was threatened if the dominoes of communism fell across Indochina. But by the late 1960s, this was a farfetched notion.

Our predicament was that North Vietnam, and, as we have by now come to realize, many other societies in the world, did not think about the good life in the individualistic manner our institutions had taught us. We could not get these societies to cooperate with us on our terms. Nor could we stand aloof from these people in self-satisfied isolation, "the sanctuary of the ideals of civilization." Like it or not, our fate was inextricably woven together with that of foreign countries whose actions we could not control.

Though the Vietnam War is long over, this basic predicament remains. It takes many different forms. Some of these are military, such as in Central America, the Middle East, and southern Africa. Others are mainly economic, as in our relations with Japan. Others are political, as in our negotiations with the Soviets over arms control. Ultimately, we can accurately describe and meaningfully respond to these predicaments—this condition of being part of a diverse world we cannot control—only if we develop a richer, better grounded, more cosmopolitan understanding of our core ideals.

We have not been quick to do this. Our first reaction to the predicament when we experienced it in the Vietnam War was, of course, to try to escape it through our conventional repertoire of individualistic responses: improve the technologies of control; develop "smart" bombs; invent better surveillance measures; and thus lower the cost of bringing a recalcitrant enemy to heel. Critics who found this impossible or intolerable were equally individualistic: identify with the enemy; associate emotionally (if not necessarily in practice) with their revolutionary redemptive cause.

We still instinctively follow such courses of response. We try to build an impregnable shield against enemy missiles. We try to find a cheap way—one that won't cost many American lives—to overthrow governments we don't like, such as Grenada or Panama.

Another common response to our worldly predicament is to constrict our ideals, to say that Americans can no longer be committed to the cause of global freedom and justice. We need to recognize our limitations, the argument goes, set our sights on surviving and on keeping our standard of living from falling too far and too fast. Through fancy diplomatic footwork, we can remain Number One, even though we can't be as far ahead of the others as in the good old days, and even though we can't claim to be the powerhouse of the ideals of civilization. The way to do this is through the balance-of-power geopolitics so brilliantly executed by Henry Kissinger and his protégés. This is now the standard thinking of most professional schools and think tanks devoted to public policy.

But ordinary Americans generally have not taken kindly to such "realistic" approaches. "My opponent's view of the world," said George Bush in his acceptance speech at the 1988 Republican National Convention,

> sees a long slow decline for our country, an inevitable fall mandated by impersonal historical forces. But America is not in decline. America is a rising nation. He sees America as another pleasant country on the U.N. roll call, somewhere between Albania and Zimbabwe. I see America as the leader, a unique nation with a special role in the world. This has been called the American century, because in it we were the dominant force for good in the world. We saved Europe, cured polio, we went to the moon and lit the world with our culture. Now we are on the verge of a new century, and what country's name will it bear? I say it will be another American century.

Either Bush had learned nothing from the forty-seven years since Henry Luce first called for an "American Century," or he thought the American people hadn't.

A less constricted understanding of freedom and justice would enable us to see how they are connected with the common good. Freedom finds its fulfillment not merely in independence from but in active engagement with the society that creates us. Justice finds its fulfillment not simply in the formal rules that enable individuals to compete but in the commitments that members of a society make to ensure one another the minimum necessities of life. This view of freedom and justice morally embraces the reality of interdependence and does not hide from it. It does not entail heroic self-sacrifice. In fact, our commitment to being radically independent calls for the most heroic— and because of its lack of realism, often tragically futile—self-sacrifice. Through the lens of more socially realistic views of freedom and justice the world would appear as it is—a small and fragile planet, divided into a multitude of economically and politically interdependent societies of vastly disparate wealth and power, often causing destructive rivalries. The United States of America is still the strongest and wealthiest nation in this world. With its economic and political strength come great responsibilities to build the foundations for order, stability, and rising prosperity. But its power is no longer sufficient for it easily to impose its will, even on its allies, much less its rivals. To maintain peace, it will have to cooperate more readily with other nations than it is used to doing. It will have to use its great but limited power wisely, responding to genuine opportunities for peaceful settlement of disputes as well as to real dangers.

It would be a mistake, for example, to abandon all caution with regard to agreements for nuclear and conventional arms control. But it would be a tragedy not to take advantage of genuine opportunities for arms control simply because our economy is addicted to a huge defense industry. And it would be self-destructively foolish to fail to deal with remediable causes of the brutal poverty afflicting so much of the world. To a significant degree this poverty is a result of an economic system that favors the wealthiest countries at the expense of the poorest. In this poverty, as we have seen, lie the seeds of violent conflict. It is in no way a matter of starry-eyed idealism to advocate an alleviation of poverty through reform of the institutions governing international finance. It is hardheaded realism. Even if the measures to reduce Third World debt led to a slight decline in the standard of living in the United States (and it is by no means clear that this would be necessary), it does not demand heroic idealism to support them. "You don't have to tell Americans that they have to be completely self-sacrificing to share their wealth with the poor," says Father Richard Alhertine, a Maryknoll missioner. "This is in people's self-interest. You can tell them that sharing more of their goods with the poor will lead to more peace, more markets for our products. What could be more in people's self-interest than that? They avoid having themselves and their families destroyed by war."

IX. A NEW SENSE OF GLOBAL RESPONSIBILITY

From deep within the American tradition comes the notion that freedom is not purely a human accomplishment but a divine gift that conveys profound responsibilities upon the recipient. Often this sense of the giftedness of our freedom, and of its attendant demand for justice and social responsibility, is conveyed in sacred stories. Perhaps the most important of these is Exodus. The Exodus story binds together all sorts of Americans from the beginnings of our history to the present. In 1988 the thirteen-year-old daughter of a Jewish immigrant from South Africa offered this text as the reading for her bat mitzvah: "When you reap your harvest in the field, and forget a sheaf in the field . . . it is to go to the resident alien, the orphan, and the widow, that the Lord your God may bless you in all your enterprises. . . . You must remember that you were once a slave yourself in the land of Egypt; that is why I am commanding you to do this" (Deuteronomy 24:19). She is retelling a fragment of a story that Americans from John Winthrop to Martin Luther King have told over and over again to make the same point. It is a story that helps to define the consciousness of our society. A good society for Americans is one in which our children may still retell such a story with hope that they can at least partially live up to its meaning. As long as we define our national identity in terms of being able to create and sustain such a society, we will have a self-understanding that can be defended and pursued in the great society of our interdependent world.

But what about societies that do not read the Bible, that tell different stories, celebrate different rituals, to signify the relation between self and society? How shall we arrive at common understandings with them about the common good of the world? How shall we cooperate with them to create new international institutions to regulate commerce, protect the environment, prevent military conflict, and defend at least minimal standards of human decency? Our schools, churches, mass media need to teach us much more about the world beyond our borders. There is no way that we can be adequately educated without being able to compare and contrast our own basic assumptions with those of other societies. In this cross-cultural encounter, ideas of freedom and justice are deepened, and we can find common ground.

This formidable task of creating a genuinely multicultural community of interpretation is easier than it would have been a century ago. Now, cross-cultural dialogue does not occur in the context of colonialism and imperialism, although remnants of attitudes from earlier times still influence it. The whole world being tied together by a common market economy offers us the possibility of setting up a common agenda for international dialogue; where marked inequalities of economic power occur, there are still significant barriers.

All over the world people ask how they can utilize the vast creative power of this market economy while protecting their own communities from its destructive power. Usually, the first answer is that a sovereign nation-state must protect its citizens from the destructive effects of ceaseless economic competition. But governments are often motivated by fairly narrow definitions of national economic, political, or military advantage. As we recognize this truth, we see the need to set moral limits on both the dynamics of the market and the power of the state.

What should those limits be, and how should they be set? Consider, for example, the international debt crisis. In the 1970s, international banks lent huge sums of money (the amount outstanding is currently more than $1 trillion) to countries in the Third World for development programs and armaments. Needing to find investments for money deposited in their banks by Middle Eastern countries after oil prices had skyrocketed, the bankers aggressively encouraged these loans. A number of factors, including rising interest rates (a partial result of the United States government's own budget deficits), left many of the debtor countries unable to pay the interest on their loans.

Up until now, the international arrangements worked out to deal with this crisis have protected the interests of the banks more than the interests of the debtor nations. Like most sets of norms governing international conduct, they were arrived at through negotiations among political elites, bankers, officials of multilateral institutions like the International Monetary Fund, and officials of the governments of the world's most powerful countries. An international financial "regime" has brought order and predictability into the world's banking system but has done so at the expense of some of the poorest people in the world.

Moral leaders like Pope John Paul II have condemned these arrangements as grossly unjust.[26] Could there be an international financial regime that would resolve this crisis more justly? Could the process of establishing norms for international financial transactions become more democratic? Representatives of the poor countries should have more say in the process, and workers in the rich countries might also have to have more influence, since, after all, the influx of cheap imports from the Third World allowed by the present international system ultimately works against their interests also. A just solution to the debt crisis is in the long-term interest of most people in the world.

A lasting solution to this and similar crises requires a global "New Deal" that, at the cost of short-term losses to the world's largest banks, would foster a healthier pattern of development in the Third World and thus a more stable, prosperous, and cooperative world order.[27] The United States is still the most influential actor in the establishment of the norms of international finance, and any comprehensive reformation of them could not happen without its support and leadership. But this support and leadership will be forthcoming only if Americans at all levels of society understand that their own identity is tied up with those of people around the world, and if they see that their ideals of freedom and justice require a broad commitment to international cooperation.

There already exists a considerable international public opinion about the illegitimacy of war as an instrument of national policy, the need to respect basic human rights, the urgency of protecting the natural environment. There already exist a host of international institutions for dealing, however tentatively, with such issues—sets of rules and meanings for defining collective purposes, establishing responsibilities for cooperative action, setting common standards of humane conduct, and resolving debate about contentious matters through reason rather than coercion. Institutions are weak, but they are not negligible. In the last fifty years, international law has developed to an extent that no one would have imagined a few generations ago; and while there are many tensions, the pressure is great to advance further.

We do not envisage the emergence of some kind of world superstate, nor do we believe that that would be desirable. Rather, we favor the gradual emergence of overlapping institutions and agreements with various sanctions and enforcement powers. This is not to say that nation-states are not important or that they will go away. Indeed, they are indispensable for the new international institutions the world so badly needs. But they are less autonomous and self-legitimating than ever before.

The United States has helped to create many of the new international institutions, although it has impeded those, like the Law of the Sea, which it suspects run counter to its economic interests. Often enough, when Americans find themselves arguing with people of other nations about the ideals that international institutions ought to embody, they find their opponents using some version of America's own ideals against them. The framers of NSC 68 were right: the idea of freedom is the most contagious idea in history. From China to the Soviet Union to Eastern Europe, Leninist-style collectivism has failed. Throughout these societies, people are using Western ideas of freedom and justice to imagine the basis of a new, good society. Indeed, Western ideas about the dignity of the individual, the right to self-expression, and the integrity of the individual conscience are familiar terms in public discourse in most societies throughout the world that are integrated into the world political economy and influenced by the mass media. The use of this language of freedom is different in different cultures, of course. There are different ways of conceiving the balance between individual initiative and social responsibility. But our highest traditional ideals are no longer by any stretch of the imagination exclusively ours. They are the common property of humankind.

It is thus quite consistent with our highest ideals that we participate in international institutions that limit our autonomy. Participation in international efforts to create a good society will often require us to submit to the discipline of our own best ideals as they are reflected back to us. It is sometimes precisely the uncomfortable tension between ourselves and foreigners who believe even more insistently than we do in our traditional promise of liberty for all that can push us toward comprehensive solutions to the problems arising from our wealthy and privileged place in the world.

X. THE CHALLENGE OF A MULTICULTURAL WORLD

Now that East-West tensions are sharply diminishing, we can better understand that the deepest chasm is between the rich and the poor nations. It would be a mistake to imagine that, even with the best will in the world, the disparities between rich and poor nations will easily be resolved. It is true that everywhere in the Third World we find people invoking Western ideals, often to criticize Western behavior, but we also find a deep resentment at the pressures on them to westernize and a profound need to be proud of their heritage. We have a long way to go before we understand the cultural dynamics of rapid social change and the terrible price that it has exacted in individual souls and in societies all over the globe.

Theodore Von Laue, in his important book *The World Revolution of Westernization*, has suggested some of the qualities we need to cope with the tensions of a multicultural world. He reminds us that the rapid social change brought on by Western incursions have had traumatic consequences for almost all the societies on the receiving end. They have come to desire many features of Western society at the same time that they deeply resent the disruptions they have experienced and the sense of futility with respect to many of their efforts to catch up with the West. Often they have engaged in "anti-Western westernization," carrying out drastic social change under the aegis of an avowedly anti-Western ideology. Communism is only the most vivid example of this trend.

In the face of this complex reality, Von Laue urges the difficult path of patience and humility:

> A better command of reality will also give rise to patience and humil-
> ity—patience not to expect quick changes and to be satisfied with slow
> progress where it counts most, in individual consciousness and wills;
> and humility to submit willingly to the necessities caused by cultural
> conditioning. From humility also will grow the compassion needed for
> coping humanely with the existing inequalities. That compassion has
> to guide both the agents and the victims of cultural change, with special
> protection offered to the human dignity of the most helpless, so as to
> ease the hardships of inevitable prestructured cultural change. All must
> humbly strive to transcend their inherited cultural limitations and search
> for more inclusive human bonds.

But while we are all in this process of global change together, there are special responsibilities required of the most affluent:

> In this change of heart, Westerners must accept the blame for the
> hardships and tragedies in the developing countries. The anti-imperialist
> radicals are right. Before the Western impact, traditional societies ex-
> isted in reasonable harmony within the intellectual, spiritual, and ma-
> terial resources at their command, in precarious balance with their
> environment. It was the Western impact which forced them, against
> their will, into a complex world beyond their comprehension and re-
> sources, destroying into the bargain the former bonds of community.
> . . . Both sides have no choice but to look forward, recognizing that in
> the global confluence of innocently incompatible cultures they face a
> huge problem never encountered before in all human experience: How
> to overcome the obstacles to inter-cultural communication in a tightly
> compressed world, how to minimize the violence caused by cross-
> cultural incomprehension?
> The initiative for such "humanization" (as Fanon called the liberating
> process) must obviously come from the West . . . the self-centered West
> so blindly convinced of its superiority must wake up.[28]

XI. ZAPATA CANYON

Consider the following scene from the boundary between our affluent society and poverty-ridden Latin America.[29] In Zapata Canyon, a no-man's land straddling the border between San Diego, California, and Tijuana, Mexico, Father Florenzo Rigoni, an Italian member of the Missionaries of Saint Charles Borromeo, stationed in Tijuana, celebrates Mass for migrants trying to enter the United States illegally. Several hundred people attend the twilight ritual, their last before attempting the illegal crossing to California. "On this evening that for many represents your last hope, the realization of so many dreams," he begins, "I invite you to join in our Mass, that Christ may accompany you." His sermon continues the theme: "I believe . . . that each one of you remembers exactly the moment when you said goodbye to your loved ones. We hope this communion will accompany you on this long, long night. . . . We hope that you can cross, that you can arrive at your destination, that you find work." He prayerfully hopes "that this Mass can be, for each of us, an encounter of brothers, brothers in a world without borders, where no one asks for papers, where dusk will fall with bread and peace for all."

Father Rigoni's prayer offers a different kind of knowledge than the articulate analysis of an economist, the proposals of a politician, the systematic reflections of a moral philosopher. He offers no practical solution to the economic and political upheavals that have made the flood of immigrants across the border a major crisis. He does not even offer guidelines on how to untangle the moral dilemmas—for instance, how to balance respect for American immigration law with the needs of the migrants. Father Rigoni's is a sacramental enactment of the ideals that most of our ancestors carried to this nation—America as the promised land of freedom, achieved through Exodus, by the grace of God.

Of course, the realist says, America can no longer be the Promised Land for everyone bold enough or desperate enough to come to these shores. For good economic and political reasons we have to keep some control over our borders. The ideals enacted in Father Rigoni's Eucharist, however, illuminate a larger reality. The liturgy signifies that this group of migrants standing in a no-man's land betwixt and between two nations, unable to claim the protection of any law, separated from family and neighbors, unemployed—that these people nonetheless belong to a transnational institution, a church that, in prayer and sacraments, proclaims the God-given dignity of all human persons. In the teaching of this institution migrants are not to be treated purely as commodities in an international labor market or as pawns in a political struggle. This vision resonates with the best of America's ideals. It also shows us that we must try to understand the enormous cultural differences that separate us even from those who share many of our ideals. As a practical matter, America can no longer—if it ever could—tame on its own the economic and political forces that cause such desperate migration. Reluctantly reminded of its ideals by such inconvenient foreigners as Father Rigoni, the United States may find the will to cooperate in the difficult, but realistically urgent, international institution-building necessary for achieving the common good of all.

Conclusion

Democracy Means
Paying Attention

From the time we were children we were told by our parents and our grammar school teachers to "pay attention!" In more or less peremptory ways we have been receiving the same message ever since. Even though we may have grown inured to this injunction and shrug it off, there are few things in life more important. For paying attention is how we use our psychic energy, and how we use our psychic energy determines the kind of self we are cultivating, the kind of person we are learning to be.[1] When we are giving our full attention to something, when we are really attending, we are calling on all our resources of intelligence, feeling, and moral sensitivity. This can happen at work, at play, in interaction with people we care about. At such moments we are not thinking about ourselves, because we are completely absorbed in what we are doing. Although such moments are enjoyable, we do not seek them out because of pleasure, but because they are things we really want to do in terms of the larger context of our lives. They "make sense." And even though they are moments of minimal self-consciousness and their purpose is not to maximize pleasure, it is in such moments that we are most likely to be genuinely happy.

While paying attention, attending, is very natural for human beings, our attention is frequently disturbed. One of the most obvious features of psychotics is that they suffer from "disorders of attention,"[2] in which they have no control over the thoughts and sensations that come flooding into their minds and cannot consciously decide to focus their attention on objects of their concern. But all of us suffer, though less drastically, from such disorders of attention. When we are doing something we "have to do," but our minds and our feelings are some-where else, our attention is alienated. In such situations of disordered or alienated attention our self-consciousness is apt to be high. We may suffer from anxiety or, today's common complaint, "stress." Working hard at something we care about, giving our full attention to someone we love—these do not cause stress. But studying a subject we're not interested in and worrying about the grade, or doing things at work that we find meaningless but that the boss requires and we must do if we don't want to lose our job, or just being overwhelmed by more than we can cope with to the point where we feel fragmented and exhausted—these cause stress, these are examples of alienated atten-tion. We attend but fitfully—inattentively, so to speak—and therefore we are not cultivating our selves or our relationships with others. Rather, we may be building up strong desires to seek distraction[3] when we have free time.

Unfortunately, many of the distractions we hope will "deaden the pain"—alcohol; restless, channel-flipping TV watching; compulsive promiscuity—do not really help, for such distractions too are forms of alienated attention that leave us mildly, or sometimes severely, depressed. We have not exercised the potentialities of our selves and our relationships, and so we have not reaffirmed our selves in the larger contexts that give our lives meaning. If, after a stressful day, we can turn our attention to something that is mildly demanding but inherently meaningful—reading a good book, repairing the car, talking to someone we love, or even cooking the family meal—we are more apt to find that we are "relaxed."

Attention is, interestingly enough, a religious idea in more than one tradition. Zen Buddhism, for example, enjoins a state of mindfulness, an open attention to whatever is at hand; but Zen practitioners know this is always threatened by distraction.[4] Mindfulness is valued be-cause it is a kind of foretaste of religious enlightenment, which in turn is a full waking up from the darkness of illusion and a full recognition of reality as it is. This idea, common enough in Eastern religions, has analogies in biblical religion as well. God revealed himself to Moses from out of the burning bush as "I am that I am" (Exodus 3:14), and Moses had a hard time getting the children of Israel, distracted by their golden calf, to see the radical truth that had been revealed to him at Sinai. Jesus preached a new reality, a Kingdom of God which he declared was at hand, though most of his hearers could not make it out. Jesus said, "Having eyes do you not see, and having ears do you not hear?" (Mark 8:18) but many were too distracted to see or hear.

This is not the place to attempt to develop a full-scale phenomenology of attention; but, as in the religious examples, we mean to use attention normatively, in the sense of "mindfulness," as the Buddhists put it, or openness to the leadings of God, as the Quakers say. On the face of it, it may seem hard to tell the difference between attention and obsession. But as we shall use the term here, attention implies an openness to experience, a willingness to widen the lens of apperception when that is appropriate, and this obsession is incapable of doing. Obsessive "attention" is in this normative sense not attention at all but distraction, an unwillingness to be genuinely attentive to surrounding reality. The genius or the saint who seems to be obsessive may be attending to a reality whose significance escapes the rest of us.

So far we have considered the issues of attention, of disordered or alienated attention, and of distraction from the point of view of the individual. Self-control and self-discipline have a lot to do with whether we can engage with life or simply attempt to escape it. But people do not deal with these questions all by themselves, as we have already noted in the area of religion, nor can one alone develop a self able to sustain attention. As we have insisted throughout this book, we live in and through institutions. The nature of the institutions we both inhabit and transform has much to do with our capacity to sustain attention. We could even say that institutions are socially organized forms of paying attention or attending, although they can also, unfortunately, be socially organized forms of distraction.

II. ATTENTION IN THE FAMILY

Americans place a high valuation on family life. But if the family is only "a haven in a heartless world," a place that provides distraction from the harshness of the rest of our lives, we are certain to be disappointed; for families require a great deal of attention to function successfully. Despite romantic fantasies, marital love is not a narcotic that soothes all wounds. Attending to each other, expressing our deepest concerns and aspirations and listening to those of the other, is fundamental in a good marriage and crucial to the satisfaction it provides. But if we only expect to be attended to and we don't attend to the other, because we've had too hard a day or whatever (and this is more apt to be a male than a female failing), we sow the seeds of marital discord and deprive ourselves of the real rewards of marriage. The fact that married people live longer than single people suggests that marriage provides a kind of attention that is very important for human beings.

Attention is important between marriage partners, but it is fundamental for children. Infants who do not get attention, in the sense of psychic interaction and love, simply cannot survive, even if they are fed and clothed. And the quality of attention that children get has a great deal to do with how they turn out. In a study in Chicago that was concerned exactly with this issue, the psychologist Mihaly Csikszentmihalyi and the sociologist Eugene Rochberg-Halton found that the children of "warm families" (families where high levels of attention were given to each member) were significantly different from children of "cool families" (families where parents were distracted and inattentive and did not relate well to each other): "Children of warm homes are more sympathetic, helpful, caring, and supporting. The next difference is Affiliation: the relevant traits here are loyal, warm, friendly, sociable, cooperative. Warm homes also breed children who are less denying, defensive, and unsure of their worth."[5] In short, attentive homes breed attentive children.

It is significant for our purposes that the attentive homes were not "havens" to which the family retreated, avoiding civic and other outside involvements. It was the members of the cool families who had few outside associations; members of warm families tended to participate in voluntary groups outside the home. The capacity to sustain attention was being generalized beyond the family.

There was one worrisome finding in the study. The authors found that a heavy responsibility for the "warmth"—that is, the high level of attention—rested on one person: the wife and mother, who typically devoted her life to her family and children. The study was done in 1977 among families with children ten years of age or older, so it does not necessarily describe how things are now. There were some indications that many of these women, however loving and outgoing (and active in local voluntary associations), felt that they were paying a price for this accomplishment—namely, their own fuller participation in the larger world, in creative and fulfilling work—and were not entirely happy about it. It was not that the fathers were not involved in family life. They were significantly more involved than the fathers in cool families, but often in stereotypically male forms that did not do much to relieve the burden on the mothers; indeed, it may have increased it by amplifying the intensity of family life.

The picture of warm, attentive and cool, inattentive families that the Chicago study draws was taken in a moment during a continuous transition. It would be foolish to imagine that Americans could simply reconstitute such warm, attentive families today. It would be equally foolish to dismiss such families as "patriarchal," lumping them in with all the historic forms of the family since the heroic age of Homer; nor would it be any better to call them "bourgeois." As Csikszentmihalyi and Rochberg-Halton point out:

> For one thing, the classical bourgeois family is held together by the heavy weight of social traditions. Economic advantages, status considerations, social controls, and expectations maintain it; they provide the constricting goals that channel the psychic energy of its members. Thus it might be a closely knit unit, but it is not necessarily a warm one because the meanings that maintain it are rigid creations of social forces. By contrast, the warm families in our midst are practically *invented* by their members. Outside constraints are relatively light; the meanings that keep these families together are woven and mended by the constant attention of those who comprise them.[6]

Now that a considerably higher percentage of the mothers of small children are part of the work force than was the case in the 1970s, many of them full-time, our family capacities for continued institutional invention are strained, even as evidence is growing of the negative consequences for children of not having an intense family life.

The psychiatric social worker Judith Wallerstein has found in a sample she studied of children of divorced parents, ten years after their parents' divorce, between the ages of nineteen and twenty-nine, that many "are drifting through life with no set goals, limited educations, and a sense of helplessness. . . . Although only a few have dropped out of high school, most have not seriously pursued higher education. . . . They don't make long-term plans and are aiming below the intellectual and educational achievements of their fathers and mothers."[7] These people suffer among other things from what they perceive as lack of attention; and their own capacity for sustained attention is weak, their capacity for building a coherent life impaired.

If an intense family life is essential both for the satisfaction of adults and for the raising of responsible children who can nurture themselves and the world they live in, then part of the solution to the dilemma is surely that family responsibilities must be shared equitably between the parents. In most cases the new situation of having both parents work has resulted in an unequal and unfair division of labor in the home. The sociologist Arlie Hochschild argues that working women come home to care for house and children at what she calls a "second shift" (in a year it adds up to one month of twenty-four-hour days of work more than their husbands), even when they hold down a full-time job. The degree of inequality in the household is a major threat to the stability of the family:

> In one . . . study, Joan Huber and Glenna Spitze asked 1,360 husbands and wives: "Has the thought of getting a divorce from your husband (or wife) ever crossed your mind?" They found that more wives than husbands had thought about divorce . . . and that wives thought about it more often. How much each one earned had no effect on a spouse's thoughts of divorce. Nor did attitudes about the roles of men and women. But the more housework a wife saw her husband do, the less likely she was to think of divorce. As the researchers noted: "For each of the five daily household tasks which the husband performs at least half the time, the wife is about 3 percent less likely to have thoughts of divorce." (The five tasks defined as taking the most time in housework were meal preparation, food shopping, childcare, daily housework, and meal cleanup.)

Hochschild draws the conclusion:

> Happy marriage is supported by a couple's being economically secure, by their enjoying a supportive community, and by their having compatible needs and values. But these days it may also depend more on sharing a value on the work it takes to nurture others. As the role of the homemaker is being vacated by many women, the homemaker's work has been devalued and passed on to low-paid housekeepers, babysitters, and daycare workers. Like an ethnic culture in danger of being swallowed up by the culture of the dominant group, the contribution of the traditional homemaker has been devalued first by men and now by more women.
>   . . . One way to reverse this devaluation is for men to share in that devalued work, and thereby help to revalue it. Many working mothers are already doing all they can at home. Now it's time for men to make the move. In an age of divorce, marriage itself can be at stake.[8]

To put Hochschild's findings in our terms, there is a crisis with respect to giving and receiving attention in the family. The care of everything and everyone, especially children, is suffering because there is not enough time. Although the solution to this problem involves changes in the larger society, in the short term there is the immediate obligation on the part of everyone in the family to restore the centrality of attention and care. Here Hochschild is surely right that the primary need at the moment is a greater participation of men, of husbands and fathers, in the care that is essential to family life.

We may note here that attention and celebration are related, an issue we shall consider further below. Many of the most time-consuming family tasks have to do with meals: food shopping, preparing, and cleaning up. But the family meal, as we noted in Chapter 3, is the chief family celebration, even a family sacrament. What happens when no one has time to prepare a meal, when for days on end the family has no common meal? If everyone joins in the common tasks, husband as well as wife, and children, too, as much as they are able, then the family can enjoy at least several common meals a week, celebrate the pleasure they have in each other's presence and the good things they have mutually helped to prepare. Mealtime, as anyone who has ever had children knows, can also produce conflicts; but learning how to resolve them, to listen and be listened to, is part of the indispensable educational function of the common meal. We can be sure that having a common meal, and one to which all contribute, results in a warmer family and an enhancement of everyone's capacity for attention.

Just as we do not want to romanticize the "warm" families of the past, of any period when family life was allegedly better, so we do not want to advocate any single form of family life. The two-parent family with children has special significance because it is the family form that has carried primary responsibility for raising children and because it has become harder and harder to sustain. But recognizing the symbolic as well as practical centrality of this family form in no way means a derogation of other family forms. Many children who are raised in single-parent households become strong, self-reliant, and loving adults. Single parents need support from the larger community (as do couples), and the dignity of their task needs to be affirmed. Similarly, committed relationships between two members of the same sex, with or without children, can contribute to a general atmosphere of love and loyalty between couples and should not be seen as a threat to something considered a "normal" family. It is a historical illusion to imagine that there has ever been only a single family form. What is important is the quality of family life, not the diversity of its forms.

But the task of restoring family life, whatever form the family may take, cannot be the family's alone. As we noted Hochschild saying, a "job culture" has expanded at the expense of a "family culture." Only a major shift in the organization of work and in American public policy with respect to it will enable us to regain a balance between job and family. It might appear at the moment, when economic competitiveness is such an obsession, that Americans "can't afford" to think about the family if it will in any way hinder our economic efficiency. Nothing could be more shortsighted. In the long run our economic life, like every other aspect of our common existence, depends on the quality of people. How effective will our economy be if it depends on a generation of listless, anxious people unable to concentrate on anything very long and unconcerned about planning a coherent life for themselves? There is literally nothing more important than the quality of our young people, yet American public policy consistently refuses to *pay attention* to this fact.

III. THE IMPORTANCE OF WHERE WE ARE

The current difficulties of the American family have a great deal to do with how isolated it is, geographically and socially. There is much talk about the various "experimental" forms of the family today—two-earner households, single-parent households, same-sex couples with children—as well as "traditional" families where husbands work and wives stay home, but there is a great deal that all these families have in common and that makes it difficult for all of them to sustain family life. As the theologian John Snow puts it:

> In all these cases the absence of generational rootedness in a certain place with a long term commitment to its community and economic life makes money—cashflow—the primary source of security.
> With professional people there is the added security of insurance, health insurance and pensions. For the rest there are welfare, social security and medicare. In all cases the bottom line of security is money, not extended family and community.
> For some families there is no bottom line at all. They may be found in shelters, and some of them are healthy young people with small children and no addiction to drugs or alcohol, sometimes with jobs, yet unable to afford rent in such cities as Boston or New York. They lack even an address.[9]

What Snow is suggesting is that stable and attentive families need commitment to a place, which in turn requires locally and regionally coherent economies. Certainly many of the experiences that make childhood enjoyable, including extended-family celebrations, get-togethers, and reunions, have become rare in our society. Snow is surely right that the cause of this condition is the pressures generated by our current form of political economy rather than the desires of people.

As Snow points out, in American society today money is essential. The first obligation of public policy is to meet the most obvious needs of those who have no money at all. But the example of more successful welfare states—in Western Europe, for example—suggests that money and bureaucratic assistance alone do not halt the decline of the family, even though they may eliminate the obvious symptoms of homelessness and disease. What the family most needs is a context of relationships and institutions that give it attention, not just money. Decentralization of the economy and other public institutions would seem to go against the whole trend of modernity; but, as we pointed out in Chapter 3, new developments in high technology offer a way to reverse long-standing trends. Where heavy equipment is no longer the basis of the economy, one can bring training and jobs to where people are rather than the reverse; this may be possible as it has not been for a very long time. Some recent experiments in local private/public initiative, as well as renewed consideration of the idea of community-development corporations first put forward by the Johnson administration, suggest models.

A new look at localism, at decentralization, at what Josiah Royce long ago, in a positive sense, called "provincialism," at what Lewis Mumford called "settlement," would be valuable for much more than family life. Localism does not imply any abdication of the responsibility of the federal and state governments for the general population—it does not insist on a devolution of major responsibilities to underfunded and wavering "points of light." But it does envision that the government would support and expand local efforts where they exist—a summer program for teenagers sponsored by a black church in a depressed neighborhood, an effort by workers to buy out and renovate a plant whose owners wish to relocate in Brazil—and also help create such efforts where they don't exist. In Catholic social teaching this is known as the principle of subsidiarity, about which there is some diversity of interpretation.[10] As we use it here, subsidiarity implies that higher-level associations such as the state should never replace what lower-level associations can do effectively, but it also implies their obligation to help when the lower-level associations lack resources to do the job alone.

Herbert Croly in 1917, well before the principle of subsidiarity was formulated, argued for the importance of what he called "supplemental centers of allegiance," such as labor unions and trade associations, that would carry out important economic functions. For Croly the state must not only tolerate such institutions, "it must seek to strengthen them when they are weak." Local associations "have independent interests and wills of their own," while the state would act "as a correspondingly strong agency of coordination."[11] The fundamental rationale is that the people closest to the situation can give it the best attention, can respond to needs in the most appropriate ways.

This is, of course, easier said than done. High-quality child care, for example, should be offered as close to those who need it as possible—for mothers who are nursing, for example, preferably at their place of work. But general standards are appropriate. We know that the number of infants that even the best-trained child-care professional can handle is small, probably no more than three. Local initiative must not be used as an excuse to lower standards, particularly since the lowered standards are apt to follow lines of class and race. In general, we want to encourage the development of practices in various contexts among people who know and trust each other and have come to see themselves as responsible for each other's welfare, and with standards of care below which no group is allowed to fall.

John Dewey believed that the vitality of face-to-face communities was essential to a functioning democracy. He did not mourn the passing of narrow and parochial local communities; he envisioned a new, more open and active localism:

Whatever the future may have in store, one thing is certain. Unless local communal life can be restored, the public cannot adequately resolve its most urgent problem, to find and identify itself. But if it is reestablished, it will manifest a fullness, a variety and freedom of possession and enjoyment of meanings and goods unknown in the contiguous associations of the past. For it will be alive and flexible as well as stable, responsive to the complex and world-wide scene in which it is enmeshed. While local, it will not be isolated. Its larger relationships will provide an inexhaustible and flowing fund of meanings upon which to draw, with assurance that its drafts will be honored. . . . Publication is partial and the public which results is partially informed and formed until the meanings it purveys pass from mouth to mouth. There is no limit to the liberal expansion and confirmation of limited personal intellectual endowment which may proceed from the flow of social intelligence when that circulates by word of mouth from one to another in the communications of the local community. That and that only gives reality to public opinion. We lie, as Emerson said, in the lap of an immense intelligence. But that intelligence is dormant and its communications are broken, inarticulate and faint until it possesses the local community as its medium.[12]

We have noted the connections that James Coleman has discovered between effective schools, effective families, and effective communities. All these connections are matters of attention, close and painstaking attention. As Dewey saw it, the school was a community in microcosm that could help children to extend their attention from their families to those around them, locally and in the larger world as well. There is an obvious tension between schools as machines for the production of competitive, skilled workers and schools as learning communities for the creation of citizens. Here as elsewhere what is done is determined by the criteria used, by the measures paid attention to. Sometimes our criteria are dictated by ease of measurement (related to utilitarian ends) instead of by intrinsic importance—math scores are easier to measure than the virtues of citizenship. This leads us back to the basic problem of complexity.

IV. CAN WE PAY ATTENTION TO EVERYTHING?

In a large, diverse society, to know what is going on is difficult even for experts and baffling for ordinary citizens. Modern Americans have developed a number of quantitative measures to help us know what is going on by summing up large numbers of events in simple numerical terms. For example, we could never run a large-scale economy without money; if we had to barter for everything, we would never know what anything was worth and we would spend our whole lives bargaining. The price mechanism, problematic as it is, is an enormous simplifier. It is also the case, however, that since money is so often an effective simplifier, we are tempted to use it where it may not be appropriate. To use a measure when it seems to simplify but actually obscures is not to pay attention but to be distracted. In a society as obsessively concerned with money as ours, money is a major form of distraction.

The most obvious form of such distraction is the idea that the value of persons is determined by how much money they make. In American society it is very hard not to translate normal human doubt about self-worth into monetary terms, and reassure or denigrate ourselves as the case may be. The extraordinary disparity in incomes in the United States, so much greater than in other advanced industrial nations, may make sense in terms of competitive markets for services, but the question remains why we ever allowed such markets to grow so powerful in the first place.

Here we come face-to-face with the central argument of our book.

The Lockean ideal of the autonomous individual was, in the eighteenth century, embedded in a complex moral ecology that included family and church on the one hand and on the other a vigorous public sphere in which economic initiative, it was hoped, grew together with public spirit. Without overlooking its many injustices, we may note that it was still a society that operated on a humanly intelligible scale. Both the economy and the government were sufficiently small-scale as to be understandable to the ordinary citizen. Looking back from our present position, we can see that citizens then were faced with two possibilities, which we may denote as "cultivation" and "exploitation." (The marvelously ambiguous word "development" could apply to both.) The pattern of "cultivation," which many Americans did embrace for a time (and some never entirely abandoned),[13] involved the creation of regional cultures in some degree of harmony with the natural environment, where individuals, families, and local communities could grow in moral and cultural complexity. New England in the early nineteenth century showed some of the possibilities of such a pattern. It was not inconsistent with autonomous individualism, when this was supplemented by religious and republican understandings of the common good, and large-scale institutions did not dominate individual decision.

But the temptations of exploitation in so new and so rich a country proved irresistible. Once the possibilities of the new industrial economy were grasped, the results were dramatic. As Lewis Mumford put it:

> Art, culture, education, recreation—all these things came as an afterthought if they came at all, after our one-sided preoccupation with industry had ruined a great many of their potentialities, both in the life of the individual, whose health and intelligence had been sacrificed to material gain, and in the life of the community. When the pioneer had skinned the soil, he moved on; when the miner had exhausted his mine, he moved on; when the timber cutter had gutted out the forests of the Appalachians, he moved on. All those social types left rack and ruin behind them. The regional planner points out that no civilization can exist on this unstable and nomadic basis: it requires a settled life, based on the possibility of continuously cultivating the environment, replacing in one form what one takes away in another.[14]

The pattern of exploitation was destructive to both the natural environment and the life of the community. It appealed to that aspect of the tradition in which individual accumulation, measured in monetary terms, came loose from other social goods and became an all-consuming concern, undercutting even the devotion to self-cultivation and the family that were originally compatible with the Lockean ideal. But what should have been even more disturbing to true followers of Locke is that this pattern of exploitation led to the development of large economic and governmental structures that grew "over the heads" of the citizens and beyond their control, making a mockery of the most fundamental principle of Lockean political philosophy: government by the consent of the governed. When this was followed not only by plundering the natural resources of the North American continent but by the development of an imperial military state, operating with the secrecy and arbitrary domination that empires always employ, the eighteenth-century notion of a republican polity, answerable to its citizens in the full light of day, was hardly recognizable.

Let us consider a concrete example of the difficulty we face—at once social and environmental—and the changes required. Let us consider the place where the overwhelming majority of Americans live their lives: the regional metropolis. New York, Los Angeles, Chicago, Houston, Miami—these and their many kindred regions are for most of us the locales in which we live out our most basic relations with nature and humankind. How we live in these places profoundly forms the way we imagine our relations with the planet. If we have difficulty knowing how we might have a new relationship with nature and our fellow human beings, perhaps it is in part because of the experience of metropolitan life. It is here that we encounter directly the patterns of cultivation or exploitation.

The American way of life is inseparable from the metropolis, which has long been the source of popular dreams and aspirations. Today and for the foreseeable future most Americans will live and die in such regions, while even those outside them feel the magnetism of metropolitan products, ideas, and life-styles. Yet most Americans, like the citizens of other industrialized nations, would rather live in smaller settlements, something like an idealized Tocquevillean town.

Why the contradiction between desire and reality, even in democratic societies? Why has the city failed to win the hearts and minds of its lifelong inhabitants? Perhaps because they find so little in it to identify with. Most of its inhabitants are drawn to the city because they see it as the site of economic opportunity. The American city is even more the result of economic forces than comparable urban clusters in other capitalist democracies, such as Britain or Scandinavia, where to a greater degree urban planning agencies buffer society from the impact of purely economic pressures. The boundaries of the American metropolis are economic rather than political, determined by the ability of the region's transportation system to get workers to their jobs and home again within a single working day. The new dispersal of population made possible by federally funded highways has spread population farther from the historic city centers than ever before. In a society in which work is simply a job, a means to personal ends, the city becomes an indifferent means to private well-being.[15]

There is a parallel between the growth of the American political economy, which we have charted in previous chapters, and that of the nation's metropolitan regions, which has transformed much of our country in ways that look more like exploitation than cultivation. Just as the American industrial system was put together over the past century primarily under the aegis of those wealthy enough to need investments for their capital, in the city real estate, banking, corporate, and development interests have been paramount. Government has not been entirely absent, of course, but it has been highly fragmented on the local level. At all levels, true to the individualist tradition, the government's role, beyond that of maintaining the defense of the nation, has been that of handmaiden to commerce, providing "infrastructure" like sewers, roads, and schools that was needed for business growth, while its function as provider of social insurance to protect the individual against the vagaries of the market, for instance, is scarcely more than a half-century old, and still meagerly understood in America as compared to other advanced nations.[16]

We sometimes experience the profound analogies between the way we relate to the physical environment and the way we relate to each other, though more often the parallels and interactions are outside our awareness. The modern American metropolis—in its physical arrangements for the human activities of living, working, and meeting and in its commercialized landscape's ecological indifference—renders into brick, steel, and concrete the invisible rule of the market. The sprawling carpet of a metropolitan landscape such as Los Angeles or Houston registers the fluctuations of the market in its random distribution of business zones, shopping malls, and residential enclaves almost always segregated by income and race. Like that of the interconnected great society that propelled it, its material growth has been dynamic and flexible, but also bewildering.

The very randomness of a city's geographic distribution of workplaces, shopping sites, schools, and homes demands from each person considerable exertion of planning and effort just to hold together the basic activities of life. While this has become more and more true for the middle class, it is a far more overwhelming problem for the poor, who so often are forced into housing (if they can find it at all) that is distant from job opportunities or adequate schools. Metropolitan Americans only sometimes live near their kin. Still, they work at neighborliness with those physically (and therefore usually socio-economically) close to them, and they work even harder at sustaining far-flung networks of friends. Although city-dwellers are able or willing to disregard traditional social patterns (more than half do not live in families, for instance), the lack of social coherence penalizes the young, the elderly, the handicapped, and the socially ungraced.[17] As reluctant metropolitans, they view their larger social environment only instrumentally, and feel little connection to the city beyond their personal networks of association. The gap in ecological attention mirrors a gap in social loyalty.

The record of city growth over the last half-century graphically demonstrates that without sustaining institutions that make interdependence morally significant, individual attention becomes fragmented in focus and delimited in scope. Vast social inequality is rendered invisible by residential separation, and an often shocking indifference to human misery and environmental degradation goes generally unremarked. As the various sectors of life of the populace have become geographically dispersed, they have also become isolated from each other. Only a few city residents are oriented to the traditional urban culture in the arts, politics, intellectual and civic life, which at its best served to make America's older cities the foci of a creative social life. Especially in the newer metropolises of the South and Southwest, the "civic infrastructure" of government services as well as regionally integrating civic and cultural institutions is poorly developed. Significantly, religious associations are among the few institutions with large memberships that partly mitigate these tendencies toward segregated lives. Even the private pleasures and personal mobility of the affluent are tainted by some of the miseries long suffered by the urban poor. Everywhere the fear of criminal violence spreads gloom over the metropolis, prompting those with means to seek, in Tom Wolfe's phrase, to "insulate, insulate!"

These trends have confirmed Lewis Mumford's forecast thirty years ago when he wrote that the dispersion of urban life from the old core cities was not realizing its positive potential to generate "a new urban constellation . . . a multi-centered city operated on a regional scale." Instead, the effect was "to corrode and undermine the old centers without forming a pattern coherent enough to carry on the essential cultural functions on anything like the old level. Within a generation," he warned, "when they lose the momentum they now derive from the historic city, the resulting deterioration will be serious."[18] For Mumford, maintaining and extending the civilizing capacities of the city was serious indeed. He viewed the historic city as the central agency of cultural evolution. The city was the medium through which people could participate in the continuity of human experience and develop both themselves and the potentials of civilization itself. As Mumford put it, "Life has, despite its broken moments, the poise and unity of a collective work of art. To create that background, to achieve that insight, to enliven each individual capacity through articulation in an intelligible and aesthetically stimulating whole, is the essence of the art of building cities."[19]

The built environment of contemporary life gives us a visible analogue for the dispersal and conflict among the elements of family, work, personal, religious, and civic life that we have examined in previous chapters. In the fate of the contemporary American city we can see the consequence of inadequate and neglected institutions and perhaps read a lesson for all of society. But the quality of life in American cities would be even worse than it is were it not for the many institutions that have striven, often against the odds, to strengthen bonds of a nonpecuniary kind. Government, relatively weak and fragmented though it usually has been, has helped to keep alive many of the people and functions of little interest to the market. And the organizations of the "third sector"—such as schools and universities, religious organizations, theaters, museums, and orchestras, voluntary associations of all kinds—have given the collective purposes of justice, mutual aid, enlightenment, worship, fellowship, and celebration some substance in metropolitan life. They have civilized commerce and enhanced metropolitan life and have saved the market from its own worst consequences. But they have done more. They are points of "focal structure," places where people can meet to focus their attention and gain a sense of the whole of life through the cultivation of memory and orientation.

It is in such organizational—and physical—spaces that conflict can be sublimated into constructive argument. Here citizens develop new hopes through the practice of public conversation and joint action. The livability of our metropolitan regions depends on the balance between the public purposes that these institutions nurture and the purely quantitative thinking of the market. The search for dynamic balance between these purposes will, in a well-ordered city, take place within corporations and banks as well as around them. If the American Century represented the pursuit of always more and bigger regardless of the costs to nature or ourselves, with the dawn of a new era that experience now seems to teach a different lesson. The quality of life, like environmental and personal health, depends on cultivating integrated and balanced purposes. The cost is very high without it.

The Los Angeles basin, which covers an area nearly the size of Ohio, was once one of the most beautiful and is now one of the most economically and culturally dynamic regions on earth. Yet today there are few places anywhere in the United States in which governmental curtailment of individual choice reaches so intimately into the lives of citizens. On any given day, government, not the individual, decides whether factories will operate, and even whether—in a region dedicated to the ideal of suburban outdoor living—people can light up a barbecue in their own backyards. All this has come about in a desperate attempt to curb the life-threatening air pollution generated by the region's dependence on automobile transportation. Ironically, the draconian measures of government are directly traceable to earlier government indifference to or encouragement of the people's half-century-long pursuit of one of the American Century's leading goals: unrestricted individual mobility.[20]

Individual frustration and collective distraction are the contradictory outcomes of the unlimited pursuit of individual purposes. Metropolitan gridlock visibly illustrates many of the social tendencies of postwar America we have described in this book. Millions got to start anew, and many prospered. But what we can now also see, in Los Angeles and elsewhere, is the enormous social and environmental cost of growth directed by such narrow goals without the counterbalance of integrating purposes.

V. THE PROMISE OF ATTENTION:
A SUSTAINABLE LIFE

What the metropolis of the American Century has lacked above all was sufficient attention to the whole. Its legacy is environmental damage, social neglect of the least advantaged, and restricted possibilities for all. What is needed for the twenty-first century is not only more and different infrastructure but the sort of "focal structure" that government, the "third sector," and public-private partnerships of business and not-for-profit institutions together can provide. The task of these focal structures is to enhance the capacity of metropolitan citizens and institutions to promote the quality of life for all citizens.

The popularity of urban neighborhood development in the 1970s was strengthened in the 1980s by public-private partnerships, which helped to revive many core cities, though we cannot forget that most of these initiatives benefited the well-to-do and that the position of the urban poor has substantially declined. Today, environmental politics offers an inclusive rallying point that brings together concerns for social justice, economic viability, and environmental integrity. Ecological sustainability as a purpose converges with the desire for safe, diverse, and economically viable communities. As the case of Los Angeles shows, these purposes join in the effort to reverse the indiscriminate sprawl of the postwar decades and aim instead toward more bounded metropolitan environments. The enlargement of our capacity for this will be the office of the democratic public. The public lives through those institutions that cultivate a constituency of conscience and vision. This constituency is the creative matrix from which city, state, and national leaders can arise; its task: to make the interdependency of modern life locally comprehensible so that responsible action is possible.[21]

Americans have pushed the logic of exploitation about as far as it can go. It seems to lead not only to failure at the highest levels, where the pressure for short-term payoff in business and government destroys the capacity for thinking ahead, whether in the nation or in the metropolis, but also to personal and familial breakdown in the lives of our citizens. In this book we have repeatedly suggested the need for a new paradigm, which we can now call the pattern of cultivation. This pattern would not mean a return to the settlement forms of the early nineteenth century, but it would be the attempt to find, in today's circumstances, a social and environmental balance, a recovery of meaning and purpose in our lives together, giving attention to the natural and cultural endowment we want to hand down to our children and grandchildren, and avoiding the distractions that have confused us in the past. Again, what has for a long time been dismissed as idealism seems to be the only realism possible today.

But how can we pay attention to all of the problems that beset us? Even the experts feel more comfortable if they can distract themselves by holding on to simple measures of the situation like GNP or comparative military strength. Fortunately, military dangers have lessened—we can expect continuing conflict in the Third World, but hardly of the magnitude of the Soviet military threat. But it would be foolish to replace a military-political fear of the Soviet Union with an economic fear. Indeed, an obsession with competitiveness against Japan or Western Europe can be just as great a distraction from reality

272 THE GOOD SOCIETY

as an obsession with communism. The whole argument about whether the United States is in decline or is as strong as ever is also beside the point and fundamentally distracting. Clearly we are headed toward a future in which a number of highly successful national or regional economies will coexist; rather than worrying about where the United States is in the hierarchy, we should be worrying about creating a humane economy that is adequate to our real purposes, and a healthy international economy that operates for the good of all peoples. As Václav Havel has been saying, we need to replace a politics of fear with a politics of trust. Trust gives us space for attention, even when what we have to attend to seems baffling, whereas fear drives us to seek distraction, the kind of reassurance that only big numbers can provide.

Money and power are necessary as means, but they are not the proper measures of a good society and a good world. We need to talk about our problems and our future with a richer vocabulary than the indices that measure markets and defense systems alone. Words like "attention" and "distraction," "cultivation" and "exploitation" may begin to encourage conversations in which we can define our priorities, our needs to strengthen existing institutions, and our needs to create new ones.

We need experts and expert opinions, and experts can certainly help us to think about the important issues. But democracy is not the rule of experts. It is basic to the education of citizens that they learn how to evaluate expert opinion. Much of high-school and college education actually does give students help in this matter, but more could be done if it was acknowledged as a central task of education. In any event, evaluating the opinions of experts is only the beginning and not finally the most important problem. Weighing the moral implications of different options is what is fundamental. Here the citizen who has learned to pay attention in the family and the local community can generalize to larger issues. When the family is a school of democracy and the school is a democratic community, then the beginnings of such wisdom have already been learned.

Our institutions are badly functioning and in need of repair or drastic reform, so that if they are to support a pattern of cultivation rather than one of exploitation, we must change them by altering their legal status and the way we think about them, for institutional change involves both laws and mores. More than money and power, these need to be at the center of our attention.

VI. ATTENTION AND DISTRACTION

We took up the idea of attention as initially a matter of individual psychology. As we followed it, we moved to ever larger social and cultural circles: from self-cultivation, to concern for the family, to our local communities and the vast cities most of us live in, to our national life and life in the world. Attention and distraction, the disturbance and destruction of attention, occurred at every point. Everywhere attention had to do not only with conscious awareness but with the cultivation of human possibilities and purposes, whereas distraction was a response to fear and exhaustion, leading to shallow escapism in some circumstances, to defensive efforts to dominate and control through power or money in others.

Attention and distraction are not merely descriptive but normative terms. Giving attention to a crying infant is something good; working at McDonald's in order to have the money to buy designer jeans rather than studying does little to develop a fuller life or the capacity to contribute to society. Attending and caring or caring for are closely related. Because we have let too much of our lives be determined by processes "going on over our heads," we have settled for easy measures that have distracted us from what needs to be attended to and cared for. One way of defining democracy would be to call it a political system in which people actively attend to what is significant.

It is doubtful whether attention has priority in America today. Much of our current politics seems to be designed to distract us from what is important and seduce us into fantasies that all is well. Worse, these politics offer solutions that only increase our distraction—as, for example, when the only answer to transportation problems is to increase the number of lanes on the freeways, or, more basically, when "growth" is offered as a universal panacea with no attention to what kind of growth or with what consequences. Attending means to concern ourselves with the larger meaning of things in the longer run, rather than with short-term payoffs. The pursuit of immediate pleasure, or the promise of immediate pleasure, is the essence of distraction. A good society is one in which attention takes precedence over distraction.

In this book we have surveyed the problems of many of our large-scale institutions, but in this chapter we have returned to the family to illustrate some of the central issues we are concerned with. Among these is what the psychologist Erik Erikson called "generativity," the care that one generation gives to the next.[22] Generativity is a virtue that Erikson initially situates in the concern of parents for children, but he extends it far beyond the family so that it becomes the virtue by means of which we care for all persons and things we have been entrusted with. With what kind of society will we endow our children and our children's children, what kind of world, what kind of natural environment? By focusing on our immediate well-being (are you better off now than you were four years ago?), and by being obsessively concerned with improving our relative income and consumption, we have forgotten that the meaning of life derives not so much from what we have as from what kind of person we are and how we have shaped our lives toward future ends that are good in themselves.

The end of the cold war, and of what may come to be called the Seventy-five Years' War of the Twentieth Century, of which the cold war was the final phase, gives us a chance to step back from these obsessions and think about the future which, perhaps, we unconsciously doubted we had. Now that the threat of the mushroom cloud is receding, we may see that many things we have been ignoring for too long need our attention.

The major problems that come to light require the virtue of generativity to solve—indeed, a politics of generativity. The most obvious problem is the perilous neglect of our own children in America: levels of infant mortality, child poverty, and inadequate schooling put us at or near the bottom in these respects among industrial nations. We fight a "war on drugs," but we do little to fight the despair that leads to the desire for drugs. It might be obvious that meaning is the best antidote to drugs and that there is no meaning if there is no future; but in our theatrical, macho politics more police, more prisons, more military interdiction are more obvious answers.

Poverty and despair fester in our own society, even though in relatively small pockets; but Third World countries know about poverty and despair on a massive scale, and many of them have been slipping backward for a decade or more rather than progressing. Their situation is certainly not "our fault," although the American banks and the American government have contributed to their problems, particularly in the handling of their enormous foreign indebtedness. Nor can we solve their problems for them, though, in accordance with the principle of subsidiarity, we can help where our help will be effectively used. But allowing the current enormous disparities to go on indefinitely runs the risk of a renewal of global conflict that will endanger all our hopes.

Finally, grave threats to the environment are obviously accumulating. To neglect these problems is to make everything else unimportant, for we will have made our planet uninhabitable. But here, too, an emphasis on the short term and the immediate payoff prevents our attending to these problems in a more serious way. For Americans environmental and social problems go hand in hand, although middle-class people are often tempted to think more about the planet than about their less privileged neighbors. The question that both issues raise is whether or not we will ever become settled on this continent. Settlement does not mean static inertia. It means a willingness to cultivate the purposes of individual and common lives rather than be swept along in the fervor of exploitation. A settled people understands its own habitat; it sees the need for wilderness and agriculture as well as cities; and it tries to think of whole regions and their needs and not just the concentrated desires of those with the most wealth and power. A settled people is concerned with the recovery of trust in family and neighborhood; with schools, museums, concert and lecture halls, which enhance its cultural life; and with enabling all its citizens to participate in these goods, so that there is no underclass living in fear and making others fearful. A settled people in the sense we are using the term is not a self-satisfied but an attentive people, concerned with drawing on its multicultural resources for the enrichment of the lives of all. A pattern of settlement and cultivation allows not only the nurturing of ethnic and racial cultures within communities of memory but an open interchange of learning between such communities, a kind of global localism. A settled people is concerned above all with living as fully as possible rather than preparing to live or fearing for their lives. Greed and paranoia, and their giant institutional forms, are enemies of settlement and cultivation.

Needless to say, settlement and cultivation are what Americans need, and they are, in richly diverse form, what troubled peoples all over the globe are also seeking. But settlement in the profound sense in which we use the term will not come as the result of aggregate private decisions; an institutional context must educate and nurture such decisions. Raising consciousness is critical, and creating new institutional patterns, formal and informal, legally and through custom, is equally critical.

Institutional change comes only as a result of the political process. An attentive democratic politics is not some extraneous demand that busy and harried citizens may ignore or attend to fitfully out of "liberal guilt." Our argument is that if we are going to be the kind of persons we want to be, and live the kind of lives we want to live, then attention and not distraction is essential. Concerns that are most deeply personal are closely connected with concerns that are global in scope. We cannot be the caring people whom our children need us to be and ignore the world they will have to live in. We cannot hide from the fact that without effective democratic intervention and institution-building the world economy might accelerate in ways that will tear our lives apart and destroy the environment. Moral discourse is essential in the family; it is also essential in the world. There is no place to hide. "Distracted from distraction by distraction" is how T. S. Eliot characterized our situation. It is time to pay attention.

VII. THE POLITICS OF GENERATIVITY

At many points we have observed how shortsighted our mechanisms for decision are. Priority in both American economics and American politics has been given to immediate return. Advertising and public rhetoric focus on the individual income, the individual house, the individual car, the individual gun. Except for invoking the ever-present term "freedom" (even when our actual future freedom is being constantly diminished by short-term decisions), our leaders show little concern for the world we are moving into or that our children and grandchildren will have to live in.

In the face of a mass culture and politics dominated by distraction, which offers not only temporary narcotics for anxiety but also a cover for those whose interests are threatened by serious change, there is an urgent need for a new politics of generativity. In recent years the Democratic party has been only half an opposition party, shifting uneasily between trying to outbid the Republicans in offering individual distractions and offering specific policies (such as legislation mandating unpaid parental leave, or national health care, or aid to education) that are at least part of a politics of generativity. But in the absence of an overall philosophy of generative interdependence (as opposed to narrowly self-interested individualism), this liberal laundry list can be taken apart and discarded at will.

The last two decades have been a time of neglect of America's material and social resources, whatever the verdict may finally be on our economic performance of those years. The breakdown during the 1970s of the informal cooperation among government, business, and labor, which had been typical of the "pluralist" politics of the years 1945–68, set in motion a general erosion of social trust. The material consequences of this regression have been profound. Investment in private and public infrastructure has slowed, especially in the public sector, with manifest consequences for our economic life. And the simultaneous disinvestment in "human resources" has already shown itself in the social decay of crime, addiction, cynicism, eroded civility, weakened education, and most shockingly, perhaps, in the pervasive indifference of youth to the world around them.[23]

This withdrawal of responsible attention has spread throughout American society, weakening our economic competitiveness as compared with that of nations such as Germany and Japan, and sapping the energies for social and political attention as well. The pattern of self-seeking indifference was begun and, as the political analyst Kevin Phillips has pointed out, promulgated by many of the wealthiest and most powerful segments of the nation, which defended and partially masked the socially regressive consequences of this generalization of distrust and self-seeking by sponsoring a revival of the nineteenth-century economic ideology of the free market.[24] In the current context of multinational finance, of course, this economic vision cannot mean a return to a world of individual entrepreneurs, however attractive this mirage has proven to some voters: it is simply a carte blanche to the owners and managers of capital to skim profits with even fewer entangling social responsibilities. At the end of the cold war, the great irony is that the Lockean United States may turn out to be more ideologically rigid than the USSR.

We know that the interdependence of modern societies is both complex and fragile. Thus, viability depends, far more than it did in the past, upon the mutual trust and goodwill of all citizens, and notably of the essential functional groups—business, labor, government, the professions, and the "third sector." Viable interdependence, as we have argued repeatedly, requires that participants integrate a cognitive understanding of their interdependence with the practical enactment of goodwill demanded in each institutional context. All-out pursuit of individual or group advantage, which is one consequence of institutional failure in the polity, quickly becomes not only pathological but threatening to the survival of all. Under modern conditions a society's economic and social development hinges essentially on ability to sustain institutions that mediate mutual trust and civic responsibility. Focusing collective attention on this capacity, developing it, and nurturing institutional reforms to promote it is the central theme of the politics of generativity.

In a postindustrial, global economic order, the old categories of (material) "base" and (institutional) "superstructure" are rapidly losing their meaning. Economic development today is the result of a ratio of "inputs" in which raw materials count for less as technological and institutional innovations count for more. It is no longer a matter of mineral deposits and low wages, as in the nineteenth-century model. Not only physical infrastructure but education, socially and environmentally sustainable communities, and managerial and political capacities are the keys to growth and prosperity.

The politics of generativity takes social inclusion and participation as a key theme—for economic no less than for moral and social reasons. Institutions of international cooperation and regulation are necessary for economic growth, even for sustainable competition, within as well as among nations. And it is the real competition among nations to develop capacities for this kind of political learning that the United States, obsessed by an obsolescent economic ideology, is in danger of losing. The Hayek-Friedman ideology of pristine, Darwinian market competition is practiced nowhere—not in international commerce and least of all by the successful trading and exporting nations, though it may serve the short-term political interests of business and investment bankers. It justifies keeping wages low as it protects the banks' disastrously imprudent international investments, but it will be catastrophic for the United States, and finally for business as well, and in the not so very long run.

We are a society that still denies to many of its citizens the supports of societal membership and dignity that are routinely extended to the privileged—and to all in many of our "competitor" nations—especially health insurance and pensions. The United States is the only advanced nation in which by law nearly all job holders can be dismissed at will.[25] With only a few heartening exceptions, American management has consistently refused to break down the barrier between those whose work allows them some discretion, trust, and the prospect of career advancement and the majority of employees, who lack these things and a secure retirement pension as well. And yet American corporations spend vast sums attempting to improve morale and limit job turnover. A politics of generativity must question and try to overcome these self-defeating failures of social learning. It can no longer assume that a policy of settlement and cultivation is utopian, and must realize that it has become one of enlightened self-interest. But it must realistically attend to the equity and inclusiveness of our institutions. Without morally informed institutional renovation, we are unlikely to develop the trust that is our most valuable social and economic resource.

It may be that, as has happened in the past when the political parties ignore major realities, a new social movement is called for. One thinks of the Green movements which have made some headway in Europe, but much more than environmentalism is required. The politics of generativity includes concerns for a good national society and a good global society as well as a good relation to the environment. A politics of generativity can develop within an existing political party, or through a new social movement, or begin with a social movement and then penetrate a political party. But it would not easily be located on the existing ideological spectrum. It would not favor big government any more than big business. It would favor effective political initiative at the federal and state levels, backed by major commitments of money and expertise, but in the service of local and regional initiatives and institutions—that is the practical meaning of subsidiarity.

Even more important, such a politics is premised on active citizen involvement and discussion—with issues of long-term purpose and consequence taking precedence over the simpler indices upon which current policy analysis focuses—public participation in administrative decisions, constituency involvement in corporate decisions, and a closer public monitoring of legislative action, through review commissions and public debates. The emphasis would be on regulation, setting limits beyond which market and monetary forces are inappropriate and administrative action without review cannot go, and on long-term planning.

The structural changes that a generative politics can produce will anchor our economic and political institutions firmly in the moral discourse of citizens concerned about the common good and the long run. This would make it harder for them to operate over the heads of the people. The achievement of such a generative politics will be to realize Robert Dahl's third democratic transformation. But none of this will happen unless a new moral paradigm—a paradigm of cultivation—replaces the old, outworn Lockean individualist one.

VIII. A PLACE FOR NEW PERSPECTIVES

Walter Lippmann, in his 1937 book *The Good Society*, from which we have taken our title, discussed the "higher law" that he believed Americans had not properly understood when they interpreted it as only the protection of the individual's absolute rights. The higher law, concerned as it is with human rights, is rooted in a fundamentally social understanding of human beings:

> The development of human rights is simply the expression of the higher law that men not deal arbitrarily with one another. Human rights do

not mean, as some confused individualists have supposed, that there are certain sterile areas where men collectively may not deal at all with men individually. We are in truth members of one another, and a philosophy which seeks to differentiate the community from the persons who belong to it, treating them as if they were distinct sovereignties having only diplomatic relations, is contrary to fact and can lead only to moral bewilderment. The rights of man are not the rights of Robinson Crusoe before his man Friday appeared.[26]

The higher law that provides the basis for human rights is not a truth complete in itself already known to select philosophers: "To those who ask where this higher law is to be found, the answer is that it is a progressive discovery of men striving to civilize themselves, and that its scope and implications are a gradual revelation that is by no means completed."[27] Nonetheless, classical philosophy and biblical religion give us our best clues as to what the higher law entails. In so arguing, Lippmann for the first time in his work married his own deeply liberal respect for individuality to older Western traditions.

In a closing section entitled "On Designing a New Society," Lippmann argued that we should be moving toward not a single homogeneous system but a society that respects and encourages diversity and attempts to "reconcile the conflicts that spring from this diversity." Such a society will indeed require virtue:

It requires much virtue to do that well. There must be a strong desire to be just. There must be a growing capacity to be just. There must be discernment and sympathy in estimating the particular claims of divergent interests. There must be moral standards which discourage the quest of privilege and the exercise of arbitrary power. There must be resolution and valor to resist oppression and tyranny. There must be patience and tolerance and kindness in hearing claims, in argument, in negotiation, and in reconciliation.

But these are human virtues; though they are high, they are within the attainable limits of human nature as we know it. They actually exist. Men do have these virtues, all but the most hopelessly degenerate, in some degree. We know that they can be increased. When we talk about them we are talking about virtues that have affected the course of actual history, about virtues that some men have practised more than other men, and no man sufficiently, but enough men in great enough degree to have given mankind here and there and for varying periods of time the intimations of a Good Society.[28]

That Lippmann turned to biblical religion and classical philosophy for elements of the new vision he thought necessary is relevant in our present situation. Recent events in Eastern Europe, as well as past experiences in our own history, suggest that the churches, synagogues, and other religious associations might be one place open to genuinely new possibilities, where cultivation and generativity have clear priority over exploitation and distraction. As an example of fresh thinking about our situation, we call to mind the American Catholic bishops' 1986 letter on the U.S. economy,[29] which argued eloquently that "the dignity of the human person" provides the moral cornerstone for social and economic life. But for the bishops the human person is not an abstract individual but one whose dignity is realized only in community. The commandments to love God with all one's heart and to love one's neighbor as oneself lay the foundations of human community. All persons have rights, but they arise from a mutual bond to care for one another as members of one creation and are rooted in "reverence for God as Creator and fidelity to the covenant." Justice begins with recognition of the need of all persons to take part in the life of a community in order to be fully human, by being united with one another in mutual activity and, finally, mutual love.

The distinctive contribution that the bishops' letter makes to public debate cuts across partisan lines and challenges the conventional bipartisan wisdom that economic well-being is defined in terms of individual levels of material subsistence and consumption, that the economy's success is measured by the aggregate and average amounts of wealth it produces and its efficiency in doing so. Most fundamentally, the bishops challenge the premise that the economy's activities, rules, and relations lie in a social sphere separate from politics and morality. Instead they propose a thick, organic connection in our moral understanding of economic, political, and spiritual life, centered around the necessity of communal solidarity and realizing the dignity and sacredness of all persons. Economic institutions should be judged not by the amount of wealth they produce but by how they produce and distribute it: in doing so do they enable everyone in the community to take part in productive work, learning, and public affairs? Human rights in general, and in particular the rights of once excluded people to take part in a good society, are rooted in a moral matrix of communal solidarity springing from creation and bound by covenant; they do not arise prudentially from the essential self-interest of individuals and their contractual exchange.

In making this argument the bishops recognize that the renewal of a shared vision of a good society must come through critically inter-relating the distinctive moral traditions of American culture instead of trying to flatten them into a uniform consensus. So the church seeks to give its own members moral guidance in terms of biblical narrative, theology, and church tradition. But it also seeks to add its voice to public debate through reasoned argument persuasive to those who do not share its own tradition of faith. The confidence that social cooperation can be sustained in public affairs, and that culturally distinctive moral efforts can be carried out compatibly, is itself an expression of faith: "The common bond of humanity that links all persons is the source of our belief that the country can attain a renewed public moral vision."[30]

Like the Protestant Social Gospel, Catholic social teachings in the past century affirm the traditional emphasis on the need to become good persons through the love of God and neighbor and also a com-mitment to reorder society's institutional arrangements so that people, flawed as they are by "original sin," may live more justly and humanely with one another. A just social system is impossible without people being just. Justice is first and foremost a virtue, and it inheres in individuals and institutions that carry out God's commandment to care for one another—to feed the hungry, heal the sick, and enable the able-bodied to work and contribute to the commonweal.[31]

In defining the institutional conditions that permit genuine com-munities to flourish, Catholic social thought underlines three princi-ples: (1) that institutions must protect the dignity and inherent sacredness of persons as God's creatures; (2) that social organizations should be ordered in interdependent and cooperative forms, with attention to the natural subsidiarity by which larger and more pow-erful political and economic institutions sustain smaller communities instead of dominating them; and (3) the necessary existence of social structures, such as the family, church, professional and civic associ-ations, that mediate between the state and its citizens without being controlled by either the will of the state or the interests of individuals.[32] The purpose of the state, then, is to serve this articulated social order by furthering the cooperation and well-being of all these groupings and institutions.

The principle of subsidiarity favors social cooperation and decen-tralized power in forms that encourage "a new experiment in partic-ipatory democracy" in the American workplace and polity (proposed in Chapter 4 of the bishops' letter). Its notion of government ordered to aid the flourishing of human beings in community harks back to America's founding ideals as a democratic republic. The principle of subsidiarity offers neither progressives nor neoconservatives a partisan blueprint for political economy. Indeed, one crucial subsidiary function of the state in this understanding is that of encouraging and heeding a moral argument in public life that moves beyond ideological stereotypes.

No political party and few political organizations have put forward so comprehensive a vision, a vision remarkably like Lippmann's analysis in *The Good Society*. In a period when one or another version of savage capitalism is pushed as the answer to our quandary about competitiveness, it is a healthy sign that the bishops' letter generated discussion of the fundamental issues of modern economic life.

IX. RESPONSIBILITY, TRUST, AND THE GOOD SOCIETY

Another key term in our moral vocabulary that is closely related to attention, and indeed to all the issues involved in the effort to create a good society, is "responsibility."

Responsibility must begin with attention. To act responsibly we must ask: What is happening? What is calling us to respond? The theologian H. Richard Niebuhr in his book *The Responsible Self* argued that all our action is a *response* to action upon us, for we are caught in an inescapable web of relationship with other human beings, with the natural world, and with the ultimate reality that includes and transcends all things—what Jews and Christians call God. In many situations we either passively accept what is happening to us or try to evade the implications of what is occurring around us. But, says Niebuhr, we must *interpret* what is happening; especially, we must interpret the intentions of the people we deal with. A third element in responsibility has to do with the effect on others of what we do, a matter that Niebuhr calls "accountability." But our actions usually are not isolated encounters with persons or things with whom we have no continuing relation but, rather, occur in contexts that are already patterned and partake of an element of *social solidarity*. Summing up, Niebuhr wrote: "The idea or pattern of responsibility, then, may summarily and abstractly be defined as the idea of an agent's action as response to an action upon him in accordance with his interpretation of the latter action and with his expectation of response to his response; and all of this is in a continuing community of agents."[33]

So far Niebuhr is being a good sociologist, for sociologists have understood human action in just such a relational context. Indeed, for sociologists, institutions are defined as those patterns which human

agents create to regulate action in a "continuing community of agents."
But for Niebuhr the idea of the moral life as the responsible life is
not just sociologically descriptive but a key to what he calls the "biblical ethos which represents the historic norm of the Christian life."[34]
Two aspects of responsibility go beyond purely sociological description: one is trust, and the other is the scope of the responsible action
to which we are called.

Trust—and here Niebuhr is being both sociologically realistic and
religiously perceptive—is never to be taken for granted. In our relation
to the world, trust is always in conflict with mistrust. Because of
previous experiences a degree of mistrust is usually realistic; yet if we
are dominated by mistrust we cannot attend or interpret adequately,
we cannot act accountably, and we will rupture, not strengthen, the
solidarity of the community or communities we live in. But how can
we trust? Erik Erikson locates what he calls "basic trust" in the child's
earliest experience with the mother (perhaps today we would better
say "parent") and suggests that if trust has not been warranted then,
it is doubtful that it ever will be adequately established in the personality.[35] Theologians such as Niebuhr suggest that behind parental
love, essential as that is, lies a deeper question: Is reality, is Being
itself, trustworthy? To argue that trust or faith is justified, that God
as the very principle of reality is good, is not obvious—not obvious
to Christians and Jews, who down through the centuries have been
supposed to believe it, and not obvious to anyone who has to live in
the world as it is. Trust or faith, like parental love, is a gift. It comes
to individuals and groups in particular experiences at particular times
and places. Niebuhr did not say that it comes only to Jews and Christians, or that it comes only to people who think of themselves as
religious, but that to whomever it comes, it comes as a gift. And when
it does come, it brings a great joy and enables us to live responsibly
with our fellow beings.

Because so much of the time we are overwhelmed with mistrust,
because it is so difficult to believe that Being is good, that, as Christians
say, God is love, yet also because to live without trust altogether
would be to be close to paranoid schizophrenia, most people try to
limit the scope of their trust. They will trust in this person or this
occupation or this ethnic group or this religion or this nation, but not
in the others. Yet every such limitation impairs the possibility of
responsible action. Since we can only attend to those we trust, we
cannot interpret accurately, we cannot be accountable to, we cannot
grow in solidarity with those we have put outside the circle of our
trust. This is no abstract argument. On it hinges the very possibility

of whether or not we can create something even partially resembling a good society. When we care only about what Tocqueville called "the little circle of our family and friends" or only about people with skin the same color as ours, we are certainly not acting responsibly to create a good national society. When we care only about our own nation, we do not contribute much to a good world society. When we care only about human beings, we do not treat the natural world with the respect it deserves. If reality itself is for us empty and meaningless, it is hard to see how our lesser commitments can be anything but brittle and transient. But as H. Richard Niebuhr put it:

> In the critical moments we do ask about the ultimate causes . . . and are led to see that our life in response to action upon us, our life in anticipation of response to our reactions, takes place within a society whose boundaries cannot be drawn in space, or time, or extent of interaction, short of a whole in which we live and move and have our being.
>
> The responsible self is driven as it were by the movement of the social process to respond and be accountable in nothing less than a universal community.[36]

Yet for none of us is it easy to override our mistrust and act responsibly in the universal community. Such a possibility is a gift; and when it comes, our response should be gratitude and celebration.

We can indeed try genuinely to attend to the world around us and to the meanings we discover as we interact with that world, and hope to realize in our own experience that we are part of a universal community, making sense of our lives as deeply connected to each other. As we enlarge our attention to include the natural universe and the ultimate ground that it expresses and from which it comes, we are sometimes swept with a feeling of thankfulness, of grace, to be able to participate in a world that is both terrifying and exquisitely beautiful. At such moments we feel like celebrating the joy and mystery we participate in. Religions at their best help us focus that urge to celebrate so that it will include all the meanings we can encompass. The impulse toward larger meaning, thankfulness, and celebration has to have an institutional form, like all the other central organizing tendencies in our lives, so that we do not dissipate it in purely private sentiment.

Institutionalization is always problematic, as we have seen throughout this book. Socially organized ways of paying attention can become socially organized ways of distraction. Nowhere is the dilemma of institutionalization more poignant than in the realm of religion. Members of biblical religions are under the obligation to listen to what God is saying in the most mundane events of everyday life as well as in the great events of world history, and to respond as conscientiously as they can to the ethical demands raised by those events. Yet it is easier to repeat old formulas, to comfort oneself with the community's familiar practices, than to risk trusting a new response to new conditions.

Yet if we are fortunate enough to have the gift of faith through which we see ourselves as members of the universal community of all being, then we bear a special responsibility to bring whatever insights we have to the common discussion of new problems, not because we have any superior wisdom but because we can be, as Václav Havel defines his role, ambassadors of trust in a fearful world. When enough of us have sufficient trust to act responsibly, there is a chance to achieve, at least in part, a good society. In the meantime, even in the world as it is, there are grounds for thankfulness and celebration. Meaning is the living fabric that holds us together with all things. To participate in it is to know something of what human happiness really is.

Appendix

Institutions in Sociology
and Public Philosophy

In the Introduction to this book we pointed out that the term "institution" is not easily understood and that it is used with various meanings. In this appendix we situate our use of the term more explicitly in the sociological and philosophical traditions that have been influential in the United States. The term "institution" is central in sociology (though its meaning is in dispute) but peripheral in philosophy. The public philosophers and theologians upon whom we have drawn did not usually use the term in a technical sense, and in many of their works it appears only in passing. It is necessary, therefore, to show that they were addressing issues that we consider institutional, even if they used different terminology.

I. THE MEDIATING ROLE OF INSTITUTIONS

It is fundamental to understand that institutions mediate the relations between self and world. Meeting another person with no institutional context is a situation of anxiety and, possibly, fear. We don't know what to expect. We don't know how to act. The first thing we do in such a situation is attempt to find some common ground, some language or even gesture, that will call up a set of mutual expectations about what is appropriate—for example, a welcoming wave or handshake that promises hospitality—after which we can negotiate what we are doing together. To put it in sociological terms, we can then organize an action that operates under the mutual expectations we have implicitly acknowledged. If we fail to establish common expectations, our anxiety level rises and it is difficult for us to engage in organized action with the other party. Indeed, at that point the interaction likely breaks down into fight or flight. But "a set of mutual expectations" is already an incipient institution, with built-in ideas about how to act and implicit notions of right and wrong.

Our relations to the natural world are also mediated by institutions. Even the enjoyment of the wilderness by a solitary hiker is mediated by a whole set of social understandings about "nature," the place of human beings in it, and the feelings nature should awaken in ourselves. Organized relations to the natural world—agriculture, mining, manufacturing, etc.—are of course mediated by institutions. This is why problems of ecology, natural or social, always involve institutions.

Institutions also mediate our ultimate moral (and religious) commitments. Not only are our moral and spiritual beliefs and attitudes learned in institutional contexts (however informal the contexts and however we may modify those beliefs and attitudes in terms of our individual experiences), but institutions themselves are premised on moral (and religious) understandings, what sociologists call ultimate values. Various institutional spheres—the economy, politics, the family, etc.—embody and specify culturally transmitted ultimate values in terms of what is right and wrong, good and bad. These normative patterns not only indicate the ends and purposes of our actions but set limits to the means used, validating only those that are morally acceptable. As we have noted, institutions operate not only through informal understandings, the mores, but also through law.

In this conception of institutions as patterns of normative, which is to say moral, expectations, the presumption is that institutions are in their very nature moral. But this does not itself legitimate their existing forms; rather it opens them to serious moral debate. Existing institutions can and frequently are challenged on two kinds of moral ground. One is that they do not live up to the moral purposes claimed for them. In this book, for example, we have criticized our free economy for not providing opportunities for livelihood and participation in meaningful work that its advocates promise, just as we have criticized our democratic politics for not empowering the active citizenship upon which it is premised. In Chapter 7 we criticized the institutions set up to fight the cold war for having partially destroyed the freedom they were supposedly set up to defend.

The other challenge calls into question some of the basic value assumptions that lie behind our institutions. In this book, for example, we have argued that Lockean individualism is inadequate, though it operates in many ways as the central American value system. If the central value system is flawed, then it is more than likely that many of its institutional specifications will be problematic as well. Institutional change must then involve changing the value system, most likely through drawing on alternative ones that already have some standing in the society—as we suggested in *Habits of the Heart*, reappropriating elements from our biblical and civic republican traditions. We have argued that our institutional problems are deeply rooted in our central values, so it follows that we believe serious institutional reform in the absence of change in the central values is not likely to succeed.

Institutions are also frequently criticized on instrumental grounds: is the American corporation, or university, or judiciary, effective? The great temptation, as we have seen, is to believe that technical fine-tuning will solve the problem. Yet the very meaning of "effectiveness" raises value questions—effective for what purposes?—that should lead to moral debate. The American tendency to think that social and institutional problems are basically technical is related to the assumption that the central value question is already settled: that institutions are there to serve the private ends of individuals. Yet we have seen that this leads to contradictions and conundrums, and obscures awareness of the many destructive consequences of our current institutional patterns.

We have derived our argument about institutions from a long history of social thought, but it owes a great deal especially to Talcott Parsons, as is evident in his early paper, probably written in 1934 but only recently published, "Prolegomena to a Theory of Social Institutions."[1] Parsons, following Durkheim and others, insisted on an essentially normative definition of institutions, and indeed on the idea that society itself is essentially normative. Parsons's "Prolegomena" is interesting in that it contains views that differ from many of those attributed to him. He does not assume, for example, that a society has a unified central value system—he gives the case of medieval Europe, where the feudal polity and the bureaucratic church were based on different and incompatible central values and the result was continuing tension and conflict. In *Habits of the Heart* we argued that radical individualism (what in this book we have called Lockean individualism) is only one of several fundamental traditions in America, and that it is basically incompatible with important elements in biblical religion and civic republicanism, which have always moderated its influence and which today we especially need to reaffirm. Nor does Parsons assume that institutions operate only on normative consensus; he sees, rather, that they are reinforced by positive and negative sanctions, rewards and punishments, although without a degree of moral legitimacy they cannot survive. In this book we argue that American economic, political, and educational institutions depend heavily on extrinsic rewards and punishments, on the manipulations of wealth and power, though their moral legitimacy is still considerable. Conflicts of interest are an essential feature of social life, as both Parsons and we affirm; but if that were the whole story, then society would collapse into a Hobbesian war of all against all. (We have pointed out that there are indeed Hobbesian sectors in our society today.)

On one important matter we have differed from Parsons, who wishes to pursue an explanatory scientific theory of institutions without becoming involved substantively in normative issues. In *The Good Society*, as in *Habits of the Heart*, we follow an older tradition, exemplified by Alexis de Tocqueville, in combining an analytic with a normative approach. We have affirmed normative positions of others—such as the "third democratic transformation" of Robert Dahl, or the "universal community" of H. Richard Niebuhr—and put forward a normative position of our own. If the central traditions of a society and its major institutions are moral, then they depend on moral argument and debate for their ongoing vitality. Parsons errs, we believe, in taking central values and institutional norms as given (although he not infrequently, and uncritically, advocates the American version of those values and institutions as he understood them), and would have increased the analytical power of his theory if he had engaged more seriously in the normative debates about the issues, which he would have had to clarify and which remain ambiguous in his argument.

For those theorists who reject the ideas that society requires some degree of shared values and that institutions are essentially normative, the cost is even higher than it is for Parsons's ambivalent approach. By adopting some version of rational choice theory—only the latest version of the old Hobbesian/Lockean emphasis on self-interest—to explain social reality, they end not only in analytic sterility but with the impoverishment of serious moral and political discussion. They become, in practice, the allies of the very manipulators they sometimes claim to be unmasking.

James Coleman's comments on Parsons's "Prolegomena," for example, show little sense of how human identity is shaped by linguistic and moral communities.[2] For him all individuals are fundamentally alike: rational actors capable of calculating the most efficient means to their ends.[3] These actors are social in the sense that they need the cooperation of others to survive and to achieve their separate interests, but not social in the strong sense that their very identity—and their very conception of what their interests are or ought to be—is shaped by the institutions of society. For him, the problem is how institutions, conceived as socially shared and enforced norms, are created by individuals whose private short-term interests conflict with common long-term interests. We, unlike Coleman, would understand this conflict as shaped by the nature of the institutions we live in. Some institutions educate us to see our selves as extensive and our truest interests as long-term and dependent on widespread social cooperation; others make us concentrate on immediate interests.

We disagree not with the empirical evidence Coleman cites but with its interpretation. Institutions are forever subject to the human corruption that comes from making means into ends, from divorcing the law from the spirit of the law—that is true. Yet it is also true that ends and means are subtly intertwined in human institutions, and it is not always clear which is which. Actions that seem quite utilitarian may also have deep symbolic significance—for example, a family meal is a means of nourishment and a "sacrament," good in itself, as well. Sometimes these patterns of institutionally directed action are, in Alasdair MacIntyre's sense, "practices," both means to a good life and also aspects of a historically constituted good form of life.[4] Sometimes the ends cannot be conceived of except in terms of the means. For us, "paying attention" is not just a means to accomplish an end but a state of being in which we participate in the end itself.

Coleman criticizes Parsons for holding to the "functionalist fallacy," that social needs generate the institutions that meet them. Whether Parsons is vulnerable to such a criticism is questionable, but we at least hold no pre-conceived view as to whether institutions are functional or not. We argue that many of our institutions are dysfunctional and that many of our common needs are not being met by institutions. And we have offered numerous criticisms of our current institutional arrangements:

(1) Americans' understanding of the ends of society is flawed so that we do not know what we want or need. We have a Lockean ideology in a non-Lockean world. We have, over the past two centuries, developed needs our Lockean ideology cannot describe. Many of our institutions (for example, corporations defined as private individuals) were constituted on the basis of now outmoded understandings of our common purposes. The authors of *The Good Society* believe that institutions are essential to help us constitute our wants and needs; they arise out of argument and action, not out of automatic responses to social needs.

(2) Institutions have become corrupt; means have wrongly been turned into ends. Even when we know what we want, we are so enamored with certain means that we are not able to make the changes necessary to get what we want. The constant preoccupation with certain means influences our conceptions of self, making it hard to transform our institutions in ways that would cultivate a different form of self.

(3) Economic institutions have invaded other institutions (politics, religion, family, etc.), making it harder for them to do what they were originally intended to do. International exchange has provided an easily universalizable language for the entire world, whereas our capacity to think about our common moral and political problems has tended, with some exceptions, such as "human rights" language, to remain embedded in local and culturally specific settings.

Our critique of contemporary social reality and particularly of the way in which economic and political institutions have become distorted and have invaded other institutions, such as the family, education, and religion, has been influenced significantly by several writers. Our earliest conception of *The Good Society* was inspired by Karl Polanyi's *The Great Transformation*, in which Polanyi described how the early capitalist economy disrupted traditional society everywhere, stimulated the growth of powerful nationalist states to cope with these disruptions, and set off destructive forces which by the middle of the twentieth century had come close to destroying civilization.[5] As our work progressed, we developed our ideas with constant reference to the writings of Jürgen Habermas, whose notion of economic and political "systems" invading and colonizing the "life-world" significantly influenced us.[6] In the end we decided not to use his terminology, which seemed to imply a sharper dichotomy between systems and life-world than we intended. In particular, Habermas's language made it difficult for us to argue for the institutional humanization of the economy and the administrative state, even though we know he shares our hope for that possibility. Yet, though we have not used his language, our substantive debt to him is great, as any knowledgeable reader will easily see. Finally we discovered R. H. Tawney's *The Acquisitive Society*, in which Tawney eloquently argued for a reordering of social institutions in accord with true human purposes. For Tawney, economic activity is

> the servant, not the master, of society. The burden of our civilization is not merely, as many suppose, that the product of industry is ill-distributed, or its conduct tyrannical, or its operation interrupted by embittered disagreements. It is that industry itself has come to hold a position of exclusive predominance among human interests, which no single interest, and least of all the provision of the material means of existence, is fit to occupy. . . . Industrialized communities neglect the very objects for which it is worth while to acquire riches in their feverish preoccupation with the means by which riches can be acquired.[7]

In the theoretical perspective we have developed, we see our present configuration of institutions not as sociologically "necessary" but as historically contingent, open to critical reflection and significant reform. We advocate taking advantage of society's institutional pluralism to escape from the logic of one kind of institution (for example, the market) by looking at it from the standpoint of another (for example, the church). If, as Mary Douglas says, institutions think, what they think about is other institutions: they translate the means and ends of other institutions into their own logic. Thus, economic institutions interpret educational institutions as a business, as we saw in Chapter 5. If we want a democratic society, we need to maintain a plurality of institutions; we need to avoid economic as well as political totalitarianism. One purpose of our book is to generate a lively dialogue among different types of institution and to cultivate the practical (in the sense of moral) reason that would make that possible.[8] We believe it is necessary to bridge the gap between theoretical reason and moral reason, and we differ in this from both Parsons and Coleman.

Just as the late writer Rachel Carson combined a disciplined knowledge of natural science with her concern for the environment,[9] we try to combine what we hope is a disciplined knowledge of society with a concern for our current social ecology. America's social institutions are damaged and threatened by many of the same forces that threaten the natural environment. We need clear standards to help us regain environmental health, and we also need clear standards to regain our institutional health: indeed, we cannot repair the damaged environment unless we also repair our damaged social ecology.

Although in this book we have leaned heavily on contemporary social scientists for many of our arguments and evidence, we have frequently turned for insight and inspiration to certain early- and mid-twentieth-century thinkers in a tradition of public philosophy that has been attenuated if not lost in recent years. We believe they were engaged in a conversation, at once analytical and normative, that we cannot afford to abandon—indeed, that we need urgently to resume. Social science and policy analysis have not taken the place of public philosophy but, instead, have regrettably strengthened the notion that our problems are technical rather than moral and political. If policy elites stand outside the world of citizens, designing social policies evaluated in terms of outcomes, efficiency, or costs and benefits, as they define them, they short-circuit the democratic process, and this is so whether they believe that people are essentially "interest maximizers" or even that they are motivated in part by "values." Politics under these circumstances becomes the art of image manipulation by expert media managers. The spinal cord of democracy, the connection between government and an enlightened public, is broken. A third democratic transformation needs to renew a serious public conversation and to strengthen the institutions that nurture and extend it. Picking up the public conversation, many of whose strands were broken a half century ago, is one way to start that renewal. It is not that the thinkers from whom we have learned spoke with one voice. They differed sharply. But the very intensity of their argument, and the degree to which it was followed by millions of people, were signs of a healthy democratic public life.

II. ALL OF US ARE IMMIGRANTS SPIRITUALLY

Uneasiness about the rapid changes accompanying modernity goes back a long time; but in the years before World War I, concern for what was happening to America's institutions and uncertainty about what would take their place became central preoccupations not only for intellectuals but for the general public. Walter Lippmann, in his 1914 book *Drift and Mastery*, commented on William Jennings Bryan's famous "Cross of Gold" speech of 1896, in which Bryan had lashed out at the incursions of the new corporate economy:

> What Bryan was really defending was the old and simple life of America, a life that was doomed by the great organization that had come into the world. He thought he was fighting the plutocracy: as a matter of fact he was fighting something much deeper than that; he was fighting the larger scale of human life. The Eastern money power controlled the new industrial system, and Bryan fought it. But what he and his people hated from the bottom of their souls were the economic conditions that had upset the old life of the prairies, made new demands upon democracy, introduced specialization and science, had destroyed village loyalties, frustrated private ambitions, and created the impersonal relationships of the modern world.[10]

This treatment of Bryan has all the brashness and certainty of youth. But by the end of his book Lippmann recognized that Bryan was not alone in this new era; that we all, as Americans, as moderns, live in an uprooted condition: "All of us are immigrants spiritually. We are all of us immigrants in the industrial world, and we have no authority to lean upon. We are an uprooted people, newly arrived, and *nouveau riche*. As a nation we have all the vulgarity that goes with that, all the scattering of soul. The modern man is not yet settled in his world. It is strange to him, terrifying, alluring, and incomprehensibly big. . . . We are blown hither and thither like litter before the wind."[11] For all the energy and excitement of the book, there is a sustained note of wonder about the new society taking shape: "No mariner ever enters upon a more uncharted sea than does the average human being born into the twentieth century. Our ancestors thought they knew their way from birth through all eternity: we are puzzled about the day after to-morrow."[12]

In these words Lippmann spoke for most of the intellectuals of late-nineteenth- and early-twentieth-century America. Some of them—Josiah Royce, John Dewey, George Herbert Mead, Reinhold and H. Richard Niebuhr—had grown up in the same kind of small town that Bryan had. Others—Charles Peirce, William James, Herbert Croly, Lewis Mumford, Lippmann himself—came from more sophisticated urban backgrounds. But all knew they were living in a society undergoing fundamental changes, in which the old verities could not be trusted or would at least have to be rethought. The new industrial economy, with its national and international scale of organization, urbanization, the rise of science and specialization, the modern university, and mass communications—all these were baffling to individuals, and they were certainly making "new demands upon democracy." Perhaps at the end of the twentieth century we are more used to the scale of modern life, but we are no less baffled by its consequences. We still have much to learn from these thinkers.

One of the striking things about most of these thinkers is their social realism, their intellectual detachment from mainstream American Lockean individualism. Classic American philosophy was consistently critical of individualism. Even William James was only a partial exception: he never saw the individual as primarily self-interested, and his critique of the American ideology of success involved a rejection of the operative Lockeanism of the day. Charles Peirce, the most original philosopher America has yet produced, was not only an uncompromising social realist but a philosophical realist as well, and he linked the two realisms through his essentially social conception of inquiry: "The real, then, is that which sooner or later, information and reasoning would finally result in, and which is therefore independent of the vagaries of me and you. Thus, the very origin of the conception of reality shows that this conception essentially involves the notion of a COMMUNITY [Peirce's emphasis], without definite limits, and capable of a definite increase in knowledge."[13] It is not necessary to trace direct lines of "influence" (though Royce drew directly on Peirce; Mead and Croly studied with Royce; H. Richard Niebuhr was heavily influenced by Royce and Mead, etc.) to recognize a general climate of opinion. Thinkers more directly engaged in practical life—such as Jane Addams (whose views we discussed in Chapter 5),

W. E. B. Du Bois, our most significant early-twentieth-century African-American public philosopher, and the feminist advocate Charlotte Perkins Gilman—shared equally in a view of society as being as real as individuals.[14] The nominalism that Locke represents both epistemologically and sociologically and that has been so dominant in most modern philosophy and social science was not appealing to the best American minds of the time. Their social realism made them think seriously not only about individual motivation and great ideas but about how the way society is organized affects both individual responsibility and cultural creativity. In this way they were thinking about institutions, in the sense in which we are using the term, even though the word was seldom central in their discussions.

III. AN INCLUSIVE PUBLIC

John Dewey expressed his social realism throughout his life, but nowhere more clearly than in his 1927 book *The Public and Its Problems*. As Eugene Rochberg-Halton comments: "There Dewey criticizes the idea of the 'natural' inalienable rights that are given prior to politics, claiming instead that inalienable rights are constituted in and through the social process. The philosophy of individualism posited individuals *apart from* the social world they inhabit, and asserted that constraints on the individual (on private property, etc.) should be severed. Yet, Dewey claimed, human rights are constituted by human relationships, and mediating institutions form the living social web of our consciousness."[15]

The Public and Its Problems offered a sharp diagnosis of the condition Dewey called "the eclipse of the public." "The same forces which have brought about the forms of democratic government," said Dewey, "have also brought about conditions which halt the social and humane ideals that demand the utilization of government as the genuine instrumentality of an inclusive and fraternally associated public."[16]

The coming of the great society tended to disintegrate the local communities that had given people their identities. While this emancipated people from the chains of dependence and tradition, Dewey sharply criticized the way the individualistic doctrine of the private market economy prevented individuals from struggling together to develop new identities drawing on the wider freedom now available. "The democratic public," Dewey complained, "is still largely inchoate and unorganized."[17] Dewey's aim was to foster the creation of a new national public through the development of communication among the partial publics thrown up accidentally by the workings of the economy. The wider public would then bring a new coherence to national development.

Dewey's goal was "liberation of the potentialities of members of a group in harmony with the interests and goods which are common." But this liberation was not identical with the expansion of individual consumer choice being effected by the new economy. "Where the realization of the good is such as to effect an energetic desire and effort to sustain it in being just because it is a good shared by all," insisted Dewey, "there is in so far a community." And "the clear consciousness of a communal life, in all its implications, constitutes the idea of democracy."[18]

IV. CONFLICT IS INEVITABLE

Dewey's devotion to democracy was matched only by his devotion to education—indeed, the two ideas for him were indissolubly linked. Only an educated citizenry, and educated not only in the acquisition of knowledge but in the capacity for active social life, would make a genuine democracy possible. In 1932, in response to the immense suffering that the Great Depression was causing to millions in America and the rest of the world, Reinhold Niebuhr published *Moral Man and Immoral Society*, an angry book that called in question the dominant secular and religious liberalism of the day and served as a reminder that society has a dark side. In the introduction there was a stinging rejection of John Dewey. Niebuhr castigated Dewey for "the assumption that our social difficulties are due to the failure of the social sciences to keep pace with the physical sciences which have created our technological civilization. The invariable implication of this assumption is that, with a little more time, a little more adequate moral and social pedagogy and a generally higher development of human intelligence, our social problems will approach solution."[19] Niebuhr found this position finally evasive and unrealistic. High-minded disinterested intelligence simply fails to come to terms with what is really happening:

> Complete rational objectivity in a social situation is impossible. The very social scientists who are so anxious to offer our generation counsels of salvation and are disappointed that an ignorant and slothful people are so slow to accept their wisdom betray middle-class prejudices in almost everything they write. Since reason is always, to some degree, the servant of interest in a social situation, social injustice cannot be resolved by moral and rational suasion alone, as the educator and social scientist usually believes. Conflict is inevitable, and in this conflict power must be challenged by power.[20]

Niebuhr argued that it was the mistake of secular liberals and the Social Gospel theologians to think that the kindness and virtue evident in the personal relations of (middle-class) individuals could be generalized to reform society. Social groups, argued Niebuhr, contain a collective egoism, self-assertiveness, and proclivity to coerce that are much less amenable to moral control than the motives and actions of individuals. H. Richard Niebuhr, though he never publicly criticized his brother's book, made a decisive objection in a private letter to him, pointing out that there is no form of egoism or even coercion that is not expressed in the most intimate relationships and that the distinction his brother was trying to make was false logically and theologically.[21] Nevertheless, the distinction enabled Reinhold Niebuhr to face realistically a harshness in political life that he could never accept in interpersonal relations.

While Reinhold Niebuhr tried to maintain a separation between the individual and society that most of the other thinkers we are considering found unconvincing, he maintained in his own way a "social realism" that, because of its insistence on the significance of power in institutions and the inevitability of conflict, made an important contribution to the ongoing conversation, and opened up a space for a more radical questioning of American institutions than John Dewey usually imagined.

V. LIPPMANN'S *THE GOOD SOCIETY*

Walter Lippmann's *The Good Society* (1937) contains some of his most profound insights into the condition of modern society, and it can help us think about our present situation. The first part of the book argued that modern society, resting on a growing division of labor and a concomitant market economy, has become a "great society" (again referring to Graham Wallas's idea) of international proportions. While the modern market economy can and should be regulated (he had much to say about that in the second half of the book), it is only under conditions of emergency, war or the preparation for war, that it can be replaced by a command economy. Lippmann argued that totalitarian states resemble democratic states in wartime: they attempt to make emergency mobilization permanent. They are thus by nature militaristic and in fact invariably plan for expansion (fascist states) or consider external attack inevitable (Russia). Lippmann believed that the effort to create a command economy in a militarized state is profoundly pathological and goes against the fundamental tendency of modern development.

From the point of view of the events of 1989, Lippmann's analysis seems remarkably prescient. Many of the dangers he had come to fear from an overly mobilized state during the New Deal became all too real in the United States during forty years of cold-war mobilization under the national security state. He concluded, as we noted in the Introduction, that in modern society all war is civil war and that, in spite of appearances, we are moving toward the abolition of war, again an insight that is more convincing in the 1990s than it was in 1937.

Lippmann celebrated "the increase of wealth by a mode of production which destroys the self-sufficiency of nations, localities, and individuals, making them deeply and intricately interdependent,"[22] and thus leads to the formation of the great society. But he was quite aware that the great society is not necessarily a good society and that the economic liberals who dogmatically defend the unfettered market overlook its grave defects:

It [the market economy] has resulted in such a substantial improvement of the standard of life, measured in command over material goods, that the modern Marxians no longer insist on the original thesis that capitalism causes increasing poverty among the working classes. But it is equally certain that the progressive increase of wealth leaves behind it a trail of misery and failure and frustrated lives which has shocked the conscience of mankind. The statistics of improvement are not sufficiently impressive to obscure the statistics of waste or to drown out the cries of the victims. While it is perfectly true that the market determines how labor and capital can be effectively invested to satisfy popular demands, the market is, humanly speaking, a ruthless sovereign. In practice those who misjudge the market must pay for their mistakes with their fortunes and by defeat in their lives.[23]

By attempting to deny rather than ameliorate the human costs of the market economy, economic liberals, according to Lippmann, opened the door to collectivist movements (nationalist, socialist, fascist) that proposed to use the power of the state to administer the economy more fairly. This was a tragic development, for there is an extraordinary potential in the new mode of production. We noted in the Introduction that Lippmann viewed the increased productivity of the modern economy as the possible basis for a much better, indeed a good, society.

Lippmann proposed what he called an "agenda of liberalism," a series of reforms considerably more radical than the New Deal, which would correct the defects of the market economy, not primarily through administrative substitution but through legal regulation—that is, institutional reform. "I have suggested," he wrote, "that the 'frictions' and 'disturbances' which the classical economists recognized—only to neglect them—were, in fact, the social problems which should have been, and in a society practising the division of labor must always be, the paramount concern of enlightened men."[24] He began his list of necessary reforms with "the conservation of the land and of all natural resources," remarking, "That anyone who thought he was preserving the system of free enterprise should have persuaded himself to believe that the law must leave men free to destroy the patrimony of their children is one of the curiosities of human unreason."[25]

Lippmann next called for the modification of the classical economic notion that "labor and capital must both be perfectly mobile. . . . Capital has to be more mobile than labor, sufficiently more mobile to compensate for the inevitable and desirable human resistance to a migratory existence." He did not defend geographical immobility, but he did point to the disruptions resulting from too massive and too constant migration. "It should, therefore, be the aim of policy to mitigate this human evil by using social controls to induce inanimate capital, rather than living men to achieve high mobility. It should be the aim of educational policy to make most men versatile and adaptable in the place where they were born, and of economic policy to make capital mobile."[26] In his own way Lippmann was consistently proposing the virtues of cultivation and settlement as against exploitation.

Lippmann's concern for inequalities in the economy led him to consider not only those whose position is too weak but those whose position is too strong. He called for a "different distribution of incomes," which under present conditions can only be obtained through a "policy which redistributes large incomes by drastic inheritance and steeply graduated income taxes,"[27] and argued that "under a regime of equal opportunity, there could not be any such gross inequality of income as obtains to-day in a country like the United States."[28]

Lippmann then discussed two fundamental premises of economic liberalism that he believed need to be reconceived if the major reforms he recommended were to be effective. These are private property and the business corporation. He insisted that private property is not "a sole and absolute dominion" but "a right established by law and enforceable at law."[29] Property indeed is a set of rights instituted by society for the common good. Just as the right of property is not absolute but involves obligations as well as rights, so, said Lippmann, is the right of incorporation: "Is it not evident that in granting the privilege of incorporation the state may fix the conditions, that it may say what the rights of an incorporated body are, that it may say that the privilege of limited liability and perpetual succession shall be enjoyed only in so far as the corporation meets certain specific obligations?"[30]

In arguing that the right of private property is not absolute and the business corporation is not "a kind of autonomous principality,"[31] Lippmann was not at all arguing for the increased power of an administrative state. Rather, he was supporting a more vigorous use of the rule of law to require owners and corporations to meet their obligations as recipients of rights that are held only for the sake of the common good. The rule of law is critical, he said, "to achieve what Plato called the victory of persuasion over force."[32]

The burden of Lippmann's argument, classic realist though he was, was to warn us against being mesmerized by wealth and power. He was urging us, half a century ago, to use moral standards, which could be embodied in laws as well as mores, to measure our institutions and to ameliorate the destructiveness of our economic and technological dynamism. It was his hope that the achievements of modernity might provide the means not for ever greater exploitation but for the creation of a good society, one really fit for human beings, in a world so interconnected that any major conflict would be a civil war.

VI. CULTURAL REVOLUTION

In 1960 the Catholic theologian John Courtney Murray, S.J., published a book entitled *We Hold These Truths: Catholic Reflections on the American Proposition.* In the foreword he spoke of "the public philosophy of America," and in the book he described public argument and public conversation in a way thoroughly consonant with the writings of Dewey, Niebuhr, and Lippmann that we have been considering. Though Murray was only fifteen years younger than Lippmann and twelve years younger than Niebuhr, he was a relative newcomer to the common conversation: *We Hold These Truths* was a collection of articles published in the 1950s. A major Catholic thinker had finally joined a discussion once dominated by Protestants and secularists, and indeed had clarified and enriched that discussion in its own terms.

According to Murray, "Society is civil when it is formed by men locked together in argument. . . ."[33] Argument involves disagreements, but to disagree is to share enough in common to have something to disagree about: "The whole premise of the public argument, if it is to be civilized and civilizing, is that the consensus is real, that among the people everything is not in doubt, but that there is a core of agreement, accord, concurrence, acquiescence. We hold certain truths; therefore we can argue about them."[34] Without a minimum of consensus the argument falters and the results for civil society are dire: "If the argument dies from disinterest, or subsides into the angry mutterings of polemic, or rises to the shrillness of hysteria, or trails off into positivistic triviality, or gets lost in a morass of semantics, you may be sure that the barbarian is at the gates of the City."[35] That the barbarian wears a Brooks Brothers suit and carries a ballpoint pen does not lessen his barbarism; for, according to Murray, "barbarism is not, I repeat, the forest primeval with all its relatively simple savageries. Barbarism has long had its definition, resumed by St. Thomas after Aristotle. It is the lack of reasonable conversation according to reasonable laws. Here the word 'conversation' has its twofold Latin sense. It means living together and talking together."[36]

Murray emphasized the core of agreement in America, what Parsons would have called common values, that makes the conversation possible. He accepted the fundamental terms of the republican order, as Catholics had done from the founding of the nation. Moreover, he was ready to enter into the public conversation more openly and more fully than Catholic intellectuals had usually been willing to do. He is often interpreted as helping to bring the American Catholic Church into a fuller integration with American society, an integration that, until Vatican II, Rome was not entirely happy about.

A close reading of *We Hold These Truths* suggests that that interpretation is severely distorted. Murray was not just trying to bring Catholics into the common conversation. He was trying, with civility and gentleness to be sure, to change the terms of the conversation. He was saying that Catholics had been excluded, or had been required to give up their identity to enter it, and that exclusion must stop. The publication date of 1960 gives *We Hold These Truths* a meaning that was not obvious at the time: it was an opening salvo in a cultural revolution. Along with the argument for civil concord, Murray made a strong argument for the legitimacy of pluralism: "The Catholic may not, as others do, merge his religious and his patriotic faith, or submerge one in the other. The simplest solution is not for him. He must reckon with his own tradition of thought, which is wider and deeper than any that America has elaborated. He must also reckon with his own history, which is longer than the brief centuries that America has lived."[37]

In describing the reality of America as against the ideal of civil argument, he spoke of an actual "structure of war":

> We are not really a group of men singly engaged in the search for truth, relying solely on the means of persuasion, entering into dignified communication with each other, content politely to correct opinions with which we do not agree. As a matter of fact, the variant ideas and allegiances among us are entrenched as social powers; they occupy ground; they have developed interests; and they possess the means to fight for them. The real issues of truth that arise are complicated by secondary issues of power and prestige, which not seldom become primary.[38]

Nor was Murray hesitant in naming those who have used their power and prestige to get what they want not by persuasion but by force: "Protestantism in America has forged an identification of itself, both historical and ideological, with American culture, particularly with an indigenous secularist unclarified mystique of individual freedom as somehow the source of everything, including justice, order, and unity. The result has been Nativism in all its manifold forms, ugly and refined, popular and academic, fanatic and liberal."[39]

Catholicism has been condemned as a conspiracy, said Murray. But, he argued, the root meaning of "conspiracy" is simply to breathe together, as persons who agree with each other naturally do. He insisted that Protestantism, Judaism, and secularism are also conspiracies. What we require is not the exclusion of any one of them but the construction of a larger conspiracy that can contain us all. Murray's use of the word "consensus" must be carefully considered. He always believed a minimum of agreement was necessary to get the conversation going, but that even the most fundamental things were open to civil argument. Consensus, then, did not mean bland agreement or a refusal to face painful conflicts in American society. On the contrary, it allowed those conflicts to come to consciousness.

Murray's argument was not new,[40] but he put it forward with an insistence that presaged a new day, and his themes were later developed with dramatic intensity by racial minorities, women, and gays. Pluralism and diversity were indeed on the American agenda. Whether we can attain the "larger conspiracy" of which Murray spoke remains to be seen.

VII. STUDYING INSTITUTIONS

John Courtney Murray has outlined the subject matter of the public argument in a way that is consonant with what we have tried to do in this book. He held that though public argument and public philosophy concern the actions of government, they are concerned more essentially with people's beliefs and practices and with how they are transmitted and embodied in some form of a good life—in the terms of this book, embodied in institutions.

From Lippmann's *Drift and Mastery* of 1914 right up to the writings of social critics today, there is a litany of concern that the beliefs and practices of the people are in disarray, that there is little agreement about, or even understanding of, the meaning of the good life, that our institutions are badly damaged. Most of the public philosophers assert that modernity itself is at the heart of our problems. We have not learned how to unite the tremendous possibilities opened up by modern technological, economic, and administrative advances with a coherent pattern of living together. In the midst of the flux we do not seem to know very well how to handle the warm commitments of our familial and personal lives or the cooler commitments of civic friendship, where Murray says the only admissible passion is the passion for justice.

We have insisted that analysis of the challenges and opportunities facing us at this critical juncture requires a revived analysis of institutions. But institutions are hard to see, and they are also hard to study. The social sciences have well-developed methods for studying individuals—the survey, the in-depth interview, life-history analysis, and so forth—and well-developed methods, from demography to survey analysis, for studying the aggregate patterns formed by individual experience.[41] We also now have rudimentary methods for studying organizations—case studies based on files and interviews,[42] surveys of an organization's members,[43] surveys based on public documents, on coding organizational characteristics from archival sources, and even on questionnaires to personnel.[44]

But how does one study institutions? Simply studying organizations is not enough. It runs the risk of confusing the organizations with institutional patterns that define their purposes and meanings.

One answer is to study the law in a given area and the way the law has worked out in practice. Since institutions are normative patterns and law is society's most explicit statement of normative patterns, the study of institutions "may be regarded as precisely the sociology of law," and as closely related to jurisprudence, as Parsons pointed out in his "Prolegomena."[45] We have relied on Mary Ann Glendon's comparative studies of family law in our discussions of institutional problems of the family in the Introduction and Conclusion.[46] Philip Selznick's *Law, Society, and Industrial Justice* is an exemplary study of the institutionalization of collective bargaining and industrial justice in American business.[47] But in the study of institutions "law" is used in the broadest of senses. It includes case law,[48] the customary law of nonliterate societies, and administrative regulations of both public and private organizations in complex societies. It also includes what Tocqueville called the mores, the informal patterns of belief and practice that regulate much of daily life.

But because institutions cover such large areas of social life and are much less easy to delimit than organizations or the actions and beliefs of individuals (which is one reason why some sociologists collapse institutions into the aggregate behavior of individuals or organizations), the study of formal and informal codes is only the beginning of the task. Intensive study of an institution may begin with formal codes but requires one to immerse oneself in how an institution works, to read widely both scholarly studies and the writings of practitioners in the area, and to interact with the participants. It almost certainly also involves a deep concern with the moral meaning of the institution and a willingness to make judgments about the justice and injustice of institutional arrangements. All social science is implicitly normative as well as descriptive, but it is particularly difficult to do good work in the study of institutions without taking responsibility for disciplined moral evaluation. This combination of wide-ranging immersion in the data and moral perception is what allows a scholar like Philip Selznick to write about law as an institution in ways sensitive both to the deeper value commitments that animate it and to its current vicissitudes.[49] We have tried to follow a similar strategy, immersing ourselves in the work of those scholars who are knowledgeable about the various institutional sectors of American society, attempting to remain sensitive to the underlying principles that animate institutions and give them their defining purposes, while simultaneously understanding their more concrete organizational difficulties. We have also occasionally relied on interviews, trying to understand the dilemmas that arise for those caught up in an institution and attempting to realize its purposes. We certainly employed no principle of sampling, and looked only for those who, from various perspectives, were struggling with the core normative issues at the heart of an institution.

We also relied on conversations with many other scholars and on our own sense of the core cultural traditions and commitments of our society. Since we believe there is a necessary link between normative theory and institutional analysis, we see a need in both the social sciences and philosophy for more explicit ways to attend to institutions. Much of philosophy, as it abandoned the concerns of classical pragmatism, has ignored institutions, treating normative matters as if they arose primarily for individuals outside a social context rather than in institutions. A novelist such as Henry James, with his keen sense that his characters act within the confines of family and class expectations, did not make that mistake, even though his primary interest was in the characters' moral dilemmas. More recent novelists, such as John Updike, chronicle the decline of those institutional expectations without ignoring their significance or the cost of institutional weakness for individuals. Both philosophers and social scientists can learn much about institutions from perceptive writers and artists.[50]

A social science with a commitment to address institutions would be a substantial contribution to a renewed public philosophy. It would be a morally engaged social science, since to address institutions is to address their core principles and values. In this book we call not only for a renewed public conversation but for a new engagement by social scientists with institutions as the focus of analysis. Such an engagement requires a deeper consideration of history and of issues of purpose and value than is usually the case in the social sciences, as well as a renewed consideration of methods of inquiry and analysis for the study of institutions.

VIII. THE SCOPE OF THE CONVERSATION

All the public philosophers on whose work we have drawn agreed that our problems will be solved in new forms of moral reflection and in practices that embody them. In a word, our problems will be solved by changes in our institutions. None of them was blind to the great achievements already attained in limiting arbitrary power, whether in the state, community, or family, and extending justice and participation to those previously oppressed and excluded. None of them believed in automatic progress, and all were impressed with modern society's terrible perversions. Yet none of them gave up the hope of a better, more just world.

It is part of Dewey's argument that the great society is impersonal and destroys local communities and cultural differences.[51] One task of the great community is to nurture the revitalization of local community and cultural difference, not in an atmosphere of exclusiveness but in an open understanding between communities as ultimately all members of the great community. On these matters John Courtney Murray, not to speak of Martin Luther King, Jr., and many others, was even clearer than Dewey.

It is often said that American culture is so diverse and so pluralistic that we cannot expect meaningful public discussion, much less agreement. Yet actual experience—for example, in discussions sponsored by the California State Legislature's Joint Senate and Assembly Committee on the Family—found large areas of agreement among all sectors of the diverse population of the state. There was no significant sector that was not concerned about the plight of the family today, nor was there any great disagreement about many of the necessary remedies. But the argument here is not so much that cultural diversity is no barrier to serious discussion about the common good as that the real danger is that America, in the form of the great society, continuously undermines pluralism and diversity, that it implacably subverts bilingualism and biculturalism (not to mention multilingualism and multi-culturalism), that the great society is an agent of homogenization, not diversity. Our most influential recent cultural institutions, television and mass higher education, have been agents of the monoculture rather than seedbeds of diversity.

Much of what today is discussed in terms of cultural "diversity" or "pluralism" really involves the politicization of identity, a well-known process in American history. For a long time political parties in many states had to make sure to "balance the ticket" when proposing candidates, and it is still true, increasingly with African-Americans, Hispanics, and Asians so included. This may make it appear that America is composed of diverse cultural "communities," each homogeneous in itself. But the very process of the politicization of identity is a sign of cultural assimilation. For example, it is obvious today that there are Irish Republicans as well as Democrats, conservatives and liberals, pro-lifers but also pro-choicers, that Irish ethnic culture has become diffuse. The same process of assimilation and diffusion occurs among the newer entrants into the game. Departments of ethnic studies in American universities were created through the process of the politicization of identity and can be defended as such. But it is poignant that many minority students learn "their" culture for the first time in their college classes because the actual communities they come from have lost the capacity to transmit that culture. Since the university—including, in its own way, ethnic studies—is so much a part of the monoculture, how much difference can a particular course here or there make? The effort to create a great community that nurtures genuine ethnic and local diversity has never been easy in America and remains a major challenge. As we argued in Chapter 5, for the university to make a significant contribution to that effort would require a much deeper consideration of the meaning of education than most of the contestants in the debate over curriculum imagine.

Dewey did not, any more than Royce, have any nostalgia for a bygone past, for what Lippmann called village America, for what the sociologists call gemeinschaft, when he used the term "great community." Dewey sought not to return to unconsidered tradition but to combine character and criticism, loyalty and debate, equality and the flourishing of individual personality. In one way or another all our major figures agreed with him. Murray, whose sense of the objectivity of truth and whose social realism are paralleled only by Lippmann's last writings, perhaps because both of them were so much influenced by Thomism, nonetheless said of the beliefs that would make the great community possible: "Neither as a doctrine nor as a project is the American Proposition a finished thing. Its demonstration is never done once for all; and the Proposition itself requires development on penalty of decadence."[52]

IX. THE PROSPECT BEFORE US

In a situation of both opportunity and threat it is imperative that we come up with new moral insights, communicatively persuasive, leading to vigorous public discussion about the meaning of the good life, and capable of being embodied in reformed institutions. We must clearly draw from older traditions, but reconceive them in ways consonant with new conditions. Such a moral argument cannot alone produce significant institutional change. Power and profit are always involved. But where moral agreement is strong enough, it will find opportunities for breaking through, and power and profit will find it advantageous to go along. Such outcomes cannot occur without conflict, when power is pitted against power. But without the moral argument, there is no steady pressure to bring potentially destructive economic and political forces to the service of human ends.

It is instructive that most of our public philosophers were accessible to a general public. Many of their books are still in print and can still be read with profit by educated lay people. Even though they understood that scientific and technological complexity was central to our form of society, they still believed that our fundamental problems are moral and political and can be solved only by public discussion and democratic decision. The vogue of modern policy analysis, which in many instances has taken the place of the reflections of our public philosophers, does not substitute for genuine democratic conversation, for it remains within the esoteric domain of experts, experts who, under the facade of democratic rituals, want to make the real decisions for us. To allow policy analysis to supplant public discussion is, in effect, to abandon the democratic undertaking altogether, and to admit that we have become the administered society our prophets have long feared we might become. The final irony would be the defeat of democracy in America just when it is gaining in so much of the rest of the world.

Finally, it is worth noting the extent to which all our figures, typically American in their several ways, transcended America. John Dewey was a philosopher of international standing whose work in China may yet prove to have major consequences. Walter Lippmann understood, as did few others in his day, how much America, even at the height of its power, was only a part of a world system: had we heeded his warnings about the limits of our capacity to police the world, we might well have avoided the tragedy of Vietnam. Reinhold Niebuhr, H. Richard Niebuhr, and John Courtney Murray always asserted a primary allegiance that entirely transcended the nation, and held America under the judgment of God. All of them invoked a vigorous public life as essential to a good society. And all of them in their own way reminded us that the purpose of the public lies beyond its own boundaries, however inclusive they may become, in the service and the celebration of the greater city, that cosmopolis, that universal community, of which all of us, our regions, our nations, are citizens.

Notes

INTRODUCTION: WE LIVE THROUGH INSTITUTIONS

1. Eli Sagan, in his book *The Honey and the Hemlock: Democracy and Paranoia in Ancient Athens and America* (New York: Basic Books, 1991), forcibly argues for the importance of psychic trust for democracy and the danger paranoia creates for democratic institutions.

2. George Grant, *English-Speaking Justice* (Notre Dame: University of Notre Dame Press, 1984 [1974]).

3. It was the Berkeley sociologist Kristin Luker who suggested homelessness as an example of the difficulty of knowing how to respond personally to a problem that one knows is institutional in origin.

4. Robert N. Bellah, Richard Madsen, William M. Sullivan, Ann Swidler, and Steven M. Tipton, *Habits of the Heart* (Berkeley and Los Angeles: University of California Press, 1985), p. vi.

5. See the Appendix for a fuller discussion of the sociological conception of institutions.

6. See especially pp. 144–47 of *Habits of the Heart*.

7. See, for example, Bernard Yack, "Liberalism and Its Communitarian Critics: Does Liberal Practice 'Live Down' to Liberal Theory?" and Jeffrey Stout, "Liberal Society and the Language of Morals," in Charles H. Reynolds and Ralph V. Norman, eds., *Community in America: The Challenge of "Habits of the Heart"* (Berkeley and Los Angeles: University of California Press, 1988), pp. 147–69 and 127–46. See also Jeffrey Stout, *Ethics After Babel: The Languages of Morals and Their Discontents* (Boston: Beacon Press, 1988).

8. Christopher Lasch in his review of *Habits of the Heart* in *In These Times*, June 26–July 9, 1985, pointed out that *Habits* was about public participation and not simply about community in the traditional American sense of that word. In his new book, *The True and Only Heaven: Progress and Its Critics* (New York: Norton, 1990), Lasch, in chapter 4, "The Sociological Tradition and the Idea of Community," points out in detail the weaknesses of the usual American use of the term "community." In chapter 3, "Nostalgia: The Abdication of Memory," he attacks another characteristic weakness of American thought.

9. Graham Wallas, *The Great Society: A Psychological Analysis* (New York: Macmillan, 1914).

10. John Dewey, *The Public and Its Problems* (1927), in Jo Ann Boydston, ed., *John Dewey: The Later Works*, Vol. 2: 1925–27 (Carbondale and Edwardsville: Southern Illinois University Press, 1984), p. 314.

11. Josiah Royce, *The Hope of the Great Community* (New York: Macmillan, 1916).

12. Walter Lippmann, *The Good Society* (Boston: Little, Brown, 1937).

13. Ibid., p. 194.

14. Ibid., p. 161.

15. Dennis McCann, "The Good to Be Pursued in Common," in Oliver F. Williams and John W. Houck, eds., *The Common Good and U.S. Capitalism* (Lanham, New York, London: University Press of America, 1987), pp. 158–78.

16. Herbert Fingarette has beautifully analyzed the institutional aspect of shaking hands in our culture in *Confucius: The Secular as Sacred* (New York: Harper and Row, Harper Torchbooks, 1972), pp. 9–10.

    Handshaking is an instance of a much more general relation between ceremony and institution. That institutions require ritual reenactment for their survival does not make them, from our point of view, equivalent to nonrational customary behavior. Healthy institutions live in the vital polarity of rational reflection and ritual.

17. David Kirp, *Learning by Heart: AIDS and Schoolchildren in America's Communities* (New Brunswick: Rutgers University Press, 1989).

18. Mary Douglas, *How Institutions Think* (Syracuse: Syracuse University Press, 1986), p. 124.

CHAPTER 1: MAKING SENSE OF IT

1. Jesse Jackson, "Common Ground and Common Sense," speech delivered at the Democratic National Convention, Atlanta, Georgia, July 20, 1988; in *Vital Speeches*, vol. 54, no. 21, August 15, 1988, pp. 649–53.

2. This description of the Open Door Community relies on the research of Peter M. Gathje. See his *A History of the Open Door Community*, unpublished MTS thesis, Emory University, 1988.

3. Reinhold Niebuhr, *Moral Man and Immoral Society* (New York: Charles Scribner's Sons, 1932). See also Richard Wightman Fox, "The Liberal Ethic and the Spirit of Protestantism," in Charles H. Reynolds and Ralph V. Norman, eds., *Community in America: The Challenge of "Habits of the Heart"* (Berkeley and Los Angeles: University of California Press, 1988), pp. 240–43.

4. Richard Nixon, *The Real War* (New York: Warner Books, 1980), p. 249.

5. Gaddis Smith, *Morality, Reason, and Power: American Diplomacy in the Carter Years* (New York: Hill and Wang, 1986), pp. 29, 32.

6. Noted in Bruce Cumings, "Chinatown: Foreign Policy and Elite Realignment" in Thomas Ferguson and Joel Rogers, eds., *The Hidden Election: Politics and Economics in the 1980 Presidential Campaign* (New York: Pantheon, 1981), p. 228.

7. Arthur M. Schlesinger, Jr., "The Theory of America: Experiment or Destiny?" in *The Cycles of American History* (Boston: Houghton Mifflin, 1986), pp. 3–22. The quotation from Stowe is on p. 14.

8. Woodrow Wilson, *Messages and Papers*, Albert Shaw, ed., Vol. 2 (New York:

Review of Reviews Corp., 1924), p. 777, as quoted in Schlesinger, *Cycles of American History*, p. 54.

9. This point is made in Gaddis Smith, *Morality, Reason, and Power*, and in Bruce Cumings, "Chinatown," in Ferguson and Rogers, *Hidden Election*, pp. 196–231.

10. For a helpful discussion of many of these issues see Sanford J. Unger, ed., *Estrangement: America and the World* (New York: Oxford University Press, 1985).

11. Daniel Bell, "The World and the United States in 2013," *Daedalus*, vol. 116, no. 3, Summer 1987, pp. 13–14.

12. *New York Times*, August 11, 1989, section 1, p. 23.

13. Jonathan Simon, "The Emergence of a Risk Society," *Socialist Review*, no. 95, 1987, pp. 61–89.

14. David Popenoe, *Disturbing the Nest: Family Change and Decline in Modern Societies* (New York: Aldine de Gruyter, 1988), pp. 57–79.

15. See also Judith Stacey, *Brave New Families: Stories of Democratic Upheaval in Late Twentieth-Century America* (New York: Basic Books, 1990).

16. Barbara Ehrenreich, *The Hearts of Men* (Garden City: Doubleday, Anchor Books, 1983).

17. Popenoe, *Disturbing the Nest*, pp. 295–306.

18. Mary Ann Glendon, *The Transformation of Family Law: State, Law, and the Family in the United States and Western Europe* (Chicago: University of Chicago Press, 1989), p. 292, quoting Alain Bénabent.

19. Judith S. Wallerstein and Sandra Blakeslee, *Second Chances: Men, Women and Children a Decade After Divorce* (New York: Ticknor and Fields, 1989), p. xxi.

20. Glendon, *Transformation of Family Law*, p. 313.

21. Arlie Hochschild, *Second Shift: Working Parents and the Revolution at Home* (New York: Viking, 1989), pp. 231, 267.

22. Lenore Weitzman, *The Divorce Revolution* (New York: Free Press, 1985).

23. Mihaly Csikszentmihalyi, *Flow: The Psychology of Optimal Experience* (New York: Harper and Row, 1990), chapter 7, "Work as Flow."

24. Gaetano Salvemini, *Italy from the Risorgimento to Fascism* (Garden City: Doubleday, Anchor Books, 1970), p. 453. Salvemini warns that there are no paradises on earth and that if we will not settle for some kind of purgatory, we are likely to end up in hell.

CHAPTER 2: THE RISE AND FALL OF THE AMERICAN CENTURY

1. Kenneth T. Jackson, *The Crabgrass Frontier: The Suburbanization of the United States* (New York: Oxford University Press, 1985), p. 248. For the context of Futurama, see also Jeffrey L. Meikle, *Twentieth Century Limited: Industrial Design in America, 1925–1939* (Philadelphia: Temple University Press, 1979).

2. Frederick F. Siegel, *Troubled Journey: From Pearl Harbor to Ronald Reagan* (New York: Hill and Wang, 1984), p. 86.

3. Lewis Mumford, *The City in History: Its Origins, Its Transformations, and Its Prospects* (New York: Harcourt, Brace, 1961), p. 486.

4. David Riesman, with Nathan Glazer and Reuel Denney, *The Lonely Crowd: A Study of the Changing American Character* (New Haven: Yale University Press, 1950).

5. William H. Whyte, *The Organizational Man* (New York: Simon and Schuster, 1956).

6. C. Wright Mills, *White Collar: The American Middle Classes* (New York: Oxford University Press, 1951), p. xv.

7. Robert S. Lynd and Helen Merrell Lynd, *Middletown: A Study of Contemporary American Culture* (New York: Harcourt, Brace, 1929); Robert S. Lynd and Helen Merrell Lynd, *Middletown in Transition: A Study in Cultural Conflicts* (New York: Harcourt, Brace, 1937).

8. Quoted in Siegel, *Troubled Journey*, pp. 110–11.

9. Ibid., p. 93.

10. Robert Reich, *The Next American Frontier* (New York: Times Books, 1983), p. 81.

11. Eric F. Goldman, *The Tragedy of Lyndon Johnson* (New York: Knopf, 1969), p. 164.

12. Thomas Pangle, *The Spirit of Modern Republicanism: The Moral Vision of the American Founders and the Philosophy of Locke* (Chicago: University of Chicago Press, 1988).

13. John Dunn, *The Political Thought of John Locke: An Historical Account of the Argument of the Two Treatises of Government* (Cambridge, England: Cambridge University Press, 1969), and *Locke* (Oxford: Oxford University Press, 1984).

14. Jean Bethke Elshtain in chapter 3 of her book *Public Man, Private Woman* (Princeton: Princeton University Press, 1981) gives a nuanced view of Locke's position on women. She points out that "Locke's justification of woman's subordination to man is explained as a result of the curse laid on Eve," but that this contradicts his firm opinion that "a grant of dominion to the patriarch is denied as having any basis in nature" (p. 125). Elshtain is convincing in arguing that Locke simply will not face the results of consistently applying his political position to the family, but that he has no theoretical basis for refusing to do so. Susan Moller Okin in chapter 4 of her *Justice, Gender, and the Family* (New York: Basic Books, 1989) gives a much less satisfactory account of Locke's views on women and the family.

15. Forest McDonald, *Hamilton: A Biography* (New York: Norton, 1979), pp. 234–35. See also Leslie Wharton, *Polity and the Public Good: Conflicting Theories of Republican Government in the New Nation* (Ann Arbor: UMI Research Press, 1980).

16. On the changing status of the corporation in American law and society, see: Alfred D. Chandler, *The Visible Hand: The Managerial Revolution in American Business* (Cambridge: Harvard University Press, Belknap Press, 1977) and *Managerial Hierarchies: Comparative Perspectives on the Rise of Modern Industrial Enterprise* (Cambridge: Harvard University Press, 1980); Thomas C. Cochrane, *Two Hundred Years of American Business* (New York: Basic Books, 1977) and *Challenges to American Values: Society, Business, and Religion* (New York: Oxford University Press, 1985); James Oliver Robinson, *America's Business* (New York: Hill and Wang, 1985); Michel Barzelay and Rogers Smith, "The One Best System?" in Warren J. Samuels and Arthur S. Miller, eds., *Corporations and Society: Power and Responsibility* (New York: Greenwood Press, 1987).

17. Herbert Croly, *The Promise of American Life* (Cambridge: Harvard University Press, Belknap Press, 1965 [1909]), pp. 21–22.

18. Ibid., p. 24.

19. Ibid., p. 25.

20. Graham Wallas, *The Great Society: A Psychological Analysis* (New York: Macmillan, 1914).

21. Croly, *Promise*, p. 104.

22. "NSC 68" in Thomas H. Etzold and John Lewis Gaddis, eds., *Containment: Documents on American Policy and Strategy, 1945–1950* (New York: Columbia University Press, 1978).

23. Robert Dahl, *Democracy and Its Critics* (New Haven: Yale University Press, 1989), especially the introduction and chapters 22 and 23. In general, *The Good Society* is an effort to consider the institutional framework Dahl's "third democratic transformation" would require.

CHAPTER 3: THE POLITICAL ECONOMY: MARKET AND WORK

1. Daniel Bell, *The Cultural Contradictions of Capitalism* (New York: Basic Books, 1976), chapter 6, "The Public Household," pp. 220–82.

2. Adam Smith, *The Wealth of Nations*, ed. Edwin Cannan (Chicago: University of Chicago Press, 1976). Smith takes a comprehensive view of the role of exchange in the history of civilization, giving weight to political and moral, as well as more narrowly economic, factors.

3. Donald Miller, *Lewis Mumford: A Life* (New York: Weidenfeld and Nicolson, 1989), p. 164.

4. Robert Dahl, *A Preface to Economic Democracy* (Berkeley and Los Angeles: University of California Press, 1985), pp. 162–63.

5. Ronald Reagan, press conference, 1983, as quoted in Jennifer L. Hochschild, "The Double-Edged Sword of Equal Opportunity," in Ian Shapiro and Grant Reeher, eds., *Power, Inequality, and Democratic Politics: Essays in Honor of Robert A. Dahl* (Boulder and London: Westview Press, 1988), p. 168.

6. Herbert Gans, *Middle-American Individualism: The Future of Liberal Democracy* (New York: Free Press, 1988).

7. Kevin Phillips, *The Politics of Rich and Poor: Wealth and the American Electorate in the Reagan Aftermath* (New York: Random House, 1990).

8. Benjamin Friedman, *Day of Reckoning* (New York: Random House, 1988), pp. 8–9.

9. David Popenoe, *Private Pleasure, Public Plight* (New Brunswick: Transaction Books, 1985), pp. 82–84. John Kenneth Galbraith gave currency to the idea of "private affluence and public poverty" in *The Affluent Society* (Boston: Houghton, Mifflin, 1958). The phrase ultimately goes back to Cato the Younger, who, in a speech against Catiline recounted by Sallust, laments the decline of republican virtue in Rome by saying, "*Habemus publice egestatem, privatim opulentiam,*" almost literally, "We have public poverty and private affluence" (Sallust, *Catilina*, section 52, subsection 22). Machiavelli in his *Discourses* makes the point when he says that well-ordered republics have to keep the public rich but the citizens poor (*Discorsi*, I.37.3; see also III.25).

10. Robert N. Bellah, Richard Madsen, William M. Sullivan, Ann Swidler, and Steven M. Tipton, *Habits of the Heart* (Berkeley and Los Angeles: University of California Press, 1985), provides a full-scale description of this situation.

11. Alan Wolfe, *Whose Keeper? Social Science and Moral Obligation* (Berkeley and Los Angeles: University of California Press, 1989), pp. 36, 32, 37–38. *The Good Society* owes a considerable debt to Wolfe's book. We have learned much from his criticism of the economy and the state in modern Western society in the first

two parts of his book. In many respects our book is an effort to develop the institutional implications of the third section, on society, of his book.

12. Adam Smith, *The Theory of the Moral Sentiments*, ed. D. D. Raphael and A. L. Macfie (Oxford: Oxford University Press, 1976), part III, chapter 3, paragraph 25, pp. 146–47.

13. Robert Heilbroner, "The Coming Meltdown of Traditional Capitalism," *Ethics and International Affairs*, vol. 2, 1980, p. 72. See also his "Reflections: The Triumph of Capitalism," *New Yorker*, January 23, 1989, pp. 98–109, where Heilbroner describes the significant achievements of capitalism compared with the command economies of the Communist nations without obscuring the serious problems that remain in the capitalist economies themselves.

14. Fred Block, *Post-Industrial Possibilities* (Berkeley and Los Angeles: University of California Press, 1990).

15. Robert Dahl, *Democracy and Its Critics* (New Haven: Yale University Press, 1989), pp. 111–12.

16. Alexis de Tocqueville, *Democracy in America*, trans. George Lawrence, ed. J. P. Mayer (New York: Doubleday, Anchor Books, 1969), vol. II, part II, Chapter 20, pp. 555–58.

17. See David Vogel, *Fluctuating Fortunes: The Political Power of Business in America* (New York: Basic Books, 1989).

18. David F. Noble, *Forces of Production: A Social History of Industrial Automation* (New York: Oxford University Press, 1986).

19. Harley Shaiken, *Work Transformed: Automation and Labor in the Computer Age* (New York: Holt, Rinehart and Winston, 1985).

20. Robert Howard, *Brave New Workplace* (New York: Viking, 1985).

21. Robert B. Reich, *The Next American Frontier* (New York: Times Books, 1983).

22. Michael J. Piore and Charles F. Sabel, *The Second Industrial Divide: Possibilities for Prosperity* (New York: Basic Books, 1984).

23. Shoshana Zuboff, *In the Age of the Smart Machine: The Future of Work and Power* (New York: Basic Books, 1988).

24. Joseph Pratt and Louis Galambos, *The Rise of the Corporate Commonwealth* (New York: Basic Books, 1988). See also Neil D. Fligstein, *The Transformation of Corporate Control* (Cambridge: Harvard University Press, 1990).

25. Charles R. Strain, "Madison and Jefferson in the Workplace: Technological Change and the Ethos of a Democratic Society," paper presented at "The Worker in Transition: Technological Change," conference, Bethesda, Maryland, April 4–7, 1989. See also "Beyond Madison and Marx: Civic Virtue, Solidarity and Justice in American Culture" in Charles R. Strain, ed., *Prophetic Visions and Economic Realities: Protestants, Jews and Catholics Confront the Bishops' Letter on the Economy* (Grand Rapids: Eerdmans, 1989), pp. 190–202.

26. Cuomo Commission on Trade and Competitiveness, *The Cuomo Commission Report* (New York: Simon and Schuster, 1988).

27. No one has spoken more eloquently than Wendell Berry on the need to reorient our lives with respect to work, the environment, and our relations to others. Two of his recent collections of essays are particularly pertinent: *Home Economics* (San Francisco: North Point Press, 1987) and *What Are People For?* (San Francisco: North Point Press, 1990).

28. R. Jeffrey Lustig, "Taking Corporatism Seriously: Private Government and American Politics," paper presented at the American Political Science Association

meetings, Chicago, September 4, 1987. See also Lustig's *Corporate Liberalism: The Origins of Modern American Political Theory, 1890–1920* (Berkeley and Los Angeles: University of California Press, 1982).

29. James Boyd White, "How Should We Talk About Corporations: The Languages of Economics and Citizenship," *Yale Law Journal*, vol. 94, 1985, pp. 1418, 1416.

30. See Ronald Dore, *Taking Japan Seriously: A Confucian Perspective on Leading Economic Issues* (Stanford: Stanford University Press, 1987), pp. 148–50; see also the discussion of a guaranteed minimum income in Fred Block: *Post-Industrial Possibilities* (Berkeley and Los Angeles: University of California Press, 1990), pp. 204–8.

31. James Stockinger, "Locke and Rousseau: Human Nature, Human Citizenship, and Human Work," unpublished Ph.D. dissertation, Department of Sociology, University of California, Berkeley, 1990.

32. Jennifer Hochschild, "The Double-Edged Sword of Equal Opportunity," in Shapiro and Reeher, *Power, Inequality, and Democratic Politics*, pp. 168–200. We have found Hochschild's probing analysis of equal opportunity helpful at several points in this chapter.

33. See Robert Coles, "The Underclass: What Is to Be Done?" *New Oxford Review*, March 1990, pp. 19–22.

34. Philip Scranton, personal communication, Fall 1988.

35. Carol Gilligan, *In a Different Voice: Psychological Theory and Women's Development* (Cambridge: Harvard University Press, 1982); Sara Ruddick, "Maternal Thinking," in Barrie Thorne, ed., *Rethinking the Family: Some Feminist Questions* (New York: Longmans, 1982), pp. 76–94.

36. *Economic Justice for All*, Pastoral Letter on Catholic Social Teaching and the U.S. Economy (Washington, D.C.: National Conference of Catholic Bishops, 1986), paragraphs 183–85, pp. 90–92.

37. Christopher Jencks et al., Inequality: A Reassessment of the Effect of Family and Schooling in America (New York: Basic Books, 1982), p. 8.

38. Jeffrey C. Goldfarb, *The Cynical Society* (Chicago: University of Chicago Press, 1991).

39. Václav Havel, address to a Joint Meeting of the United States Congress, Washington, D.C., February 21, 1990, *Congressional Record—Senate*, vol. 136, no. 13, p. S1313.

40. James Fallows, "Wake Up, America!," *New York Review of Books*, vol. 37, no. 3, March 1, 1990, p. 19.

CHAPTER 4: GOVERNMENT, LAW, AND POLITICS

1. Ronald L. Jepperson and David Kamens in "The Expanding State and the U.S. 'Civic Culture': The Changing Character of Political Participation and Legitimation in the Post-War U.S. Polity," paper presented at the annual meeting of the American Political Science Association, 1985, develop a provocative analysis of the expansion of the American "polity"—the arena in which problems are defined as public and government is expected to solve them.

2. For an exceptionally intelligent treatment of these issues from a point of view similar to that of this book, see Daniel Callahan, *Setting Limits: Medical Costs in an Aging Society* (New York: Simon and Schuster, 1987) and *What Kind of Life: The Limits of Medical Progress* (New York: Simon and Schuster, 1990).

3. See Guido Calabresi and Philip Bobbitt, *Tragic Choices* (New York: Norton, 1978).

4. Viviana Zelizer, *Pricing the Priceless Child* (New York: Basic Books, 1985).

5. See Robert Bell, *The Culture of Policy Deliberations* (New Brunswick: Rutgers University Press, 1985) for an analysis of why the language of welfare economics tends to drive out other ways of justifying policy choices.

6. There is by now a large literature on cost-benefit analysis and, more generally, on the uses of economic logic in policy making. Two sympathetic yet mildly critical introductions are E. J. Mishan, *What Political Economy Is All About: An Exposition and Critique* (Cambridge, England: Cambridge University Press, 1982), and Steven E. Rhoads, *The Economist's View of the World: Government, Markets, and Public Policy* (Cambridge, England: Cambridge University Press, 1985). Peter Self, *Econocrats and the Policy Process: The Politics and Philosophy of Cost-Benefit Analysis* (London: Macmillan, 1975), raises more fundamental criticisms. See also Steven Kelman, "Cost-Benefit Analysis: An Ethical Critique," *Regulation*, vol. 5, no. 1, January–February 1981), pp. 33–40, and Duncan Kennedy, "Cost-Benefit Analysis of Entitlement Problems: A Critique," *Stanford Law Review*, vol. 33, February 1981, pp. 387–445.

7. For analysis of relative risks, see Bernard L. Cohen and I-Sing Lee, "A Catalog of Risks," *Health Physics*, vol. 36, June 1979, pp. 707–22. For an insider's assessment of government's record of rationally reducing risk, see John F. Morrall III, "A Review of the Record," *Regulation*, vol. 10, no. 2, November–December 1988, pp. 25–34.

8. For a sense of the history, and some of the complexity, of economists' work on this issue, see Steven E. Rhoads, ed., *Valuing Life: Public Policy Dilemmas* (Boulder: Westview Press, 1980).

9. Ann Fisher, Lauraine Chestnut, and Dan Violette, "The Value of Reducing Risk," unpublished paper, Environmental Protection Agency, September 16, 1986, p. 3. See also Morrall, "A Review of the Record," p. 34.

10. A technical critique of the possibility of rationally aggregating preferences can be found in Kenneth Arrow, *Social Choice and Individual Values* (New York: Wiley, 1951).

11. Robert Bell, "Moral Order in America," paper presented to the Georgetown University Faculty Seminar on Social and Political Theory, 1988, p. 19, argues that for policy makers the economic language of liberal individualism, because it "prove[s] inadequate to describe the actual moral intuitions behind government policy or to construct a coherent and persuasive framework for reconstructing policy," can lead to "growing cynicism about morality and principle themselves, potentially challenging the fundamental ideal of government under law." See also Bell, *Policy Deliberations*.

12. Douglas Maclean, in "Comparing Values," paper prepared for National Academy of Sciences Conference on Valuing Health Risks, Costs, and Benefits for Environmental Policy Making, Washington, D.C., June 23–24, 1987, develops a careful argument against discounting lives. See also his "Valuing Human Life," in D. Zinberg, ed., *Uncertain Power* (New York: Pergamon, 1983), pp. 89–107, and "Social Values and the Distribution of Risk," in Douglas MacLean, ed., *Values at Risk* (Totowa: Rowman and Allanheld, 1986), pp. 75–93.

13. For an analysis of the effects of new social practices that treat persons statistically on social and moral understandings, see Jonathan Simon, "The Emergence of a Risk Society: Insurance, Law, and the State," *Socialist Review*, no. 95 (vol. 17,

no. 5), September–October 1987, pp. 61–89. See also his "The Ideological Effects of Actuarial Practices: *Manhart* Reconsidered," Center for the Study of Law and Society, University of California, Berkeley, no date.

14. Ronald Dworkin has been the most eloquent spokesman for the view that individual rights are the foundation of legal order and the essential complement to democratic governance. See his *Taking Rights Seriously* (Cambridge: Harvard University Press, 1977) and also *Law's Empire* (Cambridge: Harvard University Press, 1986).

15. James Q. Wilson, in "The Newer Deal," *New Republic*, vol. 203, no. 1, July 2, 1990, pp. 33–37, has noted that "there has been a transformation of public expectations about the scope of federal action, one that has put virtually everything on Washington's agenda and left nothing off. . . . Moreover, the language by which that transformation was accomplished was that of individual rights: morally superior and legally defensible claims for protections and remedies" (p. 37).

16. Charles A. Reich, "The New Property," *Yale Law Journal*, vol. 73, April 1964, pp. 733–87.

17. See Jethro K. Lieberman, *The Litigious Society* (New York: Basic Books, 1981); but note the much more cautious interpretation in Lawrence M. Friedman, *Total Justice* (New York: Russell Sage Foundation, 1985).

18. Friedman, *Total Justice*, p. 48.

19. Philip Selznick, "The Ethos of American Law," in Irving Kristol and Paul H. Weaver, eds., *The Americans, 1976: An Inquiry into Fundamental Concepts of Man Underlying Various U.S. Institutions* (Lexington: Lexington Books, 1976), pp. 217, 219.

20. The research of Joel Handler, however, shows how precarious those rights remain, given the power of welfare agencies and the vulnerability of welfare clients. See Handler, "Controlling Official Behavior in Welfare Administration," *California Law Review*, vol. 54, 1966, pp. 479–510. See also Fred Block, Richard A. Cloward, Barbara Ehrenreich, and Frances Fox Piven, *The Mean Season: The Attack on the Welfare State* (New York: Pantheon, 1987), for an analysis of how American ideology and institutions continually undermine support for social welfare.

21. See Gary C. Bryner, "Affirmative Action: Minority Rights or Reverse Discrimination?" pp. 142–76 in Raymond Tatalovich and Byron W. Daynes, eds., *Social Regulatory Policy: Moral Controversies in American Politics* (Boulder: Westview Press, 1988), for a history of affirmative action in law, policy, litigation, and public debate.

22. Mary Ann Glendon, *Abortion and Divorce in Western Law* (Cambridge: Harvard University Press, 1987). Several other works, among them Kristin Luker, *Abortion and the Politics of Motherhood* (Berkeley and Los Angeles: University of California Press, 1984), Rosalind Pollack Petchesky, *Abortion and Woman's Choice: The State, Sexuality, and Reproductive Freedom* (New York: Longman, 1984) and Carole E. Joffe, *The Regulation of Sexuality: Experiences of Family Planning Workers* (Philadelphia: Temple University Press, 1986), offer rich, empirically grounded analyses of why the abortion issue has proved so intractable.

23. See Larry Letich, "Abortion: Bad Choices," *Tikkun*, vol. 4, July–August 1989, pp. 22–26.

24. Michael Perry, *Law, Morality and Politics* (New York: Oxford University Press, 1988).

25. Selznick, "The Ethos of American Law."
26. Martin Shefter, "Party and Patronage: Germany, England, and Italy," *Politics and Society*, vol. 7, 1977, pp. 403–51. See also Ann Orloff and Theda Skocpol, "Why Not Equal Protection? Explaining the Politics of Public Social Spending in Britain, 1900–1911, and the United States, 1800s–1920," *American Sociological Review*, vol. 49, December 1984, pp. 724–50.
27. Stanley Lieberson, *A Piece of the Pie: Black and White Immigrants Since 1880* (Berkeley and Los Angeles: University of California Press, 1980).
28. This section relies heavily for both evidence and argument on Jepperson and Kamens, "The Expanding State and the U.S. 'Civic Culture.' " See also Benjamin Ginsberg and Martin Shefter, *Politics by Other Means: The Declining Significance of Elections in America* (New York: Basic Books, 1990).
29. See Norman Nie, Sidney Verba, and John Petrocik, *The Changing American Voter* (Cambridge: Harvard University Press, 1976).
30. Seymour Martin Lipset and William Schneider, *The Confidence Gap: Business, Labor and Government in the Public Mind* (New York: Free Press, 1983).
31. Edward O. Laumann and David Knoke, *The Organizational State: Social Change in National Policy Domains* (Madison: University of Wisconsin Press, 1987), document this remarkable growth in political access.
32. See Robert B. Reich, ed., *The Power of Public Ideas* (Cambridge, Mass.: Ballinger, 1988), especially Reich's own paper, "Policy Making in a Democracy," pp. 123–56; Robert B. Reich, *Tales of a New America* (New York: Times Books, 1987); and Steven Kelman, *Making Public Policy: A Hopeful View of American Government* (New York: Basic Books, 1988).
33. Judith Innes, in "State Growth Management Programs: Experiments in Collaborative Intergovernmental Planning," unpublished paper, 1990, describes these new programs in Vermont, New Jersey, Rhode Island, Maine, and Florida as well as Washington State. Tony Hiss describes a number of these efforts at the state level, especially the Massachusetts Department of Environmental Management, in *The Experience of Place* (New York: Knopf, 1990). David Osborne in his *Laboratories of Democracy* (Boston: Harvard Business School Press, 1988) has considered a number of efforts to involve citizens of various backgrounds in the process of economic development. Wallace Katz in his forthcoming *The Politics of the Public Sphere: Growth and Democracy in Post-Industrial America* argues, on the basis of the study of economic growth and democratic initiative in ten metropolitan areas, that cities are even more important than states as "laboratories" of democratic participation.
34. See the Conclusion for further reflections on the concept of subsidiarity.
35. See Bruce A. Ackerman, *Reconstructing American Law* (Cambridge: Harvard University Press, 1984).
36. Jürgen Habermas, *The Structural Transformation of the Public Sphere: An Inquiry into a Category of Bourgeois Society*, tr. Thomas Burger (Cambridge: MIT Press, 1989 [1962]), part 3.
37. Václav Havel, "New Year's Address to the Nation," in *Congressional Record—Extension of Remarks*, vol. 136, no. 2, January 24, 1990, p. E49.
38. John Dewey, *The Public and Its Problems* (1927), in Jo Ann Boydston, ed., *John Dewey: The Later Works*, vol. 2: 1925–1927 (Carbondale and Edwardsville: Southern Illinois University Press, 1984), p. 282.

39. Ronald Dworkin, "The New England," *New York Review of Books*, vol. 35, no. 16, October 27, 1988, p. 60.

40. Richard Flacks in *Making History: The Radical Tradition in American Life* (New York: Columbia University Press, 1988) analyzes both the successes and the failures of the American left as a force for genuine democratic participation. His concluding recommendations for "revitalizing the tradition of the left" include valuable suggestions for strengthening the practice of democracy in America. Norman Birnbaum surveys the radical intellectual tradition with similar intent in *The Radical Renewal: The Politics of Ideas in Modern America* (New York: Pantheon, 1988).

CHAPTER 5: EDUCATION: TECHNICAL AND MORAL

1. Aristotle, *Nichomachaean Ethics*, book 10, chapter 9.

2. Daniel Boorstin, *The Americans: The Democratic Experience* (New York: Random House, 1973), p. 478.

3. Material on early American education is drawn from Lawrence A. Cremin, *American Education: The Colonial Experience, 1607–1783* (New York: Harper and Row, 1970) and *American Education: The National Experience, 1783–1876* (New York: Harper and Row, 1980).

4. John Dewey, *The School and Society* (1899), reprinted in John Dewey, *The Child and Curriculum and The School and Society* (Chicago: Chicago University Press, 1956), pp. 9–11.

5. Ibid., pp. 24–25.

6. Ibid., pp. 28–29.

7. John Dewey, *Democracy and Social Ethics* (New York: Macmillan, 1916), p. 383; emphasis Dewey's.

8. Lawrence A. Cremin, *American Education: The Metropolitan Experience, 1876–1980* (New York: Harper and Row, 1988), p. 14; Dewey, *Democracy and Social Ethics*, p. 220.

9. Cremin, *American Education: The Metropolitan Experience*, p. 175.

10. Ibid., p. 176.

11. Jane Addams, *Twenty Years at Hull House* (New York: Macmillan, 1910), pp. 428, 431.

12. The term "Chicago school" has had a complex history. It has been applied not only, as we do here, to the circle around John Dewey in the earliest years of the university, but to Chicago sociology in the 1920s and to Chicago economics in recent decades.

13. Burton J. Bledstein in *The Culture of Professionalism: The Middle Class and the Development of Higher Education in America* (New York: Norton, 1976) describes the close relation of the expansion of higher education to middle-class professional aspirations.

14. Cremin, *American Education: The Metropolitan Experience*, pp. 242–43.

15. Reinhold Niebuhr, *Leaves from the Notebook of a Tamed Cynic* (Chicago: Willett, Clark and Colby, 1929), p. 162.

16. James A. Berlin, *Writing Instruction in Nineteenth-Century Colleges* (Carbondale and Edwardsville: Southern Illinois University Press, 1984), chapter 5.

17. Jürgen Habermas, *The Structural Transformation of the Public Sphere: An Inquiry into a Category of Bourgeois Society*, tr. Thomas Burger (Cambridge: MIT Press, 1989 [1962]).

18. Lawrence Levine, *Highbrow Lowbrow: The Emergence of Cultural Hierarchy in America* (Cambridge: Harvard University Press, 1988).

19. Bruce A. Kimball, *Orators and Philosophers* (New York: Teachers College Press, 1986).

20. Berlin, *Writing Instruction*, pp. 86, 92.

21. Ibid., pp. 73, 75.

22. Robert K. Merton, *On the Shoulders of Giants: A Shandean Postscript* (New York: Harcourt, Brace, 1965); Mary Douglas, *How Institutions Think* (Syracuse: Syracuse University Press, 1986).

23. William James, "The Moral Equivalent of War," in William James, *Writings, 1902–1910* (New York: Library of America, 1987 [February 1910]).

24. Jürgen Habermas, *The Theory of Communicative Action*, Vol. 2: *Lifeworld and System: A Critique of Functionalist Reason* (Boston: Beacon Press, 1987 [1981]), chapter 5.

25. Bruce Kuklick, *Churchmen and Philosophers: From Jonathan Edwards to John Dewey* (New Haven: Yale University Press, 1985).

26. Lewis Mumford commented incisively on the contradictory nature of the modern university. In the note to plate 56, "University City," in *The City in History* (New York: Harcourt, Brace, 1961), which is a picture of the University of California at Berkeley and its surroundings, he noted that the university city came close to embodying the full range of institutions of the ancient polis and thus performing "the most central role of the city," providing "the central nucleus of the new urban and cultural grid." Yet at the same time "the university has pushed to the point of caricature many of the worst aspects of the historic city: intense vocational compartmentalization, over-specialization, and hierarchic subordination under a pervasive bureaucratic discipline." Mumford calls for "an inner transformation: from pedagogy to paideia, from science to wisdom, from detachment to commitment." Three decades later, these contradictory impulses have only grown in intensity.

27. Sam Bass Warner, Jr., *The Province of Reason* (Cambridge: Harvard University Press, 1984), p. 247.

28. Talcott Parsons and Gerald M. Platt, *The American University* (Cambridge: Harvard University Press, 1973), pp. 103, 313. For another, slightly earlier and rather different view, see Christopher Jencks and David Riesman, *The Academic Revolution* (Garden City: Doubleday, 1968).

29. Derek Bok, *Higher Learning* (Cambridge: Harvard University Press, 1986).

30. Allan Bloom, *The Closing of the American Mind* (New York: Simon and Schuster, 1987).

31. Ibid., pp. 372–73.

32. Ibid., p. 374.

33. Quotations from William Massy are from *Stanford School of Education*, a supplement to the *Stanford Observer*, January 1989, p. 2.

34. James A. Berlin, *Rhetoric and Reality: Writing Instruction in American Colleges, 1900–1985* (Carbondale and Edwardsville: Southern Illinois University Press, 1987), p. 155.

35. Ibid., p. 169.

36. Ibid., p. 170.

37. Zelda F. Gamson and Associates, *Liberating Education* (San Francisco: Jossey-Bass, 1984).

38. Bok, *Higher Learning*, pp. 38–39.

39. Robert E. Proctor, *Education's Great Amnesia: Reconsidering the Humanities from Petrarch to Freud* (Bloomington: University of Indiana Press, 1988).

40. David V. Hicks, *Norms and Nobility: A Treatise on Education* (New York: Praeger, 1981).

41. See Bok on the core curriculum, *Higher Learning*, p. 45.

42. Thomas McCarthy, "Rationality and Relativism: Habermas's 'Overcoming' of Hermeneutics," in John B. Thompson and David Held, eds., *Habermas: Critical Debates* (Cambridge: MIT Press, 1982), p. 78.

43. James S. Coleman, Thomas Hoffer, and Sally Kilgore, *High School Achievement: Public, Private and Catholic High Schools Compared* (New York: Basic Books, 1982), and James S. Coleman and Thomas Hoffer, *Public and Private High Schools: The Impact of Community* (New York: Basic Books, 1987).

CHAPTER 6: THE PUBLIC CHURCH

1. Jürgen Habermas, *The Structural Transformation of the Public Sphere: An Inquiry into a Category of Bourgeois Society*, tr. Thomas Burger (Cambridge: MIT Press, 1989 [1962]), part 3.

2. The text of the First Amendment to the United States Constitution is: "Congress shall make no law respecting an establishment of religion, or prohibiting the free exercise thereof; or abridging the freedom of speech, of the press, or the right of the people peaceably to assemble, and to petition the Government for a redress of grievances."

3. Quoted in John R. Howe, Jr., *The Changing Political Thought of John Adams* (Princeton: Princeton University Press, 1966), p. 185.

4. John Locke, *A Letter Concerning Toleration* (Indianapolis: Bobbs-Merrill, 1950 [1689]), p. 52.

5. See, for example, John Rawls, "Kantian Constructivism in Moral Theory," *Journal of Philosophy*, vol. 77, 1980, pp. 536, 542, and "Justice as Fairness: Political Not Metaphysical," *Philosophy and Public Affairs*, vol. 14, no. 3, Summer 1985, pp. 223, 225, 226, 230. See also Richard Rorty, "The Priority of Democracy over Philosophy," Merrill D. Peterson and Richard Vaughan, eds., *The Virginia Statute for Religious Freedom* (New York: Cambridge University Press, 1988), pp. 257–82. Critics of philosophical liberalism on this point include Michael J. Perry, *Morality, Politics, and Law* (New York: Oxford University Press, 1988), pp. 57–63, 82–90; also Michael J. Sandel, *Liberalism and the Limits of Justice* (New York: Cambridge University Press, 1982), pp. 1–11, 12, 55, 58–59, 172–73, and "The Procedural Republic and the Unencumbered Self," *Political Theory*, vol. 12, 1984; and Samuel Scheffler, "Moral Scepticism and Ideals of the Person," *Monist*, vol. 62, 1979, pp. 288, 295.

6. See Perry, *Morality, Politics and Law*, pp. 85–87, for the argument that Rawls's recent introduction of the concept of an "overlapping consensus" into his theory of justice as fairness makes the Good prior to the Right (contrary to Rawls's original formulation); and it makes various conceptions of the human good within the moral pluralism of American culture prior to our democratic politics and

essential to supporting such politics (contrary to Rorty, "The Priority of Democracy over Philosophy"). Cf. John Rawls, "The Idea of an Overlapping Consensus," *Oxford Journal of Legal Studies*, vol. 7, no. 1, 1987, pp. 9–12; "Justice as Fairness"; and *A Theory of Justice* (Cambridge: Harvard University Press, 1971).

7. Robert N. Bellah, Richard Madsen, William M. Sullivan, Ann Swidler, and Steven M. Tipton, *Habits of the Heart* (Berkeley and Los Angeles: University of California Press, 1985); Charles Y. Glock and Robert N. Bellah, *The New Religious Consciousness* (Berkeley and Los Angeles: University of California Press, 1976); Steven M. Tipton, *Getting Saved from the Sixties* (Berkeley and Los Angeles: University of California Press, 1982), pp. xiv, 281.

8. Michael Novak, *Choosing Our King* (New York: Macmillan, 1974), p. 132.

9. Ann Douglas, *The Feminization of American Culture* (New York: Alfred A. Knopf, 1977).

10. By comparison, some fifteen hundred nonprofit, *non*religious associations concerned with governmental and public affairs have come into being since 1960—more than half of all such associations now in existence. Robert Wuthnow, *The Restructuring of American Religion* (Princeton: Princeton University Press, 1988), pp. 112–13.

11. Wuthnow, *Restructuring*, pp. 131, 336 n. 11.

12. Major religious advocacy and lobbying groups in Washington, D.C., grew fivefold in number from sixteen in 1950 to more than eighty in 1985. See Allen D. Hertzke, *Representing God in Washington* (Knoxville: University of Tennessee Press, 1988), p. 5.

13. See congregational case studies of parish organization, programs, and administration for an analysis of their growing internal differentiation, bureaucratization, denominational, and para-church connections; for example, David Roozen, William McKinney, Jackson W. Carroll, *The Varieties of Religious Presence* (New York: Pilgrim Press, 1984), chapters 6–9. Cf. Wuthnow, *Restructuring*, pp. 126–29.

14. Pseudonyms are used for the people interviewed in this chapter; their precise institutional identities are disguised but sketched accurately in all but incidental details.

15. Peter Steinfels, "Churches Find the Message of the Season Is Debt and Donations," *New York Times*, November 13, 1988, p. A54. Since 1975 support for the National Council of Churches from its thirty-two denominational members has remained flat in the face of inflation, halving its value and resulting in professional staff reductions of more than two-thirds over the past twenty years. Disposable personal income of most U.S. church members grew by one-third between 1968 and 1985, while their total church contributions dropped 8.5 percent and their contribution to "mission and outreach programs" beyond the local level dropped 23 percent. John and Sylvia Ronsvalle, *Study of Church Benevolence Giving, 1968–1985* (Urbana: Empty Tomb, 1988). Little fiscal evidence exists for denominational centralization since 1960, as central bureaucracies and agencies often continued to expend no more than 5 to 6 percent of their denomination's total revenues. Wuthnow, *Restructuring*, pp. 99, 335 n. 88.

16. Linda-Marie Delloff, "The NCC in a New Time (II): Structural Changes and the Future of Ecumenism," *Christianity and Crisis*, January 9, 1989, pp. 468–9.

17. Committee on Membership, Council of Bishops, United Methodist Church, Pastoral Letter, November 12, 1985, p. 1. Literature on "church growth and

decline" is summarized in Wade Clark Roof and William McKinney, *American Mainline Religion* (New Brunswick: Rutgers University Press, 1987), chapters 5, 7, esp. pp. 158–83, 230–36; and Roof and McKinney, "Denominational America and the New Religious Pluralism," *Annals of the American Academy of Political and Social Science*, vol. 480, July 1985, pp. 24–38, esp. pp. 29–32. Also see Dean Hoge and David A. Roozen, *Understanding Church Growth and Decline: 1950–1978* (New York: Pilgrim Press, 1979), chapters 4, 8, 9, 14, 15.

18. Roof and McKinney, "Denominational America," pp. 26–27, and *American Mainline Religion*, pp. 150–61, 165–75, 183.

19. On the coincidence of religious denomination and political party, see Warren E. Miller, "Disinterest, Disaffection, and Participation in Presidential Politics," *Political Behavior*, vol. 1, no. 1, 1980, p. 22; and Roof and McKinney, "Denominational America," pp. 33, 37. Cf. Roof and McKinney, *American Mainline Religion*, chapters 5–7, for its emphasis on church growth and decline in response to social-cultural changes; and Wuthnow, *Restructuring*, chapter 7, esp. pp. 88–91, 156–72, for its emphasis on growing social convergence since 1960 *across* denominations in terms of educational attainment, occupations, and middle-class status, coupled with greater social polarization *within* each of the larger Protestant denominations and American Catholicism between better-educated, younger cultural "liberals" and less educated, older cultural "conservatives."

20. William McKinney, "The NCC in a New Time (I): Finding a Place in the Culture," *Christianity and Crisis*, January 9, 1989, p. 466.

21. Roof and McKinney, "Denominational America," pp. 26–27, 34, 36, and *American Mainline Religion*, pp. 54–56; Patrick H. McNamara, "American Catholicism in the Mid-Eighties: Pluralism and Conflict in a Changing Church," *Annals of the American Academy of Political and Social Science*, vol. 480, July 1985, p. 66; William D'Antonio, James Davidson, Dean Hoge, and Ruth Wallace, *American Catholic Laity* (Kansas City: Sheed and Ward, 1989), chapters 1, 2, 5.

22. Wuthnow, *Restructuring*, pp. 131, 336 n. 11.

23. 1980–84 General Social Surveys show support for increased government spending on health, education, cities, and the environment among almost 50 percent of black Protestants and Jews, 42 percent of the unchurched, 35 percent of Catholics, and 27 percent of both evangelical and mainline Protestants. Similar levels of support exist for increased spending to "help the disadvantaged," except that such support rises to 70 percent among black Protestants and falls to 40 percent among Jews. Kenneth D. Wald, *Religion and Politics in the United States*, (New York: St. Martins Press, 1987), pp. 71, 74.

24. Arthur Keys, "National Ecumenical Advocacy: What Future?" *Christianity and Crisis*, August 14, 1989, p. 241.

25. Marjorie H. Royle, *Research Findings Pertaining to Mission in the United Church of Christ* (New York: United Church for Homeland Ministries, 1986).

26. In mid-1989 President Bush called on local volunteers and businesses to build "relationships, not bureaucracies" to combat homelessness, illiteracy, and drug abuse as part of a "Points of Light Initiative" backed by a national foundation and federal funding of $25 million annually. Americans already give some $100 billion a year, according to Independent Sector, with church members far more likely to give than the unchurched. But the poor are more generous than the well to do: households with annual incomes under $10,000 in 1988 gave 2.8

percent of that to charity, a proportion nearly double that for households earning $50,000–75,000 and higher than households with incomes over $100,000. Steinfels, "Debt and Donations"; also *Atlanta Constitution*, June 23, 1989, p. A5.

27. Arie L. Brouwer, "Stand for Truth," Report of the General Secretary to the Governing Board of the National Council of Churches of Christ in the U.S.A., Lexington, Kentucky, May 17, 1989, pp. 6–7.

28. Children (under age eighteen) displaced the elderly as the poorest age group in 1974. By 1984, the child poverty rate (21.3 percent) was nearly three-quarters greater than the elderly rate (12.4 percent) due to sharp rises since 1979; it now is approaching one-quarter of all children in poverty. In 1984 more than three-quarters of all the poor in America were either adult women or children, including almost one black child in two, more than one in three Hispanic children, one in six white children, and one in four children under age six. Daniel P. Moynihan, *Family and Nation* (New York: Harcourt, Brace, Jovanovich, 1986), pp. 111–12; Marian Wright Edelman, *Families in Peril* (Cambridge: Harvard University Press, 1986), chapters 1–2, esp. pp. 25–26.

29. Domestic Human Needs and Economic Policy Work Group, Interfaith Action for Economic Justice, *Children: The Promise* (Washington, D.C.: IMPACT Education Fund, 1987), p. 1.

30. In 1958 only one person in twenty-five had left his or her childhood church behind; by 1984, one in three had done so, according to Gallup polls. By the early 1980s roughly four of ten persons raised as Presbyterians, Methodists, or Episcopalians had switched; so had one in four Baptists and Lutherans, and one in six Jews and Catholics, led by the college-educated among every group but Jews. See Roof and McKinney, *American Mainline Religion*, pp. 172–83; and Wuthnow, *Restructuring*, pp. 88–91.

31. Jeffrey Hadden, *The Gathering Storm in the Churches* (New York: Doubleday, 1969); Harvey G. Cox, "The New Breed in American Churches: Sources of Social Activism in American Religion," *Daedalus*, vol. 96, no. 1, Winter 1967, pp. 135–50; and Wuthnow, *Restructuring*, pp. 160–61.

32. The official United Methodist statement on abortion reads in part: "Our belief in the sanctity of unborn human life makes us reluctant to approve abortion. But we are equally bound to respect the sacredness of the life and well-being of the mother, for whom devastating damage may result from an unacceptable pregnancy. In continuity with past Christian teaching, we recognize tragic conflicts of life with life that may justify abortion. . . . We cannot affirm abortion as an acceptable means of birth control. . . ." *The Book of Discipline of the United Methodist Church—1988* (Nashville: United Methodist Publishing House, 1988), paragraph 71G, p. 96.

33. See, for example, Harvey G. Cox, *The Secular City* (New York: Macmillan, 1965); Gibson Winter, *The Suburban Captivity of the Churches* (Garden City: Doubleday, 1961); Pierre Berton, *The Comfortable Pew* (New York: Lippincott, 1965); and J. Howard Pew, "Should the Church 'Meddle' in Civil Affairs?" *Reader's Digest*, May 1966, pp. 1–6. On growing theological pluralism and controversy, see Hadden, *Gathering Storm*, chapters 1–3, and Wuthnow, *Restructuring*, pp. 142–72.

34. *The Book of Discipline of the United Methodist Church—1988* (Nashville: United Methodist Publishing House, 1988), pp. 8, 45, 55–56.

35. *The Book of Discipline of the United Methodist Church—1972* (Nashville: United Meth-

odist Publishing House, 1972), pp. 68–70, paragraph 70. Cf. the 1988 edition of *The Book of Discipline*, pp. 78–81, which moves away from emphasis on recognizing theological pluralism as a principle and proclaims "The Gospel in a New Age."

36. Compare the republican ideals of William Everett, *God's Federal Republic* (New York: Paulist Press, 1988), and the procedurally regulated, strategic infighting described in Arthur Farnsley, "Majority Rules: The Politicization of the Southern Baptist Convention," unpublished Ph.D. dissertation, Emory University, 1990.

37. Sansom is referring to the American theologian H. Richard Niebuhr's well-known book *Christ and Culture* (New York: Harper and Brothers, 1951), chapter 6, where "Christ transforming culture" is one of the five types of relation between Christ and culture that Niebuhr describes.

38. Paolo Friere, *Pedagogy of the Oppressed* (New York: Herder & Herder, 1970), defines conscientization in education as a liberating process of mutual learning among democratic equals to enable persons to "name the world" as social and historical subjects. Latin American liberation theologies use the term "to name the activity of faith: becoming human in solidarity with God and with the poor," a project "of the people" and "in the world" that typically occurs in small, basic Christian communities. Rebecca Chopp, *The Praxis of Suffering* (Maryknoll: Orbis Books, 1986), pp. 21–22.

39. Writes Gustavo Gutiérrez, "Only these base-level Christian communities, rising up out of the oppressed but believing people, will be in a position to proclaim and live the values of the Kingdom in the very midst of the common masses who are fighting for their liberation. . . . [As] a tool, if you will, for the evangelization of all nations from the standpoint of the poor and exploited . . . they are transforming our way of understanding discipleship. . . ." From "The Irruption of the Poor in Latin America and the Christian Communities," in Sergio Torres and John Eagleson, eds., *The Challenge of Basic Christian Communities*, (Maryknoll: Orbis Books, 1981), p. 118.

40. Through a hermeneutic of suspicion, liberation theology seeks to reinterpret traditional religious symbols with a critical eye to their systematic distortion by sinful social conditions, and with faith in their true power to reveal and transform social reality. See Gustavo Gutiérrez, *A Theology of Liberation* (Maryknoll: Orbis Books, 1973), pp. 287–302; and Jürgen Moltmann, *Theology of Hope* (New York: Harper and Row, 1967), pp. 50–76.

41. Liberation theology draws broadly on modern theology as well as Marxism to stress the inextricably social constitution and historical transformation of humankind, a position similar to the concern for "human nature as history" in recent works that stress the narrative character of Christian social ethics—for example, Stanley Hauerwas, *A Community of Character* (Notre Dame: University of Notre Dame Press, 1981), esp. pp. 111–28.

42. Writes David Tracy: "To risk conversation with our classic texts should be more like meeting such characters as Amos and Isaiah, Ruth and Jeremiah, Oedipus and Antigone, even Medea and Herakles, than it is like conceiving the classics simply as further examples of ideology. . . . [Like Greek tragedy, they] stir one's conscience with their demands for nobility of thought and action. They expose our present inauthenticity and complacency. At the same time, they also force us to resist their own half-concealed tragic flaws." *Plurality and Ambiguity* (New York: Harper and Row, 1987), pp. 86–87; passages rearranged.

43. See Dennis P. McCann, *Christian Realism and Liberation Theology: Practical Theologies in Creative Conflict* (Maryknoll: Orbis Books, 1981).

44. Lawrence H. Mamiya, "Class Differentiation in the African-American Community and Its Implications for the Ministry of Black Churches: Some Present Trends and Issues," unpublished paper delivered at the 1989 annual meeting of the American Academy of Religion, p. 24. See C. Eric Lincoln and Lawrence H. Mamiya, *The Black Church in the African-American Experience* (Durham: Duke University Press, 1990), and Roof and McKinney, *American Mainline Religion*, pp. 90–91.

45. Mamiya, "Class Differentiation," pp. 3–12, esp. pp. 9–10. See also the class bifurcation thesis advanced by William Julius Wilson in *The Declining Significance of Race* (Chicago: University of Chicago Press, 1987).

46. Ronald Smothers, *New York Times*, July 14, 1988, p. A13, quoted in Mamiya, "Class Differentiation," p. 8.

47. Compare, for example, Concord Baptist Church in Brooklyn (more than twelve thousand members), Abyssinian Baptist in Harlem (eight thousand members), Shiloh Baptist in Washington, D.C., and Bethel A.M.E. in Baltimore (five to six thousand members each) with the black church congregation of average size, which is two hundred to two hundred and fifty active members. Mamiya, "Class Differentiation," pp. 12–14.

48. E.g., Peter L. Berger, "From the Crisis of Religion to the Crisis of Secularity," in Mary Douglas and Steven Tipton, eds., *Religion and America* (Boston: Beacon Press, 1983), pp. 17–23; also Wuthnow, *Restructuring*, pp. 130–31, 212–18.

49. *The Harris Survey*, no. 104, December 22, 1983; cited in Wuthnow, *Restructuring*, pp. 253–54. Steven M. Tipton, "Moral Languages and the Good Society," *Soundings*, vol. 69, nos. 1–2, Spring–Summer 1986, pp. 165–80, esp. pp. 167–72.

50. James Davison Hunter, *Evangelicalism: The Coming Generation* (Chicago: University of Chicago Press, 1987), chapters 2–5. Similar dynamics of assimilative rapprochement, irreducible to secularization or cultural liberalization, are at work among the American Catholic and African-American middle class. See Timothy Healy et al., "Religion and Education, *Daedalus*, vol. 17, no. 2, Spring 1988, pp. 8–32; also Lincoln and Mamiya, *The Black Church*.

51. Tipton, "Moral Languages," pp. 165–80, esp. pp. 167–72.

52. Cf. Bellah et al., *Habits of the Heart*, chapter 9.

53. Ibid., *Habits of the Heart*, p. 246.

CHAPTER 7: AMERICA IN THE WORLD

1. Paul Kennedy, *The Rise and Fall of the Great Powers* (New York: Random House, 1987).

2. See, for example, Robert O. Keohane, *After Hegemony: Cooperation and Discord in the World Political Economy* (Princeton: Princeton University Press, 1984).

3. Robert Gilpin, "The United States and the Postwar International Economy" in L. Carl Brown, ed., *Centerstage* (New York: Holmes and Meier, 1990), pp. 79–103; Gilpin, *The Political Economy of International Relations* (Princeton: Princeton University Press, 1987).

4. Walter Isaacson and Evan Thomas, *The Wise Men: Six Friends and the World They Made* (New York: Simon and Schuster, 1986).

5. NSC 68, in Thomas H. Etzold and John Lewis Gaddis, eds., *Containment: Documents on American Policy and Strategy, 1945–1950* (New York: Columbia University Press, 1978), p. 386.

6. NSC 68, p. 386.

7. Ibid., p. 387.

8. Ibid., p. 388.

9. Ibid., p. 390.

10. Ibid., pp. 388, 389, 390, 415.

11. Ibid., p. 415.

12. Ibid., p. 413.

13. Ibid., p. 391.

14. Ibid., p. 413.

15. See George Parkin Grant, *English-Speaking Justice* (Notre Dame: University of Notre Dame Press, 1985); and Alasdair MacIntyre, *After Virtue* (Notre Dame: University of Notre Dame Press, 1981), esp. pp. 227–37; Michael Ignatieff, *The Needs of Strangers: An Essay on Privacy, Solidarity, and the Politics of Being Human* (New York: Penguin Books, 1986).

16. Henry R. Luce, "The American Century," *Life*, February 11, 1941, pp. 61–65.

17. Reinhold Niebuhr, *Discerning the Signs of the Times* (New York: Charles Scribner's Sons, 1946), quoted in Daniel Bell, *The Winding Passage* (New York: Basic Books, 1980), p. 254.

18. Reinhold Niebuhr, *The Irony of American History* (New York: Charles Scribner's Sons, 1952), pp. 149–50, 174.

19. Richard Wightman Fox, *Reinhold Niebuhr: A Biography* (New York: Pantheon, 1985), pp. 238–39.

20. James Peck, "Revolution Versus Modernization and Revisionism: A Two-Front Struggle," in Victor Nee and James Peck, eds., *China's Uninterrupted Revolution* (New York: Pantheon, 1973), pp. 57–217.

21. Marilyn Young, "Contradictions," in Sara Ruddick and Pamela Daniels, eds., *Working It Out: 23 Women Writers, Artists, Scientists, and Scholars Talk About Their Lives and Work* (New York: Pantheon, 1977), p. 219.

22. See Bruce Cumings, "The Origins and Development of the Northeast Asian Political Economy: Industrial Sectors, Product Cycles, and Political Consequences," *International Organization*, vol. 38, no. 1, Winter 1984, pp. 1–40, esp. pp. 26–35.

23. Young, "Contradictions," 221, 225.

24. "Imperialism in China: An Exchange," in *Bulletin of Concerned Asian Scholars*, vol. 5, no. 2, September 1973, pp. 32–35. The quote from Young is on p. 35.

25. John K. Fairbank and Jim Peck, "An Exchange," *Bulletin of Concerned Asian Scholars*, vol. 2, no. 3, April–July 1970, p. 67.

26. Pope John Paul II, *On Social Concern* [Sollicitudo Rei Socialis] (Boston: Saint Paul Books and Media, 1987). See especially part 3, pp. 21–45.

27. See Walter Russell Mead, *Mortal Splendor: The American Empire in Transition* (Boston: Houghton Mifflin, 1987), pp. 303–46.

28. Theodore H. Von Laue, *The World Revolution of Westernization* (New York: Oxford University Press, 1987), pp. 315–16.

29. Patrick McDonnell, "Ministering to Souls on the Run," *Los Angeles Times*, January 25, 1988, San Diego County edition, Part 2, pp. 1–2.

CONCLUSION: DEMOCRACY MEANS PAYING ATTENTION

1. Mihaly Csikszentmihalyi and Eugene Rochberg-Halton, *The Meaning of Things: Domestic Symbols and the Self* (Cambridge, England: Cambridge University Press, 1981), Chapter 1. We are drawing on Csikszentmihalyi's notion of attention, further developed in his *Flow: The Psychology of Optimal Experience* (New York: Harper and Row, 1990), and Rochberg-Halton's notion of cultivation. Rochberg-Halton's views are further developed in his *Meaning and Modernity: Social Theory in the Pragmatic Mode* (Chicago: University of Chicago Press, 1986).
2. Csikszentmihalyi and Rochberg-Halton, *Meaning of Things*, p. 9.
3. Pascal in his *Pensées* speaks of "diversion" (*divertissement*) in ways similar to our use of "distraction." T. S. Eliot in a famous line from "Burnt Norton," describing the faces of people in the subway, speaks of them as "distracted."
4. "Each act must be carried out in mindfulness," observes a contemporary Buddhist teacher. "Each act is a rite, a ceremony. Raising your cup of tea to your mouth is a rite. Does the word 'rite' seem too solemn? I use the word to jolt you into the realization of the life-and-death matter of awareness." Thich Nhat Hanh, *The Miracle of Mindfulness* (Boston: Beacon Press, 1987), p. 4.
5. Csikszentmihalyi and Rochberg-Halton, *Meaning of Things*, pp. 161–62.
6. Ibid., p. 170; emphasis in original.
7. Judith S. Wallerstein and Sandra Blakeslee, *Second Chances: Men, Women, and Children a Decade After Divorce* (New York: Ticknor and Fields, 1989), pp. 148–49.
8. Arlie Hochschild, *Second Shift: Working Parents and the Revolution at Home* (New York: Viking, 1989), pp. 214–15.
9. John Snow, "Families in the Fast Lane to Nowhere," *Episcopal Life*, May 1990, p. 18.
10. The locus classicus for the discussion of subsidiarity in modern Catholic social teaching is Pope Pius XI's encyclical *Quadragesimo anno* (Forty Years After: Reconstructing the Social Order) of 1931. For a recent exposition of the idea, see Dennis P. McCann, *New Experiment in Democracy: The Challenge for American Catholicism* (Kansas City: Sheed and Ward, 1987), pp. 136–51.
11. Herbert Croly, "The Future of the State," *New Republic*, September 15, 1917, pp. 180–81.
12. John Dewey, *The Public and Its Problems* (1927), in Jo Ann Boydston, ed., *John Dewey: The Later Works*, Vol. 2: 1925–1927 (Carbondale and Edwardsville: Southern Illinois University Press, 1984), pp. 370–72.
13. Wendell Berry, in *What Are People For?* (San Francisco: North Point Press, 1990), continues his eloquent plea for a return to cultivation as the American cultural pattern.
14. Donald L. Miller, ed., *The Lewis Mumford Reader* (New York: Pantheon, 1986), p. 213.
15. David Popenoe, *Private Pleasure, Public Plight: American Metropolitan Community Life in Comparative Perspective* (New Brunswick: Transaction Books, 1985), pp. 33, 94.

16. Stephen L. Elkin, *City and Regime in the American Republic* (Chicago: University of Chicago Press, 1987).

17. Popenoe, *Private Pleasure*, p. 130.

18. Lewis Mumford, *The City in History* (New York: Harcourt, Brace and World, 1961), p. 503.

19. Lewis Mumford, *The Culture of Cities* (New York: Harcourt, Brace and World, 1966 [1938]), pp. 484–85.

20. Scott Bottles, *Los Angeles and the Automobile: The Making of the Modern City* (Berkeley and Los Angeles: University of California Press, 1987).

21. Tony Hiss in *The Experience of Place* (New York: Knopf, 1990) describes a number of efforts to make urban and rural patterns of settlement and change intelligible so that responsible action concerning them may be taken. His examples are drawn from New England, New York, and the West Coast. For a description of the problem in the San Francisco Bay area, see Larry Orman and Jim Sayer, *Reviving the Sustainable Metropolis: Guiding Bay Area Conservation and Development in the 21st Century* (San Francisco: Green Belt Alliance, 1989).

22. In *The Life Cycle Completed: A Review* (New York: Norton, 1982) Erik H. Erikson sums up his work on the place of the virtues in the life cycle. Erik H. Erikson, Joan M. Erikson, and Helen Q. Kivnick have much to say about generativity in *Vital Involvement in Old Age: The Experience of Old Age in Our Time* (New York: Norton, 1986).

23. *The New York Times* of June 28, 1990, has extensive coverage of the Times Mirror study released that month that shows a significant decline in interest in and knowledge about national and world events among young people between the ages of eighteen and twenty-four. They are less apt to read newspapers or even watch television news than people of the same age in earlier periods.

24. Kevin Phillips, *The Politics of Rich and Poor: Wealth and the American Electorate in the Reagan Aftermath* (New York: Random House, 1990).

25. "The at will rule—that workers have no rights except those they are able to extract by individual negotiation and agreement—is out of step with the systems of job protection adopted by other industrialized nations, and with international norms. All of our European competitors and Canada have statutes protecting employees against wrongful discharge and establishing tribunals in which claims can be adjudicated. A covenant of the International Labor Organization of the United Nations calls upon all participating nations to adopt such statutes, but the United States—almost alone among industrial democracies—is not party to that covenant. In this respect we stand isolated within the international community." Joseph Grodin, "Remedy Wrongful Termination by Statute," *California Lawyer*, vol. 10, no. 7, July 1990, p. 120. Grodin is hopeful that legislative action will remedy this situation in the foreseeable future.

26. Walter Lippmann, *The Good Society* (Boston: Little, Brown, 1937), p. 348.

27. Ibid., p. 347.

28. Ibid., p. 363.

29. National Conference of Catholic Bishops, *Economic Justice for All: Pastoral Letter on Catholic Social Teaching and the U.S. Economy* (Washington, D.C.: National Conference of Catholic Bishops, 1986).

30. Ibid., paragraph 27.

31. Ibid., paragraph 123.

32. Ibid., paragraph 124.

33. H. Richard Niebuhr, *The Responsible Self* (New York: Harper and Row, 1978 [1963]), p. 65; summing discussion on pp. 61–65.
34. Ibid., p. 65.
35. On basic trust, see Erik H. Erikson, *Insight and Responsibility* (New York: Norton, 1964).
36. Niebuhr, *Responsible Self*, p. 88.

APPENDIX: INSTITUTIONS IN SOCIOLOGY AND PUBLIC PHILOSOPHY

1. Talcott Parsons, "Prolegomena to a Theory of Social Institutions," *American Sociological Review*, vol. 55, 1990, pp. 319–33. See also the discussion of institutions in Parsons, *The Social System* (Glencoe, Ill.: Free Press, 1951), *Sociological Theory and Modern Society* (New York: Free Press, 1976), and other of his works.
2. James S. Coleman, "Commentary: Social Institutions and Social Theory," *American Sociological Review*, vol. 55, 1990, pp. 333–39. For a more perceptive understanding of Parsons's position, see in the same issue Jeffrey C. Alexander, "Commentary: Structure, Value, Action," pp. 339–45.
3. See James S. Coleman, *Foundations of Social Theory* (Cambridge: Harvard University Press, 1990), for a full development of his position. Talcott Parsons would have been amazed or amused to find the assumptions he thought he had laid to rest in *The Structure of Social Action* (New York: Prentice-Hall, 1937) reiterated in 1990 as the last word in sociological theory. Or perhaps he would not have been surprised after all, for he often commented on the cultural persistence of Anglo-American utilitarianism in spite of all criticism.
4. Alasdair MacIntyre, *After Virtue* (Notre Dame: Notre Dame University Press, 1981).
5. Karl Polanyi, *The Great Transformation* (New York: Rinehart and Company, 1944).
6. These ideas are most fully developed in Jürgen Habermas, *The Theory of Communicative Action*, Vol. 1: *Reason and the Rationalization of Society* (Boston: Beacon Press, 1984 [1981]) and especially Vol. 2: *Lifeworld and System: A Critique of Functionalist Reason* (Boston: Beacon Press, 1987 [1981]).
7. R. H. Tawney, *The Acquisitive Society* (New York: Harcourt Brace, 1920 [Harvest, 1948]), pp. 183–84.
8. On the moral dialogue between institutional spheres, see Steven M. Tipton, "Moral Languages and the Good Society," *Soundings*, vol. 69, nos. 1–2, Spring–Summer 1986, pp. 166–77.
9. For a particularly perceptive treatment of Rachel Carson, see Sam Bass Warner, Jr., *The Province of Reason* (Cambridge: Harvard University Press, 1984), chapter 12.
10. Walter Lippmann, *Drift and Mastery* (Madison: University of Wisconsin Press, 1985 [1914]), pp. 80–81.
11. Ibid., pp. 118–19.
12. Ibid., p. 112.
13. Charles S. Peirce, "Some Consequences of Four Incapacities," *Journal of Speculative Philosophy*, vol. 2, 1861, reprinted in Philip P. Wiener, ed., *Charles S. Peirce: Selected Writings* (New York: Dover, 1966), p. 69.
14. Jane Addams, *Twenty Years at Hull House* (New York: Macmillan, 1910); W. E. B. Du Bois, *Writings* (New York: Library of America, 1986); and Charlotte

Perkins Gilman, *Women and Economics* (Boston: Small, Maynard and Co., 1898). Gilman was a leading feminist theorist and publicist in the period before World War I. She thought deeply, if in ways not entirely convincing today, about how to get women out of the home into fuller participation in public life. She was right in seeing the family as a potential source of egoistic preoccupation that limited the larger vision of both men and women. Her main emphasis was on the need for active citizen involvement in an increasingly interdependent society.

15. Eugene Rochberg-Halton, *Meaning and Modernity: Social Theory in the Pragmatic Mode* (Chicago: University of Chicago Press, 1986), p. 18.

16. John Dewey, *The Public and Its Problems* (1927), in Jo Ann Boydston, ed., *John Dewey: The Later Works*, Vol. 2: 1925–1927 (Carbondale and Edwardsville: Southern Illinois University Press, 1984), p. 303.

17. Ibid., p. 130.

18. Ibid., pp. 327–28.

19. Reinhold Niebuhr, *Moral Man and Immoral Society* (New York: Charles Scribner's Sons, 1932), p. xiii.

20. Ibid., pp. xiv–xv.

21. Letter from H. Richard Niebuhr to Reinhold Niebuhr, n.d. (mid-January 1933), cited in Richard Fox, *Reinhold Niebuhr: A Biography* (New York: Pantheon, 1985), pp. 144–45.

22. Walter Lippmann, *The Good Society* (Boston: Little, Brown, 1937), p. 165.

23. Ibid., p. 171.

24. Ibid., pp. 210–11.

25. Ibid., p. 213.

26. Ibid., p. 214.

27. Ibid., pp. 225–27.

28. We might note that the distribution of income more than fifty years later is considerably more unequal than it was when Lippman wrote those words. Kevin Phillips in *The Politics of Rich and Poor* (New York: Random House, 1990) documents the striking increase in income and wealth disparity during the 1980s, but his figures show that the disparity has been growing steadily since 1954, the earliest year for which he gives data. See p. 13, and more generally pp. 8–23.

29. Lippmann, *Good Society*, p. 274.

30. Ibid., p. 278.

31. Ibid., p. 280.

32. Ibid., p. 333.

33. John Courtney Murray, *We Hold These Truths: Catholic Reflections on the American Proposition* (New York: Sheed and Ward, 1960), p. 8.

34. Ibid., p. 10.

35. Ibid., pp. 11–12.

36. Ibid., p. 13.

37. Ibid., p. xi.

38. Ibid., pp. 18–19.

39. Ibid., p. 20.

40. See W. E. B. Du Bois, *The Souls of Black Folk* (1903) in *Writings*, pp. 357–547. Randolph Bourne made an eloquent case for ethnic pluralism in America just before and during World War I. See his *War and the Intellectuals: Collected Essays, 1915–1919* (Harper and Row, Harper Torchbooks, 1964).

41. See Arthur Stinchcombe, *Constructing Social Theories* (New York: Harcourt, Brace,

Jovanovich, 1968), for a detailed discussion of causal models linking individual properties to aggregate-level outcomes.

42. See Alvin Gouldner, *Patterns of Industrial Bureaucracy* (Glencoe, Ill.: Free Press, 1954), and Peter Blau, *The Dynamics of Bureaucracy: A Study of Interpersonal Relations in Two Government Agencies* (Chicago: University of Chicago Press, 1955).

43. For example, see Michel Crozier's *The Bureaucratic Phenomenon* (Chicago: University of Chicago Press, 1964).

44. See the imaginative survey of methods for studying organizations in Gareth Morgan, ed., *Beyond Method: Strategies for Social Research* (Newbury Park, Calif.: Sage Publications, 1983).

45. Parsons, "Prolegomena," p. 328.

46. Mary Ann Glendon, *Abortion and Divorce in Western Law* (Cambridge: Harvard University Press, 1987) and *The Transformation of Family Law: State, Law, and the Family in the United States and Western Europe* (Chicago: University of Chicago Press, 1989).

47. Philip Selznick, with the collaboration of Philippe Nonet and Howard M. Vollmer, *Law, Society, and Industrial Justice* (New York: Russell Sage Foundation, 1969).

48. Case law can be well developed in nongovernmental institutions. There is a long tradition of case law in the Catholic Church which is called "casuistry," but need not have pejorative connotations. See the enlightening study by Albert R. Jonsen and Stephen Toulmin, *The Abuse of Casuistry: A History of Moral Reasoning* (Berkeley and Los Angeles: University of California Press, 1988).

49. See Philip Selznick, "The Ethos of American Law," in Irving Kristol and Paul H. Weaver, eds., *The Americans, 1976: An Inquiry into Fundamental Concepts of Man Underlying Various U.S. Institutions* (Lexington, Mass.: Lexington Books, 1976), pp. 211–36, and Philippe Nonet and Philip Selznick, *Law and Society in Transition: Toward Responsive Law* (New York: Octagon Books, 1978). John Meyer's work, on the other hand, though it is rich in empirical insight, avoids responsibility for normative judgment, thus weakening its conclusions with a pervasive cynicism. Meyer uses the term "institution" to describe both the structural principles that make social order coherent and enduring and the more ephemeral and incoherent ideas (which he calls rules) which define, for example, the accounting procedures, credentialing requirements, or administrative arrangements that make organizations *seem* technically efficient. See his contributions to John W. Meyer and W. Richard Scott, *Organizational Environments: Ritual and Rationality* (Newbury Park, Calif.: Sage Publications, 1983), George W. Thomas, John W. Meyer, Francisco O. Ramirez, and John Boli, *Institutional Structure: Constituting State, Society, and the Individual* (Newbury Park, Calif.: Sage Publications, 1987), and other publications.

50. On this point see Rochberg-Halton, *Meaning and Modernity*, chapter 11.

51. Whereas Dewey spoke of the transformation of the great society into the great community, Lippmann contrasted the great society with the good society, with much the same intent. Here there is a terminological issue that contains its own ironies. When, early in his presidency, Lyndon Johnson was seeking a slogan that could sum up his own vision, one of his speech writers, influenced by Lippmann's book, came up with the term "the good society." Having attained a decent standard of living and having made significant progress in extending justice for all, the new task would be to create a society concerned with the quality of

the good life. But one of the speech writers thought the term "great society" (also frequently used in Lippmann's book) sounded better. And so, almost by accident, the term freighted with moral meaning was abandoned for its opposite. (Personal communication, Bill Moyers to Robert Bellah, 1988.) The speech writers, of course, sought to give the term "great society" a moral meaning. The events of the second Johnson administration, especially the Vietnam War, returned it unintentionally to its impersonal and destructive original significance. That the war led to a total break between Johnson and Lippmann only completes the irony.

52. Murray, *We Hold These Truths*, p. vii.

Index